Forgotten Firebrand

FORGOTTEN FIREBRAND

*James Redpath and the Making of
Nineteenth-Century America*

John McKivigan

Cornell University Press

ITHACA AND LONDON

First published 2008 by Cornell University Press

Printed in the United States of America

Library of Congress Cataloging-in-Publication Data

McKivigan, John R., 1949-
 Forgotten firebrand : James Redpath and the making of nineteenth-century
America / John R. McKivigan.
  p. cm.
 Includes bibliographical references and index.
 ISBN 978-0-8014-4673-3 (cloth : alk. paper)
  1. Redpath, James, 1833-1891. 2. Social reformers—United States—Biography.
3. Journalists—United States—Biography. 4. Abolitionists—United States—Biography.
5. Redpath Lyceum Bureau. 6. United States—Politics and government—1849-1877.
I. Title.

 E415.9.R43M38 2008
 303.48′4092—dc22
 [B]

2007038281

Cornell University Press strives to use environmentally responsible suppliers and materials to the fullest extent possible in the publishing of its books. Such materials include vegetable-based, low-VOC inks and acid-free papers that are recycled, totally chlorine-free, or partly composed of nonwood fibers. For further information, visit our website at www.cornellpress.cornell.edu.

Cloth printing   10 9 8 7 6 5 4 3 2 1

Dedicated to Merton L. Dillon and W. Wayne Smith,
who taught me the historian's craft

Contents

Preface and Acknowledgments

The name Redpath was well known across the rural portions of midwestern and prairie states down to the Great Depression. For another generation or so, many residents of that region retained positive memories of the traveling Chautauqua programs annually brought to their community by the Chicago-based Redpath Lyceum Bureau. Operating under a tent capable of seating a thousand or more patrons, the typical weeklong program featured an assortment of entertainment and educational features. Musicians, humorists, magicians, interpretive readers, and other performers brought the latest in art and culture into the rural communities. The educational, or "instructive," portion of an evening's fare in the "Canvas College" would include lecturers on topics ranging from religion, travel, and art to reforms such as temperance and women's rights to political controversies of the era.[1]

Down to the first or second decades of the twentieth century, older members of the audience probably retained a vague recollection of the bureau's founder, James Redpath. This diminutive, red-headed Scottish immigrant organized the bureau in 1868 but retained its ownership only until 1875. Redpath's reputation as an intimate of such an eccentric assemblage of figures as John Brown, Mark Twain, Henry George, and Jefferson Davis and as a militant proponent of such causes as abolitionism, black rights, Irish nationalism, women's suffrage, and labor unions had originally drawn public interest to his lyceum programs. Although he abandoned his creation fairly quickly, a character trait he repeated through his life, Redpath had remained with his lyceum bureau long enough to have encouraged popular tastes for uplifting entertainment. Hoping to retain not just Redpath's vision but a bit of his charisma, the men who inherited the bureau kept his name attached to their enterprise for the following half century.

Redpath was a discerning witness to and an active participant in many of the key developments in nineteenth-century American political and cultural life. Born in Scotland, Redpath immigrated to the United States in 1849 and found work as a reporter for Horace Greeley's *New York Tribune*. In the mid 1850s, he made three journeys through the South secretly interviewing slaves and publishing their accounts of slavery in abolitionist newspapers. After his third trip, Redpath published these interviews together with his impressions of the South in a book entitled *The Roving Editor: or, Talks with the Slaves.*

In the late 1850s, Redpath moved to Kansas Territory where he reported on events for a number of newspapers and eventually edited his own newspaper, the *Doniphan Crusader of Freedom*. Redpath regularly crossed the line between journalist and participant and soon became a leader in both the political and paramilitary campaigns attempting to prevent the territory from becoming a slave state. In these years, Redpath also became a close associate of John Brown in the militant wing of the Kansas "free-state" campaign. In 1858, Brown persuaded Redpath to move to Boston to help recruit support for a contemplated slave insurrection. After the failure of Brown's attack on Harpers Ferry, Virginia, in October 1859, Redpath assisted raiders who had eluded capture to reach safety. Also sought by authorities as a suspected accomplice in the raid, Redpath evaded arrest. While in hiding, he produced the first biography of Brown within weeks of his execution. Redpath's *The Public Life of Capt. John Brown* was uncompromisingly sympathetic towards its subject and vigorously defended his employment of violent antislavery tactics.

In 1860, Redpath toured Haiti as a reporter and returned to the United States appointed the official Haitian lobbyist for diplomatic recognition, which he secured within two years. He simultaneously served as director of Haiti's campaign to attract free-black emigrants from the United States and Canada. Redpath hoped that a selective migration of skilled blacks to Haiti would elevate conditions on the island nation and thereby dispel prejudice in the United States. He abandoned the scheme, however, when he recognized that North American blacks preferred to remain at home once the Civil War seemed to promise a new day of freedom for their race.

In 1863 and 1864, Redpath redirected his energies to pioneering the publishing of cheap paperbound books primarily aimed at a reading audience of bored Union military personnel. This series featured a mixture of religious, historical, and humorous works by such authors as Louisa May Alcott, Wendell Phillips, and Victor Hugo. A particularly noteworthy title published by Redpath was William Well Brown's *Clotelle: A Tale of the Southern States,* the first novel written by a black. Another in this series was a short work by Redpath himself, *Shall We Suffocate Ed. Green?,* an early anti–capital punishment tract.

Later in the Civil War, Redpath served as a frontline war correspondent with the Union army in Georgia and South Carolina for the *New York Tribune*. In February 1865, federal military authorities appointed Redpath superintendent of South Carolina public schools. He soon had more than one hundred instructors at work teaching thirty-five hundred students of both races. His reputation as a radical abolitionist and his tentative steps toward integrating South Carolina schools caused military officials to replace Redpath after only seven months in order to remove a source of irritation to southern-born President Andrew Johnson.

After the Civil War, Redpath organized one of the first professional lecturing bureaus in the United States and had as his clients, and frequently as his friends, such notables as Wendell Phillips, Frederick Douglass, Charles Sumner, and Susan B. Anthony. Later he added musicians, magicians, and especially humorists, including Mark Twain, Josh Billings, and David R. Locke ("Petroleum V. Nasby") to his stable of stage performers. Further expanding the forms of entertainment he provided, Redpath personally organized operatic and dramatic companies and sent them on successful national tours. In the late 1870s, Thomas A. Edison hired Redpath as the principal publicist for his new invention, the phonograph.

Even while he helped to fashion the nation's entertainment industry, Redpath remained active in the Republican Party as an advocate for more concerted efforts by the federal government to protect the rights of southern freedmen. While serving as secretary of a congressional investigating committee in 1876, he generated considerable controversy by the strong language he used to denounce the campaign of violence employed in Mississippi to keep blacks away from the polls. After Rutherford B. Hayes removed the final federal forces protecting the freedmen from the South, Redpath sparked further debate by his public excoriation of the Republicans for abandoning the promises of Reconstruction.

In the 1880s, Redpath returned to his earlier career as a reform journalist, beginning with tours of Ireland to report on famine conditions in rural areas. He returned to the United States a convert to the cause of Irish nationalism and edited a newspaper, *Redpath's Illustrated Weekly*, on behalf of that cause as well as women's suffrage and organized labor. In 1886, he became a leading propagandist for the New York City mayoral campaign of the utopian reformer Henry George. During the George campaign, Redpath befriended Father Edward McGlynn and served as a vice president of the Roman Catholic priest's Anti-Poverty Society, which sought solutions for the deteriorating conditions of urban ethnic neighborhoods.

Redpath ended his professional life as the managing editor of the *North American Review* and as a ghostwriter for the former Confederate president Jefferson Davis. From among his many friends in reform circles, Redpath recruited authors for the *Review* who addressed the pressing political and social issues of the late nineteenth century, including women's suffrage, immigration, corporate monopoly, and racial discrimination. Redpath's relationship with Davis is one of the least characteristic episodes in his long career as a defender of the rights of southern blacks. After Redpath persuaded Davis to write articles for the *Review* on Confederate history, feelings of mutual respect began to develop between the two men. Redpath lived in the Davis household at Beauvoir, Mississippi, for several months in 1888 and 1889 and assisted the old Confederate to prepare an abridged edition of his history of the Southern rebellion. After Davis's death, Redpath assisted his widow to write a biography of her husband. Despite suffering a stroke in 1887, Redpath continued to lead an active public life until fatally injured by a trolley car accident in New York City in 1891.

In addition to recounting the details of this active and exciting life, this biography of Redpath serves as a lens to examine a number of significant issues in the history of nineteenth-century reform and culture in the United States. Redpath stood out among the younger generation of American abolitionists, generally neglected by historians. His intimate contact with both slaves and southern slaveholders made him almost unique among younger antislavery commentators. In his *Roving Editor* and *Public Life of Capt. John Brown*, Redpath led abolitionists in formulating a justification for the employment of violent tactics on behalf of the antislavery cause. His biography of John Brown was so influential in defining the popular image of its subject that historian James C. Malin described writing over the next half century as "the James Redpath Period of John Brown Biography."[2]

Redpath's abolitionist career also fails to conform to charges made by historians in earlier decades that white antislavery activists harbored significant degrees of paternalistic, condescending, or even racist attitudes toward the African Americans that they sought to aid.[3] During the 1850s and 1860s, Redpath not only worked with but for blacks on terms of complete equality. Redpath's involvement in the Haitian emigration movement in the 1860s put him at the center of the heated debate in the African American community between nationalists and assimilationists over how to respond to the racism that pervaded the United States. When he recognized that most African Americans opposed the emigration effort, he reluctantly abandoned it to find other means to assist their race. During the prolonged turmoil of Reconstruction, abolitionists such as Redpath came under pressure to compromise in the interests of sectional reconciliation.[4] From his efforts to integrate Charleston's public schools to his denunciation of Hayes's capitulation to Southern racism, however, Redpath's commitment to full black rights never wavered. Even Redpath's intimate dealings with Jefferson Davis, late in both men's lives, did not produce any important concession by the journalist to the old planter's views on race.

Despite the central role of race-related issues in Redpath's reform career, his social concerns expanded in the years after Reconstruction to include other oppressed groups. He actively recruited female speakers for his lyceum circuit and endorsed the movement for women's suffrage. Redpath also became a leading advocate for immigrants and labor in the 1880s. As historian Eric Foner has observed, Redpath and Wendell Phillips were the two most important bridges between the abolitionist and postbellum reform communities.[5] After they recognized the similarities between conditions confronting the Irish and the southern blacks, both men overcame longstanding anti-Catholic prejudices and took an active part in protesting the exploitation of the landless peasantry of Ireland. Close association with Irish Americans likewise fostered sympathy in Redpath for the efforts of many immigrant leaders in the fledgling labor movement. A study of Redpath's life therefore contributes to the scholarly appreciation of change and continuity in nineteenth-century American reform.[6]

Examining Redpath's life also throws light on the history of journalism, public speaking, and mass entertainment in the United States. Redpath's newspaper writing in Kansas for the *New York Tribune* is credited with popularizing the stenographic interview in the American press. His journalistic career can be studied as a prototype for later generations of newspaper writers who blended reporting with active participation in reform movements. Along with his personal friend Phineas T. Barnum, Redpath popularized the figure of the "impresario" in American culture. As already noted, Redpath's part in organizing the structure and in defining the content of professional entertainment in this country was attested by the long survival of his name in that industry. An examination of these aspects of Redpath's life contributes to scholarly appreciation of the place of entertainment and leisure activities in American cultural history.

Given Redpath's proximity to individuals and events of such significance in nineteenth-century American history, it is fair to ask why Redpath does not already fill a larger space in the annals of that era. There are many factors that help to explain this circumstance. Unlike most contemporary reformers, his activism did not operate from a strong religious or a narrow ideological base. Far from being monomaniacal, Redpath was a man of myriad interests. Rather than devoting his considerable talents to advancing one reform, he pursued many, on some occasions simultaneously. Contemporaries observed Redpath's inability to maintain a focus. For example, after Redpath's death, an old ally in many reform causes, Richard J. Hinton, sketched an insightful description of his one-time friend:

> Redpath came as near possessing positive genius, and yet just missing it, as any man it has been my fate to know intimately. He was a most attractive speaker, yet had not a scintilla of oratorical grace or continuity. He wrote occasionally both poems and *gens d'espirits* which indicated high powers in wit, imagination, and harmony, yet he seemed without capacity to develop, except in fragments. A clever businessman to initiate, he had no balance wheel. A writer of power, he never pursued a theme logically and to the end. Doing much to make the conflict between freedom and slavery inevitable, he failed utterly to make himself a perceptible factor in the great struggle that arose. His personality was as elusive as the memory that remains.[7]

In 1900 James Pond, a close friend of Redpath both in Kansas and much later in the lyceum industry, came to a similar assessment of the latter's active but erratic career as a reformer:

> Every ethical breath or cause seemed to draw him, but he did not remain to round out either the cause or his own work. But what a lot of service, according to his light, he rendered! . . . His life was full of large beginnings and alive with "divine fragments," dramatic contrasts, and active with vigorous work, so that while he moved, and where he did so, he for the time being filled the centre of the stage.[8]

Given Redpath's own dearth of introspection in the thousands of pieces of his correspondence and published writings that survive, such perceptive observations of his personality from close associates are invaluable. Both Hinton and Pond recounted Redpath's disturbingly capricious nature. Redpath's professional and personal life also provides evidence of alternating episodes of extremely heightened creative activity as well as incapacitating and occasionally near suicidal depression. Although this is far from clinically satisfactory evidence, such behavior hints that Redpath might have been affected with bipolar disorder or more likely the similar, but milder, mood disorder of cyclothymia. Even the less threatening diagnosis, however, might not fit Redpath who successfully functioned for extended periods of time in each of his various careers. Furthermore, while Redpath's professional activities shifted quite often, his underlying ideological commitments remained very consistent for forty years of public life. To the general public, Redpath might have appeared a manic character but intimates such as Twain and Whitman found him a loyal and congenial friend over many decades. In fact, Redpath's volatile personality added to the fascination of the nineteenth-century public with his activities.

Redpath's roving reformism led some contemporaries and later historians to view him as a self-promoter without firm commitment to the causes in which he participated.[9] At best, Redpath was viewed as a gadfly, darting from issue to issue looking to gather attention for his own support of those causes. Some of this seeming self-promotion was due to Redpath's need to combine making a livelihood with advocating unpopular issues. Unlike political journalists who might aspire to patronage or even elected office, reform journalists like Redpath had to find a way to profit from their literary support for unpopular causes in the mid nineteenth century.

Redpath also brought an entrepreneurial spirit to reform that blurred traditional lines between business and political activism in ways that seem striking familiar today but were uncommon in his own era. Redpath was a pioneer in cultural entrepreneurialism and helped to forge modern concepts of celebrity. In his antebellum abolitionist advocacy and his work on behalf the Haitians, Redpath used himself as his model for a politically engaged writer chronicling his own activities on behalf of an oppressed class. He was one of the first reformers to learn that his personal celebrity status could advance the causes that he advocated. Later in his lyceum bureau, Redpath invented new means to transform other reformers into well-paid entertainers and established performers into public advocates of reform movements.

In addition to the taint of self-promotion attached to his activities, Redpath never gained personal acceptance from the nation's cultural elite. As an impecunious immigrant, Redpath was an outsider seeking acceptance. His proto-Bohemian lifestyle was highlighted by a divorce, extramarital affairs, and episodes of mental collapse. His intimate connections with radical political figures from John Brown to Henry George, his advocacy for African Americans, immigrant laborers, suffragists, and Irish Catholic tenant farmers, and personal friendship with such controversial figures as the homoerotic poet Walt Whitman, the atheist Robert Ingersoll, and the many sensational artists he introduced to the lyceum stage conspired to persuade many of his contemporaries that he was a disreputable figure best forgotten.

By his mottled collage of careers and his flaunting of Victorian conventions, Redpath seemingly dared people to attempt to ignore him. While few contemporaries could successfully do so in their own lifetimes, many attempted to excise Redpath from the earliest "histories" they wrote of the era. Sadly this early censorship has caused most twentieth-century professional historians to overlook Redpath's contributions to a wide range of the most interesting features of mid- and late-nineteenth-century life in the United States. In publishing this biography, Cornell University Press has the rare opportunity to allow an author to truly rewrite some major chapters of American history and resurrect the reputation one of the nation's most colorful and unjustly forgotten characters.

———

Another reason for the dearth of earlier study into Redpath's career is the difficulty in researching his life. No biography exists for Redpath. The only previous attempt is Charles F. Horner's *The Life of James Redpath and the Development of the Modern Lyceum* (1926).[10] A former manager on the lyceum circuit, Horner was able to gather considerable information on his subject through personal interviews with surviving relatives and former employees and acquaintances. Unfortunately he provided neither footnotes nor a bibliography to the sources for this or any other material. Overall, Horner's biography is a superficial and uncritical examination of Redpath's career except for the relatively brief period of his subject's involvement in the management of the Redpath Lyceum Bureau.

Fortunately many sources have survived that deal with Redpath. In his busy public life, Redpath wrote and published six books, edited several newspapers and magazines, wrote thousands of journalistic pieces, and corresponded with a large number of contemporaries. Redpath's journalistic career was perhaps the easiest to reassemble. Sometimes with the assistance of student researchers, I painstakingly combed issues of dozens of the newspapers and periodicals that employed Redpath during his forty years as a journalist. I also traveled to scattered libraries to examine the surviving issues of the four newspapers edited by Redpath, the *Doniphan Crusader of Freedom* (1856–57), the *Pine and Palm* (1860–62, Boston), the *Boston Lyceum* (1870–75), and *Redpath's Illustrated Weekly* (1882–84, New York).

Handicapping earlier historical appreciation of Redpath has been the fact that there is no single repository of Redpath's correspondence. The only extensive collections of Redpath's letters focus on his directorship of the Haitian Emigration Bureau, but over the years these letters became scattered into collections at Duke University, Columbia University, the Boston Pubic Library, and the Library of Congress. I also located significant amounts of Redpath's correspondence in the collections of his associates in various reform movements and in the newspaper and entertainment industries. Among the most helpful of these collections were the Louisa May Alcott Papers at the New York Historical Society, the John Brown–Thomas Wentworth Higginson Collection and the William Lloyd Garrison Collection at the Boston Public Library, the Samuel Gridley Howe Papers at the Massachusetts Historical Society, and the William Whitelaw Reid Papers at the Library of Congress.

Redpath might have been singularly unfortunate in attracting a biographer too much like himself. In the more than two decades since starting this project, I have unconsciously imitated Redpath in peripatetically pursuing a multiplicity of careers and causes. Like my subject, I have bounced between participation in both conventional and radical politics; worked for the rights of minorities, immigrants, and labor; and invested heavily in friendships, romances, and marriages that alternatively produced enormous amounts of fulfillment and heartache. This book has taken a shamefully long period of time to complete; since I began work on it I have written or edited more than a dozen other books and been immersed in numerous political struggles. While friends and colleagues often shook their heads at these many delays, I remained confident that Redpath would have endorsed my choice of priorities, which allowed the partially completed manuscript of his biography to gather dust for months, even years, between the times that I could find to work on it.

Much of the early research for this manuscript would not have been completed if not for the assistance of many young scholars at Yale University who assisted me over a number of years. These individuals include Nancy Kopman, Dominic Parisi, Randy Session, Tor Ormseth, Daniel Coleman, Bruce Spiva, Andrew Lewis, Nancy Warfield, and Stefan Cohan. They tracked down innumerable leads in old newspapers, created an elaborate day-to-day itinerary of Redpath's activities, and participated in many discussions about that journalist's motivation and personality, while still finding time to excel at their class work. Stefan Cohen also generously shared with me the fruits of his own research on Theodore Holley, one of Redpath's free-black emigrants to Haiti. I was singularly fortunate in the early days of my research in the mid 1980s that a close friend, Marta Wagner, designed a computerized inventory that allowed me to organize the products of my own and my assistants' research.

In later years, my work benefited from the assistance of many friends, especially Dave Roediger, Karin Shapiro, Tony de la Cova, Tom Robertson, Jane Holtan, and Becky Bailey, who kept their eyes open for Redpath-related materials while conducting their own research. Over the years, other scholars responded generously to my requests for assistance. Jeffery Collins supplied me with key details on the life of Redpath and his family in Malden. Brent Tarter of the Library of Virginia helped me verify numerous details of Redpath's travel accounts in the *Roving Editor*. Professor W. Marvin Dulaney of the College of Charleston assisted me in clarifying details on Redpath's activities in that city. Dr. Frank Chorpenning of Delaware, Ohio, provided me valuable information on the family tree of Redpath's second wife. Very late in my work on this biography, Pat Pflieger generously called my attention to Redpath's authorship of a series of postwar children's stories.

Over the years, I delivered presentations on portions of my Redpath research at many professional meetings and received thoughtful advice from commentators and audience members. In particular, I owe a debt to the organizers of the sadly now-defunct annual Duquesne University History Forum who gave me a venue for six papers on various aspects of Redpath's career. Similar thanks are due to the editors of the following journals and presses where I have previously published short accounts on aspects of Redpath's life: *Manuscripts, Civil War History, Mid-America,* the Pennsylvania State University Press, and Greenwood Press.[11]

As this biography slowly came together, I have received valuable advice from readers of portions of the manuscript, including Madeleine Stern, Eric Foner, Karen Halttunen, John Blassingame, William McFeely, Nancy Hewitt, and Carol Wilson. I owe an especially large debt to a long-time friend Stanley Harrold, who read and extensively commented on a preliminary draft of the entire manuscript. I also am indebted to Heather L. Kaufman, Jeb Barnes-McKivigan, Merton L. Dillon, Peter Hinks, James B. Stewart, Hugh Davis, Richard Blackett, and John Stauffer for their unflagging encouragement as I struggled to bring this biography to its completion.

Forgotten Firebrand

I   *The Roving Editor*

Redpath is a common name in Berwickshire, the district along the Tweed River that separates England and Scotland. For centuries the monarchs of those two countries had fought over the region. The walled garrison town of Berwick changed hands numerous times before the crowns of England and Scotland were united in 1603. With commercial access now secured to its Scottish as well as English hinterlands, Berwick prospered as a port and service center for the region. In the early nineteenth century, its harbor bustled with ships carrying Berwickshire's exports of coal, salmon, and agricultural products. Berwick's stable population of approximately eight thousand lived in solidly built stone houses inside or immediately adjacent to the town's Elizabethan era walls. The nearby villages of Tweedmouth and Spittal along the coast also were home to prosperous fishing fleets.[1]

Over the centuries, several Redpaths had received grants of land to reward their services to the Scottish kings. There also had been numerous Berwickshire clergymen bearing that name. The most famous of these was George Ridpath, an eighteenth-century minister of Stitchill, who in 1776 published a collection of folktales from the Scottish-English countryside, entitled *Border History of England and Scotland.*[2]

Very little is known about Redpath's immediate family. James Redpath himself left behind little in the way of autobiographical writings. His first biographer, Charles F. Horner, gained a small amount of information about this portion of his subject's life from personal interviews with Redpath's younger brother, John. Unfortunately, Horner's work is riddled with minor inaccuracies. Horner's account of Redpath's early family life has not been accepted as fact, except where confirmed in surviving government and church records, town directories, and local histories.[3]

The father of James Redpath, Ninian Davidson Redpath, was born in 1806. Ninian's own father was a farmer in the Scottish lowlands near Berwick and at least one of his brothers, John, made his livelihood from agriculture. Another brother James became a shopkeeper in Berwick. Ninian apparently received a good elementary education, perhaps at the private school conducted by his mother's relative James Davidson in nearby Tweedmouth. In the 1822 directory for Northumberland, Ninian is listed as conducting his own academy on Berwick's Union Street.[4]

The Berwick vicinity supported a dozen or more small private day schools in the early nineteenth century. The sons of Berwick's wealthy received a classical education gratis from an endowed grammar school, while a system of charity schools tutored the children of the poor in a rudimentary education. In between these extremes, parents of middling means paid varying fees for their sons, and a growing proportion of their daughters, to receive a good general education at private academies such as Ninian's. A survey taken in 1821 found that more than three-fourths of the Berwick area children aged five to fifteen were enrolled in some sort of school.[5]

Despite stiff competition among schools for students, Ninian made a living as a teacher. By 1834, he had moved his day school to 79 Church Street not far from Berwick's town hall. He lived at the same address and owned the building. This property apparently did not have sufficient value to qualify Ninian as a freeman of Berwick because he is not listed among those eligible to vote in Parliamentary elections before the Reform Act of 1832.[6]

Fittingly for a border community, Redpath's mother, Maria Main, was English in ancestry. A number of her ancestors were seamen and one had achieved a small amount of fame for being shipwrecked on the Hawaiian Islands. Both Maria and Ninian were members of the United "Seceder" Presbyterian Church, a century-old sect whose founders had protested against the state-sanctioned Church of Scotland. They were married on 13 November 1832 at Golden Square Chapel in Berwick by the Reverend Robert Balmer of that church. Ninian's brothers James and John acted as witnesses for the couple.[7] A directory of Berwick businesses lists Maria Redpath as conducting a dressmaking business from the Redpaths' Church Street home in 1834.[8]

James Redpath was born in his family home in Berwick on 24 August 1833 and was baptized in the Golden Street Chapel on 22 September 1833.[9] According to Horner, he was the oldest of seven children.[10] The only other ones known to have survived to adulthood were his sisters Jane and Mary, born in December 1837 and June 1840 respectively, and his brother John, born in December 1844.[11] Increasing child rearing responsibilities forced Maria to curtail her dressmaking business by 1840.

To better support his growing family, Ninian Redpath accepted the position of schoolmaster in the nearby coastal village of Spittal at a newly opened academy supported by the British and Foreign School Society.[12] Ninian Redpath's new employer assisted several hundred academies across the British Isles. These schools attempted to provide an inexpensive elementary education to the children of the poor by employing the "Monitorial" System of instruction, developed by Joseph Lancaster. These "Lancasterian" schools reduced the cost of education by having more advanced students ("monitors") assist adult masters in tutoring younger pupils. The curriculum also incorporated a large dose of scriptural study.[13]

This "British school" in Spittal opened in 1839 after local ministers, merchants, and landowners had raised £75 to qualify for a matching contribution from the British government. During the 1840s, between 127 and 165 students annually attended classes in the small school building constructed near the beach "for the gambols of its children." Parents paid one to two pence a week per child enrolled, but a larger share of the school's budget came from wealthy local patrons. Visiting inspectors from the British and Foreign School Society praised the Spittal school as "sound throughout" and Ninian Redpath as a "sound master."[14]

Soon after accepting his new teaching post, Ninian relocated his family to Spittal. There James Redpath spent his youth. He was a small child who in adulthood measured only five feet, four inches and weighed just over one hundred pounds. Perhaps to compensate for his lack of stature, he drove himself hard physically and his health broke down several times during his life due to prolonged overexertion. Young James Redpath received most of his formal education in his father's school. He developed a fondness for reading English literature that allowed him to sprinkle allusions to such writers as Shakespeare, Milton, Bunyan, Hazlitt, and Bulwer throughout his later reporting. According to family tradition, Ninian desired that his oldest son become a minister of the United Presbyterian faith. The younger Redpath, however, balked at unquestioning adherence to any religious dogma and rejected his father's guidance.[15] Throughout his life Redpath never affiliated with any denomination, although he briefly professed his religious conversion in the early 1860s and possibly dabbled in spiritualism a decade later. He did imbibe in strong anti-Catholic prejudices in his youth but eventually overcame them during trips to Ireland in the 1880s.

After passing all of his educational tests at the age of thirteen, James ended his formal education. Rather than study for the clergyman's profession, he instead learned the printer's trade. Where he received his training as a printer is not known, but the most likely location was the offices of the *Advertiser,* Berwick's weekly newspaper. James also learned shorthand reporting—which an earlier Ridpath had helped to invent—and James, according to Horner, wrote articles for the local newspapers.[16]

The highlight on James's early years in Scotland was a collaborative project with his father. In 1848, Ninian and young James published a new edition of George Ridpath's *Border History of England and Scotland.* This work by their most illustrious ancestor had been long out of print. The father and son carefully reproduced the type and had it printed by Catherine Richardson, the publisher of the *Berwick Advertiser.*[17]

By the late 1840s, the Redpath family was beginning to experience economic difficulties. Ninian had received as much as £66 a year in the mid 1840s from the local committee overseeing the Spittal "British School."[18] Competition from new publicly funded schools, however, caused a slow decline in enrollment at Ninian's school. The British and Foreign School Society also experienced a large drop in financial contributions from some Protestant groups after 1846 when it began accepting state grants.[19] Although the school in Spittal ultimately survived into the twentieth century, its seemingly precarious state caused Ninian to consider emigration to the New World as the best way to provide for the his family's well-being.

In the 1840s, the local economy of the Berwick region, heavily dependent on seaborne commerce, also was beginning a decline due to the recent completion of a direct railroad link between Edinburgh and England.[20] Ninian's brothers, John and James, already had joined the wave of early-nineteenth-century emigration from the Scottish lowlands and adjacent Northumberland.[21] John had departed in 1837, settling first in Canada and then western New York. Less is known about James's emigration except that he had left Berwick before 1847 and bought land in Allegan County in western Michigan before 1850. John then moved to an adjacent township in Allegan around 1850.[22]

Ninian Redpath followed his brothers James and John in migrating from Scotland to Michigan in the late 1840s. The family was reunited in Allegan County, whose settlers contained many first- and second-generation Scottish immigrants. Local records also disclose a number of Davidsons settling in the region who might have been relatives of Maria's from the Berwick area. Ninian attempted to clear the forest from a tract in Martin Township and become a farmer. When the Redpath brothers, Maria Redpath, Charles and Robert Davidson, and six others formed a congregation of the Associate Presbyterian Church, the American branch of the Scottish "Seceder" Presbyterians in Martin Township in March 1852, Ninian was elected one of the two elders. Little more is known of Ninian's brief life in Michigan. In February 1855, this small church elected James to the eldership vacated by his recently deceased brother. This James Redpath thereafter devoted himself to the care of Ninian's widow and children.[23]

Sometime before the death of his father, Ninian, the younger James Redpath had discovered that he had little inclination for farm life. Within a few months of their arrival in Michigan, James separated from his family and found work as a printer and an occasional reporter, for the *Telegraph,* a weekly newspaper published in nearby Kalamazoo, Michigan. That paper was owned and edited by George A. Fitch who later gained some fame as an early advocate of the formation of the Republican Party.[24]

Redpath soon moved on to work for the *Detroit Advertiser* and thereafter his contact with his family became very erratic. His employer in Detroit was Rufus Hosmer, a former colleague of Fitch's. Well-connected in state politics,

"Roof" Hosmer was a prominent Whig in the early 1850s and later an active Republican.[25] Hosmer gave the teenage Redpath the opportunity to write on a wide range of controversial topics. In 1852, Redpath's reporting for the *Advertiser* came to the attention of Horace Greeley, the owner and editor of the *New York Tribune*. Family legend reports that Greeley wired Redpath an offer of a job on the *Tribune* and the nineteen-year-old reporter immediately set off for New York City.[26]

Founded in 1841, the *New York Tribune* was probably the most influential newspaper of the late antebellum period. When Redpath went to work for the newspaper its weekly edition had fifty thousand nationwide subscribers, making it the most read periodical in the world. The *Tribune*'s staff in the mid 1850s included an impressive assortment of literary talents. Charles A. Dana Jr., who later managed the *New York Sun,* oversaw the newspaper's editorial operations. The operatic and symphony composer, William H. Fry, and the historian, Richard Hildreth, directed the political reporting. The noted utopian George Ripley served as literary editor for the *Tribune.* By this time, Greeley, himself, wrote relatively little for the *Tribune,* except occasional editorials on behalf of one of the numerous reform causes or political movements he championed.[27]

Young reporters like Redpath labored in anonymity at the *Tribune.* At first, he worked in the city department as a "local" gathering up news items to fill a gossipy paragraph or two. Because of his stenographic training, Redpath soon gained the rank of "reporter" and attended meetings and public events to "take down" the important speeches that were reprinted at length. Editors frequently sent Redpath to the city's courts and prisons to prepare crime stories that filled many *Tribune* columns.[28] Redpath also did numerous routine office jobs at the *Tribune,* including corresponding with politicians such as William H. Seward regarding the correct text of their speeches when published.[29]

There is evidence that Redpath also did extensive research for editorials that the *Tribune* attributed solely to Greeley. He later complained that Greeley and other *Tribune* editors mistreated their staff by assuming credit for all editorial writing. Redpath publicly pledged in writing never to be guilty of such practices "if ever I become—and I give you warning that I mean to—an influential journalist."[30] After leaving the *Tribune*'s employ a few years later, Redpath wrote that "Greeley's reputation is one of the great shams of the day."[31]

Settling in New York City, the teenage Redpath developed friendships with a small circle of journalists and writers, many of them of recent British extraction. The most famous of this group was the dramatist and novelist William North, often compared to Edgar Allen Poe. A slightly older journalist who hung on the outskirts of this group was Walt Whitman. Whitman and Redpath remained close friends for life.[32] This semi-Bohemian group frequented restaurants and German beer halls, including Pfaff's, the Howe

House, and Windust's, debating, drinking, and singing late into the night. Never a temperance advocate, Redpath later admitted that at this time in his life "he had drunk enough of lager bier in German cellars to have drowned Governor Seymour and all his hosts."[33]

By early 1854, Redpath had been promoted to exchange, or mail, editor with responsibility for searching for stories in other newspapers to reprint in the *Tribune*. He later wrote this humorous description of the exchange editor's job: "He reads and mutilates newspapers from nine o'clock in the morning till six in the evening. The Tribune and the Herald have enormous exchange lists. It is as much as one can do to glance over a day's mail in a day. The situation of a mail editor on a metropolitan journal causes every one who fills it to cherish a profound contempt for partizan or personal politics, and the political press in general and in detail."[34] It was at this task that Redpath developed his first interest in the true character of southern slavery. He produced a regular feature for the *Tribune,* entitled "The Facts of Slavery," which reprinted accounts of the treatment of southern slaves.[35]

Few clues survive about Redpath's attitude toward slavery during these years. There is no evidence of Redpath's intimacy with any abolitionists during the early 1850s.[36] The best evidence available is Redpath's testimony, given a decade later to the Freedman's Inquiry Commission, that in the early 1850s he had been "an abolitionist, but a very mild one."[37]

As a result of his assignment on the "Facts of Slavery" column, Redpath developed a strong curiosity about that subject. Serious overwork at the *Tribune* caused the twenty-year-old Redpath to consider taking a leave from his job in the spring of 1854, and the idea of a pedestrian tour of the South began to develop in his mind. He later recalled: "My object in travelling was, in part, to recruit my health, but chiefly to see slavery with my own eyes, and personally learn what the bondsmen said and thought of their condition."[38] The opportunity to examine slavery "with my own eyes" would enormously intensify Redpath's antislavery sentiments along lines described by historian James L. Huston. He notes that most native Northerners and recent immigrants in the 1840s and 1850s lacked firsthand contact with slavery. At most they regarded the institution as an abstract or imagined evil. A surprisingly large proportion of leading abolitionists, Huston finds, had an "experiential basis" for their antislavery views. They had visited the South where personally witnessing the cruelties of slavery had a profound emotional impact that aroused a fervid commitment to the abolitionist cause.[39] Redpath's three tours of the South in the mid and late 1850s had just such an effect.

Redpath also had a journalistic inspiration for his southern travels. Just one year before Redpath's first tour, Frederick Law Olmsted of the *New York Times* had undertaken the first of several tours of the slave states and published travel letters describing various aspects of southern life. Olmsted opposed immediate emancipation but looked toward the eventual extinction of slavery by unfavorable economic forces. He noted a widespread southern fear of slave insurrection but never commented on its likelihood. Olmsted's letters served as a rough model for the reports Redpath would later write, but the latter's analysis of conditions under slavery would be far less dispassionate.[40]

Redpath set off for the South in late March 1854 and sailed from New York City by steamer to Richmond, Virginia. He toured the town and visited a slave auction. A high point of his stay was an afternoon spent in conversation with a free black confectionary and his wife in their store. After some hesitation, the two discoursed freely with Redpath about the conditions of slaves, the legal impediments placed on free blacks, the attitude of poor whites toward blacks, and the "African church."[41]

Redpath experienced depression while residing in Richmond, far from family and friends, and later claimed to have contemplated suicide. He recalled that he abandoned that idea on reading the novel *Alone* by a young female southern writer, Mary Virginia Terhune, who wrote under the pen name Marion Harland. Redpath immediately began a correspondence with Terhune. His first letter began by telling her: "I detest both your politics and your theology. All the same, you will make your mark upon the age. In the full persuasion of this, I write to pledge myself to do all in my power to forward your literary interests." During the next few years, Redpath quoted or praised Terhune's work in scores of newspaper articles and mailed her the clippings. Only five years later did Redpath explain to Terhune that on arriving in Richmond in 1854, he had determined on suicide and gone to the cemetery with a pistol to kill himself. He had earlier purchased a copy of *Alone* and planned to read it while waiting for darkness to give concealment and solitude to his final act. Redpath wrote Terhune that "your book held me back from infidelity. Chapter Sixteenth [containing the story of an interrupted duel] saved my life." Terhune doubted the sincerity of Redpath's story but nonetheless was charmed by the impulsive and romantic personality of the young journalist who labored so loyally to advance her literary career.[42]

Redpath departed Richmond by railroad for Wilmington, North Carolina, where he stayed three days. He then traveled on to Charleston, South Carolina, by steamship. Redpath arrived shortly before the start of the latest in a series of Southern Commercial Conventions, held from the 10th to the 15th of April 1854. The purpose of these gatherings was to promote the region's economic diversification by fostering manufacturing and improving transportation facilities. However, politicians less interested in business than in advocating southern nationalism took over the 1854 convention. Redpath sarcastically claimed that delegates had come to the Charleston gathering "to discuss the interests, and 'resolve' on the prosperity—immediate, unparalleled, and unconditional—of slaveholding trade, territory, education, Legree-lash-literature, and 'direct commerce with Europe!'"[43]

Without authorization from the *Tribune,* Redpath prepared a series of reports on this convention but all save one were drastically summarized by the paper's news editors who stated that "we have not found substance enough in the proceedings to make them worth inserting in our columns."[44] Even in abbreviated fashion, Redpath's *Tribune* reports conveyed the scene of a city working very hard to entertain and impress businessmen, politicians, and journalists who had gathered from all across the South and from some northern cities as well. In the one completely printed *Tribune* report, Redpath related that journalists had received free theater tickets and invitations to lavish balls. After taking full advantage of both opportunities, he wrote, "Thus, you see, if the strangers here are not happy and [do not] have a good time of it during the week, the fault will not be attributed to the citizens of Charleston."[45]

Despite this hospitable treatment from the city of Charleston, Redpath encountered problems in covering the convention itself. Initially he found himself well treated by the delegates, especially the well-known Reverend William G. Brownlow, who introduced Redpath to many prominent Southerners. One of these individuals inadvertently created problems for Redpath when he got the convention to accredit reporters from the northern press as honorary members.[46] The local newspapers, the *Charleston News and Courier* and the *Charleston Standard,* however, denounced the action. The next day at the convention, a delegate introduced a motion to deny Redpath, as the representative of the antislavery *Tribune,* access to the floor of the convention. A reporter for the *New York Herald,* whose paper had a reputation for friendly coverage of slavery, reported a "spicy debate" over the motion and observed that Redpath's "conduct there is unexceptionable, and the editors of the morning papers show him every attention." After a lengthy debate the resolution was withdrawn.[47] Thereupon Redpath rose, removed his delegate ribbon, and departed the reporters' seats for the spectators' gallery from which he observed the remainder of the convention. This exhibition of defiance, Redpath later explained "was due to the press to reciprocate the contempt of the politicians."[48]

After the close of the commercial convention Redpath spent another week in Charleston. He conversed with numerous blacks in the city and visited the notorious Sugar House where slaves were brought for punishment. While these talks nurtured his growing antislavery sentiments, he nevertheless became enchanted with the city itself. Redpath later recalled that Charleston's "thoroughly English appearance and construction, its old-time customs, its genial climate . . . cast a spell around my spirit during my sojourn there."[49] Only with great reluctance did he resume his southern travels.

Redpath traveled to Savannah, Georgia, where he got a job as a city reporter for the *Daily Morning News.* His very first article for the *Morning News* was a report about the Charleston commercial convention, which he signed as "Tweed." Adopting the posture of a "Southern Rights man,"

Redpath wrote a thoughtful critique of the convention's proceedings. He playfully devoted a large amount of space to chastising the convention for wasting so much of its time in attempting to expel an unnamed reporter from the *New York Tribune*.[50]

The *Savannah Morning News'* editor, William T. Thompson, was a popular humorist. He had published several collections of his newspaper columns, purporting to be the letters from "Major Jones," a Georgian tourist on a world tour.[51] Redpath copied Thompson's style of writing during his three months on the *Morning News*. He produced numerous articles that took the form of a dialogue between a "Mr. Tweed" and "Major Jones." For example, Redpath used an imaginary meeting on the street between Tweed and Jones to enliven the start of a mundane report of a visit to the Savannah waterworks. In this article Redpath also mused that "true journalists if they do not know every one and everything, always speak as if they did."[52] Redpath also wrote a letter under his own name, using with evidence gathered in his series to refute charges from a sermon reprinted in the *New York Tribune* about the moral insensitivity of Georgians.[53]

Redpath also supplemented his routine journalistic production with a running series of articles sure to have pleased "Major Jones." Redpath created the character "Berwick," a Southerner "by temperament and self-adoption,"[54] who regularly wrote Jones lengthy letters while on a visit to New York City. Using his old skills as an exchange editor, Redpath manufactured a chatty series of reports on cultural and political events in New York by scanning and reproducing items from that city's newspapers mailed to the *Morning News*.[55]

Berwick also reported on the annual anniversary week in New York City where dozens of religious and reform groups held public meetings. By this means, Redpath introduced lengthy reports on the anniversary meetings of abolitionist societies into the *Morning News*. He playfully closed one of these reports with what was, under the circumstances, a highly ambiguous condemnation: "By their fruits and by their words ye shall judge them."[56] Berwick also reprinted verbatim many northern editorials and resolutions by public meetings denouncing the Kansas-Nebraska Bill, then undergoing debate in Congress. Comparing such editorials in one article, he advised readers to regard the *New York Times* as "more obnoxious" than the *Tribune* of that city because it was "a less manly opponent of Southern institutions." Surely with himself in mind, he counseled Southerners that "an open foe is less dangerous than a secret enemy."[57]

In mid June 1854, Redpath left Savannah to return to New York City. Thompson accompanied him to the wharf and saw him off on the steamship *Knoxville*. Redpath promised to mail Thompson a new series of reports from New York, this time real ones, to be signed "Tweed." On 19 June, the *Morning News* published what was intended as the first of these "Northern Notes for Southern Circulation."[58] In a half-humorous and half-philosophical vein,

Tweed recounted the voyage northward. Sadly, this was the last piece Redpath produced for the Savannah newspaper, except for a brief and highly flattering review of Marion's Harland's *Alone,* which, it claimed, merited attention because "its literary character is as praiseworthy as its typographical, although the author, like its publisher, is a citizen of a State [Virginia] not fruitful in literature."[59]

What Redpath had witnessed in the South had made him a confirmed enemy of slavery. On returning to New York City, he decided to recount his observations of the southern institution and his conversations with its victims. Using notes from a diary he kept while on his trip, he prepared a series of articles in the form of letters recounting his contact with southern slaves.[60] Redpath also determined to make another, more extensive tour of the South and to use his travels to produce more eyewitness descriptions of slavery, loosely modeled on Olmsted's series for the *New York Times.*

Redpath took his letters first to the New York City offices of the *National Anti-Slavery Standard,* the official newspaper of the American Anti-Slavery Society. That newspaper's editor, Sidney Howard Gay—preoccupied with the illness of one of his children—let Redpath's letters go several weeks without evaluating their suitability for publication.[61] In a hurry to depart for his second southern tour, Redpath retrieved the letters and mailed them to the nation's foremost abolitionist newspaper, the *Liberator,* edited by William Lloyd Garrison in Boston. Redpath requested that Garrison publish the letters under the pseudonym "John Ball Jr." rather than his own name. This choice of a pen name is illuminating, for the original John Ball was a fourteenth-century English priest executed by King Richard II for seditious preaching that encouraged the peasants' insurrection led by Wat Tyler.[62]

To further camouflage his identity, Redpath supplied Garrison with what he called a "blind," a short letter purportedly from Ball to relatives in Iowa to be published at the start of the series, supplying false biographical information about the correspondent.[63] Redpath told Garrison that he feared that "if it were to become known that I am an 'ultra' abolitionist, my life would not be considered a profitable investment at any insurance office."[64]

The first series of John Ball Jr. letters appeared in the *Liberator* in August and September 1854 while Redpath journeyed again in the South. In addition to the "blind," there were two letters describing slavery in Richmond and one each focused on Wilmington and Charleston. Perhaps because he had become well known to so many in Savannah, he omitted any reference to his three-month stay there.[65]

Before leaving New York City, Redpath also made an agreement with Gay of the *National Anti-Slavery Standard* to send him more John Ball Jr. letters from various southern locations.[66] Fifteen of these letters appeared in the *National Anti-Slavery Standard* between October 1854 and April 1855.[67] The *Standard* paid Redpath $2.50 for each of the letters. Redpath told Gay that the salary did not meet his traveling expenses but boasted "as I am 'a fanatic' or an Enthusiast at least—I gladly gave my time to promote so desirable a Revolution!"[68] Redpath also sent the *National Anti-Slavery Standard* numerous clippings describing the mistreatment of slaves and free blacks from newspapers in the cities he visited.[69] In addition, he wrote occasional reports for publication in the *New York Tribune* but he signed these with pen names other than John Ball Jr.[70]

An abolitionist risked his well-being and perhaps even his life to enter the South to interview slaves and record their opinions about slavery for the northern press. Redpath remained fearful that some unfriendly northern colleague would recognize his hyperbolic writing style and identify him as the author of the John Ball Jr. letters and warned Gay to "never mention my name to any one—above all not to the *Times*-servers. Never let it appear in the Stand*d* in *any* connection."[71]

To avoid having his frequent correspondence with the abolitionist newspaper traced, Redpath arranged an elaborate system of third-parties, including New York City friends and Michigan relatives, to forward mail to and from him. Redpath also instructed Gay to discontinue the exchange of the *National Anti-Slavery Standard* with newspapers from the cities where he was residing in order to prevent unwanted local publicity for his reporting.[72] In case copies of his John Ball Jr. articles nevertheless reached the South, Redpath supplied false itineraries in the letters to throw the suspicious off his track.[73]

Redpath departed from New York on his second tour in September 1854, shortly before his twenty-first birthday. He visited his friend, the free black confectionary in Richmond, and discovered that the man's wife had died earlier that summer. Carrying his possessions in a carpetbag, he walked the seventy miles from Petersburg, Virginia, to Weldon, North Carolina, spending one night in the home of a planter and another in that of a small farmer. After a train ride to Wilmington, he waited there a week without receiving a draft of cash that a friend had promised to send him. By now nearly penniless, Redpath decided to set off on foot for Charleston, following the railroad line. Finding the walking difficult along railroad trestles over the swampy coastal plain, he altered his plans and proceeded on to Columbia, South Carolina, and then on to Augusta, Georgia.[74]

Redpath reached Augusta when it was in the midst of a yellow fever epidemic. Much of the city's population had evacuated the city for the healthier countryside. Redpath later explained that he had ignored warnings about the danger of entering the city because he "believed in destiny; and therefore never hesitated to run any risk of any kind anywhere."[75] Redpath spent several weeks in Augusta, working for the *Daily Constitutionalist and Republican*. Not much of his writing for that newspaper can be detected besides literary reviews, including a puff for Marion Harland's *Alone,* which he pronounced "a well written and interesting story."[76]

Despite all of his precautions to protect his secrecy, Redpath felt he came perilously close to discovery in Augusta. In November 1854, James Gardner, editor of the *Augusta Constitutionalist,* inadvertently opened a letter that one of Redpath's teenage sisters back in Michigan had mailed him in care of that newspaper. This letter contained references to the John Ball Jr. series but Gardner claimed to have read only the salutation before turning it over to Redpath. The incident nonetheless unnerved Redpath, and he quickly departed Augusta for Montgomery. In a John Ball Jr. letter sent to the *National Anti-Slavery Standard* just as he left Augusta, Redpath related: "I am suspected here of being a lover of Liberty and therefore—and as I have an innate aversion to a costume of feathers—I am preparing to fly to another state."[77]

Although Redpath had an offer of a reporter's job on a Charleston newspaper, he instead decided to travel to New Orleans, where another commercial convention was to be held in January. He left Augusta in late November and walked to Atlanta which he described as "straggling business place of about nine thousand inhabitants."[78] He hiked on to Montgomery, Alabama, where he stayed several weeks. Redpath ridiculed the city's sense of morality for auctioning off slaves six days a week but then forbidding even the sale of cigars on Sunday. Redpath entered into an arrangement with the editor of the *Montgomery Daily Mail* to send columns from New Orleans to his newspaper. Redpath then sailed down the Alabama River to Mobile and took a steamer to New Orleans.[79]

Redpath arrived in the Crescent City in January 1855. In addition to writing occasional pieces for the *Montgomery Mail,* he probably authored anonymous reports on the commercial convention for the *New York Tribune.* The *New Orleans Daily Picayune* complained that those reports had undertaken "with a brazen assumption of superiority to lecture Southern men on their habits, their modes of doing business, their agricultural pursuits, their lack of enterprise, etc."[80]

From New Orleans, Redpath wrote Gay that he had run up a large debt: "My traveling expenses have got me into serious embarrassment. It will be six months at least before I am again out of financial difficulties."[81] To regain solvency, Redpath found a full-time job as a reporter for the *New Orleans Bee* or *L'Abeille,* which was published in both English and French. The *Bee*'s editorial office was a "long, lofty room," Redpath recalled, where the editors "as ably argued and defended theories as you ever heard either in court, college, caucus, club, or social gathering" in both languages.[82]

Most of Redpath's writing for the *Bee* was anonymous. In private letters to friends, Redpath boasted of his ability to write fiery prosouthern articles despite his strong abolitionist sentiments.[83] Unfortunately no example of such a proslavery article can be detected from this period but one significant story traceable to Redpath's pen was his account of the public execution of Wilhelm Jung, the murderer by starvation of his youthful ward. Due to bungled work by the hangman, Jung took almost twenty minutes to die. Redpath reported that "it was the most revolting spectacle that we have ever saw or read of."[84] A decade later, Redpath retold the incident in an anti–capital punishment tract he wrote and published. At that later time, he bitterly denounced the callousness of the specially invited audience of one hundred who "smoked, joked, laughed, talked, swore, and spat as inconcernedly as if nothing of any consequence had called them together."[85]

Despite his revulsion at the hanging, Redpath found much to like in New Orleans. He wrote that "externally, at least, it is one of the most pleasant cities I ever visited. . . . It requires but little aid from fancy, to imagine oneself in a European city when in many of the streets of New Orleans."[86] He made friends of fellow reporters. One of them, Joseph Brenan, an editorial writer for the rival *Delta,* had been exiled from Ireland for his activities in the nationalist Young Ireland movement.[87] Redpath also busied himself on behalf of his old friends, persuading literary magazines to reprint poems by Mary Virginia Terhune and soliciting positive reviews for the novel *Slave of the Lamp,* by his friend William North, who had committed suicide the previous fall.[88]

Redpath also produced four new John Ball Jr. letters in February and March 1854. That brought to a total of fifteen John Ball Jr. letters that Redpath wrote for the *National Anti-Slavery Standard* during his second tour of the South. These letters related numerous conversations about the institution of slavery with free blacks, nonslaveholding whites, and planters. The most important feature of the letters were accounts of secretly conducted interviews with slaves about their living conditions and their contentment.

The history of Redpath's travels in the South and of the publication history of the John Ball Jr. letters helps to bolster the authenticity of Redpath's slave interviews. The newspaper articles in the *Liberator* and the *National Anti-Slavery Standard* supply the places and times of many of the slave interviews. Surviving private correspondence and Redpath's published articles in other newspapers verify his residence in southern communities at the times these interviews were reported to have taken place.[89]

Proving that Redpath had the opportunity to have conducted interviews with southern slaves, of course, does not prove that he did interview slaves or prove that if he did interview them his published interviews were true reports of what the slaves told him. There are a few facts that lend a degree of credibility to the interviews. In the *National Anti-Slavery Standard,* Redpath answered contemporary critics of the veracity of his reports:

> I defy the united slaveocracy of the South to prove that I have spoken falsely. Many facts that I have advanced will be doubted or denied; but whoever will follow in my footsteps and speak with the slaves as I spoke to them, and as frequently as I did, will find that I have been a most truthful chronicler.[90]

Since modern scholars do not have the option of actually retracing Redpath's travels, they must rely on other evidence to help validate his interviews. Some of the best evidence is the information that Redpath himself supplied about the technique of his interviewing.

In later correspondence, Redpath told New York abolitionist Gerrit Smith that he had interviewed nearly a thousand slaves during his travels.[91] Although this claim seems greatly exaggerated, how Redpath could have persuaded slaves to speak candidly is a serious question. In one John Ball Jr. letter he described the manner he approached slaves for interviews:

> Before questioning any of the slaves, or free men of color whom I have hitherto spoken with on the topic of slavery, I have invariably informed them that I am a Northern abolitionist, traveling in the South for the purpose of ascertaining the real sentiments of the African population on the subject of involuntary bondage. By showing myself to be their friend, I have elicited replies that could have been obtained by no other method.[92]

Redpath presented additional reasons why the slaves were willing to confide in him. He observed that slaves seemed more inclined to trust him because of his British origins as made obvious by his accent; a circumstance probably also true when he conversed with southern whites.[93] An even more important factor, Redpath believed, was his effort to treat the slaves as his equals in conversation: "I have been their [the slaves'] favorite and confident wherever I have gone, because I did not adopt the 'shiftless' policy of speaking as if conscious of being of a nobler race. I *could not* do so, if I would: for I, for one, am a firm believer in the equality of the African race."[94] As evidence of his freedom from racial prejudice, Redpath reported that he had spent ten consecutive nights sleeping in slaves' cabins and sharing their meals while crossing Georgia and Alabama on foot.[95]

Redpath took great pains to record accurately the responses of the slaves to his questions. To answer skeptics, he described his method:

> My conversations with the slaves were written down as soon after they occurred as was convenient; occasionally, indeed, in stenographic notes, as the negroes spoke to me. It will be seen that I do not aim at a literary reputation. I have only plain truth to tell—only plain words to tell them in. My mission was a humble one—to report. I claim no other merit than fidelity to that duty.[96]

Redpath also defended the accuracy of his interviews and of his observations of southern life on the grounds that his personal antislavery creed was not based on the actual treatment of the southern slaves. As John Ball Jr., he told readers of the *Liberator*:

> I will relate, with equal willingness, whatever I see of evil or of good in slavery as it exists here; because I regard the question of slavery as a moral question,

and therefore to be determined by pure reason, and neither by social nor historical considerations, nor by the deductions of experience. If Slavery is right, then are the sufferings of the slaves—and sufferings exist—of no moment whatever; and if, on the other hand, it is wrong, then, also, are the contentment of the slaves—if they *are* happy and content—of no importance whatever, as far as the settlement of the question of slavery is concerned.[97]

All doubts about the reliability of the slave interviews in the John Ball Jr. articles can never be laid to rest. Redpath's previous journalistic career at the *Savannah Daily Morning News* shows him to have been a highly inventive writer, quick to blend fiction with fact. Therefore scholars need to approach the John Ball Jr. letters with a degree of skepticism about their accuracy in every detail. Nonetheless, as a combination of a documentary account of conditions under slavery and a travelogue of the antebellum South by a perceptive critic, the John Ball Jr. letters demand careful attention.

In his interviews, Redpath usually questioned slaves about topics of interest to his northern readers such as work patterns, living conditions, family life, and religious practices. When Redpath asked for evidence of mistreatment by masters or by other whites, he received some exceptionally graphic replies.[98] The interviews also contain considerable slave testimony regarding violations of the sanctity of their marriages and the involuntary separation of their families.[99] Redpath evidenced little respect for the religious practices of slaves but he nevertheless quoted black complaints about white controls over their churches.[100] True to his promise to report positive as well as negative aspects of slavery, Redpath related the testimony of several slaves who, while hired out by their masters, had managed to earn money toward their eventual manumission.[101]

In response to his questioning, the slaves frequently asked Redpath for information about the condition of free blacks in the North and in Canada and about the prospects of the abolition movement. Redpath admitted that free blacks in the North faced heavy discriminatory laws and customs and reproved his northern readers "disgraceful and relentless prejudices" for not abolishing them.[102]

Invariably Redpath inquired if any slaves were content with their status. The answers to this question were quite revealing. "*Not more than one-tenth.* As few as has good masters doesn't think about freedom so much; but if they could get the offer, *all* of them would be free," replied a North Carolina slave. "Well, I never met but one. *He* said he would rather be a slave than a freeman; he, I guess, was a liar. . . . What slave-man wouldn't rather work for himself than for a boss, mass'r?" was the response from a Virginia field hand.[103]

The contents of the John Ball Jr. letters reveal significant evolution in Redpath's thinking about violent antislavery tactics. A few years later, he claimed that his purpose in touring the South had been to find means to aid the slaves obtain their freedom: "If I found that slavery had so far degraded them, that they were comparatively contented with their debased condition, I resolved, before I started, to spend my time in the South, in disseminating discontentment. But if, on the other hand, I found them ripe for a rebellion, my resolution was to prepare the way for it, as far as my abilities and opportunities permitted."[104] A close examination of the John Ball Jr. letters from 1854 to 1855, however, reveal that at the earlier period Redpath was less single-mindedly committed to slave insurrection than he was at the end of the decade.

An important feature of Redpath's John Ball Jr. letters was the number of slaves who expressed the willingness to escape or even fight for their freedom, especially if assisted by sympathetic whites. Redpath observed that slave sentiment varied from region to region in the South. He noted: "At Richmond and at Wilmington . . . I found the slaves discontented, but despondingly resigned to their fate. At Charleston I found them morose and savagely brooding over their wrongs."[105] Redpath reported that one Charleston slave had told him that "all [slaves] that I does know *wants to be free very bad,* I tell you, and *maybe will fight before long if they don't get freedom somehow.*"[106] Redpath concluded that in Charleston "the sewers of the city [would] be instantly filled with the blood of the slave masters," if the slaves believed a rebellion could succeed.[107]

Redpath also reported finding evidence of great discontent among the free-black population of the South. He published lengthy interviews with several who complained bitterly of the discrimination they endured. Redpath believed that the free blacks would need little encouragement to enlist in any insurrectionary plot.[108]

Another discontented group that Redpath uncovered during his southern travels were the nonslaveholding artisans and small merchants of southern cities and towns, especially immigrants from Britain or Germany, most of whom he believed to be "secret abolitionists."[109] The only significant exception was the Irish. The Irish immigrants, according to Redpath, "have acquired the reputation, both among Southerners and Africans, of being the most merciless of taskmasters."[110]

Redpath contended that practically all slaveholders were beyond the reach of traditional abolitionist tactics of moral suasion but believed that the nonslaveholding whites could be shown that slavery is an economic curse to them by carefully crafted literature. Once these people had been fully converted, Redpath proposed: "Let the *anti-slavery* population of the South be associated by forming a secret society similar to the Odd Fellows, or the Masons, or the Blue Lodges of Missouri, and let this union be extended over the entire country. The societies could circulate tracts, assist slaves in escaping, and direct the movements of the agents of the Grand Lodge."[111]

Redpath used the John Ball Jr. letters to defend the slaves' right to violent rebellion: "Although . . . I wish to see slavery abolished at any cost—even at the cost of a social St. Bartholomew's night, I do not say that even the majority of the slaveholders are depraved men. But the negroes have the right to that liberty to which their masters, who deprive them of it, have none: and if their owners resolutely refuse to set them free, then—let them, without mummuring, endure *the approaching massacre.*"[112]

Despite Redpath's willingness to sanction violent slave rebellion in the John Ball Jr. letters, he devoted far more space in them to advocating a more pacific way for abolitionists to assist the slaves to obtain their freedom. During his second tour of the South, Redpath began encouraging northern abolitionists to aid slaves to escape. More than year before he met John Brown in Kansas, Redpath publicly advocated a plan historians associate with the older abolitionist. Redpath publicly predicted that "A GENERAL STAMPEDE OF THE SLAVES" could involuntarily make North Carolina and Virginia into free states "if the Abolitionists would send down a trustworthy Band of 'Liberators' provided with compasses, pistols, and a little money for the fugitives."[113] In North Carolina, Redpath boasted: "If I had a good stock of revolving pistols and as many pocket-compasses, I would not leave this State until I had liberated, at least, a hundred slaves."[114] Redpath claimed to have personally given advice on ways to escape to more than a dozen slaves.[115]

Redpath proposed a secret organization to carry out his slave escape plan. He advised northern abolitionists:

> Appoint a small band of bold but cautious men to travel in the most Northern slave States for the purpose of securing the cooperation of the free-colored population in assisting fugitives; of disseminating discontent among the slave themselves, and of providing the most energetic of them who wish to escape with pocket compasses, pistols, and directions. . . . Ten or twelve such apostles of Freedom could, in one year, easily induce six or seven slaves to fly to the North; of which, if they were properly equipped, at least five thousand would escape bondage forever.

"John Ball Jr." volunteered to serve as one of these apostles for three months if provisioned, but no one backed him.[116]

Redpath claimed that only by such organized activity in the South could the abolitionists truly assist the slaves. He advised them: "Let not the Abolitionists of the North be deceived. The South will *never* liberate her slaves, unless compelled by FEAR to do so; or unless the activity of the abolitionists renders human property so insecure a possession as to be comparatively worthless to its owner."[117]

The John Ball Jr. letters document Redpath's growing commitment to abolitionism and his striving to use his journalistic skills on behalf of that crusade. With the publication of these letters, Redpath took his place among a younger generation of abolitionists, including Thomas Wentworth Higginson and Theodore Parker, who had little patience with the pacifism espoused by many of those who had launched the modern American anti-slavery movement in the 1830s.[118] But in 1855, Redpath's contribution to abolitionism still remained a secret one. Aside from his family and a few close friends, only Garrison and Gay knew the real identity of John Ball Jr.

Redpath's anonymity was essential to his journalistic mission in the South and another close call in almost being exposed helped bring his second southern journey to its end. At the end of January, he sent two incautious pseudonymous letters, describing a slave auction, to his old employer, the *New York Tribune*.[119] When copies of the *Tribune* articles containing Redpath's account of the slave auction reached New Orleans in mid March 1855, they produced an immediate uproar. The New Orleans *Delta* denounced the *Tribune* and the articles as "the boldest fabrications that were ever imposed upon a public journal, or imposed by such a journal upon a credulous people." The *Delta* also demanded that the city police detect and punish "the sneaking Abolitionists in the pay of Northern journals, who pry around our city, hunting up pretexts for their atrocious falsehoods."[120]

By this time Redpath had become intimate with many members of the small journalistic establishment in New Orleans. He also had made no effort to hide his earlier connection with the *Tribune*. The increased danger of exposure after this incident therefore caused Redpath to halt his production of John Ball Jr. letters for the *National Anti-Slavery Standard*. He remained at his job with the *Bee* until late May. At that time, the rumor of a resurgence of the cholera epidemic that had caused several thousand deaths in New Orleans since 1848 frightened Redpath. He later recalled leaving New Orleans "to escape the entangling endearments of the cholera, which already had its hands in my hair" and setting off north in the direction of St. Louis.[121]

2   *The Crusader of Freedom*

In 1859, James Redpath reminisced about the three years he had just spent in the Territory of Kansas. He claimed that he had gone there because "I believed that a civil war between the North and South would ultimate in [slave] insurrection, and that Kansas troubles would probably create a military conflict section. Hence I . . . went to Kansas; and endeavored, personally and by my pen, to precipitate a revolution."[1] Close examination of Redpath's Kansas career, however, reveals that a commitment to violent antislavery tactics was not present at the time of his first arrival in the territory. Redpath's support for violent means instead appears to have developed gradually as a result of a combination of factors. Throughout most of his Kansas residence, Redpath advocated political means to resist the spread of slavery, championing first the Free State Party and then the Republican Party in the territory. However, he became steadily more disenchanted with the low antislavery standards of Kansas's free-state politicians. At the same time, Redpath actively participated in the paramilitary groups that resisted attempts by Southerners and federal officials to establish slavery in Kansas. This latter activity drew Redpath into close contact with radical abolitionist John Brown, who sought to turn the sectional feuding over slavery in Kansas into the spark that would lead to civil war and eventually emancipation. By the time Redpath left Kansas to settle in Massachusetts in mid 1858, Brown had enlisted him in the secret plot that resulted in the Harpers Ferry Raid the following year.

St. Louis was growing rapidly in the decades before the Civil War. By the time of Redpath's arrival in June 1855, it possessed more than eighty thousand residents. Members of the older southern-born generation were now elbowed by recent arrivals from New England, Ireland, and especially Germany. While still a commercial entrepôt, the city increasingly attracted small manufacturing establishments. A vibrant and growing community in the 1850s, St. Louis competed strongly with Chicago to become the transportation hub and financial center of the Midwest. This combination of demographic and economic factors allowed an unprecedented amount of questioning of slavery for a southern city.[2]

Immediately on his arrival in St. Louis, Redpath sought out journalistic employment on the *Daily Missouri Democrat*. He chose this newspaper because it was the voice of the moderate antislavery elements in that city and the border state. The *Democrat* was owned William McKee, a printer, and two young, aspiring politicians, Francis "Frank" Blair Jr., the son of a prominent member of Andrew Jackson's "kitchen cabinet," and B. Gratz Brown, the younger Blair's cousin and law partner. Since its founding in 1852, the *Democrat* had slowly evolved from support of the aging Missouri political legend, Thomas Hart Benton, to a cautiously stated free-soil position.[3]

When Redpath arrived at the *Democrat*'s office on Locust Street between Main and Second, he was tired and tattered from his travels northward from the Deep South. The business manager Daniel M. Houser, who after the Civil War would purchase the paper and develop it into the renowned *St. Louis Globe-Democrat,* listened to Redpath's request for work. Impressed by the applicant's previous journalistic experience, if not his current appearance, Houser took Redpath to see Theophile Papin, the head of the *Democrat*'s city department. Papin gave Redpath several trial assignments.[4] Redpath produced a gossipy series of articles on the press of New Orleans that certainly appealed to the *Democrat*'s editorial staff if not its readers. About the Crescent City, he came to the interesting conclusion that "except for the summer solstice, New Orleans contains more anti-slavery than pro-slavery citizens. But the dominant party is powerful and imperious, and the actual majority are obliged to be silent."[5]

The *Democrat* hired Redpath as a staff reporter. Among his early productions was a series of articles entitled "Jottings in a Junior's Sanctum." These articles featured lengthy quotations from plays, poems, and novels that Redpath was reading. His tastes ran from German dramatist Johann Wolfgang Goethe and English essayist Matthew Carey to the popular female novelist Anna Bartlett Warner and his favorite writer Marion Harland. In a humorous aside Redpath declined to criticize one writer because he himself had more failings and listed four: "First—a love of rosy lips. Second—a still stronger passion for good cigars. Third—a weakness in favor of champagne punch. Fourth—I'm a writer for the press."[6] These jottings leave the impression of a twenty-one-year-old journalist full of energy and short on reverence.

Redpath's arrival in St. Louis coincided with the rapid increase of political debate over slavery. The previous year, Illinois Democratic senator Stephen Douglas, ambitious to secure his party's next presidential nomination, had gotten Congress to pass the Kansas-Nebraska Act. This legislation opened those territories for settlement with the provision that the question of establishing slavery would be resolved by the will of their actual settlers. This policy of popular sovereignty helped to attract thousands to the territories and soon produced heated and sometimes violent disagreements among its settlers over slavery.

The Kansas-Nebraska Act had voided the main provision of the Missouri Compromise, which had prohibited slavery within the old Louisiana Purchase north of the 36 30' parallel. The repeal of this longstanding sectional compromise angered many Northerners and caused them to form the Republican Party to oppose the further spread of slavery into the West. At the same time, Northerners formed emigrant aid societies to assist free-state settlers to reach Kansas and create a majority there opposed to the institution of slavery. Missourians and other Southerners were alarmed by the organized northern invasion of Kansas. Led by U.S. senator David M. Atchison, several thousand Missourians crossed into Kansas and voted in the 30 March 1855 election for the first territorial legislature. Because of this fraud, the proslavery forces handily won and free-state settlers refused to recognize the authority of the "bogus" legislature.[7] Subsequent quarrels between settlers from the free and slave states captured the nation's attention and the editors of the *Democrat* decided to dispatch their newest staff reporter, Redpath, to cover that story.

All press coverage of Kansas events was highly colored by the ideological question of slavery. Most of the major eastern newspapers sent reporters to the territory, where they lived a dangerous life, chronicling the descent of territorial politics into bloody civil war. Nearly all of these reporters were in their twenties or early thirties and a high percentage were of recent British origin, including Redpath, William A. Phillips, Richard J. Hinton, and Richard Realf. Most of these men held free-soil or abolitionist sentiments and several eventually became followers of John Brown.[8]

Many historians have been critical of the partisan nature of Kansas reporting in the eastern press. James Ford Rhodes charged that the free-state reporters were "ready to believe the most atrocious outrages related of the border ruffians, and apt to suppress facts that told against their own party."[9] James C. Malin accused Republican Party newspaper reporters and editors of taking "advantage of every aspect of the controversy that could be turned to their advantage."[10] Bernard A. Weisberger complained that the Kansas reporters had hastened the coming of the Civil War because they "helped to make the sectional issue, in many minds, one of absolute rights and wrongs, and whether or not disunion could eventually have been prevented, the release of such explosive forces in men's brains boded ill for any hope of compromise."[11]

It was that very reckless partisanship that led free-state settlers in Kansas to appreciate their journalistic champions. As a consequence of his steadfastness on the slavery question as well as his provocative language, Redpath quickly gained a minor celebrity status among the Kansas reporter corps. Free staters such as Governor Charles Robinson praised Redpath's reporting:

> James Redpath, the fearless, indomitable friend of the oppressed of all colors and all climes, was its [*St. Louis Missouri Democrat's*] correspondent. Neither he nor [William A.] Phillips [of the *New York Tribune*] allowed any incident to escape attention, and if every outrage by the invaders and their accomplices was not so presented as to have the greatest possible effect upon readers, it was not for lack of will, but of ability; and if any one had more ability in that line than these young correspondents, he had not appeared in Kansas.[12]

Fellow reporter, Richard J. Hinton, described Redpath as "a compound of glycerine and guncotton" on the slavery issue and reminisced that he "flamed meteor-like over this blazing field" when compared to the other territorial journalists.[13]

Redpath's initial assignment in Kansas was to report on the proceedings of the first meeting of the territorial legislature. When that body had removed itself from its first meeting place to the more congenially proslavery settlement of Shawnee Mission, territorial governor Andrew H. Reeder declared the session illegal and threatened to veto each piece of legislation it passed. The legislature nonetheless proceeded to adopt laws to govern the new territory, foster internal improvements, and most controversially protect the importation of slaves into Kansas.[14] Redpath arrived in Kansas just in time to attend the territorial legislature's first session in Shawnee on 16 July. Like many of the legislators, he boarded in Kansas City, Missouri, where the nearest hotels were, and traveled the six miles to Shawnee each day by a primitive stage line.[15] The territorial house of representatives voted Redpath a seat on its floor as a reporter for the *Democrat*. The same day, however, that body debated a motion to authorize members to "thrash" any reporter whose writings "traduce and villify" their body.[16] Although tabled, the motion gave Redpath immediate warning of the rough-and-tumble nature of frontier politics.

Redpath stayed in Kansas City for the next six weeks, mainly covering the Shawnee legislature but occasionally journeying to nearby settlements to learn more about the territory. Most of Redpath's reports were detailed accounts of the legislative process. He observed that the majority of the bills introduced had been copied from the law codes of adjacent Missouri. Redpath's reports were largely factual, but he did give disproportionate attention to legislation protecting slavery and circumscribing the rights of free blacks in the territory.[17]

Occasionally, however, Redpath used his reports to enter into the territory's political debate. When President Franklin Pierce fired Governor Reeder for failing to cooperate with the proslavery legislature, Redpath hailed Reeder's "unflinching adherence to his principles" and recommended him to the antislavery voters of the territory as a candidate for high office.[18] Redpath also sprinkled his reports with attacks on Missouri senator David Atchison, who he accused of habitual drunkenness and visiting Shawnee to attempt to dictate to the territorial legislature.[19]

Redpath's criticism of the Shawnee legislators tended to be milder and more humorous. The upper house of the legislature, he dismissed as "the old fogies" and rarely reported their activities.[20] The representatives Redpath characterized as typically conceited, frequently drunk, and occasionally lecherous. Several eastern newspapers regularly reprinted Redpath's lampooning accounts of debates in the legislature.[21] Perhaps because his reports ridiculing the Shawnee legislators took so long to reach print in St. Louis and copies of the *Democrat* to get back to Kansas, Redpath remained on cordial terms with those men. Toward the end of the session, Redpath reported attending a banquet with the legislators at Shawnee's only dining house and, after helping champagne bottles disappear "like brave soldiers before the walls of Sebastopol," awakening the next morning in the yard.[22]

Members of the proslavery press of the territory also enjoyed Redpath's company. After a visit to Shawnee, John H. Stringfellow, the editor of the *Atchison Squatter Sovereign,* reported that he founded Redpath "a printer, a gentleman, and a scholar, and, save, his freesoil principles, we would be willing to 'hitch to him.' We sincerely hope that after a residence in a Slave State, and seeing what a blessing to the slave the institution of slavery is, he may yet be persuaded to look not through a 'glass darkened.'"[23]

After a brief visit to St. Louis in late September, Redpath returned to the territory early the next month. He then produced an eight-part series for the *Democrat,* entitled "Equestrian Journeys in Kansas," as he visited the eastern portion of the territory.[24] These travels confirmed Redpath's earlier conclusion that the antislavery settlers in Kansas already formed a clear majority. Of these, the "abolitionists proper," he reported, "are a very small band; but they are earnest, bold, and influential."[25] The large majority of free staters, he complained, "adopt the doctrine which Bennett of the Herald has branded as Sewardism—they cry 'leave slavery alone where it already exists,' *but* 'No more slave States.'"[26] Nonetheless, Redpath noted that even moderate antislavery opinions outraged Missourians such as Atchison and their friends in the territory and he warned that each side was arming in anticipation of violence.[27]

Redpath's return to the territory was beclouded by a controversy over an article he had written at the end of this first stay. He had reported that Wilson Shannon, the newly appointed replacement of Reeder as territorial governor, had announced himself at a public reception in favor of Kansas becoming a slave state.[28] Henry Clay Pate, reporter of the rival *St. Louis Republican,* a pro-Atchison newspaper, was the first to question the accuracy of Redpath's account. Shannon then labeled it a "caricature report."[29]

Redpath gathered up affidavits from numerous people, both pro- and anti-slavery, who had heard Shannon's address and endorsed his report of it. As in later controversies, the editors of the *Democrat* stood fully behind the veracity of Redpath's reporting.[30]

Questions about the accuracy of Redpath's journalism, nonetheless, persisted especially after he began crossing the line from reporter to participant at free-state conventions at the end of 1855. For example, Redpath attended a convention at Topeka in mid September called by free-state leaders. The gathering at first seated Redpath as a journalist from the *Democrat* but then elected him their official "reporter." This gathering decided to authorize a second convention to draft an antislavery constitution with which free-state settlers could petition Congress for admission to the union.[31]

Redpath also attended the free staters' constitutional convention held in Topeka in late October. Again he was elected the gathering's official reporter and given a seat on the platform. In the official convention roll, he listed himself as a "Democrat and Emancipationist."[32] At this convention, some heated debates occurred between Democrats still inclined toward popular sovereignty and Republicans totally hostile toward the Pierce administration and its agents in the territory. Redpath reported with some surprise that James Lane, a former Democratic congressman from Indiana, had emerged as the leader of the latter faction. Redpath also noted, however, that most Republican delegates supported a provision to restrict suffrage to whites. Redpath's account of the convention for the *Democrat* contained relatively few of his characteristic editorial comments, other than the observation that "the complexion of this convention is so decidedly conservative in character, that it has already disappointed many who expected to see it ruined by radicalism."[33]

The Topeka Constitution was ratified by an election on 15 December, called by the "Free State Executive Committee" headed by James Lane, and regarded as illegal by territorial governor Shannon.[34] The free staters then called for another election to choose officers to serve under the new constitution. At this point, some discontent surfaced within free-state ranks. Redpath was the secretary of the Lawrence convention of free staters that chose Charles A. Robinson, an agent of an emigrant aid society, over Lane, as its gubernatorial candidate. Soon after, a "Free State *Anti-Abolition* ticket," substituted a Douglas Democrat, William T. Roberts, for Robinson and also replaced several other known Republicans with Democrats or Whigs.[35] Redpath's reports immediately denounced the bolters as "old Hunkers . . . who deserve to be politically damned."[36] Redpath not only reported rallies supporting the "Regular Free State Ticket" but he addressed one at Lawrence on 12 January 1856 on behalf of its candidates. Redpath also unsuccessfully called on the free staters to adopt clearer antislavery grounds by petitioning Congress to repeal the Fugitive Slave law, abolish slavery in the District of Columbia, and prohibit interstate commerce in slaves.[37] The results of the election on 15 January gave thirteen hundred votes to Robinson and only four hundred to Roberts.[38]

A second major topic in Redpath's reporting during the winter of 1855–56 was the farcical siege of Lawrence, known as the "Wakarusa War." At the end of November, he reported that the militia of the proslavery territorial government had been called out to suppress an alleged abolitionist "rebellion" in Lawrence.[39] Redpath was in Leavenworth when the crisis broke out and described the bulk of the militia volunteers heading to attack Lawrence as young Missourians who "care for nothing but liquor and excitement."[40] Redpath joined a small free-stater party from Leavenworth that traveled by night to assist the settlers of Lawrence. His group was captured by the militia, however, and he did not get to Lawrence until after a truce had been arranged between Governor Shannon and free-state "General" Jim Lane.[41]

Serious fighting had been averted at Lawrence but Redpath noted a major increase in violent feuding between the free- and slave-state settlers. He reported that after his departure from Leavenworth, Missourians had entered the town and destroyed the press of its only free-state paper, the *Territorial Register*, edited by Mark W. Delahay.[42] Although Delahay was a supporter of Stephen Douglas, Redpath had befriended him and applauded his denunciations of "Border Ruffianism." Redpath also reported that his own life had been threatened if he returned to Leavenworth. Noting the violence free staters faced in Kansas, Redpath called on Northerners: "Indignation meetings and patriotic resolutions won't save Kansas. Send out as soon as navigation opens, or earlier, ten thousand armed men,—mechanics, laborers, farmers, capitalists,—and then, let Congress act as it may, Kansas will be a Free State, and the mother of many more. Until the North does so, the Slave Power will rule us."[43] Redpath also reported that since the recent fighting " 'Abolitionist' has ceased to be a word of reproach with hundreds of men who previously detested the name. I have heard men who were semi-Southerners before, declare, with Garrison: 'I am an Abolitionist! I glory in the name!'—since Kansas was invaded. I have heard others hint that even Garrison himself was rather an old fogy, *because he does not go far enough in opposition to Slavery.* 'The world *does* move.' "[44]

At the end of January, Redpath left Kansas and stayed briefly in St. Louis, writing more reports about the violent state of the territory.[45] From mid February to April 1856, he returned to the East. On this trip Redpath sent back regular dispatches to the *Democrat*, which he entitled "Rough Notes of Eastern Travel." This series featured Redpath's impressions of various towns and cities along his route, including Vincennes, Terre Haute, Indianapolis, Cincinnati, Columbus, and Pittsburgh.[46] About Pittsburgh, he remarked: "If cleanliness is next to godliness, as the old proverb says, there can be very little piety in the smoky city of Pittsburgh."[47] Redpath's "Rough Notes" also sent back lengthy descriptions of the commercial and manufacturing activities of these communities with advice to St. Louis businesses about how to tap these markets.

While traveling through Missouri and Kentucky on his way east, Redpath also used the opportunity to resurrect John Ball Jr. to comment on the relatively poverty of those two slave states compared to their free-state neighbors of Illinois and Ohio. Ball reported that the chief hope of emancipationists in that area was "politico-economical arguments in favor of Free labour and Free Soil" because slavery "has deadened the moral sense" of border state whites.[48]

One major goal of Redpath's trip was to cover the Republican Party's first national convention at Pittsburgh for the *St. Louis Daily Missouri Democrat*. The gathering in mid February strove to unite all elements opposed to the administration's Kansas policy. Redpath interviewed delegates and found many very cautious in their opposition to the spread of slavery. Noting the selection of Frank Blair's father, Francis Sr., a Maryland slaveholder, as the gathering's presiding officer, Redpath concluded that "Conservatism, in fact, was king, or perhaps, I should say President of the Republican Convention."[49] The convention ultimately approved a public address condemning popular sovereignty and pledging to resist the expansion of slavery into the territories "by every constitutional means." That final highly significant qualification, coupled with the prominent role of Blair, proved deeply disturbing to many abolitionists.[50]

Redpath's reports of the convention were more positive. He strongly praised the antislavery tone of many speeches, including those by his former employer, Horace Greeley, and another by John C. Vaughan, editor of the *Chicago Tribune*.[51] A personal highlight of his visit to Pittsburgh was an evening "mass meeting" of more than one thousand delegates and others to voice support for the Kansas emigrant aid movement. Greeley spoke again and among the other orators was Redpath himself, who one newspaper noted "defied the assumption that the mass of the people of Missouri were parties to the outrages in Kansas."[52]

The Pittsburgh gathering authorized a second convention in June to nominate candidates for the presidency and vice presidency. To oversee party affairs until the next convention, the very first Republican National Committee was created and Frank Blair Jr. was selected as Missouri's representative on it. Blair could not attend the first meeting of the committee in March, and Redpath was appointed to fill his vacancy and signed his name to the call for the party's first nominating convention.[53] In private correspondence, Redpath explained to other abolitionists why he had publicly joined the Republicans: "I work with this party because its creed—altho' unsatisfactory to a genuine *antislavery* man—is as liberal as a citizen of a slave state—can safely advocate."[54]

In March Redpath visited New York City and his old colleagues at the *Tribune*. His friend North had died and Redpath obtained manuscripts of several of his poems and sprinkled them in his writing for years to come. He sent back to the *Democrat* reports of the latest political and social developments in the East.[55] At this time, Redpath began corresponding with the wealthy upstate New York abolitionist, Gerrit Smith. The ostensible purpose of these letters was to obtain financial support for fellow journalist Mark Delahay to reestablish his Kansas newspaper office sacked by Border Ruffians. It is likely that Redpath also desired to make himself known to one of the most generous patrons of antislavery activity.[56] In his introductory letter, Redpath claimed to have devoted the past two years to "advancing to the best of my knowledge & ability the . . . cause of Freedom for *all*." Redpath described his antislavery writings both as "John Ball Jr." and as a Kansas correspondent to Smith and claimed his publications had "contributed greatly in reviving & popularizing the antislavery sentiment of the North." Redpath thanked Smith for his devotion to abolitionism and promised, "If I live—I am young in years yet—I hope I shall return you more acceptable thanks—the thanks of emulation."[57]

At the same time, Redpath left indications of his intention to work hard for the Republicans. He corresponded with New York Republican senator William H. Seward and sent him intimate details about events in Kansas to use in congressional debate as well as news about the prospects of the Republican Party in Missouri. Redpath promised to distribute any political literature Seward could send him "to the press, prominent politicians of the Benton party & working classes."[58]

Before returning to Kansas, Redpath made arrangements with the *Chicago Tribune* and the *New York Tribune* to become a regular correspondent for both in the territory. The frequent reprinting of his dispatches to the *St. Louis Daily Missouri Democrat* had made Redpath a widely read celebrity journalist, a status he would unapologetically use to advance the Kansas free-state cause to northern newspaper readers. The *Chicago Tribune* noted the controversies regarding Redpath's previous reporting but claimed that the "ingenuity of the Pro-Slavery press has been exercised to invalidate his testimony; but to this day, his evidence stands unimpeached."[59] Redpath traveled up the Missouri River from St. Louis to Kansas City on the steamer *William Campbell*. In the first of his "Kansas Revisited" series, he reported back to the *Chicago Tribune* that he had shared this ship with emigrants from western Virginia and North Carolina, who he claimed were traveling to Kansas "to live where labor is honored and free speech permitted." He predicted that these white refugees from the slavery system would prosper far better in the territory than "the scions of the first families of South Carolina, Alabama [and] Louisiana" who "have been educated to despise labor and certainly had never been accustomed to work."[60]

Redpath based himself in Lawrence. Many of his early reports from the territory were accounts of the public hearings by a special investigating committee of the U.S. House of Representatives on the disputed validity of the

Kansas elections of 1855. While generally sending east verbatim transcriptions of these hearings, Redpath occasionally inserted his own rebuttal of testimony critical of the free staters under the intentionally transparent pen name "Sentier Rouge." After mocking the failed semblance of democracy in the previous year's elections, he closed one self-described "sermon," with the observation: "Squatter Sovereignty is a great institution, isn't it."[61]

Redpath reported growing violence in the territory beginning that May. He noted that the South was sending its own armed parties of emigrants to the territory and charged that Governor Shannon, at the order of Secretary of War Jefferson Davis, had secretly supplied them with government rifles.[62] Redpath was in Leavenworth when a proslavery "posse" of 750 attacked Lawrence on 21 May and destroyed its hotel, newspaper offices, and the home of free-state "Governor" Robinson. For the *New York Tribune,* Redpath described the condition of the territory as a "Reign of Terror" when "'the laws' disfranchise the Northern emigrants, and the Bench orders the destruction of their property as a 'nuisance,' when freedom of speech is a penitentiary offense, and guerrillas and horsethieves are 'legally organized' by the Executive, when armed mobs from foreign States are licensed to plunder, and backed by all the power of the Federal Government."[63] He called on Northerners to send immediate military aid and to press Congress for the prompt admission of Kansas under the Topeka free-state constitution.

Soon after traveling to Lawrence to investigate firsthand, Redpath reported that "Horrible stories" were being circulated about the murder of five proslavery settlers from Osawatomie in southeast Kansas allegedly in retaliation for the Lawrence sacking. Historians now know that the five had been killed by a party of free staters, led by John Brown. A longtime abolitionist, Brown and five of his sons had come to the territory the previous year to fight slavery. Brown had led a small company of free staters to the relief of Lawrence but learned of its sack while still en route. Seeking revenge, Brown and eight followers, including three sons, had gone to the cabins of known proslavery settlers in the middle of the night and executed them. Although Brown never acknowledged his part in the "Pottawatomie massacre," the press was soon publishing reports attributing the killings to him.[64]

Because such reports damaged the reputation of the free staters, Redpath sought to interview Brown after receiving a tip about his whereabouts.[65] Historian Hill Peebles Wilson believes the most likely source for the tip was Brown's followers John E. Cook or Charles Lenhart. Another historian, Otto Scott, believes that Lane had sent Redpath to find Brown to arrange more violent actions.[66] Redpath set out to locate and interview the most notorious of the free-state guerrilla captains.[67] On his way, a company of dragoons took him into custody as a suspected horse thief but soon released him.[68] Redpath rode to the vicinity of Ottawa Creek on 30 May and became lost in the wooded creek bottom. Suddenly he stumbled upon a "wild-looking man" armed with a revolver and "a large Arkansas bowie knife." Redpath drew his colt pistol on the stranger who turned out to be Brown's son Frederick. Frederick had seen Redpath in Lawrence and announced "You're all right," and took him on an intentionally meandering course toward the Brown camp.[69]

Frederick Brown finally led Redpath to a clearing where a dozen horses were tied and rifles and sabers were sacked around the trees. At last, Redpath encountered the elder Brown, who he found "poorly clad, and his toes protruding from his boots," in the process of roasting a pig.[70] Redpath later reported that Brown had greeted him cordially "but firmly forbade conversation on the Pottawatomie affair."[71] One of Brown's sons, Salomon, however, claimed that John Brown had told Redpath that the Pottawatomie killings had been a "summary execution."[72]

Redpath and Brown conversed for about an hour before Redpath departed. This would be the first of many meetings between the two men. Through these conversations, Redpath and Brown discovered that they shared a belief that slaves would fight for their freedom if armed and accompanied by white abolitionists. Brown had been considering instigating such a revolt for more than a decade and eventually he enlisted Redpath into his conspiracy.[73]

The day after meeting Brown, Redpath dispatched an article to the *Chicago Tribune*, presenting a very different account of the details of the Pottawatomie massacre than any previously published. While admitting that free staters had killed the five, Redpath claimed that he had information that the proslavery men had been shot while in the process of lynching an opponent. Redpath warned that the false stories of this event "will be made the excuse for arresting every man in that section of the State who has made himself obnoxious, or is likely to be a leader in defending the lives and property of Northern men."[74] Subsequently critics have charged that Redpath knew this denial was false and that he intentionally covered up evidence in order to enhance Brown's reputation with eastern supporters of the free-state cause.[75]

Two days after Redpath's visit, Brown abandoned his hiding place and attacked a band of Missourians pursuing the murderers of the Pottawatomie settlers.[76] Ironically, this group of twenty-five men was led by Redpath's principal nemesis in the press corps, Henry Clay Pate.[77] Although outnumbered two-to-one, Brown's force defeated and captured Pate's party. Three days later, a troop of U.S. cavalry caught up with Brown, freed the Missourians, and ordered both parties to return to their homes.[78] After regaining his freedom, Pate blasted not only Brown in his columns in the *St. Louis Republican* but accused Redpath of being a spy and horse thief on behalf of the free-state guerrillas.[79]

Whether Pate was correct or not, Redpath had certainly become an active partisan. Despite the efforts of the federal army to keep the free- and slave-state parties from engaging in pitched battles, many small skirmishes occurred. Redpath, who had been commissioned a "major" in the free-state militia occasionally engaged in these minibattles. William A. Phillips, a correspondent for the *New York Tribune,* reported that Redpath had led a reconnaissance party of ten free staters in early June and returned to camp with three prisoners. Another reporter, Hinton, thought Redpath's "courage was of the highest type, both moral and physical." The one surviving photograph of Redpath from this period has him posed sitting on a barrel with a copy of the *New York Tribune* in his left hand and a repeating rifle in his left.[80]

The conflict between friends and foes of slavery in Kansas took a new twist during the summer of 1856 when Missourians began to turn back all river-borne emigrants to the territory from the North. Lane already had gone East to encourage more support from the emigration aid societies when Lawrence had been attacked and the Missouri blockade begun. In Chicago, he organized his "Army of the North," a party of approximately six hundred setters who set off to Kansas overland through Iowa and Nebraska. News of the approach of this "army" reached the territory by late summer and greatly increased the excitement of all parties there.[81]

In August, Redpath traveled east to Chicago, where he assisted in the organizing of the free staters' expedition. On his way back to Kansas, he attended a Republican mass rally in Alton, Illinois, and spoke about twenty minutes on Kansas. He sent three articles about the convention to the *Chicago Tribune* but declined to note his own remarks because "if he *was* fool enough to make a speech, he isn't *quite* fool enough to report it. No sir-ee!"[82] Redpath stopped briefly in St. Louis and then rendezvoused with Lane's "army" in Iowa. By this time, that expedition had been joined by Massachusetts abolitionist Thomas Wentworth Higginson, a representative of the national Kansas Aid Society, who quickly befriended Redpath.[83] Lane placed Redpath in command of the advance guard of his party, numbering approximately 130 men and organized into four companies. Impressed by the young reporter's daring, Higginson decided to accompany Redpath's party.[84]

Lane went ahead of this party into the territory and led free staters in a series of raids against proslavery settlements. Governor Shannon's efforts to halt this round of fighting had achieved only limited success when President Pierce replaced him with John W. Geary on 21 August. The tall Pennsylvania-born Geary set out to pacify the territory with federal troops. First, he successfully turned back a new Border Ruffian invasion led by Atchison. Geary then sent cavalry patrols to intercept and arrest the scattered elements of Lane's pilgrims as they reached the territory.[85]

Redpath's party crossed into Kansas in mid September. One member of the party reminisced that at the Kansas border, Redpath "had his men fall into line. He then unfurled 'Old Glory,' the company fired a salute, and

FIGURE 1 James Redpath as a young reporter in Kansas Territory. Courtesy of the Kansas State Historical Society, Lawrence.

we passed over into the territory which was forever to be consecrated to freedom."[86] The morning after the party's arrival in Topeka, according to Higginson, a troop of forty dragoons led by Colonel Philip St. George Cook and Deputy U.S. Marshal William J. Preston from Virginia took Redpath and himself into custody. Preston's orders were to bring the prisoners before Governor Geary at Lecompton. Free-state "governor" Robinson volunteered to drive them all there in his wagon. Higginson reported that Redpath, "who would be on easy terms with the Great Mogul at the second whiff," joined Preston in the back seat, exchanged cigars and debated slavery with him during the journey.[87]

The interrogation by Governor Geary had an equally comic tone. Although Redpath's party was well-armed and carried neither artisan nor agricultural tools, Geary choose to believe their word that the new settlers intended no offensive violence in the territory.[88] Higginson reported that before the case was dismissed, Redpath's "keen wit had had ample play upon the lofty Governor, who did not for some time discover whom he had to deal with; and when they finally parted, Redpath assured the Governor that he need not apologize for his treatment of him and if their positions were ever reversed, he would certainly treat him with the same generosity."[89]

Perhaps Geary could ignore verbal abuse from a young free-state hothead such as Redpath because his program of pacification of the territory was rapidly reducing the level of violence in Kansas. One of the few unrecondite free-state guerrilla leaders was John Brown, and he became a special target of Geary's cavalry patrols. Once again, Redpath sought out Brown and found him in hiding with four sons at Plymouth, near the Nebraska border. Brown was ill and physically exhausted. While Redpath had been out of the territory, Brown had played a leading role in the small battle at Osawatomie and a minor one in the defense of Lawrence against the Border Ruffian "invasion" that Governor Shannon had aborted before blood could be shed.[90] Redpath counseled Brown to flee the territory and the old warrior crossed the border into Nebraska the same day, just a few hours ahead of a pursuing dragoon patrol.[91] Through a combination of leniency and intimidation, therefore, Geary succeeded in his pacification program by early October.[92]

It was at this time that Redpath made another trip back to the East, hoping to raise funds for the free-state movement. Instead he had to expend his own cash to settle several bills in Iowa contracted by the cause. When he got to Chicago in late October, Redpath had to suspend plans to travel on to St. Paul on account of lack of money. His fundraising efforts among Kansas sympathizers in Chicago resulted in only ten dollars to send back to the territory.[93]

Perhaps Redpath failed in his mission as a fundraiser because the attention of antislavery Northerners had turned from Kansas to the presidential election only a few weeks away. Redpath strongly supported the Republicans' first-ever presidential candidate John C. Frémont. Nonetheless, he felt it necessary to justify his stand in a letter to Gerrit Smith who was a rival presidential candidate of the tiny Radical Abolitionist Party. Redpath wrote Smith that "I am an Abolitionist of your school, but I cannot on next Tuesday vote for you. The destiny of Kansas, it seems to me is so identified with the election of the Republican candidate, that, although I am far from an admirer of the [Republicans'] Philadelphia platform, I will vote or use all my influence for him. We have no chance of electing an Abolitionist; we must choose between Buchanan & Frémont; & of two? I choose the best." Redpath promised Smith that he would work to advance the abolitionist cause by his pen as soon as the campaign was over.[94]

Although disappointed by Frémont's defeat by Democrat James Buchanan on 4 November, Redpath expressed optimism for the long-range success of the free-state cause in Kansas. He wrote the *New York Tribune* that "Republicanism in the North is a political creed—in Kansas, *a religious sentiment*. The God of the Squatters is an Anti-Slavery God, and they are the warriors of the Lord of Liberty."[95] Redpath called on antislavery Northerners to turn their attention back to Kansas affairs and to contribute to the free staters' support because "lip-philanthropy will not relieve them. It has been tried already. Dollar bills are better than good wishes, and ten dollar bills are even better than prayers. Subscribe first and pray afterward. It will help your devotion greatly."[96] Redpath reported that many free-state leaders who had gone east to campaign for Frémont were passing through Chicago on their way back to the territories in anticipation of the renewal of the contest with the Border Ruffians. Among that group, Redpath incorrectly listed John Brown, "the heroic defender of Osawatomie" as on his way back to "the scene of his romantic and daring exploits."[97]

While many of his associates were headed west, Redpath instead traveled to Boston shortly after the election to rally support for the free-state settlers in Kansas.[98] He wrote both public and private letters giving advice to the would-be settler regarding economic prospects.[99] He contacted Higginson who introduced him to many abolitionists and to antislavery politicians such as Charles Sumner. Redpath lobbied these politicians for congressional relief from the federal administration's policies in Kansas. His pen was so active for the Kansas cause, that when Higginson persuaded him not to begin a public dispute with a clerical critic of the emigrant aid movement, Redpath jokingly wrote back that "this Christian forbearance is so rare a sensation, that I am almost sick; it don't feel natural."[100] When Higginson wrote a pamphlet about the adventure the two men had shared in Kansas, Redpath playfully mailed a copy to Governor Geary with his "compliments."[101]

In the winter of 1857, John Brown also traveled east to find support. Redpath reported Brown's arrival in Boston in February to the *New York Tribune*: "Old Brown of Osawatomie is in town. He is a hale and vigorous man of fifty-seven, with a spare figure, with piercing dark-blue eyes, and face expressive of will."[102] During Brown's Boston visit, Redpath took him to meet Sumner. The Kansan requested that the senator show him the coat he had been wearing the previous year when assaulted in the Capitol by South Carolina Representative Preston Brooks. Redpath later reported that Brown examined the coat at length and "said nothing . . . but his lips compressed and his eyes shone like polished steel."[103]

While in the East, Redpath found reportial work for the *New York Tribune*, covering a "Disunionist Convention," in Worcester, Massachusetts. The meeting had been called by a group of Garrisonian abolitionists, disgruntled Republicans, and a few unaffiliated antislavery radicals. Higginson was part of the latter group and endorsed the majority position that the defeat of Frémont left the foes of slavery no choice but to quit the union with the slave states. An even more important development at the convention, which Redpath noted, was the proposal by some Garrisonians, led by Stephen S. Foster, that Northerners begin to organize revolutionary governments and unite "with the slaves against the masters to dethrone the tyrants, with the sword of the spirit if possible, but with the bayonet if necessary."[104] Redpath also covered a meeting of the National Kansas Committee in late January 1857, for the *New York Tribune*.[105] As Redpath observed, events since the passage of the Kansas-Nebraska Act had made the northern public more receptive to radical solutions to the slavery question.[106]

Also during this trip to Massachusetts Redpath married Mary Cotton Kidder on 14 April 1857.[107] She was ten years Redpath's senior and was the mother of two children from a previous marriage. Details of their meeting and courtship have been lost. Redpath's first biographer, Charles Horner, does not even allude to this marriage, which lasted two decades before ending in divorce.[108] One surviving hint of the highly romantic nature of the courtship was the poetry Redpath sent her and later republished.[109]

Mary Cotton had been born on 3 November 1823 at Cotton Valley, Wolfboro, New Hampshire. From a distinguished local family, she was sent to the Young Ladies Seminary at Charlestown, Massachusetts, for an education. In her late teens, she married Ezra Taylor Kidder of Sudbury. This union produced a daughter, Caroline Mae born in 1844, and a son, Dudley Taylor born in 1848. Ezra Kidder and his brother Francis operated a mercantile firm in Boston, which specialized in West Indies goods. Sometime after the birth of their second child, Mary and Ezra separated and divorced.[110]

Soon after Mary's marriage to Redpath, Mary's first husband attempted to regain custody of the children, and Redpath and his new family fled Boston to Mary's native New Hampshire. Redpath explained his precipitous departure from Boston to his new friend, abolitionist Wendell Phillips: "In consequence of a law of Mass. by which a Mother may be robbed of her children if she marries again, in case her former husband appoints guardians for them, I was obliged to fly out of town with my wife, her boy & girl."[111]

When his new family was resettled in New Hampshire, Redpath left them for a quick tour of Virginia in the company of the wealthy young Massachusetts abolitionist Francis Merriam, nephew of William Lloyd's Garrison's close lieutenant Francis Jackson. Redpath prepared a series of pseudonymous letters for the *Boston Daily Evening Traveller,* over the pen name "Jacobious." These letters reported on slavery much in the style of the John Ball Jr. letters, except that this time Redpath had had fewer opportunities for undetected interviews with slaves.[112]

In July 1857, Redpath returned to Kansas as a reporter for the *St. Louis Daily Missouri Democrat,* sending back articles signed "Jacobious." Redpath playfully reported himself "dying of ennui" until he started west for the territory.[113] He found a new governor there, Robert J. Walker, a veteran Democratic politician from Mississippi. Redpath soon interviewed Walker and concluded: "It is proper to add that Walker is all things to all men. To *some he represents himself as a sound anti-slavery man;* to others he is courteously conservative; he tries the Bully Brooks' style of conversation to others."[114] In later articles, Redpath ridiculed Walker's claim that slavery was geographically unsuited to Kansas, calling him "Isothermal."[115]

Redpath also condemned Walker's efforts to organize a proadministration party among northern settlers in the territory. Walker's true goal, according to Redpath, was "to destroy the Topeka constitution and government, in order to obtain for the national democracy the credit of admitting Kansas into the union as a free state."[116] Redpath also censured as "miserable doughfaces and pensioned sycophants" those free-state settlers, such as George W. Brown, editor of the *Lawrence Herald of Freedom,* who supported Walker's efforts.[117]

Redpath claimed that the large majority of free staters would be immune to Walker's blandishments. Since returning to the territory, he found the more radical free-state leaders like Lane, William A. Phillips, and Martin F. Conway now openly aligning themselves with the national Republican Party. He also reported that the territory had a new, unspokenly antislavery newspaper in the *Emporia News,* edited by Preston B. Plumb and Richard J. Hinton.[118] Events soon demonstrated, however, that Redpath's prediction of increasing radical strength in Kansas politics to have been wishful thinking.

The statehood issue came to a head in the territory in 1857. Most northern settlers balked at participating in an election in June for a constitutional convention to be held at Lecompton. The free staters, instead, held a referendum in August and reendorsed their own Topeka state constitution. Lane, as commanding general of the free-state militia, appointed Redpath assistant adjutant general of the militia unit empowered to guard ballot boxes against Border Ruffians.[119] The question of participating in an election in October for offices under the federally sanctioned territorial government, however, split the free staters.[120] A convention was called to meet in Grasshopper Falls to resolve the issue. At a local meeting in Lawrence to choose delegates to this convention, Redpath made a speech opposing voting in the October territorial election because it would be interpreted as abandoning the Topeka constitution. The meeting selected Redpath as one of its delegates.[121]

At the Grasshopper Falls convention in late August, Redpath repeated his argument against voting in October in a speech which he modestly reported only in summary fashion for the *St. Louis Daily Missouri Democrat*. Robinson spoke in favor of voting in the territorial election, claiming it did not mean repudiating the Topeka state constitution. Although many others participated in the debate, a speech by Lane in favor of voting caused the convention to endorse that course. Lane brought most of the radical free staters into the provoting block leaving Redpath, Martin Conway, and William Phillips as leaders of the small remnant still opposed. When the convention adopted a resolution for a committee to call on Governor Walker to obtain assurances the election would be fair, Redpath derided that hope, stating that "free state men must be very foolish if they believe that they have anything to expect from a hireling and tool of the slave power."[122]

Redpath did not wait in Kansas to see the outcome of the territorial election. He went north from Lawrence to the new settlement of Doniphan with the intention of rendezvousing with Lane and a party of free staters and then proceeding with them to Nebraska to meet John Brown who was escorting a shipment of weapons into the territory.[123] After meeting with Lane in Doniphan, Redpath instead headed east to St. Louis and then on to Boston where he arrived on late October.[124]

Redpath had returned east to search for funds to start his own newspaper. His meeting with Lane in Doniphan had convinced him that the free-state settlers of northern Kansas would support a strong antislavery newspaper. One person Redpath turned to for a loan was Gerrit Smith, to whom he described his intended paper: "The Crusader of Freedom will be the *first antislavery* (in contradistinction to Free State) paper in Kansas: it will be printed within pistol shot of Missouri & the heaviest slaveholding portion of it."[125] Redpath obtained sufficient money to proceed with plans for his paper and to support his family in Boston and started back to Kansas in early November.

While passing through St. Louis on his return trip, Redpath published a prospectus for the *Crusader of Freedom* in the *St. Louis Daily Missouri Democrat*. The prospectus listed seven regular contributors, including Lane, Phillips, and Conway. Other promised special features were a serialized autobiography by Lane and a series of illustrated "PORTRAITS OF KANSAS CELEBRITIES." Redpath also pledged that the paper "will endeavor, by truly reporting every diversity of opinion and policy, to make it pre-eminently the ORGAN OF THE FREE STATE PARTY."[126] He soon expanded the prospectus to include the promise that the *Crusader* would "resist the Extension of Involuntary Servitude, oppose the iniquitous Fugitive Slave Law, advocate abolition, immediate and universal, in all the domain with the Federal jurisdiction."[127] The eastern Republican press hailed the appearance of the *Crusader* and endorsed Redpath's credentials to speak for their party in the territory.[128]

By 2 December, Redpath was back in the territory, having come by foot from Jefferson City, Missouri, due to the closing of transportation on the upper Missouri River. He spoke against the proslavery Lecompton Constitution at a free-state convention in Lawrence. The reporter of the *New York Tribune* supplied the longest account of his remarks: "James Redpath said he had been travelling, and was tired, 'physically, mentally and fundamentally;' but he kept the Convention in a roar of laughter for twenty minutes with his sharp sallies."[129]

On 19 December 1857, the first issue of the *Doniphan Crusader of Freedom* appeared. The new paper was published in a building shared with both the town's school and a land development company. Redpath pressed his friends and family into writing for the *Crusader*. As promised, Conway, Phillips, and Lane became regular contributors. Henry Melrose, one of Redpath's old friends from his days as a *Tribune* reporter in New York City, sent dispatches from London as the paper's own foreign correspondent. Redpath's stepdaughter, Carrie, contributed essays for a children's section of the newspaper. Redpath wrote and published a number of undistinguished, highly sentimental poems in the *Crusader* under his "Berwick" pen name.[130] His only hired staff was an eighteen-year-old printer named John A. Martin, who would become Kansas's governor in 1885.[131]

The town of Doniphan had been founded in 1855 along the banks of the Missouri River. Although Lane had recently become a major property holder there, the community's population of twelve hundred still contained a strong proslavery faction. A band of Border Ruffians shot a free stater on the town's streets the same week the *Crusader* started publication.[132] Despite such violent episodes, Doniphan had favorable business prospects. It possessed good roads leading into the interior and enough quality timber in the vicinity to support two saw mills. In his *Crusader,* Redpath advertised good prospects for a wide variety of artisans and tradesmen in the new town. Redpath, himself, became a realtor and land speculator in Doniphan, selling lots and promising a 20 percent annual return on any money sent him to invest in Kansas land.[133] Soon after the start of the *Crusader,* Redpath's wife and stepchildren came west and joined him in the territory.[134] Despite his personal stake in Doniphan, Redpath also advertised the qualities of other Kansas settlements in exchange for deeds to town lots there.[135]

As an editor, Redpath attempted to play a prominent role in free-state politics. Redpath's first editorial declared his motto to be "Right or Fight" and urged the Free State Party not to stand "immoveably on the defensive."[136] His radical, uncompromising stand on antislavery tactics, however, isolated him even in the Free State Party. He continued to favor the maintenance of the free-state militia to guard against any future Border Ruffian depredations and to protect the property claims of northern settlers who had abandoned their land due to the constant skirmishing. Conservative free staters, however, were prepared to abandon armed tactics as no longer required and condemned Lane, Redpath, and others still committed to violent means as revolutionary "Jayhawkers."[137]

During Redpath's absence in the east, the free staters had won a majority in the territorial legislature, after Governor Walker had intervened in the ballot counting to throw out fraudulent proslavery returns. Redpath nonetheless complained that the territorial legislature, whose election he was still proud of opposing, "has done little but fritter away time, increase discord in the party, and squander the people's money."[138] In particular, Redpath complained that the legislature had spent its time aiding private economic interests and not overturning the "bogus" law code that free staters had opposed for three years. The legislature retaliated first by denying the *Crusader* any public printing and then by barring Redpath from covering its sessions.[139]

In editorials, Redpath boasted of being a Republican and criticized those who still preferred "the now almost meaningless appellation of Free State."[140] In particular he attacked George W. Brown, the editor of the *Lawrence Herald of Freedom,* as leader of the "Hunker office-seeking faction in the Free State Organization, who are now trying to organize a Democratic Party, without assuming the obnoxious name."[141] Brown, in turn, condemned Redpath for trying to divide the free staters by demanding that they all adhere to Republican Party principles. According to Brown, Redpath was "one of the leading spirits of an organized band of mercenary *letter writers,* whose business has been that of sending false accounts of events in Kansas during her struggles, to Eastern papers, and basely slandering those who have done and sacrificed most for the cause of freedom."[142]

Redpath also continued to castigate Governor Walker as "a wiley [*sic*] demagogue, unprincipled and ambitious."[143] Redpath was suspicious that the true motivation for Walker's opposition to the proslavery Lecompton Constitution, written the previous fall, was a desire to advance the political career of Stephen Douglas. Citing numerous violations of his Popular Sovereignty doctrine, Douglas had resisted the efforts of the Buchanan administration to persuade Congress to admit Kansas into the union. Douglas's position bolstered those Kansas free staters who retained Democratic Party loyalties. Nonetheless, when President Buchanan fired Walker for lobbying Congress against the admission of Kansas under the Lecompton Constitution, the *Crusader* condemned the act as "an insult and an outrage."[144]

Redpath's extreme views cost him support from the growing faction of free staters ready to abandon violence for electoral means to keep slavery out of the territory. When the free-state-controlled territorial legislature called a referendum for a January 1858 to allow Kansas voters to demonstrate their disapproval of the Lecompton Constitution, Redpath supported participation in this election. The Free State Party, however, divided over participation on the same day in an election for state officers to take power if Congress approved the Lecompton Constitution. At first, Redpath called for expulsion of anyone from the Free State Party who voted in the latter election. At a convention, held late December, he relented.[145]

The conservative free-state faction nonetheless persisted in categorizing Redpath with the opponents of voting. The *Kansas Leader* declared that Redpath's original threat to expel all voters showed him "to be deficient in the commonest kind of common sense."[146] The *Herald of Freedom* happily reported that hundreds of Doniphan residents had voted in the election despite Redpath's advice. Its editor, Brown, however, warned that Redpath's course had cost the free-state cause many votes in Doniphan County by publishing "falsehoods which should make devils blush."[147] In March 1858, Redpath supplied his enemies with further evidence of his radical course by threatening violence against the newly elected state officers under the Lecompton Constitution if they did not act to kill that document: "If the members elect do otherwise, then let us once more resolve to *rebel,* and if necessary, by the rope, the rifle and the revolver rid ourselves of the usurpers; . . . for it is not the engineers but the *engine* that we object to."[148]

More damaging to Redpath's success in Kansas than quarrels with conservative free staters was his highly publicized break with radical leader, Jim Lane. The two men had cooperated closely in founding the *Crusader,* and Lane's financial support for the new paper was a poorly concealed secret.[149] Redpath had given Lane ample space in the *Crusader*'s early issues, even beginning to serialize his autobiography.[150] Strained relations between the two apparently began when Redpath refused to endorse Lane's quixotic quest for the 1860 Republican presidential nomination and instead endorsed Francis Blair Jr.[151] After that, Lane reneged on promises to assist the *Crusader* financially, causing Redpath to charge that Lane's "word of honor is as worthless as his character."[152] One historian claims that another reason that Redpath broke with Lane was that the latter attempted to seduce his wife, Mary. Redpath did attack Lane's low sexual morals after their break but he never alluded to a personal grievance against the politician in this regard.[153]

The public explanation that Redpath gave for the rupture between the two free-state radicals would seem incredulous except in context of the preceding three years of violence in the territory. The incident began innocently enough in late January when Redpath reported having recently joined a secret society in Doniphan founded by Jim Lane. According to Redpath, the group took the Old Testament name "Danite Order," to attract the "puritanical element" in the territory. However, Redpath soon learned that Lane hoped to use the group to conduct assassinations of prominent proslavery settlers.[154] In mid March, Redpath balked at Lane's request that he incite the Danites to murder Robert S. Kelley, a proslavery editor from Atchison. Relations between the two soured immediately. Redpath made his first public reference to the problems between the two men on March 26, 1858, when he published a vaguely worded statement that he would no longer labor with Lane "to renew the disturbances in the Territory."[155] He then suspended the *Crusader* until he could find alternate financial support in the Doniphan area.[156]

Redpath took on Robert St. Clair Graham, a native of Ireland and now an Atchison merchant,[157] as his partner and resumed publication of the *Crusader* in late April. He announced an uncompromising political standard for his newspaper, declaring: "Regarding the Free State party as an organized Hypocrisy,—kept up solely for the purpose of promoting the political designs of a number of ambitious demagogues—I shall refuse to fight under that banner any longer, but will hoist the *Republican* Flag."[158] In the *Crusader* issue of 17 May 1858, Redpath finally exposed Lane's "cowardly, contemptible and hellish" plan.[159] At the same time, he reported that Lane was plotting against the life of the latest Kansas territorial governor, James W. Denver. Redpath claimed that Lane had threatened him with a "good whipping" and he challenged the "human viper" to attempt it. Redpath announced that his feud with Lane might "cost us everything we possess in Kansas; press and landed property, and business prospects; but we prefer to remain free and poor, rather than to remain in the power of an assassin."[160]

Brown of the *Herald* crowed at his rival's troubles. He dismissed most of Redpath's charges against Lane and instead portrayed Redpath's problems as a consequence of his, and a few other radicals, efforts to recast the Free State Party into the Republican Party and expel all dissenters. Brown called Redpath a "traitor" to freedom in Kansas and declared "the Free State party will never miss *Redpath,* and can with impunity dispense with all men of his calibre, who claim affinity with it."[161]

Few Kansans apparently gave credence to Redpath's charges against Lane. His vituperative attacks on the popular politician mainly served to isolate him in radical circles without winning him friends among conservative free staters. The lack of paid subscribers for the *Crusader,* plus Redpath's failure as a land speculator, forced him to abandon publication of the money-losing newspaper at the end of May.[162]

Redpath's career in Kansas had only one more brief act to play. On the evening of 27 June 1858, Redpath and Hinton were having dinner in a Lawrence hotel when "a stately old man, with a flowering white beard" came to their table. Redpath later claimed to have immediately recognized John Brown in his "patriarchal disguise."[163] The three men discussed developments that had occurred in the territory while Brown had been in the East that spring. Brown and the young reporters agreed that most free staters had abandoned the rifle for the ballot box as the way of fighting the slave interests. Brown told them of his intention to join with James Montgomery, whose small armed band still pursued a violent feud with proslavery settlers in the south of the territory.[164]

Brown did not plan to stay indefinitely in Kansas. By the summer of 1858, he already had put underway the first steps of his long contemplated plot to invade the South to incite a large-scale slave insurrection. Precisely how much of the details of Brown's plan Redpath was told is unknown. In private conversations, around this time, Brown revealed most of his plot to Hinton. It seems plausible that Brown could have done the same with Redpath, whom he had known longer and respected for his "John Ball Jr." exploits. After the Harpers Ferry Raid, Redpath claimed that, while he was still in Kansas, he had learned many of the general details of the plan from another reporter and close lieutenant of Brown's, John Henri Kagi, and from Brown himself.[165] Hinton later claimed to have told Redpath the outline the plot, without naming Harpers Ferry, in November 1858.[166] Even if Brown did not confide all of the specifics of his proposed invasion to Redpath back in Kansas in the summer of 1858, nonetheless, he seems to have recruited the reporter to return east to help raise funds for him.[167] In July, Redpath and his family departed Kansas for Massachusetts.

Redpath's newly cemented allegiance to John Brown revealed how much his years in Kansas had changed him. Just five months later, Redpath wrote that Brown had gone to Kansas "when the troubles broke out there—not to 'settle' or 'speculate'—or from idle curiosity: but for one stern, solitary purpose—*to have a shot at the South*" and claimed he had had the identical motivation for going to the territory.[168] The surviving evidence of Redpath's career in Kansas, however, makes that last claim appear to be unsubstantiated bravado.[169] Until the defeat of Frémont in November 1856, Redpath appears to have had great faith in the Republican Party's ability to deal slavery a hard blow by keeping it out of Kansas. Similarly Redpath became disenchanted with the Kansas Free State Party after 1857 as the peak of the sectional fighting in the territory passed and many leaders began to return to their original loyalties to the Democratic Party. His personal feud with the political leader of remaining free-state radicals, Jim Lane, killed Redpath's last hope of influence in territorial politics.

The deterioration of Redpath's support for political means to combat slavery was coupled in his growing enthusiasm for violent tactics. His travels in the South in 1854 and 1855 had convinced him that the slaves were prepared to revolt if assisted by sympathetic whites. In Kansas, he shed the last of his personal inhibitions against employing violence on behalf of abolition. Redpath also met men in the territory who shared his interest in inciting and supporting the slaves to revolt. It was not until Redpath was drawn into the orbit around John Brown, however, that he took any steps to act on those beliefs. In Brown, Redpath found a "Cromwell" and an "American Moses" who preached a way to battle slavery without the temporizing and compromising inherent in politics.[170] By committing himself to Brown's cause, Redpath could retroactively attach a higher purpose and greater success to his journalistic and political activities in Kansas by interpreting them as the prelude and training ground for his active participation in an even more heroic attack on the institution of slavery.

3   Echoes of Harpers Ferry

The Redpath family returned east from Kansas and settled in Malden, Massachusetts, in August 1858. Across the Mystic River from Charlestown, Malden was one of a number of Boston suburbs that were rapidly losing their original character as farming towns. In the 1850s, the town of approximately six thousand was the home of dyehouses, brickmaking plants, and several shoe factories. By the time the Redpaths settled there, newly built railroad and horse trolley lines made it possible for Malden residents to commute the five miles to jobs in downtown Boston. In March 1859, Redpath praised Malden as "a town of rare and manifold virtues," but jokingly complained that commuters experience grave doubts about "Dr. Harvey's theory of the circulation of the blood" when traveling into Boston on a winter's day.[1]

The Redpaths lived in a house on Maple Street in Malden. Redpath's relationship with his wife's children strengthened during the late 1850s. Ezra T. Kidder no longer contested his ex-wife's custody of Caroline and Dudley. In her late teens, Caroline occasionally assisted Redpath in his literary projects. Still in school in his midteens, Dudley took Redpath's last name as his own. At the same time, however, there are clues to problems in Redpath's marriage. His personal correspondence contains laments about the financial burdens he endured to support his wife and her children. Since their April 1857 wedding, the Redpaths had been separated for extended periods while James worked in Kansas. This pattern persisted after the family settled in Malden. James spent more than half of 1859 out of the country on reportial assignments.[2]

When not traveling, Redpath made his home a hive of activity in 1859 and 1860. Local legend has it that Redpath's Maple Street house was a stop on the Underground Railroad. Sojourner Truth and John Brown both visited Redpath there in 1859. Few of Redpath's old New York City associates were among the guests. A heated public controversy in the late 1850s over the literary estate of his deceased friend William North had created permanent fissures in the original Bohemian circle. One exception was Walt Whitman, who became a regular visitor to the Redpaths' home when the poet was in Boston.[3]

Once settled in Massachusetts, Redpath set to work to assist John Brown, who already had put together a loose network of eastern supporters from among contributors to the Kansas free-state campaign. Organized in great secrecy in early 1858, this small group, nicknamed the "Secret Six," became Brown's principal financial support.[4] Redpath made an excellent intermediary between Brown and this secret abolitionist group. Redpath had met one member, Thomas Wentworth Higginson, in Kansas and impressed the Massachusetts minister with his boldness on behalf of the antislavery cause.[5] He also had been in correspondence for several years with the wealthy New York abolitionist Gerrit Smith, another of Brown's key backers.[6] Other than Higginson, the members of this Secret Six conspiracy harbored doubts about the readiness of the slaves to revolt. Because of his firsthand observations of the slaves and his personal acquaintance with Brown, Redpath was able to testify to the feasibility of the proposed plan for a slave insurrection and to Brown's qualities as a guerrilla captain.[7] Redpath had also met many other leading abolitionists on his visits to the East in 1856 and 1857 while still a reporter in Kansas. As a result, he was able to introduce Brown to abolitionists and antislavery politicians when the latter made his final visit to Massachusetts in spring 1859.[8]

The most important way that Redpath sought to aid Brown was by fostering favorable northern sentiment toward slave insurrection through the republication of his John Ball Jr. letters in the form of a book. With their books, Olmsted and other travelers in the South had demonstrated a reading market for works of this nature. While the slaves in Olmsted's work appeared mainly as silent actors, Redpath awarded them center stage in the *Roving Editor* to voice their discontent and willingness to revolt. Redpath found an interested publisher in the A. B. Burdick Company of New York City. However, Ashur Burdick demanded a bond from Redpath to defray typesetting costs in case the book was a failure. A cautious man, Burdick had previously made the same requirement of Hinton Helper whose controversial antislavery book, *Impending Crisis of the South*, had become a runaway bestseller for the firm.[9] To raise this printing subvention, Redpath turned to Gerrit Smith, widely known for giving freely of his vast personal fortune to various antislavery projects.[10] Redpath wrote Smith that "the difficulty is to get a publisher for a work of a *decidedly* anti-Slavery cast, which shall advocate as I do the right of slave-theft (from their masters) & Slave Insurrections."[11] Redpath gave Smith deeds to Kansas land as collateral.

Thanks to Smith's timely assistance, Burdick published Redpath's book, *The Roving Editor; or, Talks with Slaves in the Southern States*, in March

1859. Smith later wrote Burdick that he found the *Roving Editor* "too bloody." When Redpath learned of Smith's qualms, he wrote his patron that he "thought any result, no matter how sanguinary in its progress, was infinitely preferable to the death-sleep of Slavery, and the foul stain on the nation's escutcheon, which its continuance made."[12]

Because the collected John Ball materials in the various newspapers were not of sufficient length, Redpath prepared an additional hundred pages of text describing recent developments in Kansas. Redpath's revisions and additions to the John Ball Jr. letters in the text of the *Roving Editor* revealed a significant evolution between 1854–55 and 1858 in his thinking about abolitionist tactics. In the *Roving Editor*, Redpath dismissed his 1854 plan for aiding slave escapes with pocket compasses and pistols and instead professed that "I now believe that the speediest method of abolishing slavery, and of ending the eternal hypocritical hubbub in Congress and the country, is to incite a few scores of rattling insurrections—in a quiet gentlemanly way—simultaneously in different parts of the country, and by a little wholesome slaughter, to arouse the conscience of the people against the wrong embodied in Southern institutions."[13]

In new sections that he wrote in 1858 for the *Roving Editor*, Redpath strove to demonstrate the practicality of a slave revolt. A chapter entitled "The Underground Telegraph" attempted to show the ability of the slaves to communicate secretly across great distances, a requirement for any large-scale insurrectionary plot. Another chapter, "The Dismal Swamp," contended that there were numerous nearly inaccessible locations across the South from which slave "maroons" could raid the surrounding plantations. A third chapter, "My Object," supplied the general outlines of a plan for whites to foment a massive slave rebellion.[14]

Redpath dismissed objections about the potentially great bloodshed among both slaves and their masters. Violence, he professed, was the only viable tactic in the abolitionist arsenal, declaring:

> Our duty to the slave, I think, demands that we speedily appeal to the taskmaster's *fear.* Let us teach, urge, and encourage insurrections, and the South will soon abandon her haughty attitude of aggression. . . . If we want to make good terms with the Slave Power, let us bring it on its knees first! And there is but one way of doing that: by attacking it where it is weakest—*at home.* The slave quarter is the Achilles' heel of the South. Wound it there and it dies! One insurrection in Virginia, in 1832, did more for the emancipation cause, than all the teachings of the Revolutionary Fathers.[15]

Redpath volunteered his own service in such a slave revolt: "I dismiss the argument that we have no right to encourage insurrections, the dreadful punishment of which, if unsuccessful, we are unwilling or do not propose to share, by replying that I am *not* unprepared to hazard the danger of such a catastrophe, and the chances of speedy death or enduring victory with the revolutionary slaves."[16]

Redpath noted his belief that events in Kansas in the mid 1850s had hastened the coming of slave insurrections. He declared that "the Second American Revolution has begun. Kansas was its Lexington. . . . The South committed suicide when it compelled the free squatters to resort to guerilla [*sic*] warfare, *and to study it both as a mode of subsistence and a science.*" Distancing himself from his earlier support for the Republicans, Redpath now derided that party's leadership for counseling the antislavery guerrilla bands to disband before Kansas had won admission as a free state. Redpath predicted that these well-trained former Kansas free-state fighters would provide the leadership that the slaves needed to revolt.[17]

Redpath dedicated the *Roving Editor* to Brown, with words that hinted at the latter's plans for Harpers Ferry: "You, Old Hero! believe that the slave should be aided and urged to insurrection, and hence do I lay this tribute at your feet."[18]

The Burdick firm advertised the *Roving Editor* as "the most searching, thorough, and reliable investigation of American Slavery ever published." Its advertisements noted the oral testimony of the slaves in the book but avoided allusion to the question of slave insurrection. The company reprinted endorsements of Redpath's veracity and writing skills from political friends and foes in Kansas. The most insightful of these was by J. C. Vaughan, son of the Redpath's former editor at the *Chicago Tribune,* who in 1859 operated his own free-state newspaper in Leavenworth: "Redpath could not be dull, or tame, or slavish, if he were to try; he has not an idle bone in him—and if eccentric and humorous it is all for Humanity."[19]

There is no record of the sales of the *Roving Editor.* It had a market among abolitionists, of course. Frederick Douglass promoted Redpath's book by publishing excerpts from it.[20] Not everyone was so impressed. Bronson Alcott, for example, felt the *Roving Editor*'s "portraits are overdrawn, and tempered with prejudices unjust to all parties."[21]

After turning over the manuscript of the *Roving Editor* to Burdick, Redpath departed Boston in early January for the first of two trips he made to Haiti in 1859. During this tour of Haiti, Redpath studied the country's geography, politics, and history and prepared a series of travel letters for the *New York Tribune.*[22] Accompanying Redpath on these tours as a translator was his young Boston friend, Francis Merriam.[23] Redpath returned to Malden from his first Haitian visit in late March. Redpath's growing interest in Haiti will be examined in the next chapter.

Also in spring 1859, Redpath collaborated with his friend and former journalistic colleague in Kansas, Richard J. Hinton, in preparing a short book, entitled *A Handbook to Kansas Territory.* Both recent immigrants from Britain, Hinton and Redpath would collaborate in a number of reform projects during the next decade. In the preface, the authors declared their purpose was "to present a concise and impartial view of all important particulars having reference to the material and commercial resources, the interests of emigrants, and the future prosperity of Kansas."[24] To write this short 177-page book, Redpath and Hinton relied on their own observations of Kansas, other books written about the territory, and documents collected by the Kansas Emigrant Aid Society. The *Handbook* contained practical advice about how to travel to Kansas, what to bring, and where to settle. The authors assured readers that Kansas had limitless opportunity for the farmer and the mechanic, and women as well as men.[25]

Considering the involvement of both of its authors in free-state politics and the assistance given the volume by the antislavery Emigrant Aid Society, the *Handbook* was remarkably free of discussion of the slavery question. One of the book's rare allusions to the political struggle in the territory noted that "the trials of the past are but felt as a zest to greater exertion."[26] Redpath and Hinton chose this tact because they believed that by stimulating additional emigration to Kansas from the North they would help to guarantee the territory ultimate status as a free state. At this point, both Redpath and Hinton still clung to the idea of returning to live in Kansas. Redpath wrote Kansas friends that he hoped to return to the territory in May but he never made the trip.[27] Another factor shaping *Handbook to Kansas* was the need of both Redpath and Hinton for royalties so that the irregularly employed journalists could provide for their families. A nonpolitical guidebook could attract the largest possible sales among potential emigrants.

After completing the manuscript of *Handbook to Kansas* and submitting it to the New York City publishing firm of J. H. Colton, Redpath prepared for a second tour of Haiti. This time he made arrangement to write travels letters for the *Boston Atlas and Bee,* generally regarded as the most strongly antislavery of the city's Republican newspapers. In June he sailed to the island country and rendezvoused with Merriam who had remained there, exploring the interior. After another three months in the Caribbean, Redpath returned to Boston in September.[28] Redpath began publishing accounts of this second tour just a few weeks before John Brown's attack on Harpers Ferry.

There is no evidence that Brown asked Redpath to participate in his raid on the Harpers Ferry arsenal in Virginia in October 1859. There is considerable evidence that Redpath knew many details of Brown's plan. Besides his personal conversations with Brown, Redpath had discussed Brown's intentions with Hinton as early as fall 1858. The chapters in the *Roving Editor* written at that time hinted at the general outline of Brown's attack. The following spring, Brown's associate, John Henri Kagi, sent Redpath cryptic descriptions of the preparations for the raid. Redpath knew enough specifics to recruit his friend Merriam for Brown's raiding party. Blind in one eye, physically frail, and mentally erratic, Merriam nonetheless was welcomed by Brown because the young Bostonian contributed six hundred dollars in gold to finance the raid.[29]

Merriam arrived at Brown's base camp at the Kennedy farm in Maryland, seven miles from Harpers Ferry, on 15 October, just one day before the beginning of the raid. On the evening of the 16, John Brown and twenty-one followers crossed the Potomac River and seized the federal arsenal and armory buildings. A small party sent out to liberate slaves brought back only twelve and none would join the insurrection. By the evening of the 17th, local militia and armed townspeople had cut off all of Brown's possible escape routes. The following day after a short but bloody fight, a party of U.S. marines captured Brown and six surviving raiders. Ten of Brown's party had been killed and only four, including Merriam, escaped.[30]

News of the events at Harpers Ferry was wired immediately across the nation. Newspapers in both the South and the North editorialized for the swift punishment of Brown and of all his accomplices. Documents discovered at the Kennedy farm provided clues to the extent of the conspiracy backing Brown. Fearing for their personal safety, several of the Secret Six and others implicated in the plot, including Frederick Douglass, fled the country. Gerrit Smith had a psychological breakdown that required him to be committed for nearly two months in an insane asylum. Of those closest to Brown and his plot, only Redpath and Thomas Wentworth Higginson, refused to panic, although Redpath confessed that he "could neither rest nor sleep" for days after learning the news of Harpers Ferry and Brown's capture.[31]

In this frenzied state of mind, Redpath prepared a series of articles for the *Atlas and Bee* defending the character of Brown. Newspapers all across the nation reprinted the series.[32] In the articles Redpath denied that Brown had been a madman and instead described him as a "puritan in the Cromwellian sense of the word. . . . For thirty years he secretly cherished the idea of being the leader of a servile insurrection: the American Moses, predestined by Omnipotence, to lead the servile nation in our Southern States to freedom."[33] While most of the nation's press condemned Brown, Redpath gave him unqualified praise: "Let cowards ridicule and denounce him; let snake-like journalists hiss at his holy failure—for one, I do not hesitate to say that I love him, admire him, and defend him. GOD BLESS HIM!"[34] Conscious of the moral qualms of those abolitionists possessing pacifist or nonresistant beliefs, Redpath defended Brown's violent tactics as an attempt to extinguish two centuries of southern "insurrection" that slaves had endured.[35]

Redpath's articles sketched out Brown's career in Kansas, relying heavily on his own acquaintance with the former free-state guerrilla. Redpath also provided descriptions of the lives and characters of those among Brown's raiding party whom he knew. He especially praised Merriam, who he claimed had approached him in December 1858, asking advice on how he could use his fortune to free the slaves. Redpath refrained from revealing the details of how Merriam had come to join Brown but denied that the former's uncle, Francis Jackson, a leading nonresistant Garrisonian abolitionist, was responsible. While the statement about Jackson was accurate, Redpath lied when he denied the involvement of his friend, Gerrit Smith, in helping to finance Brown's plot. Redpath admitted that he himself possessed advance knowledge of Brown's general plan but not the intended time or place for the insurrection. He called the selection of Harpers Ferry a tactical blunder, but asserted that "it is the *blunder* only that I deprecate: not the *failure,* not the *thing.* For I believe in Bunker Hill South."[36]

Even as Brown awaited trial in his jail cell, Redpath praised the accomplishments of the Harpers Ferry raid: "There is not a slave who does not to-day have a NEW IDEA; and a dangerous one, which was implanted in his mind by the outbreak of Old Brown at Harper's Ferry. Truly, if his mission was to render slavery insecure, he will die a successful man."[37] Other voices praising Brown would soon be heard in the North but Redpath had earned the distinction of being the first and the most uncompromising.

Redpath did more than defend the Harpers Ferry raid with words. Several of the raiders had escaped capture when their plot collapsed. In late October, Redpath went to Chambersburg, Pennsylvania, and then to Baltimore, Maryland, to attempt to locate these men and assist their flight. Alerted by a telegraph, he met the fleeing Merriam in Philadelphia and got him on a train northward.[38] On returning to Boston, he reported to friends that his trip had been "a decidedly wild goose chase; but whatever it was possible to do for the fugitives, I *did.*" Redpath doubted that other surviving raiders remained at large in Pennsylvania, so he felt at liberty to return home because "a dozen blacks & abols are hunting for them."[39]

Upon his return to Boston, Redpath joined with other abolitionists in plotting the rescue of Brown and six other raiders captured with him. Among the Massachusetts abolitionists involved in this plot were Higginson, Boston lawyer John W. LeBarnes, and Concord school teacher Franklin B. Sanborn. The plotters assembled a small band that included several former Kansas free-state guerrillas and made plans for an attack on jail at Charles Town, Virginia, holding Brown and the other captured raiders. In late November Redpath was supposed to go to Ohio to rendezvous with the group from Kansas but failed to make that trip for unknown reasons. The plotters became dispirited when Brown sent back word through his lawyer George Hoyt that he opposed an effort to save him. While Higginson and LeBarnes wanted to make the effort nonetheless, they finally abandoned it for lack of funds.[40]

The instant notoriety caused by the *Atlas and Bee* articles led the Boston publishing firm of Thayer and Eldridge to contact Redpath about writing a biography of Brown. William W. Thayer recalled how the firm recruited Redpath as an author: "I composed the letter. There was a certain magnetism about it that Redpath could not resist. He afterwards told us that [of] the many letters from publishers asking him to write a life of John Brown, ours was the only one he answered."[41] Redpath immediately agreed to Thayer's and Eldridge's offer and launched the project while Brown was still awaiting execution.[42] Redpath later wrote that he chose Thayer and Eldridge over other publishers because "they believed in John Brown; they wished to do him justice; and they desired to aid his destitute family."[43] Expecting competition from hastily published transcriptions of the Charles Town trial records, Thayer and Eldridge ran newspaper advertisements in November and December advising readers to "wait and get the best, the only authentic and reliable work, written by Brown's old comrade in Kansas."[44]

The public announcement of Redpath's book produced differing reactions. Lydia Maria Child, who had planned to write a Brown biography, whose proceeds would go Brown's family, immediately withdrew on learning of the Redpath project.[45] In Kansas, Redpath's old journalistic enemy George W. Brown complained that Redpath was a suitable biographer only if the intention was to make John Brown appear "as a saint, and a pattern of meekness, humility etc."[46] Redpath responded by publishing a letter in the *New York Tribune* calling George W. Brown "one of the first and most prominent traitors" of the Kansas free-state cause, and the two men engaged in a nasty public dispute during the rest of the fall.[47]

Thanks to assistance from numerous persons, Redpath was able to write his biography of John Brown in less than two months. Hinton went to Kansas where he interviewed Brown's former associates and published cards in newspapers soliciting information regarding Brown's activities there. Eager to fashion a heroic image for Brown, Redpath ignored one letter he received, praising Brown but desiring to set the record straight about his responsibility for the Pottawatomie killings.[48] Redpath, himself, visited Concord and talked to Thoreau and others who gave him eyewitness accounts of Brown's lectures in that town in 1857 and 1859. The wife of George Luther Stearns, another member of the Secret Six, gave Redpath permission to reproduce a short autobiographical sketch that Brown had composed for her son. Higginson likewise permitted Redpath to republish his essay, "Visit to the John Brown Household" in the biography.[49] Most significantly, Redpath also obtained the cooperation of the Brown family. Mary Redpath traveled to North Elba, New York, met with Mary Brown, and returned to Malden with valuable family documents and much of John Brown's surviving personal correspondence.[50]

As Redpath hurriedly completed his book, he learned that many of Brown's Boston supporters were active in a last-ditch effort to save Brown's life by presenting evidence of Brown's insanity to Governor Henry A. Wise. This act appalled Redpath, as it detracted from the moral image of his hero. He wrote Higginson that the biography would not be published "until Old B. is in heaven" and then asked "I have not the faintest hope of his escape from martyrdom: have you?"[51] Virginia authorities executed Brown on December 2. Redpath completed the manuscript of the biography shortly thereafter. He wrote to Higginson in mid December that "seven Printers are after me as hard as their fingers can move."[52] The author and publisher worked together at a remarkable pace, and Thayer and Eldridge were able to release the 407 page biography on 10 January 1860.[53]

In a notice at the start of the *Public Life of Captain John Brown,* the publishers boasted at having obtained in Redpath a uniquely qualified biographer for John Brown. They also published letters from the widow of John Brown and his son Salmon, endorsing Redpath as "THE MAN ABOVE ALL OTHERS" to write the biography of John Brown. Thayer and Eldridge announced that "a large percentage on each copy sold is secured by contract to the family of captain John Brown, and every purchaser thereby becomes a contributor to a charitable object, which appeals to all freemen with a force that is irresistible."[54]

In the introduction to the book, Redpath made clear that he wrote it to defend Brown's actions at Harpers Ferry:

> Equally at war with the cant of conservatism, of politics, and of non-resistance, and a firm believer in the faith that made Bunker Hill classic, I think that John Brown did right in invading Virginia and attempting to liberate her slaves. I hold God in infinitely greater reverence than Congress, and His holy laws than its enactments. I would as soon think of vindicating Washington for resisting the British Government to the death, as to apologize for John Brown in assailing the Slave Power with the only weapons that it fears.[55]

Aside from describing Brown's Puritan ancestry and Calvinist religious beliefs, Redpath devoted relatively little space in his book to Brown's life before the 1850s, promising to describe this "private life" in a subsequent volume. Instead he presented a detailed account of Brown's career as a free-state guerrilla in Kansas. According to Redpath, Brown and his sons went to Kansas, not to settle, but "*solely* to fight the battles of freedom."[56] Redpath hotly disputed claims that Brown had attacked the South out of a desire for personal revenge for the death of a son in Kansas. He did this, he related to Higginson because "such a notion degrades him [Brown] from the position of a Puritan 'Warrior of the Lord' to a guerilla [*sic*] chief of vindictive character."[57] He instead portrayed Brown as a nineteenth-century Cromwell reluctantly taking up the sword at the call of high moral principle.

Redpath provided lengthy accounts of Brown's participation in the "battles" of Black Jack and Osawatomie. His account of the "siege" of Lawrence in September 1856 highly exaggerated Brown's role. Most significantly, Redpath repeated his 1856 denial of Brown's participation in the Pottawatomie massacre. Redpath claimed that Brown had told him that he was not present at the killings of the proslavery settlers.[58]

Redpath also denied that Brown was either a Republican or a member of abolitionist organization. Redpath described Brown as "too earnest a *man,* and too devout a Christian" to be satisfied with the Republicans' antiextensionist platform. Brown, Redpath observed, "followed neither Garrison, nor Seward, Gerrit Smith nor Wendell Phillips; but the Golden Rule and the Declaration of Independence, in the spirit of the Hebrew warriors, and in the God-applauded mode that they adopted."[59]

The *Public Life of Captain John Brown* contained a carefully censored account of John Brown's preparation for the attack on Harpers Ferry. Redpath claimed that "it would neither be prudent nor just to trace his [Brown's] movements too minutely."[60] He named no one involved in the plot other than those killed or captured at Harpers Ferry. Redpath also stated that Brown, fearing discovery by authorities at the last minute, had advanced the date of the Harpers Ferry raid. According to Redpath, this resulted in many abolitionists discovering that the raid was in progress and Brown beyond their assistance while en route to the intended Maryland rendezvous point. There is no known evidence to verify this claim but contemporaries nonetheless repeated it frequently. Redpath might have fabricated it to frighten the South further by magnifying the specter of northern support for slave insurrection.[61]

Reversing his earlier military judgment, Redpath now defended Brown's selection of Harpers Ferry as "the spot at which to begin a war of liberation."[62] His account of the events of 16–18 October 1859 contains similar unqualified praise for the bravery of Brown's entire company. He especially singled out the blacks among the raiders as evidence that "Negroes *can* fight."[63] Zealous to prove that point, Redpath incorrectly claimed that several local slaves had joined with Brown to battle for their freedom. In contrast, the Virginians and marines fought cowardly, according to Redpath, slaying raiders who were under flags of truce or trying to surrender.[64]

Redpath strongly condemned the lack of fairness in the Virginia trial that culminated in sentencing Brown to hang. He criticized the judge for denying Brown's request for a delay until he recovered from wounds incurred in the fighting. Redpath also condemned Brown's lawyers for advancing a plea of innocent on the ground of insanity, which Brown had to repudiate in court. Redpath quoted Brown's own courtroom testimony and the candid appraisals of his interrogators after Harpers Ferry, including Virginia governor Henry Wise, as proof of the abolitionist's mental competence. Moreover, Redpath denied the right of Virginia to try Brown for crime as "an atrocious assumption . . . that the statutes of the State were just; and, therefore if the prisoner should be proven guilty of offending against them, that it was right that he should suffer the penalty they inflict. This doctrine every Christian heart must scorn; John Brown, at least, despised it; and so also, to be faithful to his memory, and my own instincts, must I."[65]

The *Public Life of Captain John Brown* concludes with a description of how Brown spent his last month awaiting execution in his Charles Town jail cell, writing his family and sympathizers. Redpath reproduced a number of those letters that demonstrated Brown's lack of despair and belief that his efforts at Harpers Ferry had not been in vain. The execution is described in gruesome detail, again emphasizing a lack of human compassion among the Virginians. Redpath ends the book on a religious note, proclaiming that "the soul of John Brown stood at the right hand of the Eternal. He had fought the good fight, and now wore the crown of victory."[66]

Redpath's biography of Brown was uncompromisingly sympathetic in its assessment of its subject. To bolster his own appraisal, Redpath included quotations from Northerners praising the courage and principles of John Brown. Redpath dedicated his book to three of these: Thoreau, Emerson, and Phillips as "Defenders of the faithful, who, when the mob shouted, 'Madman!' said 'Saint!' "[67] As Redpath intended, his biography helped to secure for Brown the lasting reputation as a martyr for freedom.

The *Public Life of Captain John Brown* was a best seller for the Thayer and Eldridge firm. The company ran advertisements and agents went door-to-door to sell advance subscriptions for the book at a one dollar price. Thayer and Eldridge claimed advance subscription sales of thirty thousand and had difficulty printing copies fast enough in the first month after the book's release. Approximate forty thousand copies were in circulation by May 1860. William Thayer estimated that the firm eventually sold seventy-five thousand copies of it. In addition, three unauthorized British editions soon appeared.[68]

The book's popularity came despite many hostile reviews. *Frank Leslie's Illustrated Newspaper* printed a stinging rebuke: "The names of the hero and his biographer render it unnecessary to explain the character of his volume. . . . In every point of view that is a detestable book. . . . It expounds the most ultra-fanaticism."[69] A Democratic newspaper from Kansas condemned the book's "fanaticism, which marks every page" and charged Redpath with writing it to incite another Harper Ferry.[70] Harvard professor Charles Eliott Norton's review in the *Atlantic Monthly* attacked Redpath for writing "in the worst temper and spirit of partisanship . . . in the spirit and style of an Abolition tract."[71]

The *Atlantic* review provoked abolitionists to defend Redpath. Garrison's *Liberator* published a letter by Charles K. Whipple who declared Redpath's book "worthy of [the] praise" of being likened to an abolition tract. Whipple predicted that the Brown biography's unapologetic abolitionist principles would "sow the seeds of many enterprises for the help of the slave, and waken many hearts to inquire what they can do, directly as well as indirectly in his behalf."[72] Franklin B. Sanborn also wrote a defense of the *Public Life of Captain John Brown*. He conceded that Redpath's book "was hastily prepared to meet a pressing demand and . . . is marred by many faults of style and some extravagances of opinion." "We do not fear to wound Mr. Redpath's vanity in saying this," Sanborn claimed, "for he has always spoken, in private and in public, of his book, with the modesty native to his character. . . . He is as willing as any one to yield place to a worthier writer, but he had a duty to perform and has performed it well."[73] Privately, Sanborn confided in Thoreau his fear that Redpath's book had "told *too much*" and might lead to the arrest of Brown's secret backers.[74]

Not all abolitionists shared Whipple's and Sanborn's positive assessment. Some voiced qualms about Redpath's persistent advocacy of the righteousness of Brown's violent antislavery tactics. The *British and Foreign*

Anti-Slavery Reporter recommended the book but considered it "disfigured by the author's constant justification of an appeal to force."[75] Unitarian minister and moderate abolitionist Moncure Daniel Conway expressed disapproval not only of Brown's violence and Calvinist theology but Redpath's "coarse pencil."[76] Republicans, such as Horace Greeley, also were pleased to be able to cite Redpath as an authority to prove that their party was not responsible for the actions of John Brown.[77]

The *Public Life of Captain John Brown* remained the most widely read Brown biography until Sanborn produced one of his own in 1885. Well into the twentieth century, many writers relied heavily on Redpath's portrayal of Brown's actions and character. The *Public Life of Captain John Brown* was so influential in defining the popular image of its subject that historian James C. Malin has described the writing of the next half century as "the James Redpath Period in John Brown Biography."[78] That judgment would have greatly pleased Redpath who confided in Thoreau that he believed his book "would do good among the masses; that is all I tried to do—for the educated have teachers enough; & over them I do not expect to have influence."[79]

About the time that the *Public Life of Captain John Brown* went to press in January 1860, Redpath became involved in a renewal of the scheme to attack the Charles Town jail. This time the goal was the rescue of the two surviving captured raiders, Albert Hazlett and Aaron Stevens, awaiting execution there. Most of the original plotters renewed their involvement. Redpath's publishers, William W. Thayer and Charles Eldridge, also became active supporters. The group arranged for Hinton to travel to Kansas to recruit potential rescuers from among the old free-state guerrilla fighters. Among those Kansans who volunteered for this daring scheme were James Montgomery and Silas S. Soule. With the permission of John Brown's widow, proceeds from the sale of Redpath's *Public Life of Captain John Brown* pledged to the support of his family were made available, if needed, to finance the return of Montgomery, Soule, and a select group from Kansas. Thayer and Eldridge immediately advanced eight hundred dollars. Establishing a base in Harrisburg, Pennsylvania, Montgomery managed to reconnoiter the Charles Town area for an escape route and the even more reckless Soule got himself arrested and made contact—in the jail—with Hazlett and Stevens. The two raiders, however, rejected the proffered assistance because they did not want anyone else's life endangered. They were executed on 16 March.[80]

At the same time as he was trying to rescue Stevens and Hazlett, Redpath, himself, came into danger of arrest by federal authorities on account of his suspected complicity in Brown's raid. On 14 December 1859 Congress launched an investigation of the Harpers Ferry incident. Authorities had located a letter from Francis Merriam to Brown, which disclosed Redpath's advance knowledge of the raid. The Senate committee, chaired by James Murray Mason of Virginia, subpoenaed Redpath on 11 January and federal marshals tried to serve a warrant at his Malden house but he was absent. On 26 January 1860, the committee questioned James Jackson, the uncle of Francis Merriam, about the latter's relationship to Redpath. This witness, however, claimed to know nothing beyond the two men's trips to Haiti in 1859. Serious problems for Redpath developed during the testimony of Charles Robinson, the one-time free-state governor of Kansas, on 10 February. Robinson claimed that in spring 1858 Redpath had told him that he supported John Brown's intention of "getting up a general disturbance in the country, and abolishing slavery by means of it."[81]

Federal marshals finally served their summons on Redpath on 31 January 1860. In a public letter dripping with insolence he refused to appear, calling the Senate committee "an inquisitorial and unconstitutional body." Redpath lectured the committee's chair that the "rules and every instinct of manhood forbid me to recognize of any negro catcher to catechise me, Senator Mason. I would not pollute my lips by speaking to you. I hold the author of the Fugitive Slave law in as infinite abhorrence as in infinite reverence I cherish the memory of its most heroic assailant, John Brown."[82] On 4 February 1860, Redpath left his home to avoid possible arrest. In mid February, the Senate committee requested that warrants be issued for Redpath, and three others who also had ignored summons to appear and testify. The full Senate authorized the warrants with just four dissenting votes. The *New York Tribune* ridiculed the act as the "dying wail" of the investigation.[83]

Initially Redpath hid in the vicinity of Boston. He then contemplated staying at the home of relatives back in Michigan. His mother had recently died and he hoped to be reunited with his brother John and his sisters Mary and Jane. This reunion did not take place. Redpath instead arranged to rendezvous with another fugitive from a Senate subpoena, John Brown Jr., on the latter's farm in Ashtabula County, Ohio. Redpath spent several weeks at the home of Brown and his wife Wealthea. During that time, Owen Brown, one of the escaped raiders, arrived and took refuge in his brother's home. Redpath became a close friend of the younger Browns and corresponded with them frequently after returning to Massachusetts. While hiding in Ohio, Redpath also met William C. Howells, a Republican newspaper editor and father of William Dean Howells, who later became a famous novelist. Redpath and the elder Howells quickly became friends and visited each other often in later years.[84]

While in Ohio, Redpath wrote a letter to James H. Lane to answer the testimony of Kansas Republican Charles Robinson to Senator Mason's Committee, charging that Redpath had given Lane and William A. Phillips advanced warning of John Brown's insurrectionary plans. Redpath began this peculiar letter by stating to Lane: "I don't like you, and you dislike me; and I have no desire to change this mutual want of admiration."[85] Nonetheless, Redpath wanted Lane to make public in Kansas his denial of Robinson's accusations. After Lane published Redpath's letter, Robinson defended the accuracy of his own testimony, and the exchange added to the longstanding hostility between Lane's radical and Robinson's conservative wing of the Kansas Republican Party.[86]

At the end of March 1860 Redpath returned to Boston, although the danger of arrest by U.S. marshals had not disappeared. On 3 April, federal officers tried to arrest Franklin B. Sanborn, another of the four men who refused to appear before the Senate investigation committee, at his Concord home. A crowd of sympathetic townspeople prevented Sanborn's arrest but a hearing was arranged for the next day before the chief justice of the Massachusetts Supreme Court. Redpath, Thayer, and more than twenty other men carrying concealed weapons attended this hearing, prepared to rescue Sanborn, in case the ruling went against him. The judge released Sanborn on a technicality, causing Redpath to fear that he himself had "not more than 24 hours' grace."[87] Redpath determined to stand his ground. From Malden, Redpath wrote Higginson: "I shall stay at home & *fire* at the first intruder on my premises. . . . That the body of a U.S. Marshal is not impervious to a bullet well directed, is a lesson that I think now needs to be demonstrated—and the times are ripe for it."[88] Thayer and Higginson organized a "League of Freedom," prepared to use force to liberate Redpath or Sanborn if state courts permitted federal authorities to take them away to Washington, D.C.[89]

Despite the preparations, no attempt was made to arrest Redpath. Federal authorities did apprehend Thaddeus Hyatt of New York, another of those who had refused to respond to the Mason committee's subpoena, and imprisoned him in Washington. In a display of bravado, Redpath went incognito to the capital to interview Hyatt in his jail cell. Redpath also wrote several letters from Hyatt's cell including a note taunting Senator Mason. To abolitionist sympathizers, he reported that Hyatt "will stand out forever" as an abolitionist hero.[90] The congressional investigating committee's final report in mid June 1860 condemned Redpath's refusal to testify but ordered no further effort to apprehend him.[91]

After his return to Boston, Redpath completed his second book concerning Brown. While writing the Brown biography he had begun collecting encomiums about Brown to be published by Thayer and Eldridge in a follow-up volume. When possible, he not only wrote to the authors for permission to publish their remarks but sent them galley sheets to correct.[92] Redpath's editing of this collection had been nearly finished when interrupted by his need to hide from federal marshals. In a short period of time after returning to Malden, he finished editing these documents and published them in May in a collection, entitled *Echoes of Harpers Ferry.*[93]

In this book's preface, Redpath again repeated his advice to abolitionists that the time for aggressive, even violent, action against slavery was at hand: "Agitation is good when it ultimates in action: but not otherwise. Sarcasm, wit, denunciation, and eloquence, are eloquent preparatives for pikes, swords, rifles, and revolvers; but, of themselves, they yet never liberated a Slave Nation in this world, and they never will."[94] He concluded his introduction with an uncompromising toast: "*Success to the next Negro Insurrection!*"[95]

Echoes of Harpers Ferry reprinted praise for Brown in the form of sermons, essays, letters, and poems by such eminent figures as Henry David Thoreau, Ralph Waldo Emerson, Wendell Phillips, Victor Hugo, Theodore Parker, and Lydia Maria Child, as well as by lesser knowns such as William Dean Howells and Louisa May Alcott. Redpath also published remarks by several critics of Brown's violent tactics at Harpers Ferry, including the Reverend Henry Ward Beecher, who Redpath denounced as "the ablest and most eloquent exponent of that hypocritical cant which *talks* of sympathy for the Slave, and, at the same time, extinguishes all effective attempts to help him."[96] When reproducing published criticism of the Harpers Ferry raid by nonresistant Garrisonian abolitionists such as John Greenleaf Whittier, James Freeman Clarke, and Garrison himself, Redpath reduced the level of vitriol in his editorial remarks. He nevertheless lectured them that Brown was a "pure Idealist" who did not go South to seek violence but to free the slaves. However, if "any man had presumed to oppose this righteous action, John Brown would have summarily resisted him to death. That was the reason why he brought pikes, and Sharpe's rifles, and revolvers."[97] Thanks to the assistance of the Brown family, Redpath was able to conclude *Echoes of Harper's Ferry* by publishing, for the first time, the text of scores of letters that John Brown had received while in prison at Charles Town awaiting execution.[98]

Echoes received many of the same type of hostile reviews that the *Public Life of Captain John Brown* had. The *New York Times* focused its attack on Redpath's preface and editorial comments and denounced the book as "essentially sectional and partisan in its view, injudicious in temper, and unnecessarily violent in tone, it adds to these unamiable qualities a degree of arrogant assumption which is not only exceeding repulsive, but wholly unjustifiable, either by the immediate circumstances under which the work is produced or by the editor's right to the rank of an accomplished writer."[99]

At about this time in spring 1860, Redpath's publishers Thayer and Eldridge decided to publish a new edition of Walt Whitman's *Leaves of Grass*. The two publishers were enthusiastic about putting the controversial work back into print. Whitman spent much of the spring in Boston and his friendship deepened with Thayer's and Eldridge's star author, Redpath. When Whitman returned to Brooklyn in June 1860, Redpath wrote to his friend a letter that the poet valued and saved:

O rare Walt Whitman! I said I would write to you about your Book when I found time to read it as it was written to be read. But I take back my promise. For if you are not sane what will writing avail? and if [you] are sane your writing are alive with richest sanity. Now, if I do *not* understand them, or any parts of them, what good will it do to say so—silence, it seems to me, is a duty till I do understand them; and then again, if I do understand them, or *when* I shall do so, what good will it do to tell you of the fact? It is a waste of breath for my friend to tell me I am healthy when my pulse records the circumstance so often every minute. I love you, Walt! A Conquering Brigade will ere long march to the music of your barbaric jawp.[100]

In the summer of 1860, Redpath used skills from his days as an exchange editor to produce his third book for Thayer and Eldridge, a 132-page work entitled *Southern Notes for National Circulation*. Using abolitionist propaganda techniques dating back to Theodore Weld's *American Slavery as It Is* (1839), Redpath attempted to embarrass the South by reproducing newspaper editorials and stories that documented the suppression of free speech in the region during the panic following the Harpers Ferry raid. Redpath explained why Northerners should learn of these recent events:

> Called on solemnly to decide whether such a Social System [slavery] shall be extended into Virgin Territories, it behooves the free voters of the Union to study it carefully, perseveringly, and with an earnest purpose. "By its fruits shall ye know it." What the fruits of Slavery are to the black man; how it curses the State, and commerce, and the non-slaveholding class, there are abundant opportunities of knowing; and as to how it infringes on the rights and liberties of people of the North, these Notes bear unimpeachable testimony.[101]

The short book abounds in republished reports of mobbings, arrests, and banishings of native Southerners for making the mildest antislavery comments and of Northerners just on suspicion of their harboring abolitionist sentiments. Redpath must have reminisced about his own experiences when describing recent southern mistreatment of suspected abolitionist travelers: "Down South where the Slave-masters so loudly boast of their hospitality, they nevertheless have changed all that; and 'Be *in*hospitable to strangers, for some have entertained Abolitionists without knowing it,' seems now to be the rule that governs them."[102]

Southern Notes also reprinted articles reporting the expulsion of ministers with northern denominational affiliations, the intensified censorship of antislavery literature by southern post offices, and the destruction of William S. Bailey's *Free South* in Newport, Kentucky. Probably the most damning material in *Southern Notes* was the strident defense of these actions offered by the southern press. Redpath rebutted those editorials on constitutional grounds, claiming that "the character of our Government . . . secures to the American citizen *equal* rights in *every* quarter of the Union. Any thing that stands in the way of these rights ought to be, must be, and *shall be* abolished! Does Slavery demand the sacrifice of these precious and fundamental guarantees? Down it must go, then, and that right speedily!"[103]

Redpath concluded *Southern Notes* with the question "How long, O voters of the Northern States, HOW LONG?" and dedicated it to "Honest Abe Lincoln, Of Illinois, who, although he has often split rails, won't allow northern freemen to be 'rode' on them . . . in the hope and belief, if he shall be elected President, that it will never again be possible or necessity to make a similar collection."[104]

In a public letter to John Brown Jr. Redpath defended his endorsement of the Republican Party in the upcoming presidential election: "Let those of us who cannot aid in inciting insurrections, labor with untiring and *systematic* zeal to obtain the control of the Republican party. It is not half so difficult to abolitionize that party as most of us suppose." Redpath assured the younger Brown that, although he now worked in the political arena, he nevertheless remained devoted "to the dissemination of methods of abolition, and also . . . to the work itself, when your father's successor shall be called on to take the field."[105]

During the remainder of 1860, Redpath turned the majority of his attention to working on behalf of the Republic of Haiti. Nonetheless, Redpath continued to labor hard on behalf of both Brown's memory and heirs. Redpath announced his intention to produce another book about the "Private Life" of John Brown, along with biographical sketches of the other Harpers Ferry raiders.[106] He also oversaw a fund for the widows and children of raiders. Much of the money for this fund had come from the profits from the *Public Life of Captain John Brown* and *Echoes of Harpers Ferry*. The fund sent a thousand dollars to Brown's widow less than a month after the first book's publication. Another thousand dollars was collected and distributed by the end of 1860. Assisted in gathering funds by Wendell Phillips and Thaddeus Hyatt, finally released after three months in prison, Redpath ultimately raised and distributed more than six thousand dollars to the families of the Harpers Ferry raiders.[107]

Redpath kept Brown's memory alive in the public mind. He helped organize a Fourth of July celebration at the Brown family farm near North Elba, New York, to reaffirm "over the grave of the Martyr of Virginia, the truth of the doctrines of the Declaration of Independence."[108] Invited abolitionists and dignitaries who could not attend sent Redpath letters praising Brown, which he published in the *Liberator*. Several of these letters also commended Redpath's work, including one from Wendell Phillips that described him as "the man whose words were bullets."[109] The ceremony attracted nationwide publicity by reuniting the Brown family, two of the surviving Harpers Ferry raiders, and many of John Brown's former supporters. Redpath could not attend the ceremonies himself, however, on account of last minute arrangements to complete before departing on his third trip to Haiti on 12 July.[110]

In fall 1860, Redpath served as secretary of Boston's John Brown Anniversary Committee, which organized a public meeting to memorialize the anniversary of Brown's death and to discuss the question: "How can American slavery be abolished?" The committee rented Tremont Temple in

Boston and obtained the presence of such distinguished orators as Frederick Douglass and Wendell Phillips.[111] In December 1860, however, the nation was in the beginning phases of the secession crisis that followed Abraham Lincoln's election as president. Frightened Boston business leaders decried the convening of an "anti-Southern" convention in their city. Such sentiment caused Massachusetts's Republican senator Henry Wilson to decline his invitation because he opposed associating "in any degree the issues concerning slavery with John Brown's lawless descent upon Harper's Ferry."[112]

At 10:00 a.m. on the morning of 3 December, Redpath walked onto the Tremont Temple stage to call the memorial meeting to order. His appearance was the signal for what the *New York Tribune* described as "a diversified mob, composed chiefly of North End roughs and Beacon street aristocrats" to attempt to seize control.[113] The *Boston Post* reported that the diminutive Redpath rushed from the podium to expel the disturbers from the hall "by the collar" but he was surrounded by opponents and a "general bustle ensued."[114] Police allowed the catcalling and fistfighting to persist for three hours before finally clearing the hall of both the mob and the abolitionists. Phillips later denounced the Boston city government for "protecting fashionable riot, and putting down unpopular free speech."[115]

Thanks more to Redpath than to any other individual, the issues raised by the Harpers Ferry raid remained vivid in the public mind during the exciting year, culminating in Lincoln's election as president and the beginning of southern secession from the Union.[116] Redpath's immediate and uncompromising defense of Brown's violent actions had stimulated debate among Northerners about acceptable antislavery tactics. His heroic portrayal of Brown and his raiders helped prevent the dismissal of Harpers Ferry as an isolated act of a few madmen. His public defiance of the Mason Committee and refusal to testify about the conspiracy behind Brown intensified southern fears of continuing abolitionist incitement of slave insurrections. Redpath's skillful propaganda magnified and prolonged the sectional turmoil that accompanied Harpers Ferry and moved the nation closer to the civil war he had long dreamed of seeing.

The years 1859 and 1860 marked the period of Redpath's greatest literary productivity. In addition to newspaper articles on Haiti and John Brown, Redpath wrote or edited five books to assist the struggle against slavery.[117] Although not yet thirty years old, Redpath had become one of the nation's best-known abolitionists. Up to this point in his life, his energies had been primarily centered on writing. The recognition and confidence he had gained by that means would allow him to enter even more active spheres of reform activity just at the time when the nation began its plunge into the Civil War.

4 Commissioner Plenipotentiary for Haiti

It should be no great surprise that James Redpath's advocacy of slave insurrection would eventually make him interested in the history of Haiti. The success of the rebellious slaves and mulattoes of Haiti in holding off Napoleon's veteran troops and eventually securing their Caribbean nation's independence was a popular story among abolitionists.[1] Redpath always claimed that his original curiosity about Haiti had been created while listening to a lecture by Wendell Phillips in Malden on the Haitian revolutionary general Toussaint Louverture. He wrote Phillips that his address had "a great influence over my life,—it sent me to Hayti."[2]

The idea of visiting Haiti emerged from conversations with Francis Merriam in December 1858. The younger man was looking for ways to assist the abolitionist movement and was attracted to Redpath's advocacy of more aggressive tactics. Merriam first suggested that the two men assemble a party of abolitionists who would capture a ship involved in the coastal slave trade in the Deep South and transport the rescued blacks to Canada or Haiti. Redpath was amused at the idea of becoming "a philanthropic pirate" but worried at its dangers. He instead proposed that Merriam travel to Haiti to study the positive effects of emancipation on the black population there. Merriam replied that he felt inadequate for the project and suggested that Redpath undertake it. Merriam volunteered to accompany Redpath in the role of translator and probably offered to pay for the voyage.[3] Redpath arranged to write two separate series of articles describing his travels in Haiti for the *New York Tribune* and for the *National Anti-Slavery Standard*. Other newspapers frequently reprinted the articles from both presses.[4]

Redpath and Merriam departed Boston on 9 January 1859 aboard the brig *Laurilla*. Redpath reported the trip to have been "two days of sickness and cold, blustry winds; eleven of warm zephers and good company and books."[5] On the morning of 23 January, the *Laurilla* arrived in the harbor of Cape Haitien, and Redpath found himself "gazing at the long cluster of mountains, grand, gloomy, mist-covered, rugged and irregular, which constitute the scenery of the Northern coast of the 'Queen of the Antilles.'"[6]

The Haitian harbor pilot brought surprising news for the passengers and crew of the *Laurilla*. During the time of their voyage, a bloody revolution had overthrown the ten-year-old "empire" of Faustin Soulouque, or Faustin the First. The new ruler, Fabre Nicolas Geffrard, a popular mulatto general, had restored a republican form of government. Redpath reported that he initially worried that this revolution was just another of the periodic clashes between the nation's cosmopolitan mulatto minority and black peasant majority but soon discovered that the mulattoes and "the blackest of the Blacks—exhibit everywhere equal enthusiasm and hilarity at the fall of Faustin."[7]

Redpath spent a little over two months in Haiti on his first visit. He and Merriam traveled by foot from Cape Haitien in the north over the mountains to Gonaïves on the western coast and then by boat to Port-au-Prince. After several weeks in the Haitian capital, Redpath proceeded by himself on horseback to Jacmel in the small nation's southwestern peninsula. None of Redpath's personal correspondence from this journey has survived but his impressions of Haiti are amply documented in his newspapers articles for the *New York Tribune* and *National Anti-Slavery Standard*.[8]

Redpath's reports devoted considerable space to describing the rugged mountains and lush tropical geography of Haiti. For his readers, Redpath recounted traveling "many leagues through magnificent gorges, crossing and recrossing stony-bedded streams, seeing everywhere the most lavish profusion of vegetation and innumerable indications of great mineral wealth."[9] He frequently remarked at the natural bounty of the land with oranges, palms, and bananas growing in abundance. At Gonaïves, he witnessed the nation's plentiful forests of mahogany and other hardwoods being cut down for their valuable harvest of lumber.[10] For his American readers, Redpath also noted that the "extraordinary and inexhaustible fertility of the soil" made Haiti ideally suited for coffee, cocoa, and sugarcane production.[11]

Despite Haiti's abundant agricultural resources, the rural regions Redpath described were very poor. Practically all of the colonial-era plantation buildings along the route of their journey had been destroyed in the country's long struggle for independence a half-century earlier. In the countryside, the two white travelers visited the bamboo peasant cabins and shared meals with native Haitians. Redpath described the average Haitian as "shabbily and very cheaply attired; negligent, ragged, and not overclean in their personal appearance."[12] Redpath believed the rural poverty in part a consequence of the fact that women had to conduct much of the agriculture because the men were called away frequently for lengthy periods of military service. He did not attribute the poor living conditions he witnessed to the Haitians' race but to the adverse climate, which he noted had had a similar deleterious effect on the "poor white trash" of the U.S. South. In this way, Redpath was espousing a variant of the environmentalist arguments that abolitionists had used for several decades to attempt to overturn pervasive racist assumptions regarding blacks.[13]

Redpath also found the Haitian cities in poor condition as a consequence of "earthquakes, chiefly, and fires, the indifference of past governments, and the want of proper workmen."[14] He noted that the extensive damage caused in the city of Cape Haitien by an earthquake in 1842 largely unrepaired and many ruined building being swallowed up by the semitropical vegetation. Port-au-Prince, he wrote, "is neither a beautiful nor pleasant city; it presents few and very faint indications of prosperity."[15]

Although obviously disturbed by Haiti's poverty, Redpath formed a high opinion of the character of its people. Although Merriam carried a colt revolver, the two travelers never felt themselves in danger. Unlike his "John Ball Jr." articles, Redpath's letters from Haiti contain very few interviews with blacks. This was probably due to Redpath's poor command of French at the start of this trip and his dependence on Merriam as his translator.[16]

As a consequence of this language barrier, Redpath's appraisal of the character of Haitians often appears to be the product of visual observation rather than conversation. For example, he remarked that "the negroes here impress every unprejudiced mind with the fact that they are a more developed race than the blacks of the Southern States. Their expression of countenance, their carriage, their address, bespeak a class who are imbued with the spirit of independence and the sentiment of equality."[17] In another report, he returned to this point, arguing that "Hayti, as far as negro character is concerned, is a great success; her citizens are many in their aspect and courteous in their address, instead of cringing, timid and fawning parasites."[18]

Redpath also was disturbed by the omnipresent role of the military in the Haitian government. The necessity of an internal passport to travel through the country struck him as contrary to the spirit of republican government and the innumerable fees charged by military bureaucrats as a barrier to economic development.[19] The formal hold of the Roman Catholic Church over the country also repelled him. "For a more licentious and rascally gang of reprobates than the priesthood of Hayti," he reported, "it is difficult to imagine, and impossible to find outside of the Pagan world."[20]

In the *National Anti-Slavery Standard*, Redpath argued that the experience of Haitian blacks presented a strong case for emancipation in the United States. He conceded that Haitian exports had fallen off greatly since the days of slavery but observed that the physical condition of the nation's blacks was now vastly superior: "The whip has disappeared, and the human auction-room, and there are now no deaths by starvation or by torture."[21] Redpath also used Haitian history as an argument for violent means to overthrow slavery: "Before I went to Hayti I advocated insurrection as an agency for liberating and developing the character of the blacks; returning—having seen the realm of the annihilation of a white race of tyrants—I endorse and applaud the career of Dessalines."[22]

Having improved his "imperfect knowledge" of French after several weeks in Haiti, Redpath separated from Merriam and visited Jacmel in the south. He later reported that the purpose of this excursion was to make a collection of Haitian proverbs. He was assisted in these tasks by an English Baptist missionary in Jacmel. Redpath reported that the Haitians thought him possibly insane for making the 120-mile trip over difficult mountain trails for such a purpose, whispering to themselves: "Monsieur petit blanc est un homme tres eccentrique."[23]

The most important incident in Redpath's first visit to Haiti occurred in Port-au-Prince in early March, when he was granted a brief interview at the national palace with the new president, Geffrard. Redpath described Geffrard as a small, nervous man of about fifty with black skin but a "Caucasian type of figure and face."[24] The content of their brief conversation, Redpath admitted, was "small talk, to be sure, as is customary on such occasions; but no American President or European sovereign could have done it more gracefully."[25]

This meeting with the Haitian president was the beginning of a very significant relationship for Redpath. Ruling Haiti from 1859 until he was overthrown in 1867, Geffrard would leave his small Caribbean nation greatly transformed. After reestablishing a republican form of government, Geffrard undertook extensive reforms of the nation's military and educational, agricultural, and transportation systems. He also negotiated a concordat with the pope that brought the Haitian church back into the official Roman Catholic fold. Although the newly amended Haitian constitution empowered Geffrard as president-for-life, he shared power with a popularly elected legislature.[26]

One of Geffrard's major goals was to revitalize the Haitian economy by updating its agricultural methods. In particular, he hoped to develop the island's cotton production through the immigration of as many as one hundred thousand skilled farm laborers from the United States. Geffrard began promoting emigration shortly after taking office and recruited several hundred blacks from Louisiana during 1859 and early 1860. These blacks settled in the fertile Artibonite Valley, which ran sixty miles east of the Haitian port of St. Marc.[27] Geffrard soon concluded that a successful large-scale migration would require a well-organized network of agents in the United States and Canada to recruit emigrants and arrange for their transportation to Haiti.[28]

At the end of his first visit to Haiti, Redpath published a public letter to free blacks advising them to "wait a little longer" and gain more information before accepting invitations to migrate to Haiti. In particular, Redpath counseled American blacks to obtain exemptions from military conscription and assistance in obtaining secure titles to good farm land before seriously considering emigration to Haiti. Redpath declared Geffrard to be of a higher character than Soulouque but felt that potential emigrants should be given more firm assurances of their safety. He announced that he already had written to Geffrard's government to try to get more explicit information.[29]

Debate over emigration had played a central part in the intellectual and political life of the American free-black community in the late antebellum period. By the mid 1850s, there were clear camps of proponents and opponents of such measures. Opposition to any form of emigration had been practically universal in the free-black community before passage of the Fugitive Slave Law of 1850. The American Colonization Society had worked since 1816 to persuade free blacks to migrate to its West African colony of Liberia. Free black leaders, however, hotly disputed the colonizationists' claim that their race could never rise above a degraded status in the United States. Joined by most white abolitionists, black anti-emigrationists also argued that leaving the United States would be treason to the slaves left behind. This strong and united opposition helped account for the minimal success of the colonizationist effort.[30]

The passage of the Fugitive Slave Law of 1850 produced great anxiety in the free-black community and encouraged a reassessment of emigration.[31] In addition, a growing spirit of black nationalism in the 1850s proved favorable toward emigration proposals. Black leaders such as Martin R. Delany and Henry Highland Garnet recommended emigration as the only possible escape for blacks from pervasive racial discrimination. Their writing and lecturing stimulated increasing support from some free blacks for separatism as a means of developing a distinct black nationalism.[32] Delany played the leading role in several emigration conventions in the 1850s and even traveled to West Africa at the end of the decade to attempt to negotiate with tribal leaders for a site for North American blacks to emigrate.[33] A second group campaigning for emigration was the African Civilization Society founded by the Reverend Henry Highland Garnet in 1858. This effort differed from Delany's in that it favored a selective rather than mass emigration and sought financial aid from the white community.[34]

Both Delany's and Garnet's efforts encountered strong opposition in the free-black and white-abolitionist communities. Claiming the United States to be their homeland by right of birth, black anti-emigrationists advocated a determined battle to win suffrage and equal civil rights. Opponents of emigration asserted that the departure of free blacks would deprive the slaves of their most dependable friends. Critics also charged that Garnet's society was a front for the American Colonization Society because it received considerable support from the white community.[35]

Although the Haitian emigration movement would encounter a large measure of the same ideological opposition as Delany's and Garnet's efforts, it benefited from the high symbolic importance that most North American blacks attached to that Caribbean nation. They professed that much of the respect their race had gained came from the role that the black-led nation played in world affairs. The fact that the island republic had won its independence in 1804 and retained it in a sea of colonial possessions was deemed an important refutation of the charge of black racial inferiority.[36] In the late 1850s, as support for violent antislavery tactics grew in the black community, the example of the Haitian revolutionaries received renewed praise.[37]

There had been interest in resettlement of U.S. blacks in Haiti prior to Redpath's efforts. In 1824, Haitian president Jean-Pierre Boyer had invited blacks to emigrate to his country from the United States and a small number had moved there during the 1830s and 1840s.[38] James T. Holly had visited Haiti in the mid 1850s and conducted inconclusive negotiations regarding immigration. After returning to the United States, Holly endeavored to keep interest in migration to Haiti alive through lecturing, pamphleteering, and letter writing.[39] Ultimately the key figure in promoting black migration to Haiti was neither Holly nor any black, but white abolitionist James Redpath.

Redpath returned home from Haiti to Boston in April 1859. Merriam stayed behind and traveled extensively through the interior regions of the country, and Redpath planned to rejoin him there later that year.[40] While at home, Redpath entered the discussion about Haitian emigration and at the same time joined a highly publicized debate between Horace Greeley and Henry James, a Rhode Island minister and moral philosopher, and the father of the novelist by the same name. In a letter to the *Tribune,* James had argued for much freer divorce laws, and Greeley had replied by comparing his position to the "free love" practices that Redpath had described in his series on Haiti. The two men then exchanged another series of letters debating Redpath's assessment of Haitian sexual behavior. This prompted Redpath to write to the *Tribune* to supply more evidence of the sexual permissiveness that he had observed in Haiti. He took pains to note that not all Haitians indulged in these practices and to blame the island's lack of Protestantism for its looser moral climate.[41]

Also while back home in Malden, Redpath responded to criticism from some abolitionists about his negative appraisal of certain features of Haitian life. Redpath defended himself by declaring that he desired to describe Haiti in his articles "as it is—not as proslavery men say it is, nor as antislavery men would wish it to be." He argued that "the Abolitionists could never serve God by concealing the whole truth."[42]

Redpath departed on his second journey to Haiti in July. He later explained that he returned because his notes from the first tour were "incomplete, and in many instances contradictory" so he desired to correct his "first impressions by more extended studies."[43] Redpath sailed to Gonaïves and then visited the settlement at L'Arachaie that had been founded by black

American immigrants to Haiti in the 1820s. Redpath then proceeded to Port-au-Prince where he rendezvoused with Merriam. Redpath remained in the capital until returning to the United States in September. Much less is known about this trip than Redpath's first one because he had waited until he had returned home to begin to publish articles about it for the *Boston Atlas and Bee*. The only two articles to appear presented a very positive assessment of President Geffrard's first seven months in office. By the time the second of the articles in this "Hayti Revisited" series was published in late October, the Harpers Ferry raid had occurred, and Redpath's attention was diverted from Haiti for many months.[44]

In July and August 1860 after the John Brown-related turmoil had quieted somewhat, Redpath made a third visit to Haiti. He stayed mainly in Port-au-Prince where he resided at the house of Adolphus Ackermann, a Swedish-born merchant with a Haitian wife, whom he had met on his earlier visits. In a private letter home, Redpath recounted that soon after his arrival in Port-au-Prince, he had gone to the national palace where President Geffrard, wearing "on his head a blue velvet smoking cap, richly decorated with rich embroidry" greeted him with "great cordiality." The president asked if Redpath had come to Haiti in response to his offer of asylum from U.S. authorities hunting John Brown's accomplices. Redpath assured Geffrard that the U.S. Senate had abandoned its attempts to arrest him. The two men, with Ackermann serving as interpreter when Redpath's faulty French needed assistance, then talked for six to seven hours. Besides discussing Brown, Geffrard told Redpath about his hopes to recruit black settlers from North America.[45]

Geffrard asked Redpath to meet with his ministers and give advice about effecting his emigration scheme. Out of these discussions, came a series of public proclamations more clearly defining the terms of emigration. Geffrard's government offered North American blacks passage to St. Marc and support there at a rate of fifteen dollars per adult emigrant until they were fully settled. The Haitian government would subsidize the costs for those unable to pay in exchange for a promise by the settler to remain a minimum of three years. Emigrants were guaranteed religious freedom, equal protection of the laws, and exemption from military service.[46] Redpath also persuaded the Haitian legislature to pass a homestead law to grant each settler five *carreaux* (just over sixteen acres) of land after one year's residence and the harvest of a crop.[47]

At this time, Haitian government officials approached Redpath to become the director of their effort to attract American emigrants. Arrangements with Redpath over the structure of the Haitian Emigration Bureau were completed in August 1860.[48] The Haitians gave him the title, General Agent of Emigration to Hayti from the United States and the Canadas at quite a generous annual salary of three thousand dollars. The Haitian government launched the project with an initial investment of twenty thousand dollars. Land in the Artibonite River Valley near the Louisiana settlers was designated for the bureau's émigrés.[49] Two high Haitian officials, Victorien Pleasance, the secretary of state for foreign affairs, and Auguste Elie, director-general of emigration, would oversee the actual settlement of the American blacks in Haiti.[50]

Redpath stayed on at Port-au-Prince until 27 September while he researched information with which to write a guidebook to attract potential emigrants. He also raised money in Haiti for the families of John Brown and the other slain Harpers Ferry raiders. On the eve of his departure for Boston, the leading dignitaries of Port-au-Prince gave Redpath a banquet, toasting him as one "whose incessant labors for the triumph of the sacred cause of Liberty, and the regeneration of the African race, we desire to honor."[51] En route back to the United States, he composed a psychologically reveling letter to his friend John Brown Jr. in which he remarked that the Haitian government expected "something like superhuman energy from me & by Jove they'll have it too."[52]

Redpath established his principal office at 221 Washington Street in Boston. He shared that building with several reform societies and was just down the street from his old publishing firm, Thayer and Eldridge. The Emigration Bureau later established branch offices in New York City, Chicago, and Chatham, Canada West. Redpath's immediate goals were to publicize the Haitian emigration project and establish a cadre of competent agents to recruit emigrants.

To begin his propaganda offensive, Redpath issued circulars that described and periodically updated the terms of emigration. Redpath's circulars made it clear that the Haitian government sought potential productive citizens, especially farmers, and did not desire traders, hairdressers, waiters, teachers, or clergymen as emigrants. The Haitians offered to advance the price of passage for those unable to pay for it, free land under a homestead provision, and remunerative work until the emigrant began independent cultivation.[53] When necessary Redpath paid editors to publish his circulars and bought extra copies of newspapers carrying the circulars or favorable reports on the bureau and had his agents distribute them widely.[54]

In his Boston office, Redpath created a library of books, newspaper articles, and pamphlets regarding Haiti. He also assembled a display of the agricultural products of that country to show to potential emigrants.[55] Redpath daily devoted hours to answering letters of inquiry from the curious about Haiti and describing the emigration project. As the correspondence mounted, he hired a young Bostonian, A. E. Newton, to serve as the bureau's corresponding secretary.[56]

Redpath also contracted with his old firm of Thayer and Eldridge to publish a 180-page *Guide to Hayti* to encourage emigration. The book appeared in print in the first week in December but Thayer and Eldridge went bankrupt soon after. Redpath found another publisher for the *Guide* but he felt personally obligated for the twenty-five hundred dollars the Haitians had lost to Thayer and Eldridge. More than ten thousand copies of *Guide to Hayti* were in print by the end of 1861.[57]

The *Guide to Hayti* opened with an invitation by Geffrard to all blacks in the Western Hemisphere to unite in regenerating the "ancient splendor" of Haiti to counteract the pervasive "prejudice of caste."[58] Redpath's introduction echoed the theme that a selective immigration of North American blacks to Haiti would weaken slavery and racial prejudice in the United States.

The *Guide* contained essays on the history, government, religion, commerce, geography, natural resources, and climate of Haiti by Redpath and several Haitian authors. It also reprinted the official proclamations of the Haitian government related to the emigration movement. An unapologetic piece of propaganda, the *Guide* minimized the potential problems an emigrant might encounter. Reflecting on his experiences preparing the handbook for Kansas, Redpath observed that "it is neither possible nor desirable to put into a Guide Book . . . all that intending emigrants will ask." His *Guide* therefore contained "essential facts only" and prospective emigrants were advised to contact the Haitian Emigration Bureau for more specific details.[59]

In March 1861, Redpath purchased the *Weekly Anglo-African,* the largest circulation black-edited periodical, and placed it under the charge of George Lawrence, a black agent of the bureau stationed in New York City. Two months later, he renamed that paper the *Pine and Palm* and made it the official organ of the emigration movement. Although Redpath placed the paper under the nominal control of a black editor, he dispatched his old friend Richard J. Hinton to work with Lawrence, and he frequently dictated the contents of editorials he wanted run in the *Pine and Palm.*[60] Likewise, he made very specific suggestions to his field agents about the articles and essays he wanted them to write in support of emigration.[61] It was soon apparent that Redpath was the guiding voice of propaganda on behalf of Haitian emigration.

One way that Redpath strove to overcome suspicion regarding the Haitian emigration movement was to present the case for the bureau in the language of black nationalism, which had become popular in the 1850s. In his *Guide* and in editorials in the *Pine and Palm,* Redpath argued that the African Americans faced "annihilation" if they remained in a North America dominated by racist whites. He declared that "pride of race, self-respect, social ambition, parental love, madness of the South, and the meanness of the North, the inhumanity of the Union, and the inclemency of Canada—all say to the Black and the man of color, Seek elsewhere a home and a nationality."[62]

Redpath argued for the superiority of Haiti to any other site for African American emigration. He rejected Liberia because if black emigrants prospered in that place it would be interpreted as "the white man's victory, for he called it into being, and has fostered it from birth."[63] Redpath claimed that Haiti was the only place where blacks would be able to demonstrate their equality: "There is only one country in the Western World where the Black and the man of color are indisputable lords; . . . where neither laws, nor prejudice, nor historical memories press cruelly on persons of African descent; where the people whom America degrades and drives from her are rulers, judges, and generals . . . authors, artists, and legislators."[64]

In his *Guide*, Redpath identified one goal of the Haitian emigration movement to be overcoming white racism: "The insolent question so often asked with us, 'What would become of the Negro if Slavery were abolished?' is answered by the fact of an independent Nationality of immovable stability, and a Government inspired with the spirit of progress."[65]

Redpath also proclaimed an antislavery mission for Haitian emigration:

> It will carry out the programme of the ablest intellects of the Republican Party,—of surrounding the Southern States with a cordon of free labor, within which, like a scorpion girded by fire, Slavery must inevitably die. There is no country in the world better adapted for the culture of cotton, sugar, rice, and other Southern staples, than Hayti. All that it needs is laborers, intelligent and industrious, to devote themselves to the work. Thus, with the lever of an enlightened immigration in Hayti, the colored men of America could greatly aid in overturning the system of chattel Slavery in the South.[66]

A close reading of Redpath's propaganda in favor of Haitian emigration reveals important facets in his thinking about the future of the black race. Redpath frequently argued that African Americans in the United States had benefited from close contact with whites and Protestant Christianity. Emigrationists, he argued, could carry those improved qualities and uplift the Haitian people. Ultimately he envisioned a world where racial intermarriage would finally erase divisive borders between black and white.[67]

Redpath tried to court the old abolitionist party. He won endorsements from the religious abolitionist leader Lewis Tappan and from the political abolitionist Gerrit Smith.[68] Redpath hoped to win favor among Garrisonian abolitionists by offering John Greenleaf Whittier a position as contributing editor of the *Pine and Palm*. Redpath guaranteed the veteran of thirty years of antislavery campaigning "absolute freedom of expression, & equal freedom as to the choice of subject, & style of expounding—whether poetry or prose."[69] As a further incentive, Redpath leant his support to the application of Whittier's brother to be appointed a commercial agent to Port-au-Prince. Despite Redpath's inducements, the old abolitionist remained aloof from the new movement.

In the *Pine and Palm*, Redpath editorialized for the immediate eradication of slavery by the federal government. In July 1861, he argued that Lincoln possessed the authority to free all slaves under his war power as commander-in-chief.[70] Redpath argued that the Lincoln administration's failure to adopt that policy left the black no choice but emigration to escape the pervasive racism of the United States. After denouncing Lincoln's policies, Redpath lamented that Haitian laws forbade the naturalization of whites and declared, "Where liberty dwells, there is my country; if I fight at all, I *prefer* to fight for Haiti."[71]

Redpath demonstrated considerable skill in selecting agents to serve the Haitian Emigration Bureau. Among those who received commissions were John Brown Jr., Richard J. Hinton, James Theodore Holly, Henry Highland Garnet, William Wells Brown, H. Ford Douglas, and Charles H. Langston.[72] The bureau paid its traveling agents an average of twenty dollars per week plus two additional dollars for each emigrant they recruited. Redpath even complied with several agents' request for advances on their salaries, explaining to H. Ford Douglas, that "every Abolitionist . . . ought to feel that the laborer is worthy of his hire."[73] The agents' duties were to publicize the Haitian emigration movement by means of speeches and lectures, to create "emigration clubs" of free blacks who showed interest in the program, and to assist would-be emigrants in making transportation arrangements to embarkation ports. Redpath instructed his agents to write twice weekly reports of their activities for him but only a few of them proved that dutiful.[74]

Among the first agents that Redpath enlisted were his personal friends, Hinton, Adolphus Ackermann, Henry Melrose, and John Brown Jr. He hired Hinton as a "special agent" and sent him to lobby abolitionists and Republican politicians on behalf of Haitian emigration before assigning him to the *Pine and Palm*.[75] Redpath's Swedish friend from Port-au-Prince, Ackermann, recruited emigrants first in Charleston, South Carolina, and then in New Orleans until Louisiana's secession made that impracticable.[76] Henry Melrose, Redpath's friend from his earliest days in New York City, lectured on behalf of the bureau in Washington, D.C., and later traveled to Haiti to represent bureau interests.[77] Redpath gave only the most general directions to Brown to conduct recruitment of emigrants in Canada, because, he wrote, "My confidence in your judgment renders further instructions unnecessary." Brown's commission from the bureau carries a similar endorsement: "Whatever he [Brown] promises in behalf of this Bureau it will certainly execute."[78] Other than these four, Redpath rejected hiring white traveling agents, believing that blacks would be more effective recruiters.[79]

Redpath's bureau also enlisted several veteran black advocates of emigration as agents. The most successful of these was Holly, who himself would immigrate to Haiti in April 1861. Although unable to obtain official sanction from the Episcopal Church for a missionary-emigration scheme, Holly received encouragement from his home diocese of Connecticut and had particular success recruiting emigrants among fellow black Episcopalians.[80] H. Ford Douglas, who as early as spring 1859 had held meetings in Chicago to promote Haitian emigration, became the bureau's principal agent for the northwestern states. A veteran of many abolitionist campaigns by 1861, Douglas had concluded that "the cause of the black man" in the United States was "hopeless."[81] Redpath also persuaded Garnet to become the bureau's resident agent for New York City. Although not abandoning the idea of immigration to Africa, Garnet pledged to labor for the creation of a "black empire in the Caribbean."[82]

Redpath also recruited some long-time black opponents of emigration as bureau agents. William Welles Brown, a Boston-based Garrisonian abolitionist and novelist, lectured on behalf of the bureau on tours of New York, New Jersey, New England, and Canada.[83] Brown warmly endorsed the bureau's mission: "To emigrate to Hayti, and to develop the resources of the Island, and to build up a powerful and influential government there, which shall demonstrate the genius and capabilities of the Negro, is as good an Anti-Slavery work as can be done in the Northern States of this Union."[84] William J. Watkins, who as Frederick Douglass's assistant editor for some years had battled emigrationists such as Delany, also changed camps in mid 1861. Watkins endorsed Haitian emigration as "a movement emanating from the branch of our own people who cannot but have the welfare of the whole race at heart. It does not fatten upon prejudice against color, nor does it sympathize with the absurd and accursed dogmas of our inherent inferiority."[85] Watkins became a lecturing agent for the bureau in Ohio and Canada.

Redpath's most important black recruit to Haitian emigration was Frederick Douglass. Douglass was a lifelong ideological opponent to plans for mass black emigration, and in the 1850s had been the strongest opponent of Delany's ideal of Pan-African nationalism and regeneration.[86] In January 1861, however, Douglass announced himself in favor of a selective emigration to Haiti: "We can raise no objection to the present movements toward Hayti. . . . We can no longer throw our little influence against a measure which may prove highly advantegeous to many families, and of much service to the Haitian Republic."[87] Douglass also vouched for Redpath's abolitionist credentials and endorsed emigration to Haiti as a way for blacks to establish a secure base to combat proslavery filibustering attempts in the Caribbean.[88] Although Douglass did not lecture for the bureau, his journalistic support was a major gain for the Haitian movement. In November 1860, Redpath was happy to report back to his Haitian employers that although Douglass "has always hitherto opposed Emigration, I am likely to obtain his aid."[89] Just before the commencement of the Civil War in April 1861, Douglass set into type an article announcing his intention to accept an invitation from the government of Haiti to tour that country together with a party of emigrants to be led by Holly.[90]

The endorsement of Redpath's bureau by Brown, Watkins, and Douglass was evidence of a significant softening of resistance to emigration from the United States among northern free-black leaders. Despair created by events of recent years such as the Dred Scott decision, the execution of John Brown, and the failure of the Republican Party to embrace an abolitionist position following southern secession caused many black leaders who had opposed earlier emigration programs to consider the Haitian program more sympathetically.[91]

Despite Redpath's success in winning support for his bureau from among leading African Americans, opposition to the Haitian emigration movement arose rapidly. Long-time black opponents to the idea of emigration from the United States such as James McCune Smith, George T. Downing, and J. W. C. Pennington promptly raised their voices against the bureau. In late July 1861, Smith helped finance the resurrection of the *Weekly Anglo-African* to oppose the emigrationist position of Redpath's *Pine and Palm.*[92]

In Canada, Mary Ann Shadd engaged in a campaign of violent abuse against the concept of Haitian emigration and especially against Redpath. Shadd, a Canadian black, had developed her ideological position as an assimilationist through a long battle with Henry Bibb in the mid 1850s. In attacking Redpath's bureau, she charged that Haiti was a death trap for blacks from the United States and Canada and that the project served to revive the discredited ideas of African colonization.[93]

Black anti-emigrationists also received important help from white friends, particularly Garrisonian abolitionists, who had campaigned with them against earlier emigration projects. In a hostile review of Redpath's *Guide to Hayti,* the *National Anti-Slavery Standard* implied that support for the Haitian emigration scheme was endorsement of the position that blacks had no place in the United States.[94] William Lloyd Garrison spoke at the invitation of the black Twelfth Baptist Church in Boston on the evening of 21 July 1861 on "The War and the Haytian Emigration Movement." In questions after the talk, George T. Downing got Garrison to make strong statements opposing all forms of emigration.[95]

The bureau's opponents employed arguments similar to those used against earlier emigration programs. Downing charged that the promoters of Haitian emigration seemed "to desire to create in the minds of the colored people the impression that they cannot be anything in this country."[96] A black Baptist convention condemned the bureau because it seemed to be "characterized by the same spirit which breathed into existence the old American Colonization Society [that being] . . . that the white and black races cannot live together upon this continent in a state of freedom and equality."[97] Redpath's opponents had only to look to the tone of editorial endorsements for the Haitian emigration movement in newspapers such as the *New York Times,* which applauded the bureau for removing "the race element which the North can so well spare," as evidence of the racism the scheme encouraged.[98]

Garrison, while not questioning the sincere intention of Redpath to aid blacks, publicly warned: "One unavoidable evil attending it [Haitian emigration] is to unsettle the minds of the colored people themselves, in regard to their future destiny; to inspire the mischievous belief, in the minds of the white people, that they can yet be effectually 'got rid of'; and to keep law and custom unfriendly to them, so as to induce their departure to a foreign land."[99] Thomas Wentworth Higginson, Redpath's close ally in the support for John Brown, agreed with Garrison that blacks should be warned about the "mischief" caused by even selective emigration: "Let one family go, and it seems to infect all the rest with the desire to go,—while the whites immediately begin to fancy that it would be very convenient to have them go."[100]

Opponents of the bureau attacked Redpath's argument that emigration to Haiti would aid emancipation efforts in the United States. One *Anglo-African* correspondent derided the bureau's claims regarding free-labor cotton as a "confidence game."[101] Another correspondent claimed that the slaveholders must approve of the Haitian emigration movement because they desire "to rid the Northern states of Free colored men so that in a case of emergency the North cannot call upon them to assist her in the present struggle, neither can they (the colored men of the North) incite their slaves to insurrection."[102] Many bureau opponents remarked hopefully that the Civil War would produce emancipation and equal rights for African Americans.[103]

An indication of the strength of the assault on the Haitian Emigration Bureau was the rapid reversal of the position of Frederick Douglass. Having postponed his tour of Haiti when fighting began at Fort Sumter, Douglass returned to anti-emigrationist ranks by midsummer and denounced Haitian emigration as "a national movement . . . [with] a national creed" and charged that it resembled the African Civilization Society and the American Colonization Society in championing "the exploded ideas of prejudice and caste."[104] Douglass's change of heart angered Redpath who explained to the Haitian government that "frederick is an able man, but can easily be bought."[105]

In addition to the opposition of anti-emigrationists, Redpath had to deal with attacks by proponents of rival emigration projects. In Canada, William P. Newman charged that the Haitians intended to enslave emigrants from North America and promoted Jamaica as a safer destination.[106] In a public letter to the *Chatham Planet*, Martin Delany refused an offer of a bureau agency made by Holly. Delany stated, "My duty and destiny are in Africa, the great and glorious, even with its defects, land of your and my ancestors." Delany also bluntly criticized the Haitian leaders: "I am surprised that in the face of the intelligent black men who favor it, . . . the government would appoint over them to encourage black immigration, a white man, thereby acknowledging your inferiority . . . and the charge recently made against them by Dr. J. McCune Smith that according to their estimate 'Next to God is the white man.'"[107]

Holly quickly responded to Delany by noting that Redpath "is not the head of this movement by the black government of Hayti. He is the white servant, Geffrard the black master."[108] Garnet also responded to Delany's attack on Redpath's role at the head of the bureau by charging Delany with inconsistency because at the convention at Chatham in 1858 he had voted for John Brown not a black to be leader of the Harpers Ferry expedition.[109]

A noteworthy part of the opposition to Redpath's bureau was the violent condemnations of the Haitian government by some black opponents of emigration. For example, the revived *Weekly Anglo-African* condemned Geffrard for negotiating a concordat with the pope that established an archbishopric and four bishoprics in Haiti. The newspaper charged that the act was a capitulation to white religious authority.[110] The same paper also blasted "the Haytien Government as the most imbecile, degrading, pretentious, that were ever set up as national defenders of a people's rights."[111] Delany joined in the condemnation of the concordat and accused the Geffrard government of "compromising their country and liberty."[112]

Much of the debate regarding Haitian emigration ultimately descended to the level of character assassination. The mercenary motivation of black bureau agents became a principal target of bureau critics. One *Weekly Anglo-African* correspondent observed that every black community "had its aspirant toadying to Mr. Redpath for an agency."[113] James McCune Smith sneered that Garnet's "position always changes when . . . offered a handsome salary."[114] Apparently the constant pressure was too much for Garnet to endure. In April 1861, Garnet resigned his bureau commission and returned to advocating emigration to Africa.[115]

Highly personal attacks also were made against Redpath. An Ohio black critic condemned the Haitian movement and Redpath: "We think the scheme is a perfect humbug inducing our best citizens to leave their homes, led on by the accomplished deceiver, the notorious Jim Redpath, who cares nothing about the colored people of this country no farther than self-interest goes."[116] A New Jersey opponent of the bureau similarly branded Redpath "the heartless trader in our people's woes."[117] An editorial in the *Weekly Anglo-African* maligned every aspect of his abolitionist career and even accused him of having gone to the South in the 1850s to seek an overseer's position.[118]

Redpath responded to these slanders by defending his motives for working for the Haitians. He wrote to Garrison that "I prize my reputation as a man of honor and an Abolitionist infinitely above my position under the Haytien government. . . . I was an American Abolitionist before I was a Haytien Commissioner; and among the various titles that friends and enemies have conferred on me, I still place that of *fanatic* as first in order."[119] To John Jones, a wealthy Chicago black supporter of the emigration cause, Redpath confided that "notwithstanding what jealous individuals may think, I assure you, my dear sir, that my post is not to be envied. Denunciations come in far faster than dollars & curses than coffers!"[120]

To the Haitian government, Redpath explained the opposition of many prominent American blacks to emigration as a product of the long oppressed

status and internal rivalries of that group. He noted that many black ministers had attacked emigration because they "are afraid of losing their places
by reason of their congregations designing to emigrate." He reported that
the vehemence opponents had shown against bureau agents such as Garnett
resulted from the "petty cliques and hostile factions" of U.S. blacks "who
hate each other more than they detest their common oppressors."[121] He
even blamed much of the opposition on the "*colored* cliques" who feared
the idea of a "*Black* nationality."[122]

Despite the criticism it encountered from elements of the black community, Redpath's Haitian Emigration Bureau had considerable initial success.
The first official immigrants to Haiti sent by the bureau departed Boston
in December 1860. At least one charted ship sailed from a northern port
to Haiti each month in 1861. Emigrants came from as far away as Kansas,
South Carolina, and Canada West. Initial estimates by traveling agents were
that at least five thousand would emigrate if they could find means to get to
the coast.[123]

One reason for the early success of the recruitment drive for emigrants to
Haiti was the distress experienced by certain black groups in 1860. The South
had reacted to the previous year's Harpers Ferry raid by greatly tightening
regulations on their free-black population. Fearing potential enslavement,
thousands of these blacks made plans to leave the slave states. Until the start
of hostilities between the Union and the Confederacy made recruitment of
emigrants impossible, Redpath had Adolphus Ackermann touring the South
as an agent. Thanks to Redpath's intimate association with John Brown,
southern whites viewed these activities with great suspicion and the bureau
was even labeled a front for promoting a massive slave insurrection.[124]

The bureau also targeted free-black refugees recently arrived in the North
from Charleston and New Orleans for immigration to Haiti. Before joining
the staff of the *Pine and Palm,* George L. Lawrence had enlisted a party
of fifty emigrants in New York City from among free-black refugees from
South Carolina. Although memories of previous racial atrocities in Haiti
bothered some southern mulattoes, the bureau was able to enlist several
hundred of these refugees for resettlement on that island.[125]

Other successes were primarily the result of the labors of skillful agents.
For example, the most interesting of the early emigrant "companies" was
a group of 111 that sailed from New Haven in April 1861 under the leadership of Theodore Holly, who been a teacher and the rector of St. Luke's
Episcopal Church in that Connecticut city before working for the bureau.
Just prior to departing on the brig *Madeira,* Holly described his party as a
"*Mayflower* expedition of sable pioneers in the cause of civil and religious
liberty," and convinced his fellow emigrants to sign a "*Madiera*" compact
while on the voyage to their new home.[126]

Redpath also approached the War Department with a proposal to provide "contraband" slaves with "a comfortable home & a farm in Hayti."[127]

Redpath assigned several agents to contact "contraband" slaves to induce them to migrate and some such emigrants were eventually recruited from occupied Virginia.[128] Redpath also explored other possible Caribbean destinations for these not-quite-freed slaves if the Haitian and U.S. government could not agree on terms of emigration.[129] When approached by his old New Orleans newspaper associate, John V. Thomas, to recruit Americans blacks for a proposed colony in Nicaragua, however, he declined partially out of loyalty to the Haitians and partially because he suspected the blacks would be exploited by Central American whites.[130]

For much of 1861, Redpath could not obtain sufficient transportation to meet the heavy interest in emigration. Redpath negotiated with several shipping firms to provide adequate accommodations and provisions for the emigrants at an affordable rate. Unfortunately those companies often broke their pledges to him in order to accept more favorable terms offered by the federal government, which was rapidly preparing for war with the Confederacy. For a time, Redpath arranged for a monthly steamer to carry emigrants between New York City and Port-au-Prince.[131] To maximize the space on the ships he could obtain, Redpath had to enact very strict guidelines on the amount of materials that each emigrant could ship along to Haiti.[132]

A related problem was that many emigrants proved unable to pay for their own transportation to Haiti. Redpath reluctantly subsidized these emigrants out of bureau funds on the understanding that they would eventually repay the Haitian government. The additional financial drain on the bureau, however, forced Redpath to ask the Haitians to add to their original appropriation of twenty thousand dollars for bureau operations. They finally sent him another five thousand dollars in August 1861. Despite these unanticipated problems, the bureau's first year had been a success. More than twelve hundred blacks from the United States and Canada had sailed to Haiti by November 1861.[133]

Much of the credit for the initial achievements of the emigration project should go to Redpath. He had devoted himself totally to advancing that cause. He described his routine in a letter to his Ohio friends, the Howells family, in February 1861: "All day long the duties of my office so engross me, that when night comes, & I should have leisure, I generally discover that my strength is exhausted; that I have not even the vigor enough left to curse with sufficient force."[134]

Although Redpath's principal assignment from the Haitian government was the recruitment of emigrants, he was also appointed commissioner plenipotentiary for the purpose of carrying out negotiations to win diplomatic recognition from the United States for the Caribbean country. The bureau did not wait for inauguration day to contact Abraham Lincoln regarding the recognition question. With the help of Governor John A. Andrew of Massachusetts, Redpath gathered signatures of merchants who did business with Haiti on a petition supporting diplomatic recognition.[135] Redpath and his assistant Hinton also made a number of visits to Washington to lobby personally for this cause. The timing for this effort was propitious. Southern secession removed the major obstacle to the diplomatic recognition of Haiti by the United States, and Lincoln endorsed the idea in his first annual message to Congress on 3 December 1861. Senator Charles Sumner of Massachusetts, who had worked closely with Redpath in the recognition campaign, introduced authorizing legislation in February, and by May 1861 Congress had voted the necessary approval.[136] In April 1862, Redpath interviewed Lincoln to bring him the message that President Geffrard was willing to send a white ambassador to the United States if Lincoln so desired. According to Redpath, Lincoln had responded, "You can tell the President of Haiti that I shan't tear my shirt if he does send a nigger here."[137]

Reports of Redpath's interview with Lincoln became further ammunition for his critics. According to their characterization, Redpath had raised the subject of the prospective ambassador's race with Lincoln in the hope of getting an answer that would enhance his own chance of being selected by the Haitians. Martin Delany wrote *Douglass' Monthly,* expressing this interpretation and voicing pleasure that in matters relating to the blacks, the government "would generally prefer our claims to be made by representations from among ourselves, to any second or third rate white man, such as would intrude themselves into positions for which neither nature nor qualification fitted them."[138]

In addition to assisting Haiti as its chief emigration agent and diplomatic representative in the United States, Redpath worked to improve the economy of the Caribbean nation in the office of its "Commercial Agent" to the city of Philadelphia. The *Pine and Palm* regularly advertised investment opportunities in Haiti. Redpath successfully negotiated with the Cotton Association of Manchester, England, for the shipment of cotton gins to Haiti to stimulate the production of the staple crop for export from that country. He defended this project as a means to attack slavery: "We practical Abolitionists are determined to break down the slave power; having once failed with lead, we are disposed to try cotton."[139]

The years of the Haitian Emigration Bureau's operations coincided with especially difficult ones for that nation's newly reestablished republican government. Geffrard had to suppress revolts in November 1861, May 1862, and September 1862. Geffrard also lost considerable prestige in 1861 when Spain reoccupied Santo Domingo on the other half of the Isle of Hispaniola and then, by a show of military force, compelled the Haitians to recognize the restoration.[140] Redpath reported to Haitian officials that many potential emigrants had been frightened away by the threat of a potential Haitian-Spanish war.[141]

Back in the United States, Redpath tried to assist the Haitian government in responding to the Spanish invasion of the Dominican Republic. He wrote the U.S. State Department to warn that a war between Haiti and Spain would jeopardize U.S. interests in the Caribbean. Noting the strategic location of the island nations, he wrote that "the Munroe [*sic*] doctrine should at once be enforced or it may soon be too late."[142] With the U.S. government too preoccupied with the Civil War to intervene, Redpath proclaimed himself ready to "raise companies of Abolitionists and colored Americans to volunteer their services" in an invasion against Cuba as a means to punish Spain.[143] Such a conflict would certainly have caused a suspension of American emigration. His old friend, Francis Merriam, traveled to Haiti to assess the military situation and returned at the end of the summer of 1861 with the reassuring news that the possibility of a war with Spain had receded.[144]

The bureau experienced other problems in mid 1861 in attempting to maintain the initial pace of emigration. An example was the bureau's difficulties in recruiting Canadian blacks. Redpath's best-known white agent, John Brown Jr., toured Canada for the bureau and attracted respectable audiences to lectures on Haiti. Before he enlisted in the Union Army in August 1861, Brown claimed that more than four hundred Canadian blacks were prepared to emigrate. Redpath replaced Brown with two blacks, Alexander Tate and Isaac C. Carey, and they formed emigration clubs in Toronto, Hamilton, and St. Catherines. The efforts of these agents bore little fruit. A major obstacle appeared to be the expense of transportation from the interior to ports in the United States, so Redpath persuaded the Haitian government to underwrite that additional cost. Although more than seventy Canadian blacks sailed in June 1861 and a party of 113 departed for St. Marc in October 1861, the bureau's efforts in Canada fell very far below Redpath's original predictions of ten thousand.[145]

A recent scholar of nineteenth-century Haitian emigration movements, Chris Dixon, has observed that Redpath displayed a number of serious personal shortcomings in his direction of the bureau. Redpath proved a difficult, even dictatorial, employer. In his reports to the Haitian government, Redpath habitually shifted blame for the bureau's failings from himself to his agents, most of whom he characterized as "second class."[146] Perhaps as a consequence of such attitudes, Redpath had difficulty finding and retaining competent recruiting agents. By the summer of 1861, Brown had joined the army, Holly had departed with his colony to Haiti, and Garnett had resigned in the face of the stinging personal assaults of bureau critics. Redpath also had to dismiss his Ohio agent J. Dennis Harris after reluctantly concluding that he "lacks energy."[147] Redpath showed no sign of hesitation when he dismissed Ackermann for exceeding his authority in contracting a vessel in New Orleans to transport emigrants.[148]

The bureau experienced a severe shortage of funds in the summer of 1861. For a time, Redpath kept his agents paid by obtaining a loan from the wealthy Boston abolitionist George L. Stearns. In June, however, he had to suspend H. Ford Douglas as an agent in the Northwest for lack of funds.[149] Free distribution of the *Pine and Palm* was halted at the same time.[150]

Redpath also experienced problems in the management of the *Pine and Palm*. In early May, Hinton began to complain bitterly about Redpath's dictatorial attitude toward the contents of the newspaper. Redpath immediately reminded him: "*I am the leader of the Haytien movement, & the editor consequently of the organ of it.*"[151] A week later he apologized to Hinton for his harsh tone but not for his assertion of editorial authority. In a very revealing statement, Redpath gave his old friend a final warning:

> I am tired of all this, Hinton. If we cannot go on without having to stop every little while to decide over our relative strengths, I think we had better go on alone—each in his own direction. I have great faith in myself. I know where my strength lies & where my weak point is. I think I shall succeed, therefore, in whatever, I voluntarily & freely do. But I do not care whether that work is great or small; it must be *mine*—I must be free to work out my own destiny. I know you need the same liberty; but we must not come in collision.[152]

After more heated exchanges, Hinton left the *Pine and Palm* and the two friends since Kansas days severed communications for a quarter century before reuniting briefly to support Henry George's New York City mayoral campaign in 1886.[153]

As a consequence of Hinton's dismissal, Redpath took greater care in handling George Lawrence. Ironically, considering his treatment of Hinton, Redpath encouraged Lawrence to assume a more active editorial role on the *Pine and Palm*. He wrote Lawrence, "Pray remember this—that you will give free expression to your own thought, not asking whether it agrees with mine or not."[154] Redpath also encouraged Lawrence to take the lead in writing to leading black and white abolitionists to solicit endorsements for the emigration movement.[155] Redpath undercut these assurances, however, by adding his longtime friend Henry Melrose to the *Pine and Palm* staff as a corresponding editor.[156]

The quality of the *Pine and Palm* deteriorated over the summer of 1861 and the editors had to resort to reprinting lengthy excerpts from Redpath's *Roving Editor* to fill their four page weekly.[157] The newspaper's circulation steadily dropped due to the opposition to its emigration doctrine and to Redpath's stinging attacks on Lincoln and his refusal to endorse participation in the Union war effort until the adoption of emancipation as a war goal. Acknowledging the latter problem, Redpath announced in December 1861 that he would halt writing any editorials on political questions other than emigration. At the same time, he implied, that "higher insight" had made him doubt his previous "war doctrines," including the advocacy of slave insurrection.[158]

This shift in reform ideology appears to have been a product of a response to religious revivalism. Redpath explained his "change in political policy" as a consequence of his "change of heart from an acceptance, full and unreserved, of the doctrines and plan of salvation of our Lord and Savior, Christ." Striking for a former supporter of John Brown, Redpath even denounced violence as a means to further emancipation. Redpath's critics ridiculed his supposed change in beliefs and charged that some economic calculation must be at its root. Whatever its motivation, Redpath's conversion to orthodox religion and especially pacifism proved short-lived, as later chapters will describe.[159]

Redpath also had problems with Captain Alexander Tate, a Haitian official who visited the United States and Canada in spring 1861. Redpath believed Tate "a self-elected spy" who was "playing a deep game to ruin me. He is an infernal hypocrite—so smooth & courteous but so intriguing & false. If he ever succeeds in the slightest degree, I will throw up my Commission quicker than lightening & *stand from under*—for if the movement is managed as he wishes it to be managed, it would all go to ruin."[160] He confided in John Brown Jr. his wish that he could accompany him to Kansas to enlist in the Union Army.

Far greater problems for the bureau came from reports of unanticipated hardships and unkept promises encountered by the emigrants in Haiti, which critics of the bureau, such as the *Weekly Anglo-African,* immediately published.[161] Worse still was the testimony of dissatisfied emigrants who had returned to the United States. The principal complaints were that the Haitian government was slow in assigning homesteads, that land when finally received proved arid and unfertile, that basic utensils and household goods were unobtainable in the Artibonite Valley, that health conditions in emigrant camps were unsanitary, and that the native Haitians were unfriendly and immoral.[162] Even Holly complained of poor medical services in Haiti that had resulted in numerous deaths in his colony, including that of his mother and a daughter. This last criticism provoked Redpath to charge that the minister had failed to follow prescribed health regulations.[163]

In late 1861, Redpath's agents began to report that they had lost many prospective emigrants as a consequence of fears caused by the stories of the returnees.[164] As evidence mounted that most of the complaints about poor treatment in Haiti were true, Redpath lashed out angrily at government officials for their failure to keep promises. His suggestions regarding ways to improve conditions in Haiti for the emigrants, however, fell on deaf ears.[165] Redpath took steps to remedy the problems emigrants encountered in Haiti. He had prefabricated houses constructed in the United States and shipped to Haiti for assembly as temporary homes for newly arrived emigrants.[166] Finally, in July 1862, Pleasance, the secretary of state for foreign relations, was dismissed for the maladministration of the emigration program, but not before irreparable damage had been done to the project.[167]

The failure to improve conditions in Haiti for the emigrants undercut further efforts by Redpath and his agents. Emigrant parties departing in fall

1861 were considerably smaller than in the spring.[168] To regain the earlier pace of emigration, Redpath sought out new areas to recruit emigrants. He sent Charles H. Langston of Ohio to represent the cause of Haitian emigration to free blacks in Kansas. He also sent an agent to explore Bermuda as a possible source for emigrants.[169] None of these new efforts bore fruit.

In May 1862, Redpath reported to the Haitians: "Thus, the Spring Emigration has been a total failure."[170] He noted that less than four hundred blacks had been sent to Haiti during the past six months of labor by the bureau, compared to twelve hundred in the preceding year. In the fall, the *Pine and Palm* was discontinued, and Redpath resigned from the bureau. In a final public statement on emigration, Redpath declared that he still believed "that the negro race, like the old Israelites will be taken out of this country, and led into fairer lands."[171] Redpath blamed the failings of the emigration movement not on "mismanagement" but on "misunderstandings" caused by differences in "language, prejudice, and characteristics." Perhaps out of pique, Redpath contended that many blacks in the United States lacked the self-reliance to undertake emigration.[172]

Altogether about two thousand blacks, most of them recruited by Redpath's bureau, went to Haiti from the United States from 1860 to 1862. Several hundred of these emigrants died, many from tropical diseases. The remainder soon returned to the United States or was absorbed into the native population.[173] By 1864, U.S. diplomatic representatives could locate only two hundred of the original emigrants in Haiti and aided fifty of them to return home.[174]

The history of the Haitian Emigration Bureau reveals the deeply divided state of northern free-black opinion at the start of the Civil War. The ability of Redpath's bureau to enlist many of the emigration advocates of the 1850s as well as such previous anti-emigrationists as Douglass, Watkins, and Brown indicates that the concept of Haitian emigration had great appeal in the early 1860s.[175] Despite persistent opposition from other parts of the free-black community, the bureau proved able to recruit and actually send approximately two thousand *voluntary* emigrants to Haiti in only two years. These numbers are a valuable clue that free-black discontent at their treatment in the North remained at a high level in the first year of the Civil War.

Despite its promising start, the efforts of Redpath's bureau stalled in late 1861 and completely collapsed by the end of 1862, ironically, just before the Lincoln administration began pouring large sums of federal money into plans for the colonization of blacks in various points in Central America.[176] Surviving evidence strongly indicates that the principal cause of the bureau's demise in 1862 was the negative reaction of the free-black community to reliable reports that the Haitian government failed to provide emigrants with sufficient land, supplies, or medical care. Although the anti-emigrationist opponents of the bureau advanced strong ideological objections to the Haitian movement, their most effective arguments were simply to repeat the testimony of unhappy settlers about inhospitable conditions awaiting un-wary emigrants.[177] Even if the Haitian government had been adequately pre-pared to receive large numbers of settlers from North America, the rapidly changing situation in the United States in the early 1860s most likely would have prevented the Haitian movement from reaching its intended goals. De-spite riots and continued discrimination against blacks in the United States, the Civil War opened up new opportunities for blacks and dispelled much of the pessimism that had encouraged many to look to Haiti as a refugee and a new homeland.[178]

What were James Redpath's contributions to the Haitian emigration movement? For more than two years, he proved an energetic administrator. Nevertheless, his effort to keep complete control of the bureau in his own hands eventually drove away some of his best assistants. A skilled propa-gandist, Redpath was able to portray immigration to Haiti as an extension of black nationalist aspirations and won a respectful hearing from at least a portion of the African American and abolitionist community. As a white spokesperson for of an essentially black movement, Redpath and therefore the bureau proved exceptionally vulnerable to suspicion about his pecuniary motivation and racial values. More than one student of Haitian emigration has concluded that a black leader in Redpath's place probably could have accomplished more.[179]

Although subjected to vicious personal attack by some opponents of the bureau, Redpath won acknowledgment among critics who had known him longest, such as Frederick Douglass and William Lloyd Garrison, of his gen-uine devotion to aiding blacks. Garrison's assessment of Redpath's partici-pation in the Haitian Emigration Bureau is a fitting appraisal of the man and the movement: "We believe Mr. Redpath has acted in good faith to all the parties concerned, with an intense abhorrence of slavery, a friendly interest in the growth and stability of the Haitian republic, and a sincere desire to promote the welfare of all emigrants."[180]

5   The Radical Publisher

After the demise of the Haitian Emigration Bureau, Redpath searched for new means to support himself and his Malden-based family. Ironically it was the financial problems of his publisher, the firm of Thayer and Eldridge, that inspired Redpath to redirect his energies to book publishing. The coming of the Civil War produced grievous financial problems for this firm. For a time, Thayer and Eldridge had been very successful in publishing works by Redpath and other abolitionists as well as literary works such as a revised edition of Walt Whitman's *Leaves of Grass*. The firm found itself greatly overextended in the winter of 1860–61, however, when southern secession caused a widespread financial contraction in the North. Its heaviest creditor, the paper supply firm of Rice, Kendall, and Company, finally forced Thayer and Eldridge to liquidate its assets in December 1860.[1]

The bankruptcy of his publisher meant that Redpath had lost several hundred dollars in royalties owed him for the various Brown books. As partial compensation from Thayer and Eldridge, he received back the plates for his books. Suspecting that a market still existed for his works on Brown and Haiti, Redpath redirected his energies to book publishing. He rented room number 7 in the Washington Building at 221 Washington Street, in Boston—the same location as his former Haitian Emigration Bureau headquarters. The building also housed the editorial offices of William Lloyd Garrison's abolitionist weekly, the *Liberator*.[2] Redpath's goals were to take up Thayer and Eldridge's mantle as Boston's most daring radical publisher and to furnish inexpensive literary works to the widest number of readers.[3]

The book publishing business had undergone tremendous change in the three decades before the Civil War, thanks largely to the introduction of mechanized printing and the improvements in transportation. Publishers were now capable of producing inexpensive book for a mass reading audience. Bibles, almanacs, and schoolbooks remained steady sellers, but the decline in the religious-led opposition to novel and other forms of fiction reading had generated tremendous new markets for publishers.[4]

Once a small and localized industry, American book publishing was becoming steadily more centralized. By the 1850s, New York City had surpassed Philadelphia and Boston as the principal center of book publishing.[5] Each metropolis boosted a number of major publishing houses: New York had Harper and Brothers, and D. Appleton Company; Philadelphia hosted J.B. Lippincott and Company; and Boston possessed Ticknor and Fields and Little, Brown and Company. Harper and the Boston firms, in particular, dominated literary publishing and traditionally emphasized quality over quantity in their publishing. In the 1840s, they had beaten off a challenge to their position from rivals who had attempted to drive down book prices by reprinting "pirated" works without compensating their authors. The established firms thereafter generally issued less expensive, paperbound versions of their literary works at the same time as they published the more "respectable" hardbound ones.[6]

While the costs of book production were dropping, publishers still faced the difficult problems of distribution and sales. Publishers attempted to reach the market for their books through a combination of advertising through the press for direct sale, engaging book agents and subscription sellers, and selling through the nation's more than two thousand bookstores in 1860. By the second quarter of the nineteenth century, annual book trade fairs sold off slow-moving titles to wholesale "jobbers" who resold the books at deep discounts. Ironically book publishers found themselves in competition with their very own products for the commerce of the more cost-conscious book buyer.[7]

A major innovation in the book publishing industry occurred in 1859, when the New York publisher Irwin P. Beadle launched the first continuously issued series of "dime novels." Bound in cheap orangish-yellow paper covers and numbered continuously, the earliest of these short novels generally recounted tales of American pioneers and war heroes in sensational and nationalistic fashion. Recognizing the potential market for these cheap novels, Irwin's older brother Erastus and his partner Robert Adams, hitherto magazine publishers, took over and expanded the enterprise in 1860. The "House of Beadle" survived the financial contraction and erratic supply of paper during the secession crisis and the start of the Civil War and continued in business for the remainder of the century publishing numerous series of dime and even nickel novels. By late 1863, other publishers, including Irwin Beadle, began printing and marketing their own dime novel series to compete for the reading market. These cheap novels felt into critical disrepute by the 1880s due to their sensational character.[8]

So paperbound book publishing had already become a highly competitive industry when Redpath intrepidly entered it with his own small Boston company. Redpath's new firm published a mixture of religious, historical, and humorous works. His intention to influence northern public opinion about the issues of the Civil War and emancipation are seen in his Books for the Times series, which included abolitionist Wendell Phillips's *Speeches, Lectures, and Letters;* J.R. Beard's *Toussaint L'Ouverture;* Louisa May Alcott's *Hospital Sketches;* William Wells Brown's, *The Black Man;* and a new edition of Redpath's biography of John Brown. Another in this series was a short work by Redpath himself, *Shall We Suffocate Ed. Green?* an early anti–capital punishment tract.[9]

To reach a mass market, Redpath sold his Books for the Times in editions priced from 50 cents to $1.25. Later he published a better bound Library Edition of many of these works at $2.25. The quality of Redpath's Library Edition caused the *Boston Post* to describe them as "a luxurious style of book-making."[10] In a few cases, such as Phillips's collected works, Redpath simultaneously issued three separate editions (a Library, Trade, and People's) at different prices. Redpath employed several means to distribute his books, including mail order, wholesale agents, and retail jobbers in major cities.[11] He published advertisements for his books in popular newspapers and magazines as well as specialized periodicals, such as the *American Publishers Circular*. Redpath also mailed circulars all across the North describing his titles.[12]

In January 1864, the Redpath firm developed a series called Books for the Camp Fires, aimed principally at a reading audience of bored soldiers. Costing only ten cents, these paperbound books were modeled after the pioneers in the mass circulation book industry, Beadle's Dime Tales, first issued the previous August.[13] These brief books, from 96 to 124 pages, were bound in distinctive green paper covers and sold by mail and in bookstores and newspaper stands. Titles in the Books for the Camp Fire series included European classics, such as Honoree de Balzac's *Vendetta,* Jonathan Swift's *Gulliver's Travels,* and Victor Hugo's *Battle of Waterloo.* American works included Louisa May Alcott's *On Picket Duty* and William Wells Brown's *Clotelle.* Religious tracts, such as the *Legends of the Infancy and Boyhood of Jesus Christ,* also were on this title list. Literary journals, such as the *North American Review,* perceived a benign influence in the wartime proliferation of the dime books series: "The success of Messrs. Beadle & Co.'s undertaking has led other publishers in New York and Boston to engage in similar enterprises. As yet none of them, so far as we are aware, has reached any great magnitude. But we wish them all success, and regard the competition thus established as likely to be of service in raising the character of cheap literature generally."[14]

Redpath's announced intention for his Camp Fires series was to supply military readers with works of superior literary merit at the same price as the dime novels. His advertisements promised "the cheapest books of real merit in the market."[15] Each work was guaranteed to be "complete and unabridged."[16] Compared to his rival's volumes, Redpath's advertisements promised, the new series was "of a much higher class than the dime publications now in the market."[17]

Redpath's newspaper advertisements also assured buyers that the selections in this series were "just the books to read to the soldiers" and "equally adapted to home fires."[18] He also encouraged northern families to purchase books for their relatives and friends in the Union army, promising, "They will be welcome visitors in the camp, and the friends of our patriotic soldiers should endeavor to supply them with a copy. . . . Our soldier boys will find them just the thing to beguile an otherwise tedious hour."[19]

In addition to these two series, Redpath published an eclectic selection of books aimed at a more general reading market. These included a study on spiritualism, *Spiritual Torrents,* by the sixteenth-century French mystic Jeanne Marie de la Motte Guyon; a translation of a classic work of Stoic philosophy, *The Morals of Epictetus,* by Ellis Walker; a manual for the new lawn game, *Croquet,* by British Army Captain Mayne Reid; a novella, *The Rose Family,* by Louisa May Alcott; and the comedic *Breakfast in Bed; or Philosophy Between the Sheets* by Cockney humorist George Augustus Sala. All of these works sold in the relatively low price range of twenty-five cents to a dollar a copy.[20]

Redpath's publishing firm was practically a one-man operation. He hired assistants only as needed, subcontracted the printing to local shops, and sold the books through the mail, commission agents, and "jobbers," including Lippincott Publishers.[21] To generate large sales, Redpath sold the Camp Fire books to news agents, peddlers, army sutlers, and other retailers for the wholesale prices of sixty dollars per thousand copies. These practices enabled sellers to market the books vigorously and still profit at the low price of ten cents apiece.[22]

Redpath's small company was always financially strapped and under heavy competition from more established publishing firms. Nonetheless he won the right to many works either through friendships built up in the abolitionist movement or through great personal attention and consideration to his authors. His very first title, issued in June 1863, was by a longtime associate in the abolitionist movement, Wendell Phillips. In publishing Phillips's collected works in the Books for the Times series, Redpath reproduced some of the strongest denunciations of slavery and the compromises that northern politicians had made to protect that institution. The volume began with Phillips's famous address at an 1837 Faneuil Hall meeting on the occasion of the murder of Illinois abolitionist Elijah Lovejoy. Redpath's own introduction to that speech created the legend that Phillips later adopted, that the then little-known Boston lawyer had gone to the event without any preparation or even intention of speaking.[23] The latter half of the volume contained addresses and letters that Phillips had produced since the start of the secession crisis. These works document the abolitionist's criticism of the Lincoln administration's failure to endorse abolition as a war goal, an opinion Redpath warmly seconded.

The *Speeches, Lectures, and Letters* of Wendell Phillips received a mixed response from reviewers. Most, like the anonymous critic in the *Atlantic Monthly,* praised Phillips's oratorical skills while quarreling with his opinions on one or more issues. Thomas Wentworth Higginson complained about Redpath's decision to reproduce expressions of audience reaction that appeared in original newspaper reports of his speeches. This editorial policy, however, enlivened the texts of Phillips's addresses as well as demonstrated the hostility that many northerners had voiced toward abolitionism just a few short years before. In a forward, revealing of his intentions in publishing the book, Redpath defended these insertions:

> This was done because they were deemed a part of the anti-slavery history of the times, and interesting, therefore, to every one who shall read this book,— not now only, but when, its temporary purpose having been accomplished by the triumph of the principles it advocates, it shall be studied as an American classic, and as a worthy memorial of one of the ablest and purest patriots of New England.[24]

Phillips's book proved a modest commercial success for Redpath's company, its sales meriting a number of printings.

Another noteworthy author for James Redpath's publishing firm was William Wells Brown, author of one of the first novels published by a black. Originally entitled *Clotel; or, The President's Daughter,* the novel told the story of a slave who was the reputed mulatto daughter of Thomas Jefferson. The novel had been published first in London in 1853 by the firm of Partridge and Oakley but poor sales discouraged all American publishers before Redpath from reissuing it.[25] Redpath had employed Brown in 1861 and 1862 as an agent in his effort to recruit black emigrants to Haiti. He also had excerpted portions of Brown's novel in the weekly newspaper of the movement, *Pine and Palm* in 1861.[26] For the "Camp Fires" series Redpath published a revised edition of Brown's novel as *Clotelle, A Tale of the Southern States.*

Redpath's influence over Brown's rewriting of this important work unfortunately cannot be documented. Most significantly, the reissued novel substituted an anonymous senator for Jefferson as the slave's father, making it less sensationalist than the novel's 1853 version. The work's inherent antislavery message, however, was in no way diluted in the later edition. Redpath added his own small note to the volume, identifying Brown as a former Kentucky slave and declaring that if the book "serves to relieve the monotony of camp-life to the soldiers of the Union, and therefore of Liberty, and at the same time kindles their zeal in the cause of universal emancipation, the object both of the author and publisher will be gained."[27] Redpath confided to Alcott that he considered *Clotelle* a "book of a second rate character" in literary terms, strongly implying the work's chief merit was its dramatic support for the antislavery cause.[28]

Redpath commissioned another work by Brown for the Books for the Times series: *The Black Man,* sketches of fifty-eight leading African Americans.[29] The volume contained both a sketch and an engraved portrait of President Fabre Nicholas Geffrard of Haiti, in whose employ both Brown and Redpath had labored to encourage emigration.[30] Among those whose lives were recounted were Crispus Attucks, Phyllis Wheatley, Ira Aldridge, Frederick Douglass, and four blacks who had already distinguished themselves militarily in the Civil War. Meant to demonstrate the African Americans' capacity for equal citizenship, the sketches were advertised as showing how their subjects had "distinguished themselves in some profession or in some crisis."[31] Frederick Douglass reviewed the book and called it "an additional installment of the black man's reply to the damaging charge of natural and permanent inferiority."[32] Brown's 312-page book sold well and went through three printings by Redpath.

Besides publishing works by black and abolitionist authors, Redpath brought several other books into print to support his political goals. He substantially edited an 1853 biography of Haitian rebel leader Toussaint Louverture, by British Unitarian reformer John Relly Beard, to make the work into a propaganda piece for the emancipation cause. Redpath described Beard as "not a friend, but an able and zealous partisan" of the former slaves of Haiti. Redpath's advertisements described the Haitian revolutionary as "the greatest military genius whom the New World has produced up to the present time."[33] In the book's preface, Redpath's argued that Toussaint's example should be considered in the ongoing debate in the North about whether blacks could make good soldiers and even good officers. Redpath predicted that greater knowledge of Toussaint's life presented in this book should "help to end" that debate.[34] As editor, Redpath removed Beard's original illustrations and substituted ones he "deemed more interesting and pertinent." He substituted frequent reference to his own *Guide to Hayti* in the place of Beard's footnotes. He denied that latter action should have the "appearance of bad taste or of 'egotism'" because his own book was "an unpretending collection of facts, to which no claim or pride of authorship can justly attach."[35]

In addition to the Toussaint biography, Redpath's firm published a tract by Henry Ward Beecher aimed at persuading the British public to support the Union cause in the Civil War.[36] Redpath also reissued his own biography of John Brown, believing the abolitionist's courage and antislavery principles worthy of the emulation of Union soldiers.

Besides publishing works to advance the cause of abolitionism during the Civil War, Redpath sought out authors of works of a more literary nature. Redpath's relationship with Louisa May Alcott was an example of the latter situation. The first encounter Redpath had with the young Concord writer was in 1860 when he requested her permission to include a poem she had written memorializing John Brown in his *Echoes of Harpers Ferry.* Alcott wrote a friend that Redpath's additional request for her autograph to be published under the poem "was such a rich joke we have'nt done laughing at it yet."[37]

The two had little contact for the next few years as Alcott developed her writing skills by occasionally publishing short pieces in New England newspapers and literary magazines. In the winter of 1862–63, Alcott volunteered as a nurse in a Union army hospital in Washington, D.C. This episode lasted only six weeks before serious illness drove her home to Concord to recuperate. While recovering, she published a series of pseudonymous letters from a Union nurse named Tribulation Periwinkle in the *Boston Commonwealth*, describing her hospital experiences attending the wounded. These letters attracted much positive attention for the young writer.[38]

In June 1863, Redpath approached Alcott with a proposal to republish her hospital dispatches in book form. The rival Boston book firm of Roberts Brothers also sought out Alcott, but she selected Redpath because of his enthusiasm for the project. Redpath also promised her five cents on each of the thousand copies in the edition as well as to make charitable contributions to war orphans from any profits he derived from his share of the proceeds. The latter stipulation also helped persuade Alcott to sign with Redpath, who she wrote expressing "perfect confidence in 'my publisher' & all good wishes for his success, as well as my own."[39] Alcott confided to her diary that when she told Redpath yes "he fell to work with all his might."[40] In August, Alcott recorded with pleasure that Redpath was proceeding "vigorously, sending letters, proof, and notices daily, and making all manner of offers, suggestions, and prophecies concerning the success of the book and its author."[41]

Redpath warmly praised *Hospital Sketches* when it appeared in print in late August. Alcott also was pleased with her first published book. She wrote Redpath that she enjoyed seeing her Concord neighbors "buying, reading, laughing and crying over it wherever I go."[42] Initial sales, however, were disappointing. Alcott wrote friends that " 'the *Trade*' think it costly."[43] Redpath responded by publishing a twenty-five cent paperbound edition intended for army readers, for which Alcott received 10 percent of the proceeds.[44] By January 1864, Redpath reported to Alcott:

> I think the sale of H.S. is pretty much over, altho' of course as you advance in reputation it will continue to sell some. Booksellers think that 2000 was a fair or rather good sale; as, although it has admirable writing in it, the quantity is slight, and new things are constantly coming out.[45]

Alcott later reminisced that *Hospital Sketches* "never made me much money, but it showed me my style."[46]

Based on the success of Alcott's first book, Redpath encouraged her to prepare another collection of writings on army hospitals. Alcott hesitated, "protesting I cannot feel that because one book goes well, happening to be on a matter in which all are interested just now, another will do the same."[47] Alcott preferred to have Redpath publish a semiautobiographical novel with the working title *Success*. She sent him all the chapters that she had finished to read, but then dispatched a sister to retrieve them. Several months later, she admitted that " 'Success' is just where I left it for though I have tried a dozen times I cannot get on with it, so must wait for inspiration. Writing books is too hard work for one who likes to finish soon."[48] Redpath advised Alcott not to "print before you are perfectly ready. Fame is easy enough acquired, once you can get the ear of the public; you can do so now, but you had better feel sure that you do your best when you have it turned to you."[49] This novel, published under the title *Work: A Story of Experience*, was not completed by Alcott and published for another decade.

Blocked on her novel, Alcott relented and agreed to allow Redpath to publish a new collection of her short stories. This work, ultimately published as *On Picket Duty*, became the first volume published in Redpath's Books for the Camp Fires series. Alcott gave Redpath carte blanche to select the volume's stories from ten that she sent him. She also promised Redpath not to delay the project with requests for revisions once the type was set: "I do *not* inherit the paternal fussiness in this respect, & a thing once in the printer's hands is such a good riddance I never care to aggravate myself or him with any but the simplest corrections."[50] *On Picket Duty* contained four short stories, including the book's namesake, "The Cross on the Old Church Tower"; "The Death of John," already published in *Hospital Sketches;* and "The King of Clubs and the Queen of Hearts," which actually is about gymnastics not card playing.[51] When Alcott received her author's copies of the new book, she wrote Redpath: "The little green backs were *very* welcome & I hardly knew my own scribbles in their new dress."[52] Redpath reported to Alcott that he had printed seven thousand copies of *On Picket Duties* in its first run and would issue a second if warranted by sales.

In late 1863, Redpath also published Alcott's fairy tale novella, *The Rose Family*, concerning three roses seeking regeneration. The Redpath firm's handling of the last book disappointed Alcott who recorded in her diary that "owing to delays it was late for the holidays, and badly bound in a hurry; so the poor 'Rose family' fared badly."[53] Alcott had earlier complained to Redpath about the appearance of the paperbound edition of *Hospital Sketches*, requesting a darker cover for future printings because she had "a maternal interest in the clothes my offspring wear."[54] The sales of the *Rose Family* also displeased Redpath who, without prior notice to Alcott, unsuccessfully attempted to sell its plates in April 1864 to the Boston firm of Roberts Brothers, which had a strong line of juvenile books.[55] Despite such problems, Alcott related to a friend her overall satisfaction with working with Redpath:

when publishers get hold of a body they give that body no peace & keep them at work like 'negro mulatto slaves' all day & every day, & are never satisfied.

James Redpath is my present overseer & a sweet time I have of it, but as money is rather a necessary of life & he hands it over with a charming ease[,] I cleave unto him, & devote my energies to the earning of filthy lucre.[56]

Such sentiments apparently led Alcott to reject an approach from James T. Fields of the Boston publishing giant, Ticknor and Fields, for her next book. Alcott wrote Redpath that she "had a sort of feeling that it wasn't quite fair of Fields to offer an engagement after another manager had run all the risks of bringing the new debutante out." She expressed the hope "that your 'faith in my ability' may be rewarded, & future books may prove a good investment for us. Both."[57] She offered him the manuscript for her new novel, *Moods,* on which she had labored sporadically for the past three years. Alcott admitted that the book needed more editing and told Redpath that "I should very much value your criticism even if you bundled the book home with 'Rubbish' written on the cover."[58]

Taking no chance with his prize author, Redpath, according to Alcott, "came flying up" to her Concord home on 4 February 1864 to pick up the manuscript and promised to have it in print by May. Alcott warned him that the volume was "odd, sentimental, and tragical," but its greatest problem proved to be its length.[59] The next day, Redpath telegraphed Alcott to come to Boston immediately. When they met, he reported that his printer had found that the manuscript was much too long for a single volume. Redpath warned that a two-volume first novel was a grave financial risk and beseeched her to shorten it. Alcott refused to make further cuts, claiming she had "already shortened it all it would bear," but promised instead to work on a shorter volume for Redpath. She proposed a volume of "Fairy Tales" and suggested several artists who could be engaged to illustrate them. Redpath contracted with one of them, Elizabeth B. Greene, for the drawings.[60] In August 1864, Redpath wrote Alcott that financial reverses were forcing him to "relinquish my claims as publisher of this book in justice to you; for while I cd arrange to have it published, I do not believe I cd do it *full* justice, according to my own idea of what that is."[61] Alcott found another publisher for *Moods* later that year but the novel proved both a critical and commercial failure. The "Fairy Tales" work only appeared in print when "rediscovered" in 1975.[62]

While ending on a negative note, the overall Redpath-Alcott publishing relationship was a beneficial one for the author. *Hospital Sketches, On Picket Duty,* and *The Rose Family* all made money for Alcott—*Hospital Sketches* alone approximately two hundred dollars. Most of all, having Redpath publish her first three books gave Alcott the valuable encouragement to devote her energies to literature.[63]

Another important writer who Redpath courted for his press was the former Thayer and Eldridge author, Walt Whitman. Redpath had encouraged Thayer and Eldridge's decision to republish *Leaves of Grass* in 1860 and became Whitman's friend at that time. In December 1862, Whitman had traveled to Washington, D.C., to find and care for his brother who had been wounded at the Battle of Fredericksburg. Whitman found conditions in the military hospitals appalling and stayed on as a volunteer nurse. In February 1863, he began to solicit friends like Redpath for financial aid to continue his labors as a hospital attendant in Washington. Redpath, in turn, wrote Ralph Waldo Emerson for contributions to support Whitman. Emerson promised Redpath to explore whether he could "find any direct friends and abettors for him and his beneficiaries, the soldiers."[64] Redpath approached other Massachusetts literary figures and philanthropists on Whitman's behalf and wrote a short article in the *Boston Commonwealth* publicizing his hospital labors. Redpath apologized to Whitman for the limited success this effort achieved and blamed it on "prejudice" in the "Transcendental School" against him: "It is believed that you are not ashamed of your reproductive organs, and, somehow, it wd seem to be the result of their logic that eunuchs only are fit for nurses."[65] Emerson confirmed that suspicion when he wrote Redpath concerning Whitman: "I am not sure that he would command aid for himself in any large class,—but his selfless[?] devotion in the hospitals & his singular success entitle him to thankful assistance of all."[66]

Redpath nevertheless persisted in his fund-raising for "Nurse Walt," even soliciting from friends he encountered on the streets of Boston. Whitman thanked Redpath and other supporters profusely for these contributions. Redpath wrote him back: "Glad to know you are now in good running trim. I will do all I can here in one direction to keep you supplied with funds."[67]

This exchange of correspondence almost resulted in an important new book for Redpath's press. When Redpath wrote him in October 1863, asking "By the Bye—how are your Hospital Sketches? Are they ready yet for press?" Whitman proposed "a little 30 or 50 ct book about the scenes, war, camp, hospitals &c (especially the &c.)."[68] Soon, Whitman mailed Redpath a longer prospectus for the work, promising to write about "the immense national hospitals—in them too radical changes of premises are demanded" as well as about "the President, Seward, Congress, the Capitol, Washington City, many of the actors of the drama." Whitman advised Redpath that "it should be got out *immediately*, . . . an edition, elegantly bound, might be pushed off for books for presents &c for the holidays. . . . It would be very appropriate. I think it a book that would please women, I should expect it to be very popular with the trade."[69]

Redpath did not share Whitman's optimism. He expressed doubts about the project: "I could easily publish a small Book, but the one you propose— to stereotype, advertise and push it—implies an expenditure that may be beyond my means. But if I can get credit, I may try. Whether I will or no[t] depends somewhat on the printer's notions as to whether the book would sell."[70] Redpath promised to try to find another publisher for the book if it proved too unwieldy for him to handle; however, for unclear reasons the volume did not appear. This prose work, ultimately entitled *Memoranda during the War,* exposed the horrible conditions endured by the wounded in Union army hospitals. Such topics proved very difficult for Whitman to write about and even after he finished the book he refused to publish it until 1875.[71] Despite Whitman's failure to produce the volume for Redpath's press, the two men remained friends. A quarter-century later, Whitman recalled Redpath's response to his book proposal: "The main factor in Redpath's letter is its friendly brotherliness—its personal rather than its publisherial fervor: he was always that way with me: the man came first on both sides: business was secondary."[72]

One more publishing endeavor by Redpath deserves note. In spring 1864, Redpath employed his press to support the anti–capital punishment movement. The previous December, Edward W. Green, the young postmaster of Redpath's hometown of Malden, a Boston suburb, shot and killed a bank cashier, Frank E. Converse, during a robbery that netted approximately five thousand dollars. After a short time, a remorseful Green turned himself in and confessed to the crime. When the judge refused his original plea of guilty to second-degree murder, the defendant reluctantly pled guilty to first-degree murder, despite its capital sentence.[73]

By the 1860s, the anti–death penalty campaign had a long history. After the American Revolution, reformers such as Dr. Benjamin Rush had lobbied state governments for more rational and humane penal codes. These efforts persuaded most states to abolish public executions and to reduce significantly the number of crimes punishable by death.[74] Not satisfied with a partial reform, death penalty opponents voiced an eclectic assortment of rationalist, evangelical, romantic, and pragmatic arguments for the complete abolition of capital punishment. An equally diverse group of reformers, including journalists Horace Greeley, William Cullen Bryant, and John L. O'Sullivan; ministers Samuel J. May and John Pierpont; and politicians Samuel H. Tilden and Robert Rantoul Jr., formed a national anti–capital punishment society in 1845, headed by sitting U.S. vice president George M. Dallas. While mainly young in age and liberal in religion, this crusade attracted supporters from both political parties. Their efforts succeeded in persuading Michigan in 1847, Rhode Island in 1852, and Wisconsin in 1853 to abolish capital punishment, and many other states to restrict its application to just the crime of premeditated murder.[75]

Massachusetts had been a leading state in the anti–death penalty campaign. In the 1830s, Gloucester state legislator, Robert Rantoul Jr. won endorsement from both Whig and Democratic governors for this movement. In 1845, Rantoul was instrumental in founding the Massachusetts Society for the Abolition of Capital Punishment. Boston Universalist minister Charles Spear edited the weekly *Prisoners' Friend* to promote the cause. Prominent abolitionists, including William Lloyd Garrison, Wendell Phillips, John Greenleaf Whittier, Henry C. Wright, and Theodore Parker, also campaigned actively against the death penalty. In response to all of this pressure, the

Massachusetts legislature passed a law delaying all executions for a year and mandating an executive order for each hanging. Later governors, however, authorized executions and the issue was unsettled at the time of the Green sentencing.[76]

Redpath therefore enlisted in an experienced campaign when he opposed Green's death sentence. Already, other Massachusetts reformers, including Methodist minister Gilbert Haven, editor of Boston's *Zion's Herald*, Samuel Gridley Howe, and Wendell Phillips, had called for clemency for Green. This outcry against Green's execution found a sympathetic hearer in Massachusetts' Republican governor John A. Andrew, a friend of Redpath's since the late 1850s. Andrew had been one of the original founders of the Society for the Abolition of Capital Punishment and had already addressed the legislature in 1861 to abolish capital punishment. The governor refused to sign Green's death warrant and ordered the state Supreme Court to reexamine the question of Green's mental competence to plead guilty to a capital offense. At the same time, Andrew again recommended that the legislature do away with the death sentence as "an intrusive reminiscence of more barbarous times."[77]

Andrew's proposal provoked an acrimonious debate over capital punishment in the state. Redpath's contribution to this debate was the short tract, *Shall We Suffocate Ed. Green?* Redpath mocked the blood-thirstiness of his Malden neighbors seeking Green's execution. He condemned the "mob" demanding revenge for Frank Converse's murder and the "Scribes and Pharisees" who refused to answer the higher call of humanity. Redpath dedicated his book to Governor Andrew, who he beseeched not to play the part of Pontius Pilate.[78]

At several points in the book, Redpath made it clear that he was not arguing for Green as a person but on behalf of principled opposition to capital punishment. Nonetheless, he noted Green's abused childhood, poor education, and low-paying post office job. Redpath also hinted at Green's mental instability at the time of the crime and observed that when the murderer's mind finally cleared he voluntarily turned himself in to authorities. Appealing to his readers' prejudices, Redpath even complained that the jailers had mistreated Green by incarcerating him in the same cell with "two rollicking Catholic Irishmen."[79]

Redpath went on to deny that executing incarcerated murderers did anything to improve the safety of society and cited Charles Spear's statistics for support.[80] He recalled executions he had witnessed in New Orleans and Haiti and disputed that they had done anything to deter further crime. Redpath derisively described the reaction of the audience to the public execution in New Orleans: "If it had any good effect at all, it was simply to arouse a feeling of transient pity, which could find vent enough in a curt—'damned shame.'"[81]

Redpath singled out many local clergymen for their defense of Green's execution. He noted a recent sermon on the text of Exodus, 21:12: "Whoso sheddeth man's blood, by man shall his blood be shed." Redpath replied that Mosaic Law decreed the death penalty for many practices now part of nineteenth-century daily life. Instead, Redpath argued that Christ's "higher law—that of Love or Forgiveness of enemies" had repealed the Old Testament's law of vengeance. He reminded his readers: "No man, weighed in the scales of the Christian morality is so good that if he had his just deserts, he does not deserve to be hanged . . . but no man, weighed in the scales of Christian charity, is so bad that he does not deserve to be the object of the Father's tenderest love and pity, and of man's earnest sympathy and help."[82]

After all of the biblical arguments presented in *Shall We Suffocate Ed. Green?* Redpath confessed that he was not a Christian, because "the true Christian is he only who conforms his life in every particular to the doctrines of his masters; and I am more painfully conscious than any other human being can be how far my practice lags behind my faith."[83] This might have been a clue of Redpath's unsettled religious state as he reached the age of thirty. At the same time, Redpath dropped strong hints in the book of the influence of eighteenth-century Swedish spiritualist and capital punishment opponent Emanuel Swedenborg on his position against capital punishment.[84] Like Swedenborg, he asserted that "human life is a thing absolutely sacred" and condemned executions by the state as another form of murder.[85]

Ultimately the efforts of Redpath and the others proved unsuccessful in saving the life of Edward Green. The prisoner's lawyers lost a number of legal appeals. Governor Andrew continued to block his execution until going out of office in 1866. The next governor, Alexander Hamilton Bullock, however, finally allowed Green to be hanged. Perhaps, their sensibilities hardened by the slaughter of the Civil War and later conflicts, the people and leaders of Massachusetts never banned that form of punishment.[86]

Despite occasional successes such as the books by Alcott, the financial difficulties of managing a small publishing firm in a highly competitive and volatile marketplace finally proved too much for Redpath. In particular, the economics of publishing inexpensive volumes in mass quantities were producing little profit for his firm. He explained to Alcott that "only after a sale of 15 to 20,000 can a publisher of Dime Books make his one cent a Vol. (his maximum)."[87] In January 1864, Redpath complained that "my debtors fail me" and delayed royalty payments to his authors.[88] Redpath's efforts to obtain a new infusion of capital from his antislavery friends proved unsuccessful. In the early summer of 1864, he abandoned the business and sold his literary rights to the Roberts Publishing Company.[89] As he explained to Alcott, "I regret to be obliged to cease to be your publisher but I sincerely hope that my loss may be your gain."[90] This proved an accurate prediction as Roberts Brothers eventually published Alcott's most famous and profitable work, *Little Women*.[91]

While lasting slightly less than two years, the management of his own publishing firm proved an important step in Redpath's evolution toward the latter phase of his public career. While Redpath would always remain active in reform or journalism or a combination of both, an increasing portion of his energies began to shift during the Civil War toward supplying the cultural needs of the nation. In time, he would develop the means to blend that goal with his former pursuits and become an important agent in developing and shaping the American popular entertainment industry. Before he took that step, however, Redpath had more acts to play as an abolitionist.

6   Abolitionizing the South

With a wife and two teenaged stepchildren to support in his Malden household, Redpath experienced serious personal financial difficulties following the failure of his publishing business. As a solution, he successfully sought work as a war correspondent for the *Boston Daily Journal.* That newspaper sent him to join General William T. Sherman's army in Georgia during the summer of 1864. After Sherman's capture of Atlanta in September, Redpath covered General George Thomas's campaign against the Confederate army of John Bell Hood in Tennessee that culminated with the Union victory at Nashville in December 1864. Soon after Thomas's victory at Nashville, Redpath accepted a new reporting assignment from the *New York Tribune* to travel to Savannah, Georgia, and cover the campaigns of General Sherman's army along the Atlantic Coast. He accompanied the first Union army detachment to enter Charleston in February 1865 and sent the *Tribune* one of the first descriptions of the fall of the highly symbolic cradle of southern secession. In addition to reportorial duties for the *Journal* and the *Tribune,* both Republican Party newspapers, Redpath sent occasional dispatches to such abolitionist journals as the *Liberator* and the *National Anti-Slavery Standard.* Although he generally signed his reports under the penname "Berwick" after his Scottish hometown, the newspapers usually informed the readers of the identity of their well-known reporter.[1]

Aside from his past abolitionist activities, Redpath's background was rather typical of that of the more than three hundred reporters who accompanied the Union army and navy. Like most of them, he was relatively young (his early thirties), well educated, and a veteran journalist or writer. To be effective, a reporter had to accompany northern troops in the field and share the rigors and dangers of their campaigns. In addition, good reporters competed strenuously with each other to be the first to send their paper news of important military developments.[2]

Many of Redpath's experiences were common to journalists traveling with the Union army. Transportation was a constant problem for war reporters. Redpath frequently had to wait several days for permission to ride on railroad lines run by the federal army in Georgia because General Sherman had ordered his officers to keep "sickly sycophantic meddling" reporters off the trains.[3] At the time of the Battle of Nashville, he rented a horse to ride closer to the action. The only one available he described as a "gaunt, hungry-looking bag of bones," blind in one eye. Nevertheless, when Redpath climbed a hill to observe the movement of the armies through a set of opera glasses, even that pathetic animal was stolen from him.[4]

Sometimes Redpath sent off on foot. One night, when walking back to his camp from Union lines near Atlanta, Redpath was detained by jittery sentries as a possible spy. After being interrogated and released by one provost marshal, he was rearrested by an officer from another unit. Redpath was kept under guard out-of-doors for three-and-a half hours during a rainstorm until a colonel examined his pass from Sherman's headquarters and ordered him released. Redpath told his readers that after "being imprisoned, questioned, drenched, searched, a-hungry, a-thirsty, and tired-out in body and in mind," he finally reached safety in the rear at dawn.[5]

Transportation problems cost Redpath his biggest potential scoop of the war. He was at Hilton Head Island, the principal Union army staging point on the Sea Islands off South Carolina, when news arrived that Sherman's maneuvers had just forced the Confederates to evacuate their garrison in Charleston rather than allow it to be cut off. Hoping to be the first northern reporter to enter the fallen enemy citadel, Redpath immediately boarded a steamer to Charleston harbor where he hurriedly transferred to a navy ship. To his chagrin, instead of landing at Charleston the ship steamed on to Hilton Head. When Redpath finally got to Charleston two days later it was in the company of numerous other reporters.[6] Soon after, Redpath failed in his assignment to join Sherman's army as it rapidly pushed on toward North Carolina. As he explained to his "greatly disappointed" *New York Tribune* editor, the military had delayed giving him a pass in time for him to reach Sherman's army before it had broken contact with Union forces on the coast.[7]

Like other reporters, Redpath also was dependent on highly unreliable telegraph and mail services to get dispatches to his editors. In Georgia and Tennessee, the Confederate cavalry of Nathan Bedford Forrest frequently disrupted the communications of both the Union army officers and reporters with their northern superiors. As a consequence, Redpath's dispatches often arrived and were published out of order.[8]

Redpath's dispatches experienced problems with army censors. Sherman, in particular, possessed what one historian has labeled an "anti-press fixation," often threatening to hang reporters as spies.[9] While Sherman believed the Confederates would benefit from reading news reports of Union military operations, Redpath felt that political considerations also shaped censorship policies. Redpath reported that federal military censors acted on the theory "that no startling news should be permitted to go North that may have a tendency, unexplained and perverted as they would be, to increase the excitement of the Presidential canvass."[10]

The Atlanta campaign occurred in the midst of the 1864 presidential contest in which Republican incumbent Abraham Lincoln was challenged by Democrat George B. McClellan. In late 1863 and early 1864, Redpath had actively supported the movement by antislavery radicals such as Wendell Phillips to replace Lincoln as the next Republican presidential candidate with someone regarded as more sympathetic toward abolitionism. On 4 May 1864, Redpath's name was published on a list of men calling for a mass convention in Cleveland of opponents of Lincoln's renomination. Redpath was not reported present at that ill-attended gathering which nominated John C. Frémont for president.[11] By the time he had joined the Union army in Tennessee, however, Redpath's political opinions regarding the election seemed to have changed. Redpath's reports already had noted that the Confederates were rooting for McClellan's victory. Fearing that the Democrats might use defeatism about the war to prevent Lincoln's reelection, he never objected to the censorship.[12] Redpath was in Nashville on election day and reported the strong support for Lincoln in Union regiments. If Redpath still opposed Lincoln's reelection, he did not let his opinions slip into his wartime reporting.[13]

One additional problem that Redpath shared with many other reporters covering the Union army was receiving what they considered fair compensation for their risky labors. Typically reporters in the field received weekly salaries ranging from fifteen to thirty-five dollars plus expenses. Skilled compositors back in northern cities, at the same time, received wages over fifty dollars a week. A sharp rise in the cost of newsprint forced stringent economies on newspapers in 1864 and 1865. At the *New York Tribune,* business manager Samuel Sinclair began to scrutinize every expense voucher from the field, rightly suspecting that many reporters were attempting to augment their meager income.[14]

In February 1865, Redpath learned that Sinclair regarded his own reimbursement claims as "extravagant." Sinclair ordered no further advances to the reporter. Redpath angrily wrote his editor Sydney Howard Gay to complain about Sinclair:

> I have had quite enough of this—quite enough; and I do not mean to stand for it. . . . I have not spent a dollar more than was requisite, & not a dime have I charged or shall I ever charge that is not right. I know that this is not the custom of correspondents; but I shall do what I believe to be right & only that. And know this, I shall resent the slightest imputations either on my honor or my carefulness.[15]

Redpath threatened to send his notice to the *Tribune* and find another newspaper for which to report before he "let his family suffer" by having to pay
his own expenses in the field. Gay quickly resolved the dispute to Redpath's
satisfaction, but while Redpath waited in Charleston for new funds from the
Tribune he lost his opportunity to rendezvous with Sherman's army moving
north into North Carolina.[16]

Redpath made no pretense to military expertise. In fact, he labeled his first
series of dispatches to the *Boston Daily Journal* "An Unmilitary Reconnaissance."[17] He confessed ignorance about the meaning of many of the military
terms frequently reported in the press. He complained that veteran "war Correspondents know so much about the Art of War that they never condescend
to teach us who don't what they mean by the terms they use so freely."[18]

To educate himself, Redpath visited Union military camps in the South.
There he located old friends now in the service as well as the sons of others,
including Boston abolitionist William Lloyd Garrison. He found that many
soldiers knew of his abolitionist reputation.[19] In these camp visits, Redpath
developed a solid respect for the common soldier. Inspecting Union army
trenches before Atlanta, he found the soldiers "sun-burnt, and dirty, their
uniforms are faded and soiled." Nonetheless, he reported, that they possessed high morale and confidence in their generals, especially Sherman and
Thomas.[20] Redpath found even the youngest soldiers to be good teachers
about the art of war. Following a visit to the Union lines before Atlanta, he
remarked that "it is wonderful to see . . . how old the eyes of the youngest
look—how much older than their faces. The z-z-zipping of the bullets cuts
short minorities, and makes the boys adults before they are twenty-one."[21]
After the Battle of Nashville he observed that "old soldiers never expose
themselves for the mere fun of it. Brave men never do. The veteran has
found out that bullets hurt."[22]

Apparently forgetting these lessons, Redpath displayed considerable personal daring as a reporter. On several occasions, he joined Union cavalry
units for raids deep into Confederate territory in Georgia and Alabama.
At the Battle of Nashville, he ignored the warnings of Union soldiers and
climbed over their breastworks into heavy enemy rifle and cannon fire in
order to employ his opera glasses to better observe a federal charge. He
concluded that report: "It was the grandest thing I ever saw men do. I hate
war, but I worship daring."[23] That attitude led Redpath to voice occasional
praise for the courage and perseverance of the common Confederate soldier
who marched and fought on scanty rations.[24] Nowhere in Redpath's reporting is there a hint of the evangelically inspired pacifism that had appeared
in some of his *Pine and Palm* writings in early 1862. He seems to have fully
reverted to his earlier stance as an abolitionist of supporting violent tactics
as the only possible means to end slavery.

While Redpath's dispatches covered the same military details as those
of fellow war correspondents, what makes them of particular historical

significance is the attention he devoted to political developments in the South and to the conditions of blacks in the Union military and in "contraband" camps that followed their armies. Redpath reported the military performance of black army units to be high. For example, he praised the courage of black regiments in the Battle of Nashville in December 1864 and declared that "the notion that the negroes cannot be made gallant soldiers is now thoroughly exploded in this department."[25] Redpath also praised the black Fifty-fourth Massachusetts Infantry Regiment for its valor in the famous attack on Fort Wagner outside Charleston in July 1863 as well as for its disciplined behavior as garrison troops in the same city after its capture.[26] Redpath denounced the Confederates for their mistreatment of captured black Union soldiers and excoriated Confederate general Nathan Bedford Forrest as "the murderer of Ft. Pillow" for his massacre of the black garrison of that Tennessee Union fortification in April 1864.[27] He also bitterly denounced a Union army colonel for surrendering his all-black unit and returning those "poor men, all loyal, and desirous to fight" to slavery.[28]

As in his "John Ball Jr." letters to abolitionist newspapers in the 1850s, Redpath frequently published interviews with southern slaves. In September 1864, he accompanied a Union cavalry detachment on a raid into Confederate territory in Alabama. Redpath asked slaves about their treatment since Lincoln had issued the Emancipation Proclamation and was told that the slaves continued to be severely whipped by their masters. Redpath boasted that he had personally guided twenty-five slaves belonging to one such brutal master back to Union army camps "where they will help to swell the scanty loyal population of Middle Tennessee."[29] Redpath assured Northerners that runaway slaves behind the Union lines were ill-fed and clothed but eager to work. Nonetheless, he complained, many Union army officers treated the "contraband" with the same contempt masters had shown their slaves. This appears to have been an accurate characterization. Racial opinion in officer ranks toward blacks varied greatly. The most progressive generally were found in officers volunteering to serve in the regiments of the U.S. Colored Troops raised in captured Confederate territory, but the officers and men on many of the white regiments from northern states harbored strong prejudices against the runaway slaves who followed their army.[30]

In contrast to his praise for blacks, Redpath made southern whites now living under Union army occupation targets for his journalistic barbs. He noted that most of the slave-owning "chivalry" of Tennessee and Georgia dwelt in places where "no farmer in New England whose place and possessions are worth $5000 would consent to inhabit . . . cheerless, semi-barbarous and uncouth are the homes of the chivalry."[31] Redpath ridiculed the appearance of southern white women who he described as " sitting at the doorways of their cabins, their old-fashioned, straight-backed, rush-bottomed chairs tipped back, with a short cutty pipe stuck between their lovely lips, enjoying their after-dinner smoke."[32] Redpath applauded Sherman's total war tactics and made no apology for the sufferings the rebels endured. He visited the earthen bunkers in which Atlanta civilians had endured the siege and expressed the hope that the "wives and daughters of New England [never] have to seek such places of refuge."[33] After touring the entire city, however, he admitted that "one is astonished that, with such a long cannonading, so little permanent injury has been inflicted on the town."[34] On the other hand, the extent of damage in Charleston stunned Redpath:

> No pen, no pencil, no tongue can do justice to the scene. No imagination can conceive of the utter wreck, the universal ruin, the stupendous desolation. Ruin—ruin—ruin—above and below; on the right hand and the left; ruin, ruin, ruin, everywhere and always—staring at us from every paneless window; looking out at us from every shell-torn wall; glaring at us from every battered door and pillar and veranda; crouching beneath our feet on every sidewalk. Not Pompeii nor Herculaneum, nor Thebes nor the Nile have ruins so complete, so saddening, so plaintively eloquent."[35]

Despite the sufferings Southerners had endured, Redpath protested against leniency shown toward former Confederate sympathizers in Union-occupied territory. Instead, he believed that the slaveholders must be humbled if they ever were to become loyal again, noting that "this war is saving the South in spite of itself."[36] Yet Redpath possessed little faith in those non-slaveholding Southerners who professed to be Unionists. When he encountered a "Home Guard" unit in Dalton, Georgia, he wrote that its members could never become more than semilawless "Federal bushwackers [*sic*]."[37] Whether "Rebel or loyal," the poorer southern whites had "no love of culture, of civilization, of truth," he reported, because slave owners had discouraged all attempts to educate them.[38]

Rather than express sympathy for southern whites, Redpath reminded his readers of their mistreatment of the slaves and quoted the Bible: "Truly, the Lord liveth and heareth the cry of the poor, and avengeth those who call on Him in their distress."[39] Redpath's venomous reporting soon reached the desk of the editor of the *Richmond Enquirer* in the Confederate capital, and he branded it "wild intoxication" and reassured his Confederate readers that Redpath had forgotten that "Lord Cornwallis and the British also occupied the city of Charleston for a while."[40]

Redpath used his "war reporting" as a way to encourage northern public opinion to demand a thoroughgoing "reconstruction" of the South when the Confederacy was finally defeated. In his first report to the *Journal* in August 1864, Redpath counseled Northerners that "no peace can be had—no peace should be even dreamed of, excepting alone on the basis of the instant and entire 'abandonment of slavery.' For thus alone, as all our history shows, and as this cruel war has written in blood can 'the *integrity* of the Union be secured and perpetuated.'"[41] He also advised that the "old South must either be independent or subjugated—its ruling elements exterminated."

To do so, he prescribed the following policy: "Search out the poor Unionists and educate them; divide the large plantations between the soldiers, black, 'white trash,' and settlers from the Northern States. Thus, and thus only, will a new South be created, worthy of the glorious summer land, loyal, free, intelligent and incorruptible."[42]

Redpath advocated a thorough economic reconstruction for the South. One cornerstone of his program was a large-scale redistribution of the planters' landholdings. He argued that both the freed slave and the poor whites in the many refugee camps could become self-sufficient rapidly if "we act justly to all men—giving homesteads and equal chance to everyone would will work."[43] Redpath also contended that another key to southern economic recovery was "the Northern enterprise, intelligence, and virtue, which will flock here if the needed encouragement were given."[44] Redpath's views were very much in line with calls for permanent confiscation and redistribution of plantation lands made by congressional Radical Republicans such as George W. Julian and Thaddeus Stevens and a systematic educational plan for the former slaves already launched by numerous northern "freedmen's aid" societies.[45]

In his articles, Redpath devoted more attention to policies for political than economic reconstruction. Like many abolitionists, Redpath condemned the restoration of citizenship rights to ex-Confederates who took oaths of loyalty to the federal government, doubting their true reversion back to Union cause: "That policy of the government at Washington only [condones] perjury, and is slowly and surely digging the grave of the Republican party. It is the farce that comes before the tragedy. You will see."[46] Most white southern Unionists, Redpath claimed, seek "a restoration as nearly as possible of the old state of things," including slavery.[47] Nonetheless, Redpath voiced pleasure when Tennessee's Unionists voted to remove slavery from their state's constitution in February 1865. He judged this as evidence that "the number of 'Southern men with Northern principles' is increasing very fast."[48] Redpath's appraisal appears overly optimistic, because a modern analysis of the Tennessee referendum found the turnout of voters to have been fewer than 20 percent of that in the 1860 election.[49]

Redpath regarded the political situation in Tennessee as exceptional. In Alabama, for example, he observed that "you can always tell the native loyalist of Alabama as far as you can see them. Their physical organization is peculiar and well-defined. They have all black or yellow skin and kinky hair. Sometimes you find a white, straight-haired man who has been true to the Union of his fathers, but these exceptions are so very rare that they can be counted on your fingers in any of the towns you choose to name."[50]

In November 1864, Redpath advised the Republican Party to enfranchise the ex-slaves immediately. He reported from Nashville that "the colored population held an informal election and voted 8000 odd against *one* for McClellan! If the Union party do not take this hint and confer the right of suffrage on all loyalists without distinction here, they will display a want of shrewdness (to speak of no higher lack) which the Democracy have never yet been guilty of."[51] In addition to land redistribution and black suffrage, Redpath argued that a free public education system was an essential to the creation of a New South. "Ignorance," he reported, had been the "mental Fort Sumter" of slavery.[52]

As a military correspondent, Redpath failed to stand out among his numerous contemporaries. His accounts lack significant insights regarding the performance of the armies or generals he accompanied. Although instinctively aggressive, Redpath failed to produce any "scoop" of his fellow reporters about Union army achievements. His accounts often provided colorful commentary about army life but the best of these dealt with the reporter's own adventures and misadventures, near or behind the fighting lines.

Where Redpath's wartime reporting gained significance was in areas that primarily were extensions of his antebellum abolitionist career. He worked hard at documenting the conditions of southern blacks during the war. His dispatches were filled with positive appraisals of the "contrabands" as willing workers and as brave soldiers. Redpath also warned that southern whites in occupied territories refused to accept either military defeat or the emancipation of their slaves. More than a year before the war's conclusion, Redpath advised northern readers to adopt a tough-minded reconstruction of the South.

Redpath's career took an unexpected turn a few days after his arrival in the newly occupied city of Charleston, in late February 1865. Colonel Stewart L. Woodford, the Union military commander of the city, approached Redpath about taking charge of the creation of schools for the newly liberated slaves of Charleston. Redpath later reported to northern abolitionists that

> Col. Woodford at first offered me the superintendence of the colored schools; but I gave him my reasons for refusing to have anything to do with separate schools, in a municipality in which colored people had been taxed to build and support buildings into which their children were never admitted.[53]

The military officials relented and permitted him to take possession of all public school buildings in the city and "to open them of a basis of equality."[54] On 27 February 1865, "General Order No. 4" from the Union army headquarters for Charleston announced that Redpath had been appointed superintendent of education for the city and Kane O'Donnell, a reporter for the *Philadelphia Press,* his assistant superintendent.[55]

Redpath reopened five public schools on 4 March 1865 and during the first week enrolled more than fifteen hundred "all white, black, and yellow students, alike."[56] Eighty percent of the initial students were black, however, because the former teachers at those schools encouraged white parents to keep their children at home. On the day the schools reopened, the few white students were mainly from the city's Irish and German immigrant communities.[57] Because of "considerable opposition" from native whites, Redpath had to stop short of the total integration of the public schools. He reported to northern friends that "I am obliged to have separate rooms, and white teachers for the white children,—but all our friends here regard it as a great victory in getting the two classes into the same building."[58] He defended his limited action as "a great step toward destroying the prejudice against the colored people. All the colored people are delighted at this arrangement,—or rather they are in ecstasy about it."[59]

The initial rush of blacks to the schools surprised Redpath. At the end of March, he reported to one freedmen's aid group, that "the colored people are a unit in favor of learning at once and all together. Everybody from six to sixty is already out, or ready to turn out as soon as I can handle them."[60] A persistent problem for the schools that spring, however, was the rapid turnover of black students as many moved through the city with their parents on the way to the Sea Islands or other destinations.[61]

By May, Redpath had more than a hundred instructors at work. Of them, thirty were from the North, twenty-five were southern blacks, and forty-five were southern whites.[62] Redpath questioned the restored loyalty of many of the last group and actively recruited replacements from the North. Redpath also found competent teachers from Charleston's prewar free black elite, who had operated private schools for African American children in the city before the war. Aided by O'Donnell, Redpath supervised nine schools with a total enrollment of nearly four thousand students of both races.[63]

Three northern philanthropic societies paid the salaries of Redpath's teachers: the National Freedmen's Aid Association, the New England Freedmen's Aid Society, and the American Missionary Association. According to one visiting observer, Redpath's "sagacity and firmness" brought about a system of cooperation among the freedmen's groups, rather than competition that flared in many other southern states.[64] Redpath's secular attitude, however, did generate some tension with the American Missionary Association's Charleston manager, Thomas W. Cardozo. Redpath complained that the missionary group's schools started each day with prayer and bible reading despite the fact that the still illiterate students "did not pay strict obeisance to them." Cardozo, in turn complained that Redpath had hired teachers rumored to be "godless or Unitarians."[65] Redpath's willingness to accept teachers supplied by aid societies sponsored by both sides of the long-standing divide between Garrisonian and evangelical wings of the abolitionist movement prevented the friction found in the earlier freedmen's education projects such as those at nearby Port Royal.[66] To supplement the regular day-time school programs, Redpath organized evening classes for adults. By the end of April, more than five hundred students, mostly blacks, attended these sessions in basic literacy, which were taught by army officers and local educated free blacks as well as Redpath's regular cadre of teachers.[67] In addition, Redpath created a "normal school" in order to train older local blacks to be teachers.[68]

The northern teachers recruited for the Charleston schools gave tribute to Redpath's labors. A teacher paid by the New England Freedmen's Aid Society reported that "Mr. R. has done all in his power to make our situation pleasant. I think he is doing a great work here, and deserves much praise."[69] Redpath also drew compliments from supporters in the North. The New England Freedmen's Aid Society's monthly magazine applauded him for maintaining "the principle, that the negroes should share equally with the whites in the occupation of the schoolhouses, and in all the benefits of education."[70] A visiting reporter for a Boston newspaper claimed that Redpath and his teachers in just four months had created the most effective freedmen's schools in the entire South, "literally bringing order out of chaos."[71]

Throughout Redpath's tenure as superintendent, black and white students continued to attend the same school buildings but in separate classrooms. At the largest school on Morris Street, black and white students had their classrooms on separate floors but played together in the schoolyard during recess.[72] One northern-born teacher visiting from Port Royal praised Redpath's efforts to integrate the Charleston school system: "The successful working of the schools, and the harmony with which white and colored teachers work together in the same schools, will be a powerful aid in bringing about a feeling of social harmony in this community, and a disposition to acknowledge the great principle of political equality."[73] A scandalized native white teacher, however, complained that "the place is now an African Heaven, Redpath, a John Brown desiple [*sic*] has all the Schools open and the negro and whites Pell Mell altogether, his zeal in behalf of this race is remarkable. [He is] a low ill bread [*sic*] person both in manners and appearance."[74] Protests against Redpath's policies persuaded Colonel Woodford to turn the school buildings back to their native white trustees, but Redpath successfully appealed to General John P. Hatch, commander of the military district of South Carolina, to leave them under his control.[75]

Redpath defended the important role of the public schools, especially the night schools for adults, in the reconstruction of the South. He traced the political dominance of the former slave-owning aristocracy to "the enslavement of the poor blacks, and the ignorance of the poor whites. By educating everybody we will take care to prevent a war of races, which the old ignoblesse would bring about, if they dared and could, by prohibiting Free Schools for all."[76]

Redpath founded other institutions in addition to schools to assist the freedmen. Soon after his arrival in Charleston, a persistent black woman approached Redpath about the need for an "orphanage" where she and others could leave their children while working on farms in the state's interior.

In early April, he received permission from military authorities to start an orphanage for black infants. Redpath repaired two deserted buildings on Mary Street nearly the city's principal train terminal and named the new institution, the "Col. Shaw Orphan House," to honor the commander of the famous black Fifty-fourth Massachusetts Infantry regiment, killed in the assault on Fort Wagner. Possibly because of the well-selected name, General Hatch enthusiastically supported this project and ordered it supplied with military rations. Redpath asked a nearby black church for volunteers to clean the buildings. Soon a "society of colored ladies" formed to sew clothes for the children. The institution later was taken over by the Freedmen's Bureau and ultimately became the Shaw Unit of the Boys and Girls Club.[77]

However, the most significant organization that Redpath helped create for the Charleston black community was its "home guard" battalion. Hatch authorized Redpath to found the unit and to select its original white officer corps. Local whites protested the arming of blacks to the newly appointed military commander of the city, Colonel William Gurney, who tried to disband the battalion of black home guards. Redpath's appeals to Hatch saved the important organization.[78]

Redpath actively encouraged blacks to participate in Charleston's civic events. When a delegation of leading antislavery Northerners—including William Lloyd Garrison, Henry Ward Beecher, Theodore Tilton, Henry Wilson, and William D. Kelley—visited the city in mid April, Redpath brought more than two thousand of his students to a mass outdoor public reception. With the city seemingly aswarm with abolitionists, Redpath playfully told his *Tribune* readers, "Babylon has fallen!"[79]

In May 1865, Redpath gained national attention by sponsoring public ceremonies that were widely copied and evolved into today's Memorial Day observances.[80] These services took place at the Charleston race course, which had been the site of a prison for captured Union army soldiers. There the bodies of more than two hundred and fifty deceased military prisoners had been buried in four long, unmarked trenches.[81]

After he had visited the site in late March, Redpath related to *Tribune* readers his outrage at the accounts he heard of the prisoners' mistreatment and the "disrespect shown to the resting place of the bodies of our martyrs."[82] He founded a committee to arrange for enclosing the graveyard and erecting a suitable monument. Two newly formed local black groups, the "Friends of the Martyrs" and the "Patriotic Association of Colored Men," built and painted a fence for the graveyard with materials donated by the U.S. Army.[83]

On 1 May, Redpath and his wife, Mary, who had joined him from Massachusetts, arranged a public ceremony to dedicate the gravesite. More than ten thousand persons, most of them black, attended. After a memorial service in a black church, Redpath led a two-mile procession from the downtown area to the race course. Mary Redpath later recalled riding in a carriage with her husband and General Hatch "under avenues of cypress trees hung with moss" ahead of blacks "awaving their flowers and singing the weird, stirring songs of their race."[84] First in the line of marchers were nearly three thousand students from the public schools, followed by members of several Charleston black community organizations, and then the other attendees. One of the northern freedmen's teachers, Elizabeth G. Rice, later recalled that each "person in passing threw flowers, which had been brought for the purpose of decorating the burial-ground, till it was entirely covered."[85]

While standing around the graves, the students sang patriotic songs such as "John Brown's Body," which they learned at Redpath's schools. After an invocation, the assembly elected Redpath chair of the proceedings, and he made a short address that was followed by those of several military officers and a number of local blacks. A brigade composed of three black regiments, including the Fifty-fourth Massachusetts, concluded the services by marching past the graves of their fallen comrades. Redpath then led the crowd to a nearby site for a picnic, which lasted until dusk.[86]

Redpath's support for the right of blacks to attend and participate in political meetings led him into heated clashes with local whites and with some Union army officers. The most serious of these occurred on 11 May 1865, when Colonel William Gurney, who had replaced Woodford as military commander of the city, gave permission for a public meeting to be held at Hibernian Hall to discuss the reorganization of the South Carolina state government. The meeting's white organizers claimed that Gurney had approved only an all-white gathering and expelled blacks in attendance from the hall. The only Union army officer in the building, a Lieutenant A. S. Bodine in command of a small military detachment sent to guard this meeting, echoed that order to the blacks. Redpath arrived a few minutes later and led the blacks, now congregated outside, back into Hibernian Hall. He confronted Bodine and demanded that blacks be allowed to participate in the meeting. While the officer equivocated, most of the whites abandoned the idea of holding the meeting and departed. Ultimately, the 40 remaining whites and 150 blacks conducted a meeting and passed a series of resolutions, pledging loyalty to the Union.[87]

The complaints of Redpath and others ultimately forced the military to conduct a court-martial of Lieutenant Bodine, who was an officer of the 127th New York Volunteers, a "Zouave" infantry regiment formerly commanded by Gurney. Redpath was the principal witness against Bodine, and the military court found the officer guilty of disobeying orders from Gurney to permit a public meeting open to all citizens. Bodine's punishment, however, was only a written reprimand that military authorities subsequently withdrew.[88] Redpath later reported that Gurney and most of the white units under his command harassed public meetings of blacks. He also complained that Gurney hesitated to punish members of white units for assaults on black soldiers in the city's garrison.[89]

The long hours of work at the superintendent's post and the constant struggle with local military authorities began to tell on Redpath. At the close of the regular school year, he and his wife decided to escape the summer's heat by returning to Massachusetts for what was announced as a "vacation." The Redpaths sailed for Boston in mid June.[90]

Shortly after his departure, students, teachers, and Charleston blacks met in the Charleston's Zion Church to pass resolutions of praise for Redpath. This meeting unanimously resolved "that the loyal citizens of Charleston, owe a debt of gratitude to him, for his labors of love and mercy in their behalf, which language cannot express, and which gold and silver can never cancel." The meeting also declared that Redpath's "return to us again will be hailed by us all as an omen of future good, and a guaranty for the perpetuation of the exalted privileges which we have enjoyed at his hands."[91] A contradictory review of Redpath's performance came from the office of the city military commander Gurney, who angered by constant battles with Redpath over freedmen's rights, issued an order on 30 June relieving him and his assistant O'Donnell from their responsibilities for Charleston's schools.[92]

All indications are that Redpath hoped to return to Charleston in time for the reopening of public schools on 1 October. In his absence, however, the Bureau of Refugees, Freedmen, and Abandoned Lands, better known as the Freedmen's Bureau, was moving to give centralized direction to the myriad efforts to educate the former slaves. After less than a month at his home at the Boston suburb of Malden, Redpath began corresponding with the bureau regarding arrangements for his return to the South. In mid July, Redpath wrote the head of the bureau, Major General O. O. Howard, to request an official commission. Howard replied that Secretary of War Edwin Stanton refused to allow him to commission civilians for bureau posts as long as there were so many military men seeking them. Nonetheless, Howard promised to seek some other way to reemploy Redpath in South Carolina. Furthermore, Howard promised that if the bureau's commander in that state, General Rufus Saxton, would fund a post for Redpath, he would approve that action.[93]

In the next few months, Redpath inadvertently undercut his chances of being restored as head of Charleston's schools through both his private correspondence and his public writing. On 21 July, Redpath wrote Howard to complain about reports that the white soldiers in the 127th New York Infantry Regiment continued to mistreat Charleston's freedmen. Redpath noted that he had complained of such behavior to local military authorities before he sailed north, claiming that he threatened to seek the court-martial of General Gurney, if necessary, to force him to discipline white troops for such actions. Redpath recommended the replacement of Gurney and several other Union commanders he deemed "unfriendly to the only loyalists whom S.C. has produced."[94] Redpath's warning about the racism of troops in 127th New York proved well-founded. Clashes between its troops and black soldiers stationed in Charleston finally led to the unit's transfer from the city for mutinous and insubordinate behavior. Members of its replacement, the 154th New York, proved little better. An armed clash in the Charleston market, between the New Yorkers and black soldiers from the Twenty-first U.S. Colored Infantry and the Fifty-fourth Massachusetts regiments might have been the city's first race riot. Throughout the summer after Redpath's departure, tensions remained high and small-scale racial skirmishes recurred frequently.[95]

Also in July, Redpath used the northern press to praise Union officers who had been supportive of African-American advancement in Charleston and to expose those who had not. To the *Liberator*'s readers, Redpath declared Saxton to be "as radical as any of us [abolitionists] in theory, and none of us are more brotherly in our intercourse with the freedmen than he."[96] In the same issue, he went public with his complaints about General Gurney and noted that officers who had shown friendship for the freedmen, such as Colonel Edward N. Hallowell of the Fifty-fourth Massachusetts Infantry Regiment, had been passed over for promotion. For the *National Anti-Slavery Standard,* Redpath similarly wrote that General Hatch had been of major assistance to him in integrating Charleston's schools and protecting the rights of freedmen. However, a week later, Redpath wrote a second letter to complain that he had just learned that Hatch had denied Charleston blacks the right to participate in celebrations of the Fourth of July.[97]

The following month, Redpath raised his sights to begin attacking the first steps by President Andrew Johnson to reconstruct the former Confederate states. While a reporter covering the war in Tennessee, he had earlier criticized Johnson, as head of the state's military government, for his lack of respect for the rights of freedmen. Now Redpath warned Johnson against too hastily pardoning planters for their treasonous secession.[98] Redpath was among the first to decry Johnson's policies that curtailed black liberties and restored ex-Confederates to power in the South. By the year's end, Redpath, most abolitionists, and many Republicans would openly break with the new administration over issues of Reconstruction.[99]

As time approached for the reopening of schools, Redpath again corresponded with Freedmen's Bureau officials. On 5 September, Redpath wrote Howard, that although the Boston-based New England Freedmen's Aid Society had elected him their secretary, he preferred to return to Charleston in the position of superintendent of schools of South Carolina and Georgia. He claimed that the commander of that military district, General Saxton, was "anxious that I sh*d* [sic] go." Redpath noted that the bureau was paying the salary of a civilian as superintendent of schools for North Carolina and inquired why the same arrangement could not be made for him.[100]

Howard replied that he had decided to leave the selection of superintendents to district commanders and that Saxton could pay him if he chose. Howard warned Redpath, however, that financial problems in the bureau meant that "in most cases the Supts. will have to be military men, for the present, at any rate."[101] Perhaps sensing Howard's misgivings about him, Redpath then changed tack. Although again noting that the bureau was paying a civilian fifteen hundred dollars a year as school superintendent in North Carolina, he expressed willingness to accept any salary Howard or Saxton deemed appropriate. He also requested a pass for military transportation to Charleston, probably hoping to confer in person with Saxton. An aide of Howard's wrote back to Redpath that a pass was out of the question until Saxton had sent an endorsement for Redpath's appointment. On the same day, Howard wrote to Saxton to advise him to reject Redpath's entreaties because "from the difficulties we are now contending with, and from what I know of him, I think him the worst man to put in as Superintendent of schools."[102]

Although cryptic, Howard's advice was clear to Saxton and Redpath's appointment to a position in the South Carolina schools was effectively blocked. Howard and Saxton ultimately selected a civilian for the South Carolina school superintendency, the less controversial Pennsylvania Quaker, Rufus Tomlinson, a veteran teacher of blacks on the Sea Islands.[103]

A possible explanation for Howard's action toward Redpath comes from his modern biographer, William S. McFeely. In the summer of 1865, Howard was struggling to avoid confrontation between his young bureau and the southern-born president Andrew Johnson. At that time, Howard had hopes that Johnson might endorse the bureau's plan to redistribute farmland from the ex-Confederate planters to the freedmen. Howard recognized that if Redpath was given an official position with the bureau, his problack views and practices would inevitably irritate the president. As a consequence, Howard used Congress's failure to appropriate money for nonmilitary agents to exclude Redpath and other "radical" civilians, such as Lincoln's son Robert, from his agency.[104]

Redpath's banishment did not mean an end to northern assistance to educating the freedmen, but it did result in the halt of many of his practices that had offended local racial mores. As early as November 1865, a reporter of the *Nation* visiting Freedmen Bureau schools in Charleston found the student body all black, except for the children of several white teachers.[105] Moreover, military sanction for black participation in public political meetings remained a matter of contention between African Americans and various district commanders appointed by President Johnson until the beginning of congressional Reconstruction in 1867.[106]

Redpath's experiences in South Carolina were an early sign of the serious social and political struggle over the status of the newly freed slaves that would dominate the postwar scene. The hopes and efforts of prewar abolitionists such as Redpath to win equal rights for black Americans very quickly ran into the hostility of southern whites, the indifference of many white Northerners, and the inadequate assistance given to help prepare slaves for freedom. Although Redpath embarked on many other activities after the Civil War, black civil rights would always remain an important cause to him. The frustration and depression he would ultimately suffer in the campaign on behalf of those rights was typical of the fate of abolitionists who lived to see much of their work undone.

7   The Redpath Lyceum Bureau

The refusal by the Freedmen's Bureau to employ Redpath once again left him in a difficult financial situation. In what became a lifelong pattern, he attempted to solve that problem by returning to journalism. During late 1865 and early 1866, he supported himself and his family as a freelance correspondent for a number of eastern newspapers. To O. O. Howard's chagrin, Redpath returned to South Carolina before the end of 1865 as a reporter for the *New York Tribune*.[1] Redpath's abolitionist ally, Sydney H. Gay of the *Tribune*, in turn supported by his employer, Horace Greeley, had rapidly soured on Andrew Johnson's policies and sought eyewitness evidence of the need for a more thoroughgoing Reconstruction policy.[2]

Redpath's new series of dispatches detailed the actions by South Carolina blacks to win equal political and civil rights, denounced the local white "Chivalry" for resisting such moves, and excoriated as "Legree[s] in Uniform" the numerous occupation officials who sided with the ex-Confederates.[3] In particular, Redpath described the efforts of Freedmen's Bureau officers to coerce the freed blacks back onto the plantations to labor in conditions not far removed from servitude. Redpath's journalistic expedition through the defeated South for the *Tribune* was one of many such conducted by northern reporters. William Whitelaw Reid, J. T. Trowbridge, Sidney Andrews, J. R. Dennett, and other northern reporters generally confirmed Redpath's account of lingering southern white antagonism toward the Union and hostility directed toward the freedmen.[4]

After his return to South Carolina, Redpath concluded, "I have lately more than questioned the utility of the Freedmen's Bureau under its present imperfect and inadequate organization. I have now no doubt that, feeble as it is and almost penniless, it is the only protection that the negro can have, in this unholy state."[5] Perhaps Redpath's softened attitude toward the bureau was a product of his personal inspection visits to freedmen schools in Virginia and South Carolina. While he found no integrated schools like those he had started in Charleston, he was cheered by the increasing number of black teachers and principals. The education of the freedmen, Redpath believed, would hasten the day "when capacity not color, experience not the epidermis, the sharpness of the faculty not the sharpness of the nasal feature, shall determine position."[6]

Back in his suburban Boston home by spring 1866, Redpath wrote articles for the *Tribune* and for such other publications as the *National Anti-Slavery Standard* and the newly launched *Nation,* condemning the accommodation of the Johnson administration to the racism of southern whites. He soon resumed his criticism of the army's and the Freedmen's Bureau's failure to protect the freedmen adequately, concluding that "there are several States in which it would be better for all parties, black and white, for the Bureau to be abolished." He singled out Howard for special criticism for not resisting Johnson's systematic replacement of officers sympathetic to the freedmen, such as Rufus Saxton, with more conservative ones, concluding that "Johnson has a certain brutal courage which entitles him to respect; but Howard seems willing to lose his character rather than his place."[7]

During this period, Redpath also produced a series of eight semischolarly articles detailing the history of Brazilian slavery and implicitly calling for its abolition. Specifically Redpath set out to test the widely held opinion that Brazilian slavery was "a milder type of bondage" than that recently abolished in the United States. In a conclusion that modern studies echo, Redpath contended that despite legislation outlawing the worst forms of abuse, on the large estates, at least, "the guarantees of law were mere phantom barriers around the bondsman, which *seemed* to protect him, but vanished instantly under the tigerly glare of the slave-master."[8] Also throughout 1865, Redpath produced a series of brief pieces for the *Youth's Companion,* recalling his prewar southern travels as well as his more recent experiences as a war correspondent and a southern school superintendent.[9]

Already a friend of Senator Charles Sumner and Governor John A. Andrew, Redpath moved farther into Massachusetts Radical Republican political circles. In summer 1867, Sumner gave Redpath an exclusive interview, reprinted in newspapers nationwide, in which the senator freely criticized more moderate Republicans. The following year, Redpath publicly quarreled with Massachusetts's other U.S. senator, Henry Wilson, by accusing him of hypocrisy in endorsing both temperance and the nomination for president of heavy-drinking Ulysses S. Grant.[10] Redpath's closest associate in Radical Republican ranks was former Union army general Ben Butler. Redpath traveled as a reporter with Butler across the North as that politician shadowed and harassed Andrew Johnson's famous "Swing around the Circle," when the president unsuccessfully attempted to create a new political party loyal to his Reconstruction policies.[11]

When Butler traveled to Pittsburgh to address a "Soldiers and Sailors Convention" of Union veterans in September 1866, Redpath accompanied him as a reporter for the *Boston Evening Telegraph*. While in Pittsburgh, Redpath joined the famous black abolitionist Frederick Douglass in addressing a public meeting of local African Americans. Redpath denounced the timidity of many Republican politicians in hesitating to enfranchise black voters. He promised Republican leaders that if they allowed the black man to vote "they need never lose their sleep of nights for fear of Democratic triumphs. It was not Democrats, for they had killed themselves, but Conservatives calling themselves Republicans that the North had to fear."[12]

Also in late fall 1866, Redpath wrote a series of articles seconding Butler's calls for the impeachment of Johnson on at least thirteen counts of unconstitutional actions. In the same articles, Redpath called for "another forward movement" by "the Radical skirmish line" to "abolish the Regular Army, the entrenched Supreme Court, and the Senate of the United States." Redpath argued that "as long as these three standing menaces to popular rule, these three fortified garrisons of aristocracy, are permitted to exist, we will constantly be called on to waste our time and strength and opportunities in doing battle against them."[13]

When impeachment became a real possibility, Redpath endorsed it as a means of getting a Radical Republican, Ohio senator Benjamin Wade, into the White House. Redpath was not so much enthusiastic about Wade's ability as hopeful that the new president would appoint Charles Sumner his secretary of state. Redpath also wrote that a Wade presidency might be the only way for Radicals to block Ulysses S. Grant from the Republican nomination in 1868. Redpath advised Republicans to double Grant's salary "and increase his military honors and his dearly beloved stud to any extent, than to seek to repay his services in the field by making him the guardian of the National wards and a powerful obstacle, as he would probably be, to the speedy triumph of radical ideas."[14] In a lengthy three-part series for the *National Anti-Slavery Standard* in spring 1868, Redpath reviewed Sumner's congressional leadership during the war and Reconstruction and made it clear that the senator was his first choice for the Republicans' 1868 presidential nomination.[15]

In June 1866, Redpath lost a valuable friend at the *New York Tribune*, when Sydney Howard Gay resigned as that newspaper's managing editor. Redpath wrote Gay that he had seen the latter age visibly at his job and had worried that he was "getting old far too fast." He praised Gay's ability to direct the massive newspaper office and yet remain a gentleman. Thanking Gay for all of his past services, Redpath concluded his letter: "I very seldom express gratitude to associates or employers—I prefer to show it in facts— but in your case, I feel it wd be a wrong to myself not to do so."[16] After Gay's departure, it would be over a decade before Redpath again wrote for the *Tribune*.

When Ben Butler won a seat in Congress from Essex County, just north of Boston, in fall 1866, he had Redpath named clerk for a special congressional committee to investigate Lincoln's assassination. This "smelling committee" concentrated on searching for evidence to tie Andrew Johnson to Lincoln's murder. Butler charged that earlier investigations into the assassination conspiracy had been overly restricted by legalities. He hoped to uncover fresh evidence by offering immunity from prosecution to encourage new witnesses to come forward. Opponents charged that Butler's committee was attempting to bribe witnesses to perjure themselves against Johnson.[17]

Despite its questionable tactics, Butler's investigations failed to turn up sufficiently incriminating evidence and never issued a report. The work of the assassination committee, however, added to the intense acrimony in the capital that finally led to the unsuccessful impeachment drive against Johnson.[18] Little information has survived about the personal relationship between Redpath and Butler, but the journalist's employment by the politician was in keeping with the former's striving to find ways to support his financial obligations and his political principles simultaneously whenever possible.

Perhaps even more shadowy than Redpath's involvement with Butler's "smelling committee" was his widely rumored role as the ghostwriter for Elizabeth Keckley's *Behind the Scenes; Or, Thirty Years a Slave, and Four Years in the White House* (1868). A slave who had purchased her freedom by earning money as a seamstress, Keckley had worked as Mary Todd Lincoln's personal servant in the White House and eventually became the First Lady's confidante. She accompanied the widow back to Illinois after the president's assassination. When heavy debts forced Mary Lincoln to sell many of her expensive gowns, she entrusted Keckley with conducting the private sales in New York City. The press learned of these sales, and the two women had an acrimonious falling out. During the winter of 1867–68, Keckley dictated her memoirs which included gossip about Mary Lincoln's extravagances while First Lady. The book also consciously demonstrated the achievements of its purported author and asserted the many talents of her newly emancipated race. Critics professed to see the hand of an unswerving abolitionist guiding Keckley's story. Intimates of Keckley later claimed that it was Redpath who had visited with Keckley for many evenings and had her dictate her recollections to him. Keckley later charged that she had entrusted Redpath with several personal letters to her and that he had added them to the book as an appendix without her authorization. Redpath never took credit for the assisting in the preparation of this book and some historians credit other newspapermen with acting as Keckley's ghostwriter.[19] Even if false, the strength of the rumors connecting Redpath to Keckley was an indication of how prominently the public ranked his name among leading abolitionists.

In mid 1867 Redpath returned to Boston from Washington and took a position as a feature writer for the *Boston Daily Advertiser*. Although he still participated in a few projects supporting Reconstruction and the newspaper was a Republican vehicle, Redpath rarely wrote on political subjects for the *Advertiser*.[20] Instead his columns concentrated on such topics as travel, photography, literature, and the stage. One early example of these articles was a four-part series, entitled "Grapes from Martha's Vineyard," describing a summertime visit to that island. Redpath reported being quite impressed with the cottage community that had sprung up there to house the thousands of attendees at the Vineyard's "brown sugar Methodist lemonade mixers."[21]

The following summer, Redpath described a press junket from Boston to the railhead of the Union Pacific Railroad in Colorado in a series entitled "Westward Ho-ing." He reported great economic improvements on the prairies since his Kansas days a decade earlier. Echoing his old boss Horace Greeley, Redpath observed that "it is a sad waste of our young men, without friends or capital, to struggle on in our sterile New England States, when, by a few years of economy and industry, they could make comfortable homes and assure themselves of future competence in these growing Trans-Missourian communities."[22]

Aside from such travel features, most of Redpath's *Daily Advertiser* articles focused on Boston people and events. His series was entitled "Walks and Talks around Town" and bore Redpath's by now familiar pen name "Berwick." The current projects of local artists, writers, and inventors were a recurring topic of this series. His column also praised his friend Samuel Gridley Howe's School for the Blind as well as the poetry of the latter's wife, Julia Ward Howe. The work of women writers inspired Redpath to encourage women to enter public life:

> They will make their power felt at once by the repeal of every law which gives, as most of our laws give, the advantage to man in his relations to woman; they will render it impossible, I hope, for the crew of gamblers, drunkards, and rowdies who now disgrace our Congress to go there; but on all *other* questions, as women are naturally conservative as their habits of life increase their dread of great changes, they will steady the ship of state instead of driving it more recklessly onward.[23]

Redpath was not above frequently using his *Daily Advertiser* series to promote the interest of his stepson Dudley's new employer, the chromolithographic firm of Louis Prang. On one occasion, he wrote: "It is certain that Mr. Prang's publications, which have undoubtedly had a very wide circulation, will do much to increase and purify the taste for art among the American people, and will displace many cheap daubs and wretched engravings."[24] Redpath went so far as to proclaim Boston "the modern

Athens" based on the availability of so many high-quality and inexpensive art reproductions.[25]

The "Walks and Talks around Town" articles proved an important bridge to the next phase of Redpath's career. Redpath occasionally reported on public lectures delivered in Boston.[26] In the winter of 1868, the celebrated British novelist Charles Dickens made a well-publicized lecture tour of the United States. This tour included several visits to Boston where Redpath heard Dickens speak. His published reports of the author's talks noted Dickens's apology for the criticisms of the United States he made in his earlier *Martin Chuzzlewit* and *American Notes*. Redpath observed that "the peculiarities which Mr. Dickens ridiculed were partly the result of moral obliquity which we have since done our best to reform, and partly of crudity of manners which we have done our best to mend."[27] The enthusiastic reception shown Dickens, Redpath felt, indicated that reconciliation between Americans and the English author had occurred.

Under those auspicious circumstances, Redpath regretted the disorganization of Dickens's tour and the author's complaints about the difficulties a traveling speaker experienced trying to manage all of the complicated arrangements for lecture halls and hotel accommodations.[28] Those complaints gave birth in Redpath's mind to the idea of a professional agency to make such arrangements between speakers and the nation's hundreds of lecture halls and lyceum committees. He later recalled declaring the morning after hearing Dickens speak in Boston:

> There should be a general headquarters, a bureau for the welcome of literary men and women coming to our country for the purpose of lecturing. They should be made to feel at home among us, and the business of arranging routes of travel and dates for lectures and so forth be in charge of competent workers, and an established fee agreed upon.[29]

Within a few weeks in late 1868, Redpath, with the clerical assistance of his stepdaughter Caroline Mae Morse and the financial aid of old abolitionist friend Samuel Gridley Howe, had established an office in Boston to launch such an agency.[30]

Previous scholars have disputed Redpath's motivation for undertaking this new enterprise. Historian Carl Bode implies that Redpath saw a "golden opportunity" and reaped a "rich harvest."[31] Charles F. Horner, Redpath's previous biographer, ambivalently concluded that "his underlying motive was a desire to assist in reforms to which he had consecrated himself. The immediate cause which impelled him was his impulse to be of assistance to prominent men who desired to speak to the people."[32] Marjorie H. Eubank, who conducted the only intensive study of the Boston Lyceum Bureau, agreed with Horner that for money to have been Redpath's "primary motive" in the lyceum venture would have been "completely out of character" of the reformer.[33] Characteristically unreflective, Redpath himself failed to comment on this point. To resolve this question there must be a close inspection of Redpath's activity from 1868 to 1875.

The American lyceum had come on age in the 1830s and 1840s. Local committees, dominated by ministers, educators, and businessmen, had arranged programs of lectures on topics deemed "instructive" and morally uplifting. Most antebellum lyceums preferred "lectures free of controversy and partisanship and radicalism."[34] Priced at twenty-five cents or less for a lecture, the lyceum audience was heavily composed of professionals, clerks, mechanics, and artisans, but rarely factory operatives or laborers. Significantly, the lyceum hall was also regarded as an appropriate forum for adult women to attend. By the 1850s, an estimated 400,000 people a week attended a public lecture during the late fall to late spring "season." Seeking entertainment as well as knowledge and uplift, this audience and the lecturers who served it helped launch an American "culture industry."[35]

Most of the early speakers were ministers, lawyers, or teachers already experienced in public presentations. In the 1840s and 1850s, they also were mainly drawn from a region near a lyceum. Improved transportation, however, opened the opportunity for lecturers to travel to address audiences in numerous communities across the North. There followed a rapid proliferation of the number of men and women offering their services to lecture. Only a few star performers, such as Ralph Waldo Emerson, Henry Ward Beecher, Wendell Phillips, and Anna Dickinson, delivered large number of lectures or commanded large fees.[36] Others complained of small houses and swindling, ineffectual, or dishonest managers or of the great difficulty of negotiating fees and making travel arrangements for their lecturing.[37]

In 1864, many lyceums and literary societies in the Midwest had begun cooperating in a common association to coordinate schedules for itinerant lecturers. The leading lecturers reported great satisfaction in the efforts of the Associated Western Literary Societies, but few eastern lyceums joined the venture. In spring 1868, Thomas Wentworth Higginson observed that in the western states the lecture system was "most thoroughly organized, and takes its most characteristic forms."[38] Thanks to Redpath, that situation was about to change.

Redpath's Boston Lyceum Bureau announced itself to public speakers and lyceum managers through newspaper advertisements and printed circulars. Established lecturers soon came to the bureau asking for Redpath to arrange their tours. Among his earliest clients could be counted such notable popular lecturers as Wendell Phillips, Charles Sumner, Frederick Douglass, Henry Ward Beecher, and Julia Ward Howe.[39] These individuals in turn steered other lecturers to the bureau for subsequent seasons.[40]

Unlike the Associated Western Literary Societies, Redpath's bureau represented these lecturers, not the lyceums that employed them.[41] Redpath guaranteed lecturers that local committees would not attempt to withhold a portion of an agreed on fee due to poor attendance as frequently occurred. Working for a percentage of that fee, Redpath had the incentive to get the highest dollar for his speakers. His bureau also organized their itineraries to produce the most engagements with the least travel. For the lyceums, Redpath's bureau guaranteed the appearance of the lecturer. If unavoidable weather or health problems caused a speaker to cancel, Redpath offered the lyceum either a rescheduled performance or a suitable substitute. The Redpath Bureau dropped lecturers who missed engagements without adequate reason. Redpath also offered discounts to lyceums willing to schedule an entire series or season of speakers with his bureau. The goal of Redpath's bureau, according to one scholar was to create a professional business structure for the lyceum industry that "would be ethical and equitable for the performers and the local committees."[42]

By the spring of 1869 the Boston Lyceum Bureau, renamed the Redpath Lyceum Bureau in 1874, was making bookings for lecturers all across New England. Within two years, the bureau opened New York and Chicago branch offices, and offered its services nationwide. The bureau's commission was 10 percent of the lecture fee but in return it took full responsibility for arrangements and publicity.[43] Redpath promised would-be clients that "my facilities for giving wide publicity to announcements through the Press are not equalled, I can confidently state, by those of any other agency for lecturers."[44] The annual bulletin of the Redpath Lyceum Bureau, entitled simply *The Lyceum,* soon became the most effective means for lecturers to advertise their availability to lyceum committees. The bureau also regularly mailed out circulars to Lyceum committees and theater managers encouraging them to book their seasons early because Redpath's performers generally filled all of their engagements for the winter and spring season by September.[45]

Redpath lecturers worked hard, speaking five to six times a week during the October to May season, for fees ranging from fifty dollars to the well-publicized record high of a thousand dollars a performance paid Henry Ward Beecher.[46] Lyceum managers or theater owners charged from fifty cents up to five dollars for a seat for a "star series."[47] An affiliation with the Redpath Bureau could prove very lucrative. Humorist David R. Locke, for example, grossed more than thirty thousand dollars in one lecturing season. The young former abolitionist orator, Anna Dickinson, became the "queen" of the lyceum, and made twenty-three thousand dollars in 1872.[48] For decades, the Boston Brahmin abolitionist Wendell Phillips had delivered many of the same lectures, such as "Lost Arts," "Street Life in Europe," "Daniel O'Connell," and "Toussaint L'Ouverture," to packed lyceum halls. Under Redpath's management, he drew a salary of five hundred dollars an engagement, often twenty times what he had made before working for the bureau. In December 1870, he wrote Redpath that "so far all well & secretaries delighted with large audiences & smiling over comforting profits."[49] Redpath claimed that Phillips could have made considerably more at lecturing if his wife's health had permitted him to travel farther from his Boston home.[50] Of course, not all of Redpath's clients became wealthy. Former Massachusetts governor Nathaniel P. Banks toured for Redpath for a hundred dollars an evening in 1874. The bureau could not find a sufficient number of engagements for Banks to pay off pressing debts, so he returned to the more lucrative field of politics.[51]

Redpath concentrated on recruiting new talent for the bureau and left the more tedious work of finalizing schedule arrangements to his partner George Fall in Boston and to his Chicago office manager, George Hathaway. The greatest burden of work at the bureau was dealing with the huge volume of correspondence coming in from lyceum committees across the country. As a consequence, the bureau staff in Boston sequestered themselves in the morning until 10:00 a.m. and from late afternoon until well into the evening to respond to their mail.

Fall proved a far-better money manager than Redpath and also specialized in making the crucial transportation arrangements to get the speakers to their appointments. Bureau lecturers came to rely on Fall's scheduling acumen. Mark Twain once teased Fall's methodical attention to details by addressing him as "the infallible."[52] It also was Fall who had insisted that the bureau expand into the Midwest and open the Chicago office. Hathaway was an Australian-born immigrant to the United States who had served as an enlisted man in the Union army and worked in the woolens industry in Massachusetts before going to work for Redpath's bureau in 1870. Redpath described Hathaway as having a "cultivated and scholarly mind" that many of his clients greatly appreciated.[53]

Although it had a number of more regionalized competitors, the Redpath Bureau by the early 1870s had both the largest number and the best-known lecturers to offer to local bookers. Of this success, Senator James G. Blaine said that "although not a native-born citizen, he often thought of Mr. Redpath as a typical New Englander, for he organized speech into a mercantile staple, a feat that he thought nobody but a natural Yankee could ever have even thought of, far less of doing."[54]

Thanks to his active participation in the antebellum antislavery movement, Redpath was able to win the confidence of many reformers. As expected, former abolitionists such as Phillips, Douglass, and Thomas Wentworth Higginson lectured on the subject of Reconstruction. Republican Party leaders, including Charles Sumner, Benjamin Butler, and Nathaniel P. Banks, delivered political discourses on "The Lessons of the Hour."[55] In need of money to support his expensive Washington household, Sumner lectured for the bureau at two hundred dollars per lecture for forty-five nights in 1869 and thirty-eight nights in 1870. After he broke with the Grant administration, Sumner hoped that Redpath could arrange a lecture tour to rally his supporters around the North. When ill-health forced Sumner to cancel the tour, he wrote his loyal friend, "Mr. Redpath, this is the saddest act of my life."[56]

Many Redpath Bureau lecturers advocated the temperance cause from the lyceum stage. For example, John B. Gough, a recovering alcoholic and prohibition advocate, who had been what Redpath described as "an intimate friend" for many years, contracted with the bureau for tours from 1869 to 1875.[57] Gough's specialty was reenacting his suffering during his alcoholic youth. An acrobatic orator, Gough typically left the stage after his two hours soaked with perspiration. In just one year, Redpath claimed, the bureau received more than fifteen hundred requests to engage Gough's services. In his best season under the bureau, Gough made more than thirty thousand dollars.[58]

Black abolitionist Frederick Douglass, already a veteran of the lyceum circuit, became one of Redpath's clients in spring 1869. By that fall he wrote Redpath, complaining of exhaustion because the bureau had "done all and more than all I could ask in the number of New England appointments you have made for me."[59] A couple of years later, Douglass confided his frustration to Redpath that the public was interested only in hearing him relate his personal history, saying that "I shall never get beyond Fredk. Douglass the self educated fugitive slave." Douglass also observed that the audiences "do not attend lectures to hear statesmanlike addresses, which are usually rather heavy for the stomachs of young and old who listen. People want to be amused as well as instructed. They come as often for the former as the latter, and perhaps as often to see the man as for either."[60] In the mid 1870s, Redpath noted the Douglass was the only African American lecturer who consistently drew in large mixed-race audiences.[61]

Thanks to his combination of eloquence and humor, Brooklyn Congregational minister Henry Ward Beecher, brother of novelist Harriet Beecher Stowe, was probably the biggest draw of any of Redpath's speakers. His famous thousand-dollar fee for a single performance in Boston, which Redpath personally guaranteed, was the bureau's lure to get Beecher to agree to an exclusive lecturing arrangement for the fall of 1874. The total offered by Redpath and accepted by Beecher was twenty thousand dollars for sixty-two lectures during October, November, and December 1874.[62] At the lectern, Beecher advocated a range of reforms though often cautiously. In Redpath's estimation: "Beecher is always a preacher first, not a reformer and then a preacher; and a preacher implies a congregation to be gathered up and *kept together*."[63]

One reluctant lyceum star successfully courted by Redpath was Mary A. Livermore, famous for her Civil War activities in the U.S. Sanitary Commission. Livermore later recalled her first impression of Redpath was that he "was brainy to his finger tips, magnetic in speech and manner, and could concoct more schemes over night than a dozen men could manage."[64] Redpath not only persuaded the young writer to deliver public lectures but, as she recalled, he, "understanding the popular taste as I did not," also "suggested lecture topics, made engagements, and, altogether, was the most indefatigable of agents."[65] With Redpath's coaching, Livermore's temperance lectures drew large audiences in the mid 1870s.

Redpath was important in bringing women to the lyceum platform. Besides Livermore and former abolitionist Anna Dickinson, he arranged tours for Julia Ward Howe, author of "The Battle Hymn of the Republic." Redpath also arranged speaking tours for leading female suffragists including Lucy Stone, president of the American Woman Suffrage Association, and Elizabeth Cady Stanton and Susan B. Anthony, leaders of the rival National Woman Suffrage Association.[66] Anthony in turn attempted to recruit Redpath to write occasionally for the latter group's monthly magazine, *The Revolution*.[67]

Commercial considerations, at least sometimes, made Redpath more careful in using the lyceum platform to advocate reform. In the fall 1869 season, Redpath's "Union Course" in Boston arranged a program in which opposing speakers on such controversial issues as temperance, women's suffrage, and free trade spoke on alternating nights.[68] Mary Livermore recollected that Redpath advised her to avoid "the two vexed questions, Woman Suffrage and Temperance" if she desired to become wealthy at lecturing. While she acknowledged the business acumen prompting that advice, she nevertheless ignored it.[69] Redpath then went ahead and offered her services to the public as a debater supporting women's suffrage.

Besides reformers, Redpath engaged numerous "literary" men and women. While some of these, such as the poets Will Carleton and James Whitcomb Riley, read their own works, most lectured on the lives of famous authors or historical figures or presented dramatic readings from the plays and novels of others.[70] For example, John Hay reminisced on Abraham Lincoln.[71] Russell H. Conwell lectured on Chinese civilization.[72] Moses Coit Tyler spoke on "castes."[73] Professor Moses T. Brown of Tufts read excerpts from Charles Dickens's writings.[74] Henry James Sr., with whom Redpath had quarreled in the 1850s over Haiti, now used the bureau to book his lectures on Thomas Carlyle.[75] Popular biographical and historical writer James Parton experienced difficulty on stage because he read his lectures despite Redpath's advice that "I have always insisted that no man should ever *read* to a public audience. I should as soon think of making love to a woman by writing my opinion of her and reading it to her."[76]

In 1873, Redpath traveled to Britain to recruit additional lecture talent from its "literary men." The Redpath Bureau briefly maintained a branch office in London at No. 1 Longacre.[77] For several seasons the British radical Edward Jenkins lectured for the bureau on the Coolie question and on literary subjects such as Jonathan Swift.[78] Other British talents recruited by Redpath included novelist Wilkie Collins, who read excerpts from Shakespeare; poet George MacDonald, who lectured on Robert Burns; and William Parsons, an Irish orator.[79] One of Redpath's biggest catches in England was historian and Anglican minister Charles Kingsley. Kingsley was induced by Redpath with promises of five hundred dollars to a thousand dollars profits a week to make a tour of the United States in 1874, lecturing on "Ancient Civilizations," "Westminster Abbey," and "The Norse Discovery of America."[80] Although his newspaper reviews were mixed at best, Kingsley was so pleased by the steady stream of income from lecturing that he praised Redpath as a "good fellow."[81]

Travel speakers also proved popular as Redpath Lyceum Bureau lecturers. For example, the pioneer anthropologist, Paul B. DuChaillu, described his own African expedition as did Isaac Hayes about his Arctic exploration.[82] Journalist Thomas W. Knox spoke on his "Six Months in Siberia." Redpath arranged for his Malden neighbor Gilbert Haven, a Methodist minister and later bishop, to lecture on "Men and Mountains in Switzerland."[83] In Boston, Redpath even arranged a "Young America Course," that featured lecturers and other performers of interest to a juvenile audience.[84]

As years passed, humorists played an increasingly large part in Redpath's repertoire. His "Boston Lyceum Course" in his home city featured all of the leading humorists, including Henry W. Shaw ("Josh Billings"), David R. Locke ("Petroleum V. Nasby"), and Samuel Clemens ("Mark Twain").[85] Humorist Josh Billings already was an established figure on the lecture circuit but found that the Redpath Bureau could schedule more performances at better prices that any previous agent.[86] Billings delivered a burlesque caricature of country language and manners. He used a mix of mangled grammar and illogic to reduce audiences to hysterical laughter. Redpath claimed that Billings was "one of the men of genius whom the people have recognized, although the cultivated classes reject him."[87]

Beginning in 1866, Locke, in the persona of the rural Ohio observer, Petroleum V. Nasby, delivered humorous lectures on current political issues. An ardent Republican, he often offended a portion of his audience. Nevertheless, Locke's popularity remained high enough to demand a minimum of two hundred dollars a performance. When the Cleveland YMCA lyceum committee could not pay Locke the full sum agreed for a lecture already delivered, he demanded and received the balance from the bureau.[88] In response to a newspaper interviewer's question whether he would ever quit the lecture platform, Locke quipped that "Redpath of the *Boston Bureau* says actors, the demi-monde, and lecturers never reform, so I really can't say."[89]

The humorist whose lecturing career Redpath deserves the most credit for developing was none other than Mark Twain. While still a struggling newspaperman in December 1863, Twain heard the era's leading comedic lecturer, Artemus Ward, perform on stage in Virginia City, Nevada. Inspired by Ward, who died in 1867, Twain attempted lecturing in the Far West. When Twain visited New York City in 1867, a fan of his writing hired the Cooper Institute and distributed hundreds of complimentary tickets to drum up a good audience for the unknown lecturer. Twain spoke about a visit to the Hawaiian Islands. The following winter, he lectured about forty times through the Midwest and along the East Coast, reading excerpts from his forthcoming *The Innocents Abroad*. The good press reviews these lectures received came to Redpath's attention in Boston.[90] The next year when he started his bureau, Redpath convinced the young journalist to give up newspaper writing for the more lucrative lecture circuit. In the spring of 1869, Redpath worked to build up Twain's reputation in the East as a humorist by persuading friendly editors to republish samples of Twain's California newspaper writing.[91]

During the summer of 1869, however, Twain purchased a partnership in a Buffalo newspaper and planned to quit lecturing for good. Redpath protested that the bureau already had booked too many engagements. Twain finally relented but put so many conditions on when and where he would lecture that even George Fall complained about the difficulties of scheduling. After a couple of try-out deliveries in Pittsburgh and Providence, Twain debuted before a New England audience in the four-thousand seat Boston Music Hall with Redpath personally introducing him. Twain's lecture on Hawaii drew both popular and critical applause. His reputation quickly established, Twain demanded that Redpath always get him a salary for each performance equal or better than a town ever paid his friendly rival Nasby.[92]

Twain told practically all of his friends that he hated lecturing and feared becoming trapped in the profession, like Nasby and "the other old stagers."[93] After Twain married in 1870, Redpath had to labor harder and harder each year to induce his star to perform.[94] Twain wrote Redpath soon after his wedding: "DEAR RED,—I am not going to lecture any more forever. I have got things ciphered down to a fraction now. I know just about what it will cost to live, and I can make the money without lecturing. Therefore, old man, count me out."[95] Redpath in his bureau bulletin, *The Lyceum,* announced Twain would not be available for the coming season because "the fate of Midas has overtaken this brilliant lecturer. He lectured—and made money, he edited—and made money, he wrote a book—and made money. . . . Under these disenheartening circumstances he cannot be made to see the necessity of lecturing: 'Just for a vault of silver he left us!' "[96]

Twain quit his newspaper work in Buffalo in 1871, and financial pressures soon forced him to resume his lecture career. Twain nevertheless set demanding terms for bureau engagements. In preparation for the 1871–72 season, Twain barraged Redpath with several letters setting down numerous and contradictory conditions. Twain also abandoned several advertised lecture topics before settling on reading excerpts from his forthcoming books *Roughing It*.[97] He finally apologized to the exasperated Redpath and Fall in a humorous note:

> I am different from other women; my mind changes oftener. People who have no mind can easily be steadfast and firm, but when a man is loaded down to the

guards with it as I am, every heavy sea of foreboding or inclination . . . shifts the cargo. See? Therefore . . . one week I am likely to give rigid instructions to confine me to New England; next week, send me to Arizona; the next week withdraw my name; and the week following modify it. You must try to keep the run of my mind, Redpath, it is your business being my agent, and it always was too many for me.[98]

The strain of the lecturing tour exhausted Twain. When it ended in February, Twain wrote Redpath: "If I had another engagement I would rot before I would fill it."[99]

One way Redpath found to get Twain to lecture was to advance him money for his new home in Hartford, Connecticut. The following season, Twain toured to pay off Redpath and other creditors. He wrote to Redpath in January 1872: "Have paid up $4000 indebtedness. You are the last on my list. Shall begin to pay you in a few days and then I shall be a free man again."[100]

In the winter of 1872–73, Redpath tried with a promise of seven thousand to eight thousand dollars in engagements to persuade Twain to return from a trip to England to lecture, but the author replied: "When I yell again for less than $500 I'll be pretty hungry, but I haven't any intention of yelling at any price."[101] Nevertheless, Twain again relented and publicly announced that he must depart England due to the demand of the American public.[102]

After repeated entreaties from Redpath the following year, Twain finally consented to leave his young wife for a few lectures in Boston in early 1874. Before the last of these, Twain telegraphed Redpath: "Why don't you congratulate me? I never expect to stand on a lecture platform again after Thursday night."[103]

Despite Twain's solidly established reputation, Redpath used every opportunity to attract favorable publicity for his client. In fall 1874, as a prank, Twain wired Redpath that he had decided to walk from Hartford to Boston in the company of his friend Reverend Joseph H. Twichell. Redpath released the telegram to the press and the Associated Press covered this pedestrian expedition. Twain found the pilgrimage exhausting and soon abandoned it. Redpath read Twain's final wire from the road to a Boston lecture hall: "We have made thirty-five miles in less than five days. This demonstrates the thing can be done. Shall now finish by rail. Did you have any bets on us?"[104]

Redpath and Twain developed a warm regard for each other and "Mark" always addressed his manager as "Red." Years later in his autobiography, Twain praised his former manager: "The chief ingredients of Redpath's make-up were honesty, sincerity, kindliness and pluck. He wasn't afraid."[105] In a private letter from the 1870s, Twain described Redpath as "competent good company of an evening & companionable in his working methods."[106]

Twain also sought out Redpath's editorial assistance on several of his writing projects during the 1870s, including a one character burlesque version of Hamlet.[107] On another occasion, however, Twain rejected out of hand Redpath's proposal that he write humorous lectures for other persons to deliver.[108] Undoubtedly Redpath assisted Twain in becoming a nationally known figure. In return, Redpath gained a loyal friend who generated significant revenue for the bureau.

Redpath's lecturers used the Boston office of his bureau at 36 Bromfield Street as a kind of clubhouse. His female lecturers often received friends and other callers there.[109] Wendell Phillips occasionally brought William Lloyd Garrison with him to Redpath's offices to share stories of the antislavery movement with younger reformers. Clemens, Billings, and Locke would lounge together during the daytime at the bureau, smoking cigars and swapping high tales, before taking a late afternoon train to the nearby towns where they were booked to lecture that evening.[110] Many of the lecturers also boarded at Young's Hotel close by the office and formed an intimate social circle for several months each year.[111]

As Twain recalled, each "season" began early in October, when the lecturers gathered in Boston. For several weeks Redpath scheduled them in smaller communities in the nearby countryside where new lectures could be tried out and improved. In Twain's opinion, "the country audience is the difficult audience; a passage which it will approve with a ripple will bring a crash in the city. A fair success in the country means a triumph in the city."[112] When a lecture was satisfactorily honed, Redpath scheduled it for the mammoth Music Hall in Boston. A good "debut" there enabled him to get top dollar for the lecturer the remainder of the season.[113]

Many of the bureau's lecturers were social guests at Redpath's home. After returning from Charleston in 1865, James and Mary Redpath resumed residence in their house at 54 Maple Street in Malden, a Boston suburb. Mary's daughter Caroline worked for the bureau for a short time at its inception and later married William F. Morse, a merchant, and moved to New York City.[114] Mary's son, Dudley, adopted Redpath's last name after the Civil War. As already noted, Dudley worked as an agent for Louis Prang's lithographic company in the late 1860s. During the 1870s, he held a patronage job at the Boston Custom House, undoubted benefiting from his stepfather's connections with Massachusetts Republican leaders. Dudley established his own residence in the city in 1871 but never married. He died in 1895.[115]

Among the visitors to the Redpath home in Malden was the British lecturer and Anglican prelate, Charles Kingsley. Kingsley was greatly impressed with Mary Redpath's views on religious subjects. According to her obituary, Mary Redpath was "eclectic" in religion "seeking truth in every form, and finding much to accept in all. . . . She delighted to expound the sacred writings according to her own interpretation."[116] Kingsley reportedly sat for hours with Mary listening to her "unusual powers of conversation and intuitive transcendentalism."[117] Walt Whitman also frequently visited the couple in Malden. Local residents recalled Whitman and the Redpaths strolling after dinner to a local park, named "Sunset Rock." There the poet and his friends would converse until past dark.[118]

The Redpaths also had a number of personal friends among Malden residents. Redpath was intimate with Methodist clergyman and abolitionist Gilbert Haven. Later a bishop, Haven for many years edited a Methodist newspaper, *Zion's Herald,* headquartered in the Wesleyan Building on Bromfield Street in Boston, adjacent to the office of the Redpath Lyceum. During the Civil War, the two men had leading roles in the unsuccessful effort to block the execution of Malden murderer Edward Greene. Redpath later arranged speaking engagements for Haven.[119]

The Redpaths also were close to another Malden couple, William S. Robinson and Harriet Jane Hanson Robinson. Robinson had been an antislavery editor before the war and remained an influential leader in the Radical wing of the state's Republican Party. William Robinson's "Warrington" columns on Massachusetts politics and politicians ran for almost twenty years in the *Springfield Republican.* Harriet Robinson, a former Lowell mill worker, was active first in the antislavery and then the women's rights movement. She authored six books, including a memoir of her years at Lowell. The Redpath and Robinson families visited each other's homes frequently and the wives worked together in philanthropic projects.[120]

Perhaps it was Redpath's deepening roots in the Malden community that led him to take an active part in local politics in the fall 1872 election. The Massachusetts Republican Party in the early 1870s was divided into bitterly contentious factions over both local and national questions and over personal competition for office. The state's most powerful politician of the period was Ben Butler. After reconciling with President Grant in 1869, Butler received control over most of the federal patronage in Massachusetts. He used his Washington connections to build up a powerful political organization inside the Massachusetts Republican Party, but also acquired enemies rapidly. Butler alienated conservative Republicans by his support for inflationary and prolabor legislation as well as his persistent courting of the Irish-American vote. When Butler sought the Republican gubernatorial nomination in 1871, all of his opponents united to defeat him by a vote of 643 to 464 at the Republican state convention.

Butler bounced back quickly. Although displeased with Grant's selection of Massachusetts U.S. senator Henry Wilson as his running mate, he loyally supported the Republicans' 1872 ticket and denounced the bolt of many "Liberals" to the camp of Horace Greeley. A Grant victory in fall 1872 would further strengthen Butler's power and possibly enable him either to succeed Wilson in the Senate or win the governor's seat in 1873. As a strong supporter of "Radical Republicanism" on both the state and national level, Redpath worked hard to advance Butler's standard.[121]

At the 1872 Malden Republican caucus called to select delegates to the various regional conventions that chose the party's local and statewide candidates, Redpath challenged the "ring" of leaders who had long controlled town politics. He charged that the ring had selected delegates opposed to Ben Butler to the Republican state convention at Worcester the previous year by "as deliberate an attempt to swindle the people as he ever saw in the South, or on the border."[122] Redpath wrote regularly for the *Malden Tribune,* attacking the dominance of the "Ring" and calling for reform of the town's Republican Party apparatus. Besides the issue of "fair play," Redpath also attacked the Malden Republican leaders for their willingness to allow Democrats to vote in the caucus. He warned that ring leaders would not energetically turn out Republican voters for Grant in the fall election.[123]

As a consequence of the conflict Redpath had generated in Malden Republican ranks since early September, the party convened another caucus on the Saturday before the Tuesday, November 5 election. Redpath spoke in favor of a pro-Butler candidate for state representative. The meeting finally balloted for its choice in this race and Democrats present were not permitted to vote. When the tellers announced that the ring's candidate had triumphed, some younger men declared their intention to bolt the ticket. In the following Tuesday's election, Grant defeated Greeley in Malden by a three to one margin as did most of the Republican candidates for statewide office.[124]

After the election, Redpath continued his series of articles in the *Malden Tribune* on local politics. He lectured the bolters from the Republican ticket, saying that he preferred to achieve reform "with as little bitterness of spirit, with as little resistance from the wrong-doers as is possible. It is better to win over your opponents than to knock them down."[125] He called for reform in the candidate selection procedure to free future elections from controversy.[126]

Besides electoral reform, Redpath made an appearance at town council meetings in late 1872 to advocate that Malden purchase the local gas works in order to supply gas to the citizens at cost. The *Boston Globe* applauded this idea as one that the city also should adopt. Redpath also attacked the Boston and Maine Railroad. He charged that the "powerful corporation" had "murdered dozens of persons" in Malden by its lax safety and had "wrung out thousands of tax dollars" from the municipality.[127] Redpath's positions echoed the populist economic stance taken by Butler's "Radical" wing of the Republican Party. The following year, however, Butler again failed to win the Republican gubernatorial nomination and conservatives gradually gained ascendancy in state politics.[128] Although Redpath resided in Malden until the end of the decade, there is no record that he again played a prominent role in town politics.

In many respects, the early 1870s marked the highpoint of Redpath's power and reputation. His pioneering work in professionalizing the lyceum industry brought him wealth and influence. His bureau had the power to select which of the hundreds of individuals interested in lecturing it would represent and thereby guarantee a full season of engagements at the top fees. This ability to choose among lecturers and indirectly among lecture topics gave Redpath great influence over the content of the American speaking industry. His open mind and his committed support for many of the reform movements of the period allowed Redpath to make the lecture platform an important progressive force in American life.

Although his influence was greatest in the cultural sphere, Redpath also had developed a measure of power as a political journalist. An unwavering supporter of Radical Republican causes and candidates, Redpath published numerous articles in both local and national publications advocating fair treatment of African Americans and a complete Reconstruction of the South. As a journalist and then as an aide to Ben Butler, he had worked to topple Andrew Johnson. Although he would have preferred a more "Radical" Republican in the White House, Redpath loyally backed Ulysses S. Grant over his former employer Horace Greeley in 1872. Growing dissension in the Republican Party in the early 1870s, however, was the signal that years ahead would prove stormy ones for all Radicals, including Redpath.

8   *Entertainment Innovator*

By the 1871–72 lyceum season, Redpath became aware that, except for a few "stars" of the caliber of Henry Ward Beecher, the original cadre of lecturers was no longer drawing the full houses of just two years before.[1] The audiences for the "instructive" lecturers were clearly being eclipsed by that for humorists and other less serious "entertainers."[2] Redpath studied the public's shifting tastes and attempted to adjust the programs offered by his bureau to fit it.

Redpath did not mourn the decline of the old-style "instructive" lecture because he believed that "the penny press has called up thousands of brilliant writers to do that duty. The penny press killed all mere essay-reading in public. In order to be heard, a lecturer, now, must not only have something to say but know how to say it; he must not be a mere humdrum reader of a manuscript but a magnetic orator who can kindle thought and entrance his audience."[3]

In an interview he gave to his old antebellum employer, the *St. Louis Democrat*, Redpath shared one lesson he had learned about the lyceum: "As a rule, authors and clergymen make poor lecturers. They deliver essays or sermons, not lectures. Literary men write for the eye, not for the ear; the oratorical and literary styles ought to be different; and clergymen mostly lengthen out sermons and call them lectures, and deliver them as well as write them, not in a democratic but in a theocratic . . . style."[4] For example Redpath dismissed western folklorist Bret Harte as a lecturer: "He is a good poet and a better novelist or sketch writer, but he lacks the power to inspire an audience—what we call 'magnetism' in ordinary talk."[5] He regarded the charismatic Beecher among the clergymen as one of the few to achieve greatness on the lyceum platform.

Another lesson Redpath had learned was that most English lecturers were poorly received by American audiences. He personally considered British author and clergyman Charles Kingsley as "the worst speaker I have ever listened to."[6] The *Boston Daily Globe* agreed, calling Kingsley's delivery "very peculiar, being a strange combination of slow and rapid utterances, monotone and nervous exclamation."[7] Kingsley's letters home record that "I draw not the mob, but the educated, & R[edpath] confesses that none of *his* men had such 'high toned' audiences before."[8] However refined, Kingsley's audiences usually proved disappointingly small during his 1874 tour, and Redpath had to discount admission prices and place what the lecturer felt were "insane notices" in the press to bring in respectable sized crowds.[9]

To improve the financial health of the lecture system, Redpath's bureau promoted the professionalization of that field. Redpath advised his agent George Hathaway:

> The only way to "revive" the lecture system, (if it needs reviving) is to get orators to adopt lecturing as a profession instead of law, and medicine, and the pulpit. A lecturer can do nothing more than study for his winter's course, if he desires to meet the just expectations of a lyceum audience. Big fees are essential to keep up a high standard of lyceum oratory. . . . The complaint about big fees to lecturers is a sign that managers do not know their business. It has been the cheap people who have killed the lecture system in towns where it has failed.[10]

Redpath reacted to changing public tastes in an innovative manner by shifting the forms of entertainment he provided. The bureau's announcements for the 1873–74 season listed only 48 lecturers, down from a peak of 121 in 1869–70. In place of those lecturers, Redpath offered a much wider range of performers. The bureau had always represented a few solo musicians among its clients, but Redpath now organized musical and dramatic companies and sent them on national tours. In 1870, the Mendelssohn Quintette Club was the first concert company offered by any "lecture" bureau. On one occasion in Boston, Redpath billed the group together with a Mark Twain lecture as "Double Grand Entertainment."[11] In 1874, the bureau paid German-American violinist Max Strakosch, himself a classic music impresario, ten thousand dollars for ten concerts.[12] Another violinist, Camillo Urso, toured for the bureau with a small company in 1874 and 1875. A few years later, the Redpath English Opera Company introduced Gilbert and Sullivan to the American stage.[13] Redpath himself caught the performing bug, occasionally acting small parts in plays booked by his bureau.[14]

Redpath also recognized the appeal of the exotic and arranged appearances for foreign mystics, bands of Indian warriors, and other such acts. In 1875, he presented two Chinese scholars who debated the religious philosophies of Confucius and Zoroaster. Redpath promised the audience that while these speakers "don't get up much of a heathen revival . . . it is amusing in the most orthodox minds to see the tables turned on them to hear heathen missionaries trying to convert us."[15] The Ottoman counsel general in New York City appeared on stage in his native dress and demonstrated some of the Muslim worship rituals. Harry Kellar, the first great American-born stage medium and illusionist, proved another large draw.[16] In 1875, Redpath presented a band of Modoc Indians fresh from their famous battles with the cavalry in the Lava Beds on northern California. Redpath promised that these Indians would prove that they had been justified "if ever any man is justified, in seeking to redress his wrongs by war."[17]

Another new Redpath Bureau feature was the stereopticon, an instrument that could project a three-dimensional image on a screen, each with an accompanying lecture on the subject of the visual display. John L. Stoddard, who lectured on traveling through the Rocky Mountains, soon became the bureau's leading stereopticon performer.[18] The success of this new medium in drawing in audiences emboldened Redpath to find a "name" attraction to enter lyceum ranks employing it. He selected a difficult target when he tried to persuade the stage-shy political cartoonist Thomas V. Nast to lecture. Eager to engage the cartoonist, Redpath booked passage on the same ship as Nast bound for England in 1873. Redpath told his friend, New York journalist Theodore Tilton, that he was taking this passage as "a fisher of men of note."[19] Nast could find nowhere to hide aboard ship from the agent's blandishments. One of Redpath colleagues reports that Nast had declared to Redpath: "Well, you have got me where I cannot run away; but it's no use—I won't lecture."[20] By the time the ship docked, however, the cartoonist had reluctantly agreed to allow Redpath to send out a circular to test public interest in a Nast lecture. The response was encouraging, and Nast contracted with historian James Parton to prepare a text, entitled "American Humor," to accompany illustrations that he would sketch as he spoke.

Redpath traveled with his novice performer to his early engagements during the fall of 1873 and sat with him on the stage nightly. On the evening of his first performance, Nast is reported to have declared: "Now, Redpath, you got me into this scrape and you will have to go on the platform with me."[21] The tour netted Nast more than forty thousand dollars, although he canceled more than five thousand dollars of engagements at its end. Nast was so pleased that he tipped Redpath an additional five hundred dollars on top of his standard agent's fee of 10 percent. Despite this financial success, neither Redpath nor any other manager was able to get Nast to lecture publicly again.[22]

Redpath had less luck in attracting another well-know visual artist of the era, Vinnie Ream, to the lyceum stage. An attractive young sculptress who had won several important commissions from the federal government, Ream was the center of considerable gossip that her commissions had come through political influence rather than artistic merit. In May 1871, Redpath tried to recruit Ream promising that "the great reputation that both your friends & enemies have given you wd make your success as a lecturer, at the best prices, assured."[23] Ream declined, but that did not stop Mark Twain from caricaturizing both her and Redpath in his first novel, *The Gilded Age: A Tale of Today,* coauthored with Charles Dudley Warner in 1873. The novel portrays a ruthless lecture manager, "J. Adolphe Griller," persuading Laura Hawkins, a character with Ream's congressional lobbying skills, to make a disastrous lecturing debut. The novel's description of Griller shows him to resemble Redpath in both character and appearance:

> He was a small man, slovenly in dress, his tone confidential, his manner wholly void of animation, all of his features below the forehead protruding—particularly the apple of his throat—his hair without a kink in it, a hand with no grip, a meek, hang-dog countenance. He was a falsehood done in flesh and blood; for while every visible sign about him proclaimed him a poor witless, useless weakling; the truth was that he had the brains to plan great enterprises and the pluck to carry them through. That was his reputation, and it was a deserved one.[24]

Griller sent Hawkins onto the stage before an audience so hostile, that she fled and committed suicide later that evening. Twain probably was having fun with his friend Redpath by blaming lecture managers for heartlessly booking speakers before unreceptive audiences.

Redpath's recruitment of Ann Eliza Young, the twenty-seventh wife of Brigham Young, as a lecturer on Mormon polygamy caused many complaints about the declining moral tone of the lyceum circuit. Young, an attractive mother of two, had created a national sensation in 1873 when she had filed suit for divorce from the Mormon leader, forty-three years her senior and reputed husband to dozens of other women. Soon after, she was brought to the bureau by James Pond, a journalist Redpath had befriended in Kansas in the 1850s.[25] Redpath helped Young prepare for her debut as a lecturer on "Mormonism and Polygamy" by arranging a series of newspaper interviews. Hostile elements of the press, however, insinuated that Young and her chaperon Pond were lovers. Redpath publicly vouched for his lecturer's honor as well as her veracity as he introduced her at her first lecture in Boston's Tremont Temple. Young recalled that Redpath's remarks to the audience "inspired me, it was so kind, so reassuring, so generous, and above all, so just. He had never heard me speak, but he was so bitter an enemy to this horrible system, as indeed he is to every wrong, that he was willing to take me for my work's sake."[26] Public attitudes about Young remained deeply divided but that did not keep away large audiences, who produced considerable wealth for both the lecturer and the bureau. It also was the start of a business association between Redpath and Pond that later changed the history of the bureau.[27]

Serious problems began to surface for Redpath in the mid 1870s. He experienced increasing published criticism of his bureau's domination of the lyceum business and of the high fees he charged both lecturers and local sponsors. For example, the *Chicago Times* complained that even a mediocre lecturer "must be compensated by the modest sum of $150 or thereabouts for merely reading an hour and a half from a manuscript!"[28] Josiah Gilbert Holland, the editor of *Scribner's Monthly*, in an article entitled "Lecture-Brokers and Lecture-Breakers," assailed the bureau for driving up lecturer fees, which resulted in higher ticket prices and reduced profits, if any, for lyceum committees. Holland, author of the sentimental "Timothy Titcomb" letters, had had modest success himself as a lyceum lecturer in the late 1850s. He now held the bureau responsible for the proliferation of "dead weights" on the lyceum stage, "literary jesters, montebanks, readers, singers, etc., etc." Holland argued that "only second and third rate men . . . have any real use for the bureau."[29]

Redpath responded in his bureau's circulars and in newspaper interviews to such critics. He made no apology for encouraging new lecturers to enter the field: "Our success depends to a great extent in introducing new blood into 'the system' just as fast as the old blood stagnates." Furthermore, Redpath argued, "the lyceum was not established as a genteel workhouse" and therefore speakers are engaged on account of ability to "draw audiences." To be financially successful, he advised lyceums to follow the example of the courses that his bureau directly managed in major cities in always mixing "instructive" and "entertainment" features. He warned committees organizing lecture programs that "lyceums that are afraid of all political and other living questions are sooner or later consigned to bankruptcy."

Redpath also responded to Holland's charge that his bureau had financially abused lecturers and lyceums and debased the quality of the industry:

> Our aim is *not* merely a financial one. We must succeed as business-agents, in order to have an intellectual influence on lyceums. . . . We have already succeeded in increasing the popularity and exalting the standard of the system, by bringing out new, instructive, and eloquent speakers; by recommending descriptive, historical, literary, and scientific lectures, in preference to the spread-eagle or buncombe, and spread-owl or sermony style of discourse, which was the prevalent character of one-half of the lectures a few years ago. . . . If we had no other purpose than a business one in conducting the Bureau, we can assure the doctor that it would soon be for sale to the highest bidder.[30]

Mark Twain wrote Redpath supporting him against Holland and wanted the bureau to advertise the large fees being offered for his lectures: "Because I am 'going for' Timothy Titcomb in one of the magazines & I would like him to chaw over that little evidence that 'buffoons & triflers' are not scorned by everybody."[31] Twain was offended by Holland's audacity in assailing the intellectual quality of other lectures, when his own under the Titcomb pseudonym had obtained the reputation, according to a later critic, of being filled with "truisms insipid enough for a young ladies' boarding school and religious enough for the most bigoted sectarian."[32]

Years later, when writing his autobiography, Twain conceded the accuracy of some of Holland's charges against Redpath's management of the lyceum field. He recalled that besides the small number of "stars" in the bureau, Redpath represented many more "men and women of light consequence and limited reputation." This arrangement ultimately played havoc with the lecturing industry, Twain recalled, because

> all the lyceums wanted the big guns and wanted them yearningly, longingly, strenuously. Redpath granted their prayers—on this condition: for each house-filler allotted them they must hire several of his house-emptiers. This arrangement permitted the lyceums to get through alive for a few years, but in the end it killed them all and abolished the lecture business.[33]

Redpath's protestations that the bureau was not altering the high intellectual character of the lyceum also failed to convince an even more veteran showman, P. T. Barnum. Barnum lectured one season on temperance for the Redpath Bureau. He claimed to have initially resisted Redpath who bragged about the quality of the speakers he planned to present by stating: "You see, Mr. Redpath, that all of these men are celebrated, while I am simply notorious."[34] Both men knew it was the latter quality that drew audiences to hear Barnum. In an abbreviated season of lecturing, Barnum earned nearly ten thousand dollars for engagements made by the bureau. The two men had a falling-out, however, when Barnum demanded and received an extra five dollars from a lyceum committee in Troy, New York, to pay his hotel bill. Redpath regarded it as unseemly for a lecturer to squabble over a fee after the bureau had contracted for an engagement and never booked Barnum again.[35]

Also in the mid 1870s, the bureau was embarrassed by an acrimonious quarrel over fees with the popular women's rights lecturer Anna Dickinson. Redpath had regarded Dickinson as the female star of the lyceum circuit and praised her speaking style for having "the pace of a mustang pony, sturdy, swift and short-stepping."[36] The performer and agent initially had a friendly, even flirtatious, relationship in which Redpath addressed his correspondence to Dickinson as "Dear Queen" or "Dear Eagle." He encouraged Dickinson to deliver her lecture on "The Bungling Sex," which assailed "the majesty of man."[37] Eventually Dickinson began to believe that the bureau's 10 percent fee was unjustified. Because the bureau refused to set a dangerous precedent by discounting the fees for one star, Dickinson angrily quit the lecture platform to attempt a career as an actress. Her public accusations that the bureau retained money due her also caused several other performers to quit Redpath.[38]

A quite different kind of financial development cost the bureau other clients. By the mid 1870s, Redpath's bureau had made so much money for the humorist trio of Twain, Nasby, and Billings that they either stopped or greatly curtailed their lecturing. Twain's reluctance already has been discussed. Nasby had used his lecturing profits to open both a publishing house and an advertising firm, leaving him little spare time to lecture. Billings also had invested well and declined to lecture any more outside the immediate New York City area.[39]

As the combined consequence of these incidents, the bureau began to experience financial troubles in the mid 1870s. Management of the bureau also became more difficult as its principal itinerary organizer, George Fall, retired due to ill health in 1873. Fall attempted to return to the bureau the following year but died before he could resume his full responsibilities. Redpath praised his deceased partner's integrity and skill: "As a business man, he was trustworthy, exact, methodical, clearheaded, punctual and truthful, and all in the highest degree. His system was so admirable that he was a synonym among those who knew him for clerical infallibility."[40] Redpath brought George Hathaway back to Boston from the Chicago office and gave him complete control of business correspondence, but the loss of Fall was a serious blow to the bureau's smooth operations.

During this same period, a nationwide economic downturn added to the bureau's problems. A combination of speculative investing and commercial overexpansion produced a financial panic in fall 1873. Banks failed, businesses closed, and unemployment rose to approximately 15 percent. Full recovery did not occur until 1879. These economic problems affected the entertainment industry. As Redpath related to an old antislavery associate in November 1874:

> The lecture season this winter is very dull all across the country, and the same is true of every kind of amusement, for the people begin now to feel the effects of the last year's panic, and are everywhere economizing. They seem to have conceived the wicked and absurd theory, that it is easier to do without lecturers and concerts than pork and beans; and in consequence of this abominable theory, I do not think I shall be able to make as much money as I expected.[41]

Redpath also experienced a number of personal problems at mid decade. His reputation took a severe buffeting in 1875 when he was called as a star witness in the highly publicized Tilton-Beecher adultery scandal. Redpath had been a personal friend of New York City newspaper publisher and reformer Theodore Tilton since the time of the Civil War and sometimes was a houseguest in the latter's home in Brooklyn. The Reverend Henry Ward Beecher was the bureau's most profitable client. In the late 1860s,

Tilton had drifted away from religious orthodoxy and his wife had turned to Beecher, her minister, for spiritual guidance. According to a confession by Libby Tilton, Beecher had used the occasion to seduce her. Theodore Tilton had learned of the affair in the early 1870s and the couple had attempted a reconciliation. Theodore never managed to forgive the betrayal and soon began hinting in conversations and eventually in writing about the details of the affair. Soon gossipy rumors of the Beecher-Tilton affair were circulating in northeastern religious and reform circles. The scandal became public when free love advocate Victoria Woodhull exposed it in her short-lived weekly newspaper in November 1872. Forced to investigate the morals of its minister, Brooklyn Plymouth Congregational Church exonerated Beecher after Libby Tilton recanted earlier statements on the affair. In 1875, Tilton sued Beecher for alienating the affection of his wife. The trial that resulted in a hung jury was the most publicized legal proceeding of the decade.[42]

Redpath's part in this melodrama proved highly embarrassing. While a houseguest of the Tiltons in early 1873, Redpath had received from Theodore a written statement largely confirming the allegations made by Victoria Woodhull. Soon after, Tilton and a close advisor Frank Moulton persuaded Redpath to act as a go-between in unsuccessful negotiations between Tilton and Beecher. Redpath twice met with Beecher but accomplished little to end the controversy.[43]

Although Redpath testified on behalf of Beecher's defense at the 1875 trial, the *New York Tribune* reported that "fiery glances of Mr. Beecher's friends and counsel, gleaming from frowning and clouded brows, indicated . . . that there lurked in their minds a suspicion of treachery."[44] In fact, Redpath gave a sympathetic account of Tilton's state of mind in the midst of the crisis, revealing that a friendship had existed between the two men. As Redpath's testimony continued, however, he reported that Beecher had denied any wrongdoing and had called Tilton a "scoundrel." When Tilton's lawyer asked Redpath if Beecher had explicitly denied the adultery, Redpath replied: "I did not ask him, because I did not believe it."[45] The *Tribune* reported that Redpath spoke in "in low tones and faultless English . . . calculated to stimulate interest in his statements." It concluded that "it was difficult to tell after the testimony was all in whether it was more damaging to plaintiff or defendant; the climax pleased the latter rather than the former."[46] From Redpath's perspective, one unfortunate consequence of the trial was that Henry Ward Beecher felt that the hung jury conclusion of the trial failed to calm public suspicion of him. Redpath tried to revive his client's self-confidence by sending him a series of telegraphs in Latin. Although his legal defense had cost him $118,000, Beecher ignored Redpath's entreaties and withdrew from the lyceum circuit for the 1875–76 season.[47] Feeling financially hard-pressed, Redpath called in some old favors. In September 1875, Twain wrote William D. Howells that "Redpath *beseeches* me to lecture in Boston in November— telegraphs that Beecher's and Nast's withdrawal has put him in the tightest kind of place." Twain agreed to dig out his old "Roughing It" lecture for a few special performances that winter.[48]

Redpath had great trouble quelling the gossip touching him from the Beecher-Tilton scandal because he had himself separated from his wife and seemed on the verge of a divorce. Redpath's marriage to Mary Cotton had suffered from his peripatetic work habits. Since their marriage in 1856, Redpath had spent many long periods living apart from his wife while on journalistic projects. As Redpath entered his early forties, however, the greatest source of discord with his ten year senior wife was another woman, Katharine Sherwood Bonner McDowell, who wrote under the pen name of Sherwood Bonner.

Bonner was the daughter of an Irish immigrant who studied medicine in Philadelphia and ultimately became a wealthy Mississippi planter. Bonner started publishing short stories as a teenager during the Civil War. At twenty-two, she married Edward McDowell, scion of another prominent family from Holly Springs, Mississippi, and they had one daughter. McDowell proved an alcoholic ne'er-do-well and the two separated. Desiring a literary career, Bonner left her daughter with relatives and moved to Boston in 1873. She was taken in by Henry Wadsworth Longfellow who hired her as a secretary and encouraged her writing. Soon Bonner's stories on southern life began to appear in the periodical press. Redpath met the twenty-five-year-old, blond and shapely writer sometime in 1874. She was sixteen years younger than Redpath, who a friendly journalist had recently described as "below the medium height, wiry in frame, sympathetic in features uniting gentleness in no ordinary degree, electrical in both facial and bodily movement."[49] No correspondence between Redpath and Bonner has survived, so much of what can be known about their relationship is inferred from a heavily autobiographical novel, *Like unto Like*, that Bonner subsequently wrote and published. In the novel, Blythe Herndon, a rebellious young southern woman with literary ambitions, meets the much older Roger Ellis, a Scottish-born former abolitionist and now a journalist-reformer. Herndon (Bonner) found Ellis (Redpath) "a brilliant and witty talker," a "man of wide experience," and a "kindred spirit."[50]

Although apparently much impressed by the worldly Redpath, who helped her to gain entrance to many important social and literary circles, Bonner did not intend to encourage romantic feelings in Redpath. She still nursed hopes of eventual reconciliation with McDowell. While entertaining some avant-garde notions, she regarded divorce as improper. Nonetheless, Bonner was flirtatious in her behavior toward Redpath and he responded in kind.[51]

In May 1875, Redpath assisted Bonner in writing a satirical piece "The Radical Club: A Poem, Respectfully Dedicated to 'The Infinite' by An Atom," published in the *Boston Times* and later as a pamphlet. Longfellow had gotten Bonner invited to attend the gatherings of the aging band of

Transcendentalist philosophers and reformers who met for lectures and companionship at the home of the Unitarian minister John T. Sargent. With Redpath's encouragement, Bonner described the gatherings in a parody of Edgar Allen Poe's "The Raven." The poem broadly ridiculed the group's pretensions:

> In their wild Eutopian dreaming and
> impracticable scheming
> For a sinful world's redeeming, common sense flies
> out the door,
> And the long-drawn dissertations come to—words
> and nothing more,
> Only words and nothings more.

The poem also caricatured many of the club's members, calling Sargent "Mr. Pompous," Bronson Alcott "an ancient Concord bookworm," and writer and reformer Ednah Dow Cheney "another *magnum corpus,* with a figure like a porpus." A few Radicals came off better: Thomas W. Higginson "a Colonel, cold and smiling, with a stately air beguiling" and Julia Ward Howe "a lady fair and faded, with a careworn look and jaded."[52]

The poem was an instant sensation and won Bonner considerable praise in Boston's younger "Bohemian" circles. The city's older literary "Brahmin" circles, however, were outraged by this display of rudeness and ingratitude. Many blamed Redpath and some accused him of being coauthor of "The Radical Club." While certainly not Bonner's collaborator, Redpath probably regarded her satire as fair revenge against the pretensions of the high-brow critics of the declining intellectual tone of his Lyceum Bureau's offerings. When Bonner encountered ostracism from many in Boston's literary elite, she blamed Redpath's influence for causing her to make this great social faux pas. In August 1877, she wrote Longfellow, "I could even find it in my heart to wish that I had not written the 'Radical Club.' I want no more enemies; but only friends among those who are strong and good."[53]

In the summer of 1875, Bonner journeyed back to her parents' home in Holly Springs to be with her child. In August, Redpath arrived for a visit. Ostensibly he had come to Mississippi to try to persuade Jefferson Davis to participate in a bureau lecture series together with other leading figures from the Civil War.[54] The state was in the midst of its bloody "redemption" from Republican political rule, and Redpath was regarded as a northern spy. Redpath's radical political views on Reconstruction were not appreciated by Bonner's Mississippi friends and relatives. They angrily rejected Redpath's suggestion that southern whites should join the Republican Party because "that was the country."[55] In the midst of this political disputation, a more personal crisis occurred. Redpath proposed to Bonner but was rejected.

She apparently rebuffed her still legally married suitor graciously because the two remained close. Redpath departed by train for Boston on 6 September.[56]

Again the novel *Like unto Like* provides clues regarding what had transpired between Bonner and Redpath. The fictional Herndon and Ellis become engaged but the young southern woman realizes that her northern lover is far too radical for her. She is critical of his heavy involvement in Reconstruction politics and appalled by his treatment of African Americans as his social equal. The young writer also worries that Ellis is too domineering a personality for her to be able to establish her own independent identity and voice. In perhaps the unkindest cut, Herndon finally concludes that Ellis is "a little bald," "a little gray," and "too ole an' ugly" for her.[57] Bonner herself soon departed for a year-long European tour, residing mainly in Italy. She remained in contact with Redpath via the mails.[58]

It was under these troubled personal circumstances that Redpath made the rash decision to sell the lyceum bureau on 5 October 1875 to two long-time business associates, James Pond and George Hathaway. His motivation for this action remains unclear. The bureau's financial problems were not beyond solving. Redpath had expressed great confidence in the assemblage of speakers that the bureau was ready to present to the public in fall 1875.[59] A few years later, he explained that he sold the bureau because he "was threatened with an attack of softening of the brain, and upon the peremptory advice of my physician, quit the business."[60] Health concerns might have influenced Redpath because he ultimately did suffer a series of strokes in the next decade. Most likely, his separation from his wife of nearly twenty years in the hopes of making himself more attractive to Bonner prompted a strong desire in Redpath to relocate from Boston. As soon as the bureau's sale was completed, he left that community for New York City.[61]

Under the new management, the Redpath Lyceum Bureau continued in business into the twentieth century. Pond who specialized in recruiting foreign celebrities for the American stage quit the bureau within a few years to manage "talent" independently based in New York City, which was fast becoming the center of the entertainment industry. Hathaway remained head of the Redpath Bureau and shifted the bulk of its operations into the Midwest where the lyceum remained a vital cultural institution for rural communities into the 1920s. Many former managers of the Redpath Bureau also played key roles in launching the traveling chautauquas in the late 1870s.[62]

In his seven years as the head of the Redpath Lyceum Bureau, Redpath had converted the amateurish field of public speaking into a modern industry. At his peak, Redpath had a firm grip on the nation's leading speakers and could guarantee incomes as high as forty thousand dollars a year to his stars. This is similar to the centralizing trends occurring throughout all parts of the culture industry as well as in commerce and manufacturing after the Civil

FIGURE 2 Redpath Chautauqua and lyceum workers in front of Evanston, Illinois, office. Redpath Chautauqua Collection, The University of Iowa Libraries.

War. Redpath's ability to produce smaller but nonetheless steady incomes for hundreds of other lecturers, humorists, singers, and musicians helped make entertainment a viable profession. By linking together diverse performers as parts of the same series in first-class houses, Redpath significantly broadened the definition of respectable cultural entertainment. "Redpath," according to historian Merle Curti, "insisted that entertainment must always be clean, free from anything that might endanger public welfare, and congenial to the basic American devotion to religious observance, the sanctity of the home, the spirit of neighborliness, and the Constitution."[63]

Redpath and his bureau facilitated the commercialization of the lyceum and of stage entertainment in general. Financial pressures encouraged him to rely less on traditional "instructive" lecturers and more on varied new types of "performers." In retrospect, we can see that the influence of market forces would drive the entertainment industry in many directions unforeseen by its early reform-oriented pioneers like Redpath. By the mid 1870s Redpath's bureau was busy erasing the distinction between the old lyceum and the antebellum "variety" stage, where dancers, magicians, singers, and other artists had appeared as ancillaries to stage entertainment. When theater managers in the 1860s largely abandoned such brief entertainment acts to emphasize the dramatic performance, "variety" artist found employment largely in working-class saloons. Along with a few veteran variety managers such as Benjamin Franklin Keith and Tony Pastor, Redpath reintroduced "variety" acts to middle-class audiences by removing them from the connections with working-class drink and sexuality and put their acts into safe bourgeois theaters and lecture halls. In such a way, Redpath deserved recognition as one of the fathers of the institution popularly known by the century's end as "vaudeville."[64]

In many ways, Redpath followed the example of his erstwhile lecturer client P. T. Barnum in establishing the role of the "impresario" in American entertainment. Like Barnum, he sought to uplift and instruct the public, but he accepted the verdict of the public as expressed through their attendance or lack of it as to determine what forms of entertainment his bureau should provide.[65]

Even while he helped to fashion the nation's entertainment industry, Redpath remained active in the Republican Party as an advocate for more concerted effort by the federal government to protect the rights of southern freedmen. By the mid 1870s, alarms were sounding that the political and economic transformation of the former slave states envisioned by the abolitionists was failing. Calls for a large-scale confiscation and redistribution of plantation lands had been rejected by Congress. Other federal programs to aid the emancipated slaves such as the Freedmen's Bureau had seen their funding terminated. The Republican Party in the southern states had achieved some limited successes in the fields of education, transportation, and civil rights. While black males achieved the franchise, their influence in most state politics remained handicapped by the prejudices of white Republican colleagues. Most troubling for the future of these Reconstruction efforts was the rise of an organized push by a majority of southern whites to restore as much of the old racial order as possible. Employing violence and intimidation as well as exploiting divisions in Republican ranks, white conservative Democrats "redeemed" state after state from Republican rule. The extremely bloody redemption of Mississippi in fall 1875 left only Louisiana, Florida, and South Carolina in Republican hands while President Grant became increasingly disinclined to intervene to protect what remained of Reconstruction.[66]

The aging cadre of abolitionists responded in different ways to the crisis over Reconstruction. In 1872, many surviving abolitionists had abandoned an aggressive Reconstruction policy and joined the Liberal movement, which emphasized sectional reconciliation over freedmen's rights. In the middle of the decade, northern visitors to the South, including former abolitionists and Free Soilers such as James Freeman Clarke, William Dean Howells, and James S. Pike, published reports that the freedmen lacked the abilities to sustain honest governments in that region.[67] Redpath knew the importance of northern public support if Reconstruction was to survive. In articles in the

New York Independent, he warned that the doctrine of state sovereignty had been resurrected by ex-Confederates and their doughface allies who plotted to win the fall 1875 election by deceiving and dividing the North while simultaneously extinguishing black suffrage in the South. He called for a Republican victory to prove that the nation knew "neither North nor South, East nor West, black man nor white, but only America and Americans."[68]

In spring and early summer 1876, Redpath served as the secretary of a congressional committee, headed by Massachusetts senator George S. Boutwell, charged to investigate intimidation and violence in the recent state elections in Mississippi. He traveled with that committee to various southern states where they gathered evidence and then returned to Washington for further public hearings. Redpath subsequently generated controversy by the strong language he used in a series of newspaper articles for the *New York Times,* detailing and denouncing the campaign of violence the Mississippi Democrats had employed the previous year to keep blacks away from the polls.[69]

Redpath's inflammatory reporting offended Sherwood Bonner's relatives who had sent clippings to her while in Europe. She stood by her friend nevertheless and wrote back to a sister:

> Poor R____ I am wretched about him. Yet I know him to be sincere—He has run into this extreme from the ardor of his nature—& remembers it is Southern politicians, not Southerners he hates. At all events now when he is under such clouds *I* shall not turn on him. He has been a true friend and I must stand by him.[70]

A series of letters by Redpath to the *New York Independent* from the same period reveal that this investigation of conditions in the Deep South had produced grave despair about the future for Reconstruction. His first letter repeated criticism of the southern Democrats' campaign of political terror but it also blamed southern blacks and their northern allies for the deplorable conditions. Redpath presented a bleak account of government in formerly Republican-controlled Mississippi: "Our reconstruction policy is a failure; . . . the illiterate Negro of Mississippi is as corrupt as the illiterate Irishman of New York; . . . the county governments there were burlesques of republican rule." The North, according to Redpath, had failed the freedmen: "We ought never to have given the Negro a vote, or we ought to have forced him to learn to read and built a school for him in every township. He has shown that he is not fit to rule in Mississippi." Unless the blacks were quickly elevated by compulsory education, Redpath expressed grave doubts about further use of federal military power to keep them in power: "If we give complete military protection to the Negroes in all elections in South Carolina, Mississippi, and Louisiana where there is a large black majority we shall establish a system of government which no white race on the face of the earth either ought to endure or will endure."

Acknowledging that his diagnosis would not please northern friends of the blacks, Redpath nonetheless argued that "we must do something. Masterly inactivity means dastardly surrender. To begin with, we must comprehend the situation, and, above all, we must not lie about it."[71]

Redpath's analysis appeared so bleak that the editors of the *Independent* declared that he had "no hope for the Negro voter."[72] This led Redpath to compose a second letter on the "Lessons of Mississippi" for that paper in which he declared, "Sentimental abolitionism was well enough in its day; but Mississippi owes its present condition as much to sentimental abolitionists as to fiendish Negro-haters. The blacks were ruined as good citizens by the chronic prattle about their rights, and they were never roused to a noble manhood by instructions to their duties." Redpath retained hope in the power of education: "It is not by denunciations even of the Mississippi assassins, but by earnest and vigilant efforts to educate [the black man], that we shall ever be proud of him as a Republican citizen."[73] To Redpath's chagrin, within weeks, Democrats were quoting his *Independent* articles as justifications for the campaign of repression in the South.[74] Despite his evident despair, Redpath joined in one last battle to preserve southern Reconstruction. During the presidential election in fall 1876, Redpath moved to western North Carolina to campaign on behalf of the Republican Party. Compared to its fellow southern states, North Carolina had witnessed power shifts back and forth between Republicans and conservative Redeemers during Reconstruction. Conservatives had won control of the legislature and impeached Republican governor William W. Holden in 1871. The Republican lieutenant governor who succeeded Holden, however, had won reelection in 1872 at the same time that Grant carried the state by a comfortable margin in the presidential race.[75]

Realizing the potential closeness of the presidential contest between Republican Rutherford B. Hayes of Ohio and Democrat Samuel Tilden of New York, the Republican National Committee dispatched party workers to North Carolina. Barely a month before the election, Redpath was hired and dispatched to western North Carolina to use the press to persuade former white Unionists in the state's western mountains to stand by the Republican banner. In the mountainous region, Republicans hoped that economic issues would override the white supremacist campaign being waged by the Democrats' gubernatorial candidate Zebulon B. Vance, the former wartime Confederate political leader. In particular Redpath believed that Republican support for homestead exemptions for small farms threatened by debts might hold poorer whites in the party. Redpath reported that "there were no more loyal men in all this broad land . . . who were more devoted to the Union than these Southerners of the mountains of North Carolina."[76] Desperation forced these mountaineers to work together with blacks in the state's eastern counties, according to Redpath, because "the election of Tilden does not mean reform, but expulsion, as far as they shall be affected by such a disaster."[77] Redpath's labors proved in vain as the Democrats carried the state and national elections in North Carolina by narrow margins, Tilden pulling 125,427 to Hayes's 108,484.[78]

Redpath then returned to Washington, D.C., and produced a second series of articles for the *New York Times*, documenting the unfair and coercive tactics that the Democratic Party had used to sweep the South. Dubbing this the "New Rebellion," Redpath claimed that the Democratic "victory" in the presidential election in Mississippi, Louisiana, and Georgia "was characterized by fraud and terrorism as universal and unblushing as the infamous [Mississippi state] election of 1875."[79] In his articles, Redpath called for an investigation to invalidate these election returns: "Order can come only from justice; prosperity can come only from security; and we must put down the banditti in order to bring order and justice [to the South]. Let her banditti vote be thrown out."[80] He also complained that the only signs of "military interference" in this election had been the endorsement of the Democratic ticket by many high-ranking army officers.[81] Redpath's reports were cheering to old abolitionists such as Garrison who were striving to rally northern support for the validity of surviving Republican state governments in the South.[82]

In January 1877 in the capacity as a newspaper reporter, Redpath accompanied a U.S. Senate committee to South Carolina where hearings were held on the recent election. He returned to Washington after three weeks without a doubt that the election had been stolen by "the South Carolina Rifle-club Democracy."[83] Given his earlier statements it was surprising that Redpath's reports on these hearings for the *New York Times* lacked a call for federal authorities to use force to sustain the Republican administration of Republican governor Daniel H. Chamberlain against the superior armed force of its Democratic rivals. The absence of such a call was evidence of Redpath's growing despair about the viability of the few remaining southern Republican state governments. Redpath left further evidence of his changed mind in a private letter to Whitelaw Reid, the editor of the *New York Tribune* who had succeeded Horace Greeley, in which he proposed to travel to New Orleans to gather evidence about frauds in Louisiana's 1876 election. Rather than attempt to salvage the outcome of that state's election for the Republicans, Redpath told Reid that he hoped his reports would "advise the antislavery element in the North to acquiesce in white supremacy in Louisiana *for the sake of the blacks.*"[84] Reid steered clear of the controversial Redpath, ending his reporting on Reconstruction.

The presidential election of 1876 ultimately was resolved by an Electoral Commission that saved the White House for the Republicans. By a strict partisan vote, the commission awarded the disputed electoral votes of South Carolina, Mississippi, and Florida to the Republican candidate. The new president, Rutherford B. Hayes of Ohio, already had discreetly assured the South that federal troops would no longer be used to sustain the remaining

Republican state governments there. Hayes held what proved a futile belief that a conciliatory policy toward southern whites would win over large numbers of former Whigs to the Republican Party. He extracted no solid assurances from southern whites that blacks' rights in the region would be respected.[85]

After the Electoral Commission ruled for Hayes, Redpath answered a letter from Merrimon Howard, a deposed Mississippi Republican sheriff, and sent his reply to numerous newspapers. Despite his own previously voiced despair over the ongoing viability of Reconstruction, Redpath denounced the "New Southern Policy" of Hayes and the Republican leadership.[86] But, considering the tenor of the new administration and the uneven balance of forces in the South, he advised Howard and other southern blacks to make the best available terms with their new Democratic political masters. Redpath recommended that the remaining Republican governors in South Carolina and Louisiana turn over authority to the Democrats, arguing "it is better for the sake of the blacks that the surrender should be made quietly and quickly."[87]

Redpath concluded his letter to Howard with thoughts about future political action. Redpath's advice was startling. He wrote that southern blacks

> should be taught that the men who fought for their freedom are now in a helpless minority in the Republican party; that the blacks owe it no allegiance whatever now; and that its recognized leaders, who wield the power of the Government, are to-day the recreants who advocate and defend and decree their abandonment. . . . There is absolutely no difference whatever, now, between the Democratic Party and the Republican Party, (as represented by Hayes) on the question of the rights and condition of the negro, excepting in one important particular. That exception is a vital one. It points out the path of safety to the black voter. It points out, also the path of duty. We owe allegiance where we receive protection. The Democrats protect the democratic negro; the Republicans abandon the republican negro.[88]

Based on this analysis of the dismal conditions in the South, Redpath's advice was to "urge the black men of the South, if my voice could reach them, to join the democratic party."[89] He also revealed decisions about his own course:

> For myself, being a white man, and a Northern man, I propose to remain in the Republican party to do my part to purge it from the thieves on the one hand and the pedagogues on the other hand who now infest it; but if I were a negro and in the South, I should join the democratic party at once and vote for its candidates whenever they were reputable men. Whenever they were bandits I should refuse to vote at all.[90]

Redpath's advice contained elements of the accommodationism Booker T. Washington would advocate at the end of the century: "Pay less attention to politics and seek power through business. . . . Cease to array yourselves against the whites in politics, but, at the same time quietly and everywhere and always insist on the right of securing an education for your children. Securing that right, your children will secure all others, by and bye."[91] In his unabating faith in education, Redpath remained a true son of his schoolmaster father.

Publishing his letter to Merrimon Howard destroyed whatever opportunities Redpath might have had for preferment from the new Republican administration. In fact, office-seekers wrote to Hayes denouncing Redpath's "gross and uncalled for attack" on the president and enclosing their own published rebuttals. Hayes was advised to ignore abolitionist critics, such as Redpath, and continue his work to restore national peace and prosperity.[92]

The Howard letter revealed the degree of James Redpath's disillusionment with Reconstruction. In 1877, he joined a small band of veteran abolitionists, including Wendell Phillips and William Lloyd Garrison, in denouncing the Republican Party's leadership for abandoning the freedmen to the mercy of the region's Democratic "Redeemers." Little unity existed among the steady dwindling ranks of former radical emancipationists, however, about future efforts on behalf of the southern blacks. Some eventually came to Redpath's position that economic and educational assistance rather than political or military intervention would best serve the freedmen's long-range elevation to genuine equality.[93]

Redpath also experienced a number of professional reverses in these years. His efforts to launch a Washington-based newspaper feature syndicate failed. This was a period when a number of such syndicates flourished briefly by selling "boiler plate," or stereotyped plates one column wide, that any editor could insert as "filler" into his paper. Also the galley proofs of new pieces of short fiction were widely sold by feature syndicates to small newspapers which could set them into type themselves. With wide contacts in both the literary and journalistic field, Redpath appeared well-positioned to make a mark in the syndicate industry. However, established syndicates such as Ansell Kellogg's Chicago Newspaper Union already had more than eighteen hundred clients by the mid 1870s, and this competition apparently discouraged Redpath away from the project.[94]

Redpath then returned to the lecture-promotion business. He personally managed the famed atheist Robert A. Ingersoll in a coast-to-coast tour lecturing on the Bible. An Illinois lawyer, Civil War veteran, and minor politician, Ingersoll had won nationwide recognition as an orator for his "Plumed Knight" nomination speech of James G. Blaine for president at the 1876 Republican convention. In a series of essays and lectures prepared after the Civil War, Ingersoll advanced rational and scientific arguments against the belief in God. A frequent target of editorial attack, Ingersoll's notoriety made him a much-sought-after lyceum speaker. Describing Ingersoll as his "best card" of all times, Redpath arranged 138 appearances for his lecturer in 1877–78. Ingersoll lectured on a variety of topics, including the recent Electoral Commission, Robert Burns, and Thomas Paine. Ingersoll drew large, mainly male, audiences in the cities but active opposition from local clergy often suppressed attendance in smaller communities. When Redpath accompanied Ingersoll to a lecture, the two men often sat conversing until after midnight. Redpath displayed no hesitation at being publicly associated with such a controversial figure as Ingersoll.[95]

At the conclusion of the lyceum season, Redpath was hired by Thomas A. Edison to publicize the latter's new invention, the phonograph. Following close on Alexander Graham Bell's patent of the telephone, Edison devised a hand-crank powered machine for recording sounds on a tinfoil cylinder by means of a vibrating diaphragm. Edison had maintained a high degree of secrecy about the design of his ingeniously simple invention until the patent application was filed. This policy was reversed immediately after the organization of the Edison Speaking Phonograph Company and the hiring of Redpath in May 1878.[96]

Based at the new company's two-room office at 203 Broadway Avenue in New York City, Redpath arranged for public exhibitions of the phonograph all across the country. He even contracted for original music to be played at the exhibits, including "The Song of Mister Phonograph." To satisfy public curiosity, Redpath divided the country into territories and leased demonstration rights. Many old acquaintances from the lyceum business received territorial franchises from Redpath. To amazed audiences, Edison's machine played recordings of current popular tunes, such as "Old Uncle Ned," "The Wandering Refugee," and "La Grande Duchesse," as well as tales and poems by popular storytellers. These exhibits proved quite profitable; the one in Boston netting nearly two thousand dollars in a week. But the reproduction quality of the early phonographs proved crude and its novelty appeal soon declined. Only a small number of the tinfoil phonographs were manufactured and sold at a hundred dollars apiece. After the U.S. Patent Office rejected Edison's application, he reorganized the company and halted exhibitions while turning most of his attention to the laboratory to perfect the electric light bulb. Redpath was let go.[97]

During his brief association with Edison, Redpath occasionally visited the inventor's laboratories at Menlo Park, New Jersey, sometimes bringing celebrities from the lyceum circuit with him. One of these visits gave rise to an amusing anecdote. In the summer of 1878, Redpath was present at the first public trial of one of Edison least-well-remembered inventions, the "Megaphone." Intended to transmit voices great distances, the invention consisted of two enormous ear trumpets of nearly six feet in length and a mouthpiece. After carrying one of these horn-shaped instruments a mile across a meadow from Edison's main laboratory, one of the experimenters spoke into the mouthpiece unit. Redpath, who had remained on the laboratory porch, manned the ear trumpets of another megaphone aimed at the experimenters. When asked what the message was, Redpath replied "John Brown's body lies moldering in the grave," to the amusement of all present who remembered him as the abolitionist's best-known biographer. Redpath then exclaimed: "This is really telegraphing without a telegraph."[98]

Neither the Ingersoll nor Edison business ventures proved sufficiently financially rewarding to the always impecunious Redpath. During the summer of 1879 he laid plans to hire a variety of musical and theatrical companies to perform in a circuit of twelve New York and New Jersey cities that fall. By early September plans for "Redpath's Elysian Nights" entertainments were well advanced and among the performers booked were the Emma Abbott Opera Company, the Criterion Comedy Company, Saulsbury's Troubadors, and similar types of variety acts. Redpath committed all of his available money to reserve theaters and engage these performers.[99]

At the same time, Redpath endured a major personal crisis. During the past three years Redpath had had little or no direct contact with Sherwood Bonner. On her return from Europe, Bonner went directly to Galveston, Texas, where her husband now resided. There she began writing *Like unto Like,* to which she originally gave the revealing title of *The Prodigal Daughter.* The work was intended as a "character study" of her own earlier self in which she simultaneously explained and repudiated her treatment of her husband and child and her "affair" with Redpath.[100] Claiming the need for a better writing environment, Bonner returned to Boston in October 1877 and again worked at Longfellow's home. Eager to quell criticism of her bohemianism, Bonner brought her daughter north with her this time. She finished writing *Like unto Like* and Longfellow persuaded Harper and Brothers to publish it. Apparently unaware of the content of Bonner's yet-published novel, Redpath finally called on her in March 1878 but in the company of Ingersoll.[101] In August, Bonner rushed back to Holly Spring to nurse family members struck down by a yellow fever epidemic. Both her father and brother fell victim to and died in the epidemic. Bonner cabled Redpath for help and he arranged with friends in the military for her to pass through the quarantine lines and return by train to Boston.[102] Bonner traveled back to Holly Springs in November just before release of *Like unto Like.* Regrettably we know nothing about Redpath's reaction to the novel's portrayal of himself and Bonner's rejection of his feelings for her. There were reports of Redpath behaving erratically that summer. Some credited this to romantic issues, most blamed the pressures of arranging for his new entertainment series.[103] Word of Redpath's behavior apparently reached Bonner in Boston by way of a mutual friend who had visited with him in early August. Bonner felt compelled to go to console Redpath. She stayed in New York City for about a month.[104]

The amount of relief Bonner provided Redpath is not known. Neither left a record of this meeting. It is very likely that Bonner's appearance in New York City produced an extremely complicated personal situation for Redpath in mid 1879. Separated but not yet divorced from Mary Cotton Redpath, his wife of twenty years, and spurned soon after by Bonner, Redpath appears to have turned his affection to a third woman. In 1876–77, when Redpath based himself in Washington to report on the demise of Reconstruction, he had boarded at the home of Carrie Mae Chorpenning. Born Carrie Mae MacLellan, she was the widow of a Captain Dunlap, a deceased Civil War officer. In December 1864, she had married George Chorpenning, one of the pioneers of the western overland mail business. They had one child, a daughter, born in 1870. In 1878, Redpath relocated to New York City to work for Edison. At the same time, Carrie Chorpenning left her husband who she soon divorced and also moved to that city. In 1879, Redpath was again listed in city directories as a boarder of Mrs. Chorpenning, at 505 Lexington Avenue in New York City. The two would marry in 1887.[105]

How Redpath managed this difficult personal situation is not known. The news that Bonner's husband Edward McDowell was on route to New York City to meet his wife appears to have caused a major psychological crisis for Redpath.[106] On Friday, 3 September 1879, Redpath visited his Manhattan office in the University building, dressed in a light flannel suit, low cut shoes, and a straw hat. Departing there with a small valise and less than fifty dollars, he disappeared. By mid September, the press began to speculate on his whereabouts and intentions. Some rumors claimed that Redpath had committed suicide when he became unable to honor the financial commitments made for his upcoming "Elysian nights." In advancing that theory, the *New York Times* gave an unflattering assessment of Redpath's personality:

> Mr. Redpath was a man of singularly nervous and sensitive nature and domestic trouble, which some years ago drove him from his home, continued to pursue and harass him. He was irregular in his habits of work and of life, often working day and night when he had one of his great enterprises on his hands, eating and sleeping irregularly, and scarcely resting at all. His mental unhappiness contributed much to this disregard of the conditions of health and made him reckless of consequences. For some months he had been more than usual, troubled with dyspepsia and sleeplessness, and had exhibited in his conversation indications of mental aberration which caused solicitude on the part of his friends.[107]

In response, Redpath's business agent, Charles A. Newton, claimed that sufficient funds were on hand to meet all of the obligations of the Elysian Nights series set to begin the next month, but refused to pay either theater managers or performers without Redpath's authorization. Friends made public statements avowing Redpath's unblemished record of financial integrity and denied the likelihood that he had either committed suicide or fled his creditors.[108] On account of the impresario's continuing absence, the planned extravaganza completely unraveled by late September.

When Redpath surfaced a month later in Jamaica, he claimed to have suffered a bout of amnesia caused by a carbuncle. He recounted wandering the New York City streets for a day in a daze caused by a pain behind his left ear. On the docks, he reported, "My eyes fell on the steamer *Atlas* posted for Jamaica, and without any reasoning power went on board. The name seemed, no doubt, in my condition to be connected with a surcease of pain and sorrow."[109] Redpath stood by this story, although he later added the detail that betrayal by financial backers had threatened the failure of his "Elysian Nights" series and led him to breakdown mentally for some months.[110]

While Redpath's health and financial problems probably were genuine, the timing of events in late summer 1879 points to personal factors as the precipitant for Redpath's collapse. Sherwood Bonner's trip to New York City in August 1879, about to be trumped by the arrival of her husband, made it impossible for Redpath to continue his complicated arrangements of romantic relationships, real or merely flirtatious. When added to his physical exhaustion and business stress, the psychological dissonance caused by these relationships could quite plausibly have produced some type of breakdown.

Redpath would never again see Bonner. He spent most of the next few years outside the United States. Bonner finally divorced her husband in 1880 but was soon stricken with the cancer that killed her in July 1883. In 1890, Redpath planned to visit Bonner's grave in Holly Springs but had to cancel the trip. He wrote her sister and inquired about the well-being of all of her relatives. Surprisingly, he revealed that he had tried to assist Edward McDowell just a few years earlier when the latter was engaged in a gold-mine scheme. Such an act reveals that Redpath's affection for Bonner had endured and even extended to the other men in her life.[111]

Instead of returning to New York City in 1879, Redpath traveled on to Panama and then California. As to why he had not gone back, Redpath gave the dubious explanation that California had been as near Jamaica as New York and his business plans for the fall were obviously "gone."[112] To finance his return east he produced a series of gossipy recollections for the *San Francisco Chronicle* about his years as the leading figure in the entertainment industry. While these articles hinted at a return to the entertainment industry, Redpath's career was about to take another dramatic turn as the 1880s began.[113]

9 The Adopted Irishman

Redpath returned to New York City from San Francisco in January 1880. His residence again became the Lexington Avenue house owned by Carrie Mae Chorpennig. Although he would continue to travel frequently, Redpath made New York home for the remainder of his life.

New York City had grown substantially since Redpath had first arrived there as an aspiring young journalist from Michigan more than a quarter of a century earlier. From 1850 to 1880, the city's population had doubled to 1.1 million, not counting hundreds of thousands more in Brooklyn and the other surrounding boroughs. Even more striking than its sheer growth was the dramatic shift in the city's ethnic composition. At the earlier date, the city had just absorbed hundreds of thousands of refugees from famine-stricken Ireland. Lacking the financial resources to establish themselves as farmers in this country, these immigrants became the largest element in the city's unskilled labor pool, helping to supply the human capital for its rapid development as a manufacturing and transportation center. By 1880, continuing immigration had swelled the Irish and second- and third-generation Irish American population to nearly 40 percent of the city's total. A small "lace curtain" Irish American middle class had emerged, featuring professionals, entrepreneurs, clergy, and Tammany Hall politicians. The large majority of the city's Irish remained in the working class, although many had risen into more skilled and better paying jobs in the woodworking, metal, construction, and clothing trades.[1]

The Elysian Nights debacle had left the forty-six-year-old Redpath in dire need to reestablish his professional reputation and personal finances. To support himself in the changed New York City environment, Redpath continued to write biographical sketches of colorful figures on the lecture circuit for a variety of publications. This activity proved to be his entree to rejoining his original profession as a journalist. The New York City newspaper business in the 1880s was dramatically different than the one Redpath had known thirty years earlier. The era when the major papers unapologetically reflected the egos and ideologies of their editors had ended with the deaths of Henry J. Raymond of the *Times* (1869), Horace Greeley of the *Tribune* (1872), and James Gordon Bennett Sr. of the *Herald* (1872). Only Charles A. Dana at the *Sun* remained of the earlier luminaries, but his paper's influence waned as its editor became increasingly disenchanted with politics. The psychologically unstable James Gordon Bennett Jr. had briefly treated the *Herald* as his personal vehicle to lash out at all enemies, real or imagined, but a sex scandal had caused his self-exile to Paris in 1877.[2]

A new journalistic world was emerging. The editorial pages of the New York City dailies remained politically partisan but the papers contained more fact-laden and objective news stories. Perhaps unsure of his way in this new environment, Redpath turned in the most familiar direction, the *Tribune*. Following Greeley's death that newspaper had come under the control of Whitelaw Reid, four years Redpath's junior. While a successful war reporter, Reid had come into his own as Greeley's assistant in managing the *Tribune*. With the aid of a loan from the notorious financier Jay Gould, Reid had won control of the *Tribune* following Greeley's death. To mark the start of a new era, Reid had Greeley's old Tribune Building completely rebuilt by leading architect Richard Morris Hunt. Redpath's old nemesis in the paper's business office, Samuel Sinclair, quit and Reid reorganized its administrative department. He also relentlessly battled with the *Tribune*'s printers over wages, eventually driving out their union. Reid also cut salaries in his newsroom while hiring several prominent special correspondents, including Henry James, William Dean Howells, and Bret Harte. Eschewing Greeley's reform crusading, Reid made the *Tribune* a bastion of Republican Party orthodoxy.[3]

The one thing that Reid had failed to do was to rebuild circulation to the dominant position it once held, as the *Tribune*'s sales lagged behind most of the rest of the city's dailies. An obvious way to attract more local readers in the 1880s was to publish more stories of interest to the city's swelling Irish-American population. Under Greeley, the *Tribune* had flirted with nativism, and Reid's conservative brand of Republicanism expressed little sympathy toward the aspirations of the city's largely working-class Irish American citizens. In addition, the paper's foreign correspondents did little to hide their Anglophilia. Reid must have been pleased, therefore, to receive a written proposal from Redpath in late January 1880, which seemed to offer the *Tribune* a new means of attracting Irish American readers.

In a letter marked "Personal," Redpath told Reid that he had not yet completely recovered from his maladies of the fall: "I find that while my health is restored . . . my strength is not equal to daily or prolonged hard work. I want a sea voyage. I can endure any amount of physical work & from 4 to 5 hours hard mental work: but I don't dare to task myself beyond that."[4] Redpath proposed that Reid hire him to tour Ireland and report on the recent reoccurrence of famine in the western part of that island. Redpath promised Reid that this topic could be "worked up by an experienced hand into an old-style Tribune feature."[5] Redpath also requested permission to later republish his *Tribune* dispatches along with additional materials on Irish politics in book form. He told Reid that "I wd go if little more than my expenses were paid—for I shd expect my real remuneration in restored strength and in whatever profits a book might bring." Reid noted that he was "rather impressed" by the proposal and hired Redpath for the project.[6]

In Ireland, the years 1874–78 had been relatively prosperous, but starting in 1879 agriculture suffered poor harvests, steep price declines, and as a consequence, an increase in evictions. In some counties of western Ireland economic conditions became worse than even at the height of the Great Famine of the 1840s. Consolidation of landholdings in this region hitherto had trailed that in the rest of the island but now economic distress sparked disputes between the tenant and landlord classes.[7]

Almost immediately on his arrival in Ireland, Redpath became a convert to the cause of the Irish Land League. Led by the colorful Charles Stewart Parnell, the Land League campaigned for major reforms in British laws that governed Irish tenantry, ultimately desiring the transferal of the land from the largely Protestant and frequently absentee landlords to the Roman Catholic peasants.[8] Parnell represented the conservative wing of the Land League movement. Some popular leaders, such as Michael Davitt, sought to transform the movement into a challenge to the power of the capitalist class while still others, including John Devoy, hoped that league would revive the Irish independence cause.[9]

Redpath produced a blistering series for the *Tribune* that exposed the suffering of the Irish peasants and the need for land reform.[10] He solicited testimony from scores of ministers and other local leaders in western Ireland detailing the extent of the distress. Redpath interviewed Lord Randolph Churchill for several hours but left unimpressed with the effectiveness of the British relief efforts he was directing for the peasantry. Redpath gleefully informed Reid that the Irish viewed the *Tribune*'s archrival, the *New York Herald,* as "championing the landlords whose greed makes prosperity impossible."[11] Redpath described the Irish land system to Reid as "feudalism without the duty of lordship" and promised that a strong exposé of its abuses would give the *Tribune* "a big strike among Irish Americans."[12]

Michael Davitt years later recalled Redpath's initial encounter and then conversion to the Land League cause: "He introduced himself at the Land-League offices one day, saying he wished to look at our books and correspondence in order to find out where 'the distress, if any,' was located. To his manifest surprise his request was immediately granted, and a somewhat skeptical inquirer was disarmed by this show of confidence, and was soon, as he himself expressed it, turned into a convinced Land-Leaguer."[13] Davitt also provided one of the best descriptions of the middle-aged Redpath:

> Redpath was an intensely interesting personality. He was under medium height, with a face full of character, from which two large, gray eyes looked out at you with a deep, penetrating expression of suffering and sympathy. It was a strong but sad face—one of those faces which appear to be forever searching after a something that is not to be enjoyed in this life—a place of rest where no wrong is to be found and into which no tale of human misery could come. He had, in a marked degree, the typical American manner of independent bearing and frank speech, with a dry, caustic humor."[14]

Redpath initially stayed in Dublin to acquaint himself with the general situation. After about a month of conversing with both Irish leaders and British officials, he took off on a tour on the western counties. A few months later, back in the United States, Redpath told an audience of the powerful impact that this tour had upon him:

> I went to Ireland because a crowd of calamities had overtaken me that made my life a burden too heavy to be bourne. But in the ghastly cabins of the Irish peasantry, without fuel, without blankets and without food . . . in the West of Ireland, I soon forgot every trouble of my own life in the dread presence of the great tidal wave of sorrow that had overwhelmed an unhappy and unfortunate and innocent people.[15]

In his travels, Redpath's dispatches for the *Tribune* described scenes of extreme rural poverty and the struggling relief efforts. From the start, Redpath's articles focused not on the immediate problem of famine but on the deeper issue of tenant-landlord relations. He repeatedly emphasized the similarity of the exploitation of the Irish peasantry and the southern Black sharecropper. Reminding his readers of his antebellum travels in the slave states, he charged that "the landlords of Ireland are just as bad a lot as ever the worst of our southern slaveholders were."[16]

Redpath also warned that failure to remedy the economic problems of the Irish tenants would cause an unwanted mass migration to the United States. As these Irish laborers emigrated "in vast multitudes to America and settle down in the great cities of the East, the first effect will be to lower the wages of all of the Irish-American laborers of both sexes now there to the starvation level of Ireland."[17] Controversies soon arose concerning the impartiality of Redpath's reporting. Anglo-Irish representatives such as the wealthy County Mayo landowner Walter Bourke charged Redpath with distorting accounts of the famine and inadequate relief efforts. Redpath generated another controversy when he was widely quoted denouncing Lord Beaconsfield (former prime minister Benjamin Disraeli) as "the descendant of an oppressed race

FIGURE 3 James Redpath in the mid 1880s. Courtesy of the Kansas State Historical Society, Lawrence.

who gloried in his oppression and tyranny over another oppressed race."[18] Redpath explained to Reid that Disraeli merited "utterable scorn and contempt" for whipping up anti-Catholic prejudices against the Irish considering his own heritage.[19] Redpath privately thanked Reid for standing up for him in all of these matters.[20] In public interviews, Redpath declared, "The *Tribune* has behaved quite handsomely . . . my facts and the theories I expressed conflicted with the position that the *Tribune* had previously taken. Most editors would have thrown their correspondent's letters into the waste in such circumstances."[21] Redpath's *Tribune* articles were an important turning point in the Irish campaign to win sympathy from the hitherto largely pro-Protestant and pro-British press opinion in the United States.

Redpath returned to the United States in early April 1880. He reported to Reid that his expenses in Ireland had been much higher than anticipated. When he returned from Ireland to New York City, he asked Reid for a short-term loan and for permission to write pieces for the *New York Independent*, focusing on Ireland's Protestant community. Soon after arriving back, Irish American editors also approached Redpath for stories on Irish conditions. Because the *Tribune* had paid for his passage there, he felt obliged to ask such permission from Reid.[22]

At the same time, Redpath launched a speaking tour on behalf of relief for the Irish famine victims. He called on the Protestant clergy of the North not to be blinded by religious prejudices but to denounce the immoral behavior of Irish landlords as they once had condemned that of Southern planters.[23] The *New York Times* reported that Redpath addressed an audience composed largely of Irish Americans and Democrats at New York City's Cooper Institute in May 1880. The *Boston Pilot* praised Redpath's lecture in its home city: "During its delivery the speaker was visibly affected by his recital of the sufferings of the poor, and rugged men and fragile women wept in unison at the graphic portrayal of Ireland's wrong."[24] Redpath wrote Reid that "I find—very much to my surprise—that I have succeeded as a lecturer: and that I have numerous offers to lecture in the Fall."[25]

Also in spring 1880, Redpath assisted the touring Michael Davitt and John Devoy to make contacts with sympathetic Americans. In a welcoming speech in New York City, Redpath compared the courage of Davitt to that of his old abolitionist associate John Brown.[26] Redpath assisted Davitt in finding an office in the University Building at New York City's Washington Square for the newly created American branch of the Land League. He also found an associate from the lyceum bureau days to serve as Davitt's secretary.[27] Redpath's zeal for the Irish cause so impressed Davitt that the latter gave the journalist his own return ticket to Ireland because he believed it "important [that] he shld go their [*sic*] personally in order to depict the eviction scenes and understand the system responsible for them."[28]

Redpath returned to Ireland in July and wrote a second series of reports on Irish conditions for the *Tribune* as well as additional feature stories for the

New York Independent, the *Chicago Inter-Ocean,* and the Irish-American *Boston Pilot.*[29] At the end of August, Redpath reported back to Reid that "I have seldom worked harder in my life." He assured Reid that his current series of reports "presents the most thorough inside view of landlord rule in Ireland that has been hitherto appeared."[30]

On this second tour, Redpath immediately made contact with officers of the Land League. He reported very favorably to them on the success that Davitt was making in organizing local branches of the league in the United States.[31] In his dispatches to American newspapers, Redpath strongly endorsed the Land League's latest program of encouraging tenants to refuse to pay more rent than they judged fair as a means of compelling land reform. Landlords had retaliated by evicting local Catholic farmers. The resulting increase in tenant evictions angered Redpath. He told American readers that that "Irish landlord power is the exact counterpart of American Ku-Kluxism—only it is Ku-Kluxism codified and sanctioned by law, and enforced, not by disguised bands of midnight marauders, but by disciplined detachments of the Royal Constabulary."[32]

The most famous incident in the Land League's 1880 campaign occurred in County Mayo in September where Captain Charles Boycott, agent of Lord Erne, ejected "striking" tenants and attempted to replace them with Protestant farmers imported from Ulster.[33] To discourage this practice, the league's rural supporters members undertook a total social shunning of the interloping tenants and their families. This practice had been advocated by Land League speakers all summer.[34]

In August 1880 Redpath gained international celebrity status by popularizing the term *boycott* in his speeches and reports to describe the Land League tactics against Irish landlords. At a rally attended by two thousand Land League supporters near Ballintaffey in County Mayo on 15 September 1880, Redpath advised the Irish: "If a man is evicted, don't let another man take his farm. If he is so mean as to take it in spite of your protest, don't shoot him, but don't speak to him or his children—have nothing to do with him or say to him. . . . Keep from him as if he had the small-pox. Let him feel and know your avoidance of him, and why, and he'll have to move."[35] At a Land League rally at Ennis, four days later, Parnell followed Redpath's lead in encouraging the western Irish peasants to adopt the boycotting tactic. In his public statements, Redpath repeatedly compared the Irish "boycott" to the "color line" ostracism that he witnessed being practiced against carpetbaggers and scalawags during Reconstruction. In another address in September, Redpath went further than Parnell and most leaders of the Land League, declaring "I cannot understand how any Irishman would be satisfied even with the land for the people and Home Rule. If I were an Irishman I should never cease to work for the independence of Ireland."[36]

Redpath's role in coining the term *boycott* quickly became shrouded by layers of Irish legend. On a number of rainy evenings while reporting on the

Land League protests against Captain Boycott in County Mayo, Redpath visited the parochial house of a local priest and tenant supporter, John O'Malley, in the village of Neale. The two men sometimes shared a glass of Bushmills from a bottle Redpath carried. O'Malley later recalled them discussing their feeling that the term *social ostracism* then employed to describe the shunning tactics was not clear enough to either the protestors or their supporters. O'Malley suggested: "How would it do to call it to boycott him?" According to the priest, the term pleased Redpath who shook the priest's hand and promised "to use and reuse the word until the whole world comes to know what it means." As promised, Redpath immediately adopted "boycott" in his dispatches that were circulated widely in both Ireland and the United States.[37] Redpath's central role in popularizing the "boycott" was so great that many contemporaries and later historians mistakenly credit him with inventing it.[38]

A British government crackdown on the league occurred in November 1880. Redpath was at lunch with Parnell at Dublin's Imperial Hotel, when the British police arrived to arrest the latter. The officer handed Parnell an indictment for nineteen counts of conspiracy. Parnell accepted the indictments with a smile and resumed his lunch with Redpath. Thirteen others were also indicted with Parnell for inciting tenants to not pay their rent.[39] Parnell's incarceration made him a national hero and thereby gave him sufficient moral authority to negotiate a compromise land reform program with the British government headed by Liberal William Gladstone.[40] But for Redpath, who narrowly escaped prosecution, there was only a hasty trip back to the United States.

Yet on his return to the United States, Redpath found himself a hero to Irish Americans and a sought-after speaker. He toured the Northeast and the Midwest on behalf of the Land League.[41] In the following weeks, Redpath's lecture "Ireland's Land War: What I Know About Boycotting" drew thousands to rallies in Providence, Brooklyn, New York City, Boston, Chicago, Louisville, Omaha, Cincinnati, and elsewhere. In addressing these audiences, Redpath blended in a strong Irish nationalist message with his support for land reform:

> The doom of Landlordism is coming and I call upon you to be its executioners. [Great Applause.] You can make it die by upholding the Land-League. When the Irish get ownership of the soil and home rule they will then wait and watch England's difficulty. They will wait for her difficulty, and the next thing will be the unfurling of the green banner of the Republic. [Tremendous Applause.][42]

When Redpath prepared for a third tour of Ireland in the summer of 1881, it was as the exclusive reporter for the *Boston Pilot*, a committed pro–Land League newspaper, edited by a Fenian veteran John Boyle O'Reilly.[43] The New York City chapter of the Irish National Land League hosted a farewell dinner at Delmonico's restaurant for Redpath. The society's tribute to the departing reporter pronounced that "your noble resolve once more to confront the demon of landlord tyranny in its stronghold, regardless of all consequences or considerations of personal safety, sets forth your character in the brightest light of true patriotism." Redpath responded that he had twice before been honored by a banquet. The first time was by Haitians in Port-au-Prince, to salute his work to uphold "the principle of equal rights, without respect to color or creed or condition." The second had been the previous year in Cork, Redpath recalled, "because I had always loved liberty everywhere and for everyone, and because I had wept over the sorrows of Ireland and had cursed her oppressors."[44]

In this same address, Redpath reminisced about his abolitionist activities and remarked that

> I never uttered a kind word—I never expected to be able to utter a kind word—about American slavery or American slaveholders; but after visiting the west of Ireland I found I could say with absolute truth, and I do say that, as compared with Irish landlords, our southern slaveholders were noble philanthropists! . . . I never saw a southern slave so meanly lodged, or so poorly clad, or so badly fed as three millions of industrious and virtuous Irish peasantry are lodged and clad and fed at this very hour.[45]

Redpath sailed to Liverpool in mid June and then to London to interview Irish parliamentarians. After a brief side trip to Paris, he arrived in Ireland at the end of the month. The *London Times* covered Redpath's travels and the British Home secretary Sir William Harcourt branded him a dangerous agitator. In an address to a Land League meeting in Dublin, Redpath denied Harcourt's charge that he had called for the assassination of landlords visiting the United States but also denied that Britain could demand that the United States extradite Fenians for alleged violent acts.[46]

Despite a promise to concentrate on reporting, Redpath devoted considerable time to delivering speeches on behalf of the Land League during this tour of Ireland.[47] He reported that Land League activities had become disorganized because many of its leaders had been jailed, but nonetheless the spirit of the movement remained unbroken.[48] A carriage accident in Donegal forced Redpath into a convalescent bed in Letterkenny for several weeks and seriously impeded his writing.[49]

In fact, Redpath prepared so few articles for the *Pilot* while on this tour that he continued to write for that paper about his observations for several months after returning home. As the economic distress of the past two years ebbed, Redpath wrote more about the continuing process of tenant evictions. He compiled statistics to demonstrate that rents had increased approximately fourfold on the island since the start of the century. He argued that the rents had to be cut "at least one-half before there is even an approximation of justice" to the tenants.[50] Most of Redpath's *Pilot* articles, however, concentrated on describing political developments. In one piece, he twisted the British lion's tail with an intemperate attack on Queen Victoria, denouncing her as a "vulgar, imperious and selfish woman" for her opposition to all land reform proposals.[51] Redpath also called on American friends of the Irish to boycott "anything that is brewed, or distilled, or woven, or manufactured, in England."[52] In a letter to the *Kerry Sentinel*, Redpath counseled against any temptation to compromise, proclaiming: "This crusade is not a Donnybrook Fair fight, to break the heads of the landlords . . . but a democratic uprising for immediate and total abolitionism in Ireland. It is not a riot against men, but a holy war against a system."[53]

An interesting anecdote of this third Irish tour concerned Redpath's success in making an important convert to the Land League cause. One of Redpath's old Lyceum Bureau stars, David R. Locke ("Petroleum V. Nasby"), was touring Ireland at the same time as Redpath. Nasby confessed that until that trip he had been "the most prejudiced man against the Irish that live[d] between earth and sky."[54] Redpath took Locke on a quick tour of southern and western Ireland where peasant poverty soon melted the lecturer's heart. Redpath reported that Locke now regarded the landlords as "agrarian miscreants, for whose sake Ireland has been kept in pauperism and robbed alike of her prosperity and population for ten generations."[55]

Redpath returned to the United States in November, still not fully recovered from his carriage accident. By mid February 1883, after additional convalescence in New York City, he was ready to resume lecturing on behalf of Irish causes. His old lyceum bureau, now headed by George Hathaway and James Pond but still carrying the Redpath name, arranged this speaking tour. He wrote out a series of lectures to avoid repetition but, following his old advice to lyceum clients, he refrained from reading directly from his text.[56] Redpath described the land reform legislation under debate in Parliament but declared that "we do not want any system of modifying landlordism, because we want to abolish it altogether."[57] Redpath's favorite topic was the boycott. He wrote John Devoy in a boastful mood: "We've got them where the wool is short! Boycotting is *my* contribution to the Irish Cause. It is working effectively in Ireland as it did in the South. It drove out the carpet-baggers there and it is driving out the rent-eaters there."[58]

The Redpath activity that attracted the most press comment at this time was when he allegedly refused to endorse resolutions at a public meeting in New York City's Cooper Union, denouncing the recent assassination in Dublin's Phoenix Park of Lord Frederick Cavendish and T. H. Burke, respectively the British secretary and undersecretary for Ireland. Redpath's speech recalled the killings of unarmed Irish peasants and their families in the course of tenant evictions and condemned those acts as far more heinous than the slaying of British officials. The hostile *New York Herald* denounced Redpath, declaring that he "profoundly admired the nihilists of Russia, and in the tone of a camp-meeting ranter he cried 'God bless dynamite in Russia!' at which a vigorous round of applause came from one section of the audience."[59] Redpath issued a public denial of this report and declared that he "denounced political assassination of every character—whether done by crowned or common murder."[60] Redpath also had a significant break with his long-time employer the *New York Tribune*. He wrote several public letters to the *Tribune*'s editor Whitelaw Reid, complaining of the pro-British bias of its most recent Ireland correspondent, George W. Smalley. He chided Smalley for abandoning the principles of his abolitionist father-in-law, Wendell Phillips. Redpath lectured Smalley that the Land Leaguers and the abolitionists "were soldiers in the same great battle for equality of rights which has been waged and must continue to be waged until feudalism in every part of Europe is abolished."[61]

To promote the cause of Ireland, Redpath launched his own newspaper in July 1882. With the help of unidentified friends, Redpath responded to the published offer by a young New York City journalist, Maurice Francis Egan, to sell his newspaper, *McGee's Illustrated Weekly*. Founded in 1876, this paper's masthead declared itself: "Devoted to Catholic art, literature and education." In the 18 July 1882 issue, Egan announced to readers that the paper's editorship would immediately pass to "a gentleman whose name is a household word in every Irish home—the celebrated journalist and vindicator of the Irish race—Mr. JAMES REDPATH."[62]

Renamed *Redpath's Illustrated Weekly,* the sixteen-page paper was published each Saturday and claimed a circulation in 1883 of fifteen thousand. Not revealed was that the old owner also passed along thirty-five hundred dollars of the paper's debts to Redpath.[63] Redpath published a prospectus promising that every issue would contain "pictures of Irish Life and Scenery, by pen and pencil, and Portraits of prominent Irishmen and Irish Americans." He noted that "every other illustrated newspaper in America ridicules . . . the Irish race and the Irish cause." Redpath promised to write exclusively for his own press, pledging that the paper in "Irish politics . . . will support the Land League and its leaders; in American politics, it will be independent and unpartisan." *Redpath's Illustrated Weekly* also guaranteed at least one piece of fiction on an Irish subject and a full illustrated page on the latest fashions in each issue. The latter feature was to be "edited with notes by a lady of refined taste and culture, thoroughly familiar with the latest styles of New York."[64] That Ladies' Department editor turned out to be none other than Carrie Chorpenning, writing under her maiden name of Carrie Dunlap.

Launching a publication for the Irish American audience in the mid 1880s was an enterprise fraught with many potential pitfalls. Serious internal quarrels developed within the Irish and Irish American community on the proper tactics to solve the island-nation's longstanding problems with Britain. Michael Davitt had sought national ownership rather than peasant ownership of the land. He opposed the land reform settlement negotiated between Parnell and Gladstone, which would gradually move Ireland toward peasant proprietorship. Davitt's steadfast opposition deeply divided the Land League movement.[65] At the same time, the Irish argued bitterly over the issues of violent versus parliamentary tactics and the possibility of obtaining Ireland's complete independence or just a degree of home rule from England. Inevitably Redpath's weekly editorials caused offense to one or another of the proliferating factions. As early as 1881, Redpath had quarreled with O'Donovan Rossa, head of the United Irishmen. This small group represented the remaining Fenians committed to revolutionary action to win Irish independence. In his *Weekly* and elsewhere, Redpath explained his opposition to the United Irishmen's program: "The reason I am opposed to an insurrection in Ireland is because the Irish people have no chance, and that is the only reason."[66] He editorialized that "England is making war on the Irish race and I never yet heard of a war in which men on both sides did not get killed."[67] Redpath equated the attackers with those of his old Kansas free-state friends and declared that "Americans who laud John Brown's career and purity of motive are hypocrites or cowards if they deny the same laudation or apology to the Irish Invincibles."[68]

The debate over violent tactics added to the public quarrel between Redpath and his former *Tribune* employer Whitelaw Reid. Redpath complained that the *Tribune* unfairly attempted to attach the Phoenix Park murders to Parnell. Redpath chided Reid: "We Americans have amazing impudence when we presume to be shocked at the Irish." Redpath listed the numerous murderous assaults on blacks during Reconstruction and called on Reid to editorialize for the prosecution of those individual, now often prominent politicians, before crusading against Irish militants.[69]

From his editorial chair as well as the lecture dais, Redpath became an increasingly outspoken advocate of ultimate Irish independence. He disclosed that he had originally opposed such a policy but had "seen so much and learned so much of English hatred and tyranny and bigotry" that he had come to favor independence. Acknowledging that this position was not held by all, Redpath endorsed a gradual movement toward independence and endorsed the more moderate goal of "Home Rule as a means—not as an end."[70]

The dispute between Davitt and Parnell over the best disposition of Irish lands caused problems for Redpath. In late 1882, he accused Davitt of treason to the Irish cause for opposing Parnell. This prompted Irish Americans, such as the editor of the *Catholic Telegraph* of Cincinnati to ask "by what right Mr. fiery Redpath sets himself up as the censor of Mr. Davitt or any other leading Irishman?"[71] In the highly competitive field of Irish American journalism, Redpath suddenly found his commitment to the cause questioned and had to respond to maintain his hold on his readers.[72]

Redpath tried to heel such feuding by praising the character of Davitt as well as Parnell and Dillon:

I have known nearly all the public men of America for the past thirty years—known a large number of them intimately—and I have never met a more honest and sincere and self-sacrificing band of men in any part of America than the present leaders of the Irish people. They are worthy to be ranked in history with the American abolitionists, for purity of purpose, fidelity to principle, and earnest desire for ameliorating the condition of the poor.[73]

Events in Ireland worked to Redpath's advantage. The negative popular reaction against the increasing wave of political violence allowed Parnell to outmaneuver all challengers for leadership. In 1883, he reorganized the Land League into the Irish National League and kept it tightly under his control. Redpath participated in the merging of the American branch of the Irish Land League with other Irish American societies into the Irish National League of America. At the Philadelphia convention where the merger took place in May 1883, Redpath squeezed onto the planning committee by the subterfuge of naming him the Arizona representative. In keeping with his reputation as an advocate of violence, Redpath joked to the convention that he was honored to be "chosen representative of Arizone [*sic*], the Tombstone district, which was, he believed, also represented at present by the late Messrs. Cavendish and Burke [the Phoenix Park murder victims]."[74] Redpath supported the election of Alexander M. Sullivan of Chicago to head the new organization because "as long as the conservatives controlled the policy of the new League O'Donovan Rossa would have to take a back seat."[75] By maintaining his long-held support for Parnell's leadership, Redpath had kept himself and his publication successfully aligned with the majority opinion of Irish Americans. Safely navigating through the shoals of American political disputes, however, would prove much harder.

In addition to participating in the debates over Ireland's future, the *Redpath Weekly* editorialized on issues of American politics. For example, Redpath dismissed calls for civil service reform, declaring "the cure for inefficient governmental service in a republic ought *not* to be sought in appointing as its officers young men with good memories, but in universal education and simplifying the public service and reducing the number of its functions and duties."[76] Redpath also endorsed women's suffrage, arguing that the "patriarchal business is bankrupt. What women want is not protection, but justice—not gallantry, but equal rights. . . . Let us cease to be hypocrites. We have failed as protectors. Let us give them equal right! *Place aux dames!*"[77] Redpath also announced in his columns that he had abandoned a lifelong commitment to free trade after visiting Ireland and witnessing its desultory effects on the island's farmers and artisans. Redpath also editorialized against greedy landlords who he blamed for the slum conditions in U.S. cities and proclaimed that "no man, and no body of men should have the right or the power of perverting the system of private property in land into an instrument of social injustice."[78]

Redpath had to adapt his strongly expressed opinions to the tastes of his mainly Irish American readers. His principal problem proved in squaring his long-time commitment to the Republican Party to his largely Democratic readership. In 1882, Redpath joined the editors of most other Irish American newspapers in condemning Republican president Chester Arthur for not protesting the imprisonment of Land League agitators by the British government. Redpath supported Democrat Grover Cleveland, the overwhelming choice of Irish-Americans, in the New York state gubernatorial election of 1882. In addition to his anti-Arthur sentiment, he justified the decision as based on the hope that Irish Americans could wean the Democratic Party away from their free trade position. He applauded the victory that fall not only of Cleveland, but his old friend Ben Butler, who had run for Massachusetts governor as a Democrat.[79]

While attempting to overcome challenges in both the foreign and domestic political sphere, Redpath struggled to find a format for the *Weekly* that would make it profitable. Within two months of taking over the editorial helm, Redpath decided that he was no more able than former owner Egan to publish the weekly with all of its expensive illustrations at a three dollar annual subscription price. Announcing that he could not publish a "first-class illustrated paper" and keep it within the price range of his intended audience, "the Irish workingmen of America," Redpath decided to cut his subscription price to $2.50 a year while reducing the number of illustrations per issue to an affordable level. The following January, the paper's masthead was changed to read simply *Redpath's Weekly.*[80]

Throughout 1883, Redpath's newspaper continued to publish numerous illustrations of Irish scenes and Irish and Irish American leaders, but their size diminished. Likewise Carrie Chorpenning's column on women's fashion was retained, but with far fewer accompanying illustrations.[81] Seeking more readers, the *Weekly* shifted to printing fewer political and more fictional items on Irish subjects.[82] Redpath also called on his friends to form clubs to buy, circulate, and discuss his weekly. None of these efforts bore fruit. By spring 1883, Redpath was publicly complaining that he had "received no more practical support from my Irish friends than if I had been an enemy of the Irish."[83]

In August 1883, financial pressures forced Redpath to transform the *Weekly* into primarily a literary magazine. Political subjects became even rarer in its columns and Carrie Dunlap's fashion column disappeared. While Redpath continued to publish numerous stories and poems with Irish themes to hold his original readers, the literary range of the paper broadened to attract new ones.[84] Thereafter there were fewer works such as William Lyman's serialized novel, *Mick McQuaid*. Instead, the *Weekly* featured stories, poetry, and reviews by popular distinguished writers such as Charles Dickens Jr., Harriet Lewis, William Holborn, and Margaret Wilson Oliphant, and translated fiction by Jules Verne and Guy de Maupassant. To further economize, Redpath moved the *Weekly*'s office twice, abandoning its original prestigious Park Avenue address for a two-room suite on the corner of Pearl and Centre Street.

In a marketplace already flooded with literary magazines, *Redpath's Weekly* failed to distinguish itself. Despite its availability at newsstands across the greater New York City area, it did not win a significant new readership outside the Irish American community. To retain that base, Redpath in early 1884 offered his readers a discounted joint subscription of *Redpath's Weekly* and *United Ireland,* the official organ of Parnell's National League.[85] While Redpath's political editorials on Ireland remained popular among Irish American readers, his views on United States domestic politics ultimately undercut that support. During the summer of 1884 when the Democrats nominated Cleveland for president, Redpath attacked the candidate for having refused as New York governor to pardon John Devoy for a charge of libel brought by wealthy financier August Belmont. Redpath said Irish American Democrats should not forgive Cleveland and advocated that they support James G. Blaine, the Republican candidate.[86] The endorsement of the Republican ticket cost Redpath much of his remaining readership and the *Weekly* suspended publication in September 1884.[87] A similar fate befell Devoy's *Irish Nation* when it also endorsed Blaine in 1884. Redpath commiserated with Devoy that their commercial failure at least spared them from accusations of having sold their editorial support to the highest bidder.[88]

Despite such unpleasant experiences, Redpath remained a supporter of Parnell and eventually of the Irish Home Rule cause. He wrote public letters defending violent protests by Irish peasants against the landlords, declaring "whenever iniquity is framed into a law, equity sometimes assumes the semblance of a mob."[89] He looked for every opportunity to "twist the lion's tail" in newspaper writing and speeches.[90] When Redpath made a fourth reporting tour of Ireland in 1889, two years before his death, he received a warm reception.[91]

The journalistic activities of former abolitionist Redpath on behalf of the Irish peasantry demonstrate the interest of many Protestant American reformers in issues that spanned the Atlantic. By drawing parallels between the persecution of the southern freedmen and the Irish peasantry, Redpath sought to overcome the northern white Protestant middle class's ethnic prejudices against the Irish.[92] In attempting to revive memories of the antislavery campaign of earlier decades, Redpath sought to mobilize that former constituency behind a different emancipation campaign. Through these various journalistic activities, Redpath served as an important link between the antebellum and postbellum reform traditions in the United States.[93] Also by his labors Redpath well earned the sobriquet repeatedly quoted in his obituary notices: "The Adopted Irishman."[94]

James Redpath's intimate contacts with Irish Americans led him to a greater interest in the burning post–Civil War labor question. Redpath had first encountered many of the city's Irish American labor leaders when the latter enlisted to support the Irish Land League.[95] Coincidence in the mid and late 1880s placed him in a position to observe and participate in some critical incidents that would shape the direction of the American labor movement for decades to come. Although only a minor actor in these events, Redpath's activities reveal many important obstacles that blocked a productive interaction between middle-class reformers and the working class in these crucial years.

Before the Civil War, Irish immigrants had made up the largest element in New York City's unskilled labor pool, particularly in service and domestic jobs. While many Irish still worked at unskilled jobs in the 1880s, tens of thousands had made their way into skilled trades and a smaller number into the ranks of the professionals and small entrepreneurs. Irish American also held key posts in the city's Roman Catholic hierarchy and Tammany Hall.[96]

In his speaking tours on behalf of the Land League, Redpath became a friend of Terrance V. Powderly, the leader of the Knights of Labor.[97] Affiliated either in trade or mixed assemblies, the Knights represented thousands on the city's first- and second-generation Irish Americans. In addition, thousands more working-class Irish Americans enrolled in the trade unions that would form the American Federation of Labor in 1886. Both types of groups cooperated in the city's loosely federated Central Labor Union.[98] From his editorial chair at *Redpath's Illustrated Weekly*, Redpath could not help but be drawn into the rising tide of labor disputes affecting the city.

The first New York City labor dispute that attracted Redpath's personal involvement was a newsdealers' "strike" occurring in fall 1883. Irish Americans were heavily represented in the ranks of the three thousand to four thousand vendors who sold the daily newspapers all over the city. The newsdealers were small businessmen who acted as middlemen making a small profit by buying the papers at bulk and reselling them to customers on the city streets. The St. Louis newspaper publisher Joseph Pulitzer had invaded the New York newspaper scene in early 1883 with his purchase of the *World* and introduced his distinctive brand of sensationalist journalism and outspoken sympathy for immigrants and workers. As *World* sales soared, first the *Times* and then the much larger circulation *Herald* and *Tribune* reduced prices of their issues from three to two cents apiece to undercut the upstart Pulitzer. George Gordon Bennett Jr., the *Herald*'s Paris-based absentee owner, cut the newsdealers' share of sales price down to 1/3 of a cent per copy, when the other papers paid 1/2 cent or better. Bennett's 1883 price cuts practically erased any profit that newsdealers could extract and they protested vociferously.[99]

Redpath had relied on these newsdealers for much of the local circulation of the *Redpath's Weekly*.[100] A combination of his new friendships with Irish

Americans and a calculation of his paper's economic interests led Redpath to take a highly visible role in support of the protest. Redpath addressed a large rally of newsdealers and their supporters at Cooper Union and denounced the *Herald*:

> James Gordon Bennett is the small son of a great father. . . . He has a right to sell his paper for 1 2–3 cents, but he has no right to compel you to do so. I once made a speech in Ireland, where I introduced Boycotting—well, introduce Boycotting right here. Boycott the *Herald*.[101]

The *Herald* reporter at this meeting predictably ridiculed Redpath's speech, calling it "rich with wild and impassioned gesticulation" and full of gratuitous attacks on local politicians.[102] The newsdealers did attempt a boycott but the major dailies, led by the *Herald,* threatened to set up their own street corner distribution system. Bennett ultimately did create almost five hundred newsstands to sell the *Herald* exclusively, but the independent newsdealers held firm and forced him to compromise over profits in summer 1884.[103]

The success of the newsdealers' agitation was just one indication of New York City labor's growing power in the early 1880s. Labor groups had increasing success in economic disputes through employment of boycotts in such trades as hatmaking, shoemaking, typesetting, brewing, and baking. Worker groups learned quickly that boycotts of local shops producing goods for sale in the city could be more effective than strikes in winning concessions on such key issues as wages, hours, or job security. The Bureau of Labor Statistics for New York offered an explanation for the proliferating use of the boycott, "the strike is negotiation, the boycott is action."[104] These boycotts had two focuses. Union sympathizers were encouraged not to buy the goods produced by companies whose workers were on strike. The Irish roots of the boycott, however, were more apparent in its form, described by Knights of Labor officer Patrick Doody as "almost driving and starving a man to death, driving him out of the world, extermination."[105] To carry this out, blacklists were created and distributed giving the names of those not adhering to the strikes.

The hostile reaction of businessmen and government officials alike to the boycotts produced a series of arrests and unfavorable court decisions in 1886.[106] By means of questionable interpretatios of the New York penal code, the police arrested hundreds of boycotters and labor leaders for a variety of crimes, most commonly conspiracy, coercion, and extortion. Bitterly opposed to organized labor, judges generally found in favor of the prosecution.[107]

Redpath's personal associations with Irish-American labor leaders drew him into involvement with the Central Labor Union's boycotting campaign. Among the boycotts sanctioned by the Central Labor Union in 1886 was one against the beer garden owned by George Theiss on Fourteenth Street in Manhattan. Both musicians and waiters had protested that Theiss paid employees less than the prevailing union wage scale. The beer garden was picketed and the Central Labor Union distributed leaflets in the neighborhood calling for a boycott. The boycott soon expanded to the George Ehert Brewery that supplied Theiss and then to other taverns serving Ehert's beer. Ehert quickly began to pressure Theiss to settle and the beer garden operator capitulated by hiring only union men and paying a thousand dollars to the Central Labor Union marked for the "expenses of the boycott." Theiss subsequently went to the district attorney and a hastily conducted trial found the boycott leaders guilty of "extortion and unlawful combination" and sent five of them to Sing Sing penitentiary for terms up to four years.[108]

The quick conviction of the boycotters was an indication of growing middle-class fear of labor assertiveness. Realizing that the Theiss decision created a legal precedent that was quickly being followed by judges in other boycotting cases, the Central Labor Union formed a special committee to draft an appeal to New York governor David B. Hill to pardon the convicted boycotters. Redpath was appointed to head this five-member committee that also included Roman Catholic priest Edward McGlynn.[109]

Redpath, McGlynn, and the other committee members prepared a lengthy appeal, documenting the facts of the case, and arguing against the legality of the boycotters' conviction. The appeal asserted that the boycotters believed "they were doing a perfectly legal act." It also noted that there had been no force used against Theiss or nonunion men during the boycott. Finally the appeal denied that the thousand dollars had been extorted from Theiss but was only his "equitable share of the expenses actually incurred as [the boycotters] claimed, by reasons of his acts." The appeal concluded with the statement:

> The committee earnestly desire that their labors may help to restore harmony between those who have been temporarily alienated, and they join with General Master Workman Powderly in the hope that future differences between employers and employed may be settled by other agencies than strikes, lock outs or boycotts, and that conciliation and arbitration adapted to the needs and intelligence of American citizens.[110]

Governor Hill responded favorably to this appeal and commuted the sentences of all of the boycotters on the grounds that they did not knowingly disobey any law. Hill's ruling, however, stated that these commutations did not absolve any future boycotters from prosecution and that he would not repeat such clemency.[111] Hill's action signaled a renewed wave of prosecutions of boycotters. The legal setbacks that boycotting Irish Americans workers encountered in New York City in 1886 helped set the stage for a political rebellion.

The unprecedented militancy of Irish American labor threatened traditional voting alignments in the city. Long a bastion of "machine politics,"

New York City's political "bosses" had facilitated the rapid and often illegal naturalization of tens of thousands of Irish immigrant voters in the 1850s and 1860s. In return for their quick incorporation into the city's political community, Irish American voters had traditionally given their support to the Democratic Party. With their rapidly expanding numbers, the Irish began to play an increasingly influential role inside the party's Tammany Hall political machine after the Civil War, culminating in the selection of "Honest John" Kelly as Tammany leader in 1872.[112]

Generally having arrived in the middle class, Irish American political leaders proved more conservative than their working-class counterparts on labor, fiscal, and most social issues. In large part, this was due to the needs of the political "machine" to build a broad-based electoral coalition as well as to placate the city's business community. Because most political efforts to "reform" New York City politics in this era carried a strongly nativist tinge, Tammany leaders also developed strong ties to the hierarchy of the city's Roman Catholic Church, especially its new archbishop Michael Corrigan, who shared their middle-class Irish American background.[113]

In August 1886, working-class anger over the repressive treatment of boycotters led 402 representatives of Knights' assemblies, trade unions, socialists, and middle-class reformers to meet and found the "Independent Labor Party of New York and vicinity." In the early fall, committees met to draft a platform while potential candidates were sounded out for running in the city's November election. On 23 September, the official nominating convention of the infant party listened to a rousing keynote address from Father McGlynn and then selected economic reformer Henry George as its mayoral candidate.[114]

Originally a San Francisco newspaperman, George had come to national attention on account of his analysis of the causes of the cyclical depressions in the U.S. economy. George blamed the periodic hard times on increasing concentration of wealth, and especially of land. He preached that if land alone were taxed, on the basis of whether the land was used or not, the resultant spur to economic productivity would solve the problem of poverty. This "single-tax" theory was put forward in many newspaper articles and pamphlets and a best-selling book entitled *Poverty and Progress*.[115]

Along with many other New York City middle-class reformers, Redpath had embraced George's single-tax crusade in the mid 1880s. Several editorials in his *Weekly* endorsed portions of George's program. In December 1884, Redpath had drawn applause from reform and labor circles for a lecture, entitled "The People to the Front," which revealed considerable influence of George's economic theories. Redpath denounced "all monopolies—in land, in transportation, in finance, in taxation, that is, in the earth itself, in the products of the earth, in the transfer of those products, and in the agencies of exchange." Redpath likened the "Money Power" to the "Slave Power" of old and declared that the "Slaveholders have been succeeded by the

Bondholders: Legree by Shylock; Gen. Lee by Vanderbilt; Stonewall Jackson by Jay Gould." He called on labor to lead a political uprising to destroy the power of those economic monopolies and their political tools, the Republican and Democratic parties. He reminded his audience that "as long as workingmen wear the collars of party serfs, just so long will they be robbed by the monopolies that use their party as their constable!"[116]

A coalition composed of trade unionists, Knights, socialists, and middle-class reformers rapidly mobilized behind George. For example, the local Knights of Labor, led by James E. Quinn, organized parades and public meetings for George.[117] The mainly Irish American leadership of the city's trade unions likewise had embraced George in the early 1880s as a fellow Land League supporter and now welcomed him as a champion of their own cause. Non–Irish trade union leaders such as Samuel Gompers also addressed almost daily labor meetings and helped to organize Henry George clubs in working-class precincts.[118] Daniel DeLeon brought his small Socialist Labor Party into the coalition.[119] Patrick Ford's *Irish World* broke with Tammany and Catholic hierarchy and gave George a cautious editorial endorsement.[120] Reform-minded clergymen such as McGlynn, Father Michael J. Phelan, the twenty-five-year-old Reverend Walter Rauschenbusch of the Second German Baptist Church in New York, and the Reverend John W. Kramer of St. John's Episcopal Church, were prominent speakers at George rallies.[121] Scorned by nearly all the press, the campaign could afford to launch its own daily newspaper, the *Leader*. It was edited by Louis J. Post, like Redpath, a journalist and former carpetbagger in South Carolina.[122]

Redpath played a prominent role in George's campaign. He was one of the signers of the call for the mass meeting at Cooper Union Hall on 5 October to ratify George's nomination for mayor by the Independent Labor Party.[123] George used that rally attended by more than eight thousand partisans to accept the nomination formally. At the same meeting, it was announced that Redpath would be part of a ten-member committee charged with coordinating middle-class support for the Central Labor Union's George campaign.[124] Redpath also was active in a hastily formed Henry George Newspaper Men's Political Club and spoke at several of their outdoor rallies, including one on the steps of the Federal Treasury Building on Wall Street.[125] At another mass meeting, Redpath read a letter he had solicited from his friend and former lecturing client Robert Ingersoll endorsing the George candidacy.[126] On 18 October, Redpath addressed a Chickering Hall rally of more than a thousand people. One paper reported that

> Mr. Redpath predicted that Henry George would first be Mayor and two years hence would be President. This sentiment put the house in a roar of applause. He also denounced the police of this city, saying that they were second in infamy to the loyal constabulary of Ireland, and were made so by Tammany and the County Democracy.[127]

Redpath was in the midst of that speech when he was interrupted by a loud prolonged ovation for George as the latter entered the hall. A *New York Sun* reporter joked at Redpath's dilemma: "Mr. Redpath was soaring on a flight of eloquence, and the applause which greeted the popular hero quite took the wind from the pinions of Redpath. For a minute there he hung suspended in the air, as it were, and then, circling rapidly, flopped down upon the stage."[128]

John Swinton, a fellow Scot immigrant who had worked for both the *New York Times* and *Sun* before founding his own prolabor weekly newspaper in 1884, relates a humorous anecdote about Redpath's activities in the George campaign. McGlynn and a number of other ministers had just addressed the audience at an October rally, and Swinton, in the chair, jokingly introduced the next speaker as "the Rev. James Redpath." Almost immediately Redpath began receiving letters addressed to him with that title. After a couple of months, Redpath wrote Swinton, warning "if this keeps up, you may expect a challenge, and as for weapons you can have the choice of earthquakes or tidal waves." Swinton, who had already printed many favorable remarks about Redpath, published a notice to his readers assuring them of Redpath's lay status and praising the "shining genius" of the "Only Naturalized Irishman."[129]

The issue of religion proved no laughing matter in the closing weeks of George's mayoral campaign. A week before the election, the vicar-general of the New York City Roman Catholic diocese declared that George's "principles, logically carried out, would prove the ruin of the workingmen he professes to befriend."[130] Tammany representatives sent out fliers in Irish neighborhoods claiming that a vote for George would be against the church's wishes. The George campaign tried to counter this attack on George. At a late October rally, for example, Redpath told the crowd that he vouched for George "being a good friend of Ireland. He had the approval of such men as Archbishop Cooke, Bishop Nulty, Michael Davitt and Patrick Ford."[131] Such efforts, however, came too late to prevent serious damage to the labor candidacy.

George finished second in the race, garnering sixty-seven thousand votes to ninety thousand for Democrat Abram S. Hewitt and sixty thousand for Republican Theodore Roosevelt. George had drawn well among Irish Americans, taking about half of them away from their traditional Democratic allegiance.[132]

Just days after the election, George called a mass meeting of his supporters at the Cooper Union. Hoping to capitalize on the energy still circulating from the campaign, George sought to create a permanent political party. Acting without consultation of his labor or socialist allies, George sought to mold the new party around his land reform program. Redpath was one of the featured speakers at the postelection evening meeting. An executive committee of three, Father McGlynn, labor leader John MacMackin, and Redpath were chosen to organize a permanent political organization to be named the Progressive Democracy.[133] The committee set up offices in the Cooper Union and sent out numerous tracts across the nation. The three men also set about organizing "Land and Labor Clubs," to advance George's single tax doctrines. Critics noted that while membership in such clubs was mainly working class, leadership came from middle-class "intellectuals."[134]

Under pressure from the Central Labor Union, the new party finally adopted the name United Labor Party. As the George faction struggled with other groups for control of the new party, bickering and factionalism replaced the enthusiasm and cohesion of the campaign. In August 1887, George's backers purged the United Labor Party of all members of the Socialist Labor Party. Middle-class George followers such as Redpath and Father McGlynn supported this move that ironically pitted Redpath against his old Kansas free-state colleague, Richard Hinton, now a committed socialist journalist.[135]

The United Labor Party also rapidly lost support from the city's labor leaders. At the same time as George quarreled publicly with the city Roman Catholic archbishop Michael Corrigan, Knights of Labor leader Powderly sought a rapprochement with the church hierarchy by separating his group from the new party. Trade union leaders like Gompers also lost patience with George's single-minded focus on land reform.[136] As a consequence of heavy defections from labor, the United Labor Party received only seventy-two thousand votes statewide in the fall 1887 election, when it ran George for secretary of state. Redpath remained loyal to the new organization until 1888 when George endorsed Democrat Grover Cleveland for president.[137]

Undaunted by growing dissension in the George movement, McGlynn delivered an address in March 1887, entitled "The Cross of the New Crusade," calling for Social Christianity. Along with other United Labor Party supporters, McGlynn then founded the Anti-Poverty Society to promote such causes as child labor and antimonopoly laws. The society declared its object

> to spread by such peaceable and lawful means as may be found most desirable and efficient, a knowledge of the truth that God has ample provision for the need of all men during their residence upon earth, and that involuntary poverty is the result of the human laws that allow individuals to claim as private property that which the Creator had provided for the use of all.[138]

McGlynn was chosen president and George vice president of the new society. Meetings were held on Sunday evenings at the Academy of Music near Union Square. Beside McGlynn, the Reverend Hugh O. Pentecost from Newark's Belleville Avenue Congregationalist Church spoke regularly, giving the meetings a strong religiously tone. The group was open to members of all religious faiths, however, and soon established several chapters in New York and others in nearby cities. Addresses by George or McGlynn often filled the twenty-seven-hundred-seat academy to capacity, and the overflow was directed to nearby Irving or Steinway halls where speakers rotated among the audiences. The choir of McGlynn's St. Stephen's Church frequently entertained.[139] The Anti-Poverty Society strove to expose the deteriorating conditions of urban ethnic neighborhoods and advocated reforms such as stringent child labor laws.

In late February 1887, Henry George appeared at the weekly society meeting to ask permission of the audience to carry its greetings to Redpath, who he described as a dying man. George proceeded to praise Redpath as "a man who devoted his younger years to the freedom of the black man," did "good work for the Irish cause," and had been a founder of the Anti-Poverty movement.[140] Only a few weeks later, the Georgite New York *Standard* reported Redpath's "almost miraculous recovery . . . due to the skill and care of Dr. S. W. Dana." Few details survive on Redpath's illness but apparently he had suffered a mild stroke. Friends visited the recovering reformer at his home on Eighty-sixth Street in the "Hell Gate" neighborhood near the East River and opposite today's Roosevelt Island, then known as Blackwell's Island. Carrie Chorpenning faithfully nursed Redpath through this period.[141]

When the pope, at Corrigan's urging, excommunicated McGlynn in July 1887, the Anti-Poverty Society staged a protest parade and rally attended by approximately twenty-five-thousand, mainly Irish American workers.[142] McGlynn defended his political activism in public meetings of the Anti-Poverty Society where the recovering Redpath was regularly accorded a prominent seat on the dais.[143] To squash support for McGlynn among the Catholic clergy and laity, Corrigan declared attendance at Anti-Poverty Society meetings sinful.[144] The Catholic hierarchy's strong condemnation of McGlynn eventually caused cautious labor leaders such as Powderly of the Knights to drop their support for the defrocked priest rather than risk his organization's attempt at a rapprochement with the Roman Catholic Church.[145]

The dispute between Powderly and the Anti-Poverty Society was another indication of the steady disintegration of the labor-reform coalition in city politics. The Anti-Poverty Society faithfully backed George's 1887 campaign for New York secretary of state. George's disappointing showing in that election coupled with Archbishop Corrigan's anathema, however, caused a drop-off in membership in and contributions to the Anti-Poverty Society. In 1888, George endorsed Grover Cleveland's reelection as president, largely on account of the Democrat's opposition to trade protectionism. McGlynn denounced him for defecting to the Democrats the following year.[146] Redpath had abandoned his support for free trade after visiting Ireland earlier in the decade. He sided with McGlynn and was elected the vice president of the Anti-Poverty Society to replace George. A second minor stroke in January

1888, however, curtailed Redpath's political activities. His left side remained somewhat stiff and he never fully recovered his skills on the podium.[147] The break with George, added to the disputes with the Catholic Church and the Knights, caused attendance to dwindle further at Anti-Poverty Society meetings. Although the Anti-Poverty Society faded from public sight by the decade's end, Redpath and McGlynn remained fast friends.

The decline of the Anti-Poverty Society was just a sign that the great labor insurgency of the mid 1880s was rapidly receding. Redpath had been an active participant in the unprecedented effort to forge an alliance among trade unionists, socialists, and middle-class reformers to contest the growing political and economic power of American capitalism. Henry George's New York City mayoral campaign was only the most publicized of more than two hundred independent "labor" political candidacies from 1885–87. Redpath's compromised health in 1887 and 1888 greatly reduced his participation in the unfortunate collapse of that effort. His career was emblematic of the tragic impact of factionalism on that once powerful coalition as Redpath parted company with one-time allies first in the trade unions, then the socialists, then the Knights of Labor, and finally the middle-class followers of Henry George. Only his alliance with the social radicalism of Father McGlynn and his small band of Irish American supporters survived. Unable to forge lasting partnerships with working-class organizations, Redpath and his Anti-Poverty Society allies are best viewed as the immediate ancestors to the urban middle-class reformist vision that would be revived by the Progressive Movement at the turn of the century.[148]

It was during his recovery from his strokes that Redpath married his former landlady Carrie Chorpenning. She had divorced her husband and moved to New York to be with Redpath at about the time he founded the *Illustrated Weekly*. The wedding was performed by the Reverend Reginald Starr, an assistant minister at St. Thomas Episcopal Church, at the house of Frederick Weaverson. Only a few personal friends of the bride and groom attended. The couple made no announcement of the wedding and did not take a honeymoon. When the press learned of the marriage, Redpath was reported as declaring that "he had no desire to keep the fact of the wedding a secret, but his object was not to parade his personal affairs before the public."[149] The *New York Herald* described the new bride as "a lady of middle age, highly talented and attractive."[150]

From 1880 to the time of his strokes, Redpath had been near the center of a number of major reform movements. His most important role in these movements was to act as a bridge between the labor and immigrant radicals and the middle-class, Protestant reform community in the Northeast. Redpath's critique of the Irish tenant system was purposely phrased in a language to appeal to the generation of reformers raised on abolitionist rhetoric and still concerned with the fate of the black sharecroppers. His pointed analogy between the problems of the Irish and of the blacks helped many reformers overcome their prejudices against the "Papists." Redpath also called on the native middle-class reformers to reexamine their attitudes toward the heavily Irish American working class. He encouraged them to accept the need for both active government intervention and a trade union movement as essential for the solution of such problems as poverty, immigration, and industrial monopoly. Redpath's talents as a propagandist had propelled him once again into the leading ranks of American reformers.

10 *Jefferson Davis's Ghostwriter*

During the same period that Redpath was heavily involved in supporting Henry George and then the American Anti-Poverty Society, he derived his livelihood from his old pursuit of journalism. Soon after he suspended *Redpath's Weekly*, Redpath was at work preparing a series of interviews with "Men of Note" such as George Washington Cable to sell to the press.[1] In June 1885, Redpath found employment as managing editor of the *North American Review*. Under the editorship of James Russell Lowell in the 1860s and of Henry Adams (aided by a young Henry Cabot Lodge) in the 1870s, that venerable periodical had recovered much of its original reputation as the nation's premier intellectual periodical. Each quarterly issue contained lengthy articles on history, literature, and science, but the *Review's* low circulation of around a thousand copies meant annual deficits for its publisher, the Boston firm of James R. Osgood and Company. In October 1876, Osgood apparently forced the resignation of Adams and Lodge, after the latter editors had written an article for the *Review* endorsing support by independent voters for the presidential candidacy of Democrat Samuel Tilden.[2]

Very soon after, Osgood sold the *Review* to Allen Thorndike Rice, the twenty-three-year-old heir to a textile fortune. Rice moved the *North American Review's* editorial offices from Boston to New York and changed its format from that of a literary quarterly to a monthly covering an eclectic range of topics. His guiding plan for resuscitating the *Review* was to make it "the mouthpiece of both sides of every question."[3] He quickly attracted a wide readership by hiring "men of action" rather than journalists to advocate the newest positions in politics, sciences, and the arts.[4] In little more than a decade, Rice had elevated the *Review's* circulation to more than fifteen thousand copies per issue and derived an annual profit of more than fifty thousand dollars from the periodical.[5]

By the mid 1880s, Rice had tired of the day-to-day editorial operations of the *Review*.[6] Rice allowed Redpath as his managing editor broad powers in soliciting materials for the *Review* and for a North American Review "syndicate." The latter sold press-ready articles, book reviews, and literary pieces to subscribing newspapers, which included some major dailies such as the *New York Sun*, the *New York Tribune*, the *Philadelphia Times*, and the *Philadelphia Press*, as well as many smaller enterprises. The syndicate offered those papers articles by famous writers who individually they could not have afforded.[7]

Redpath recruited authors from among his many friends in reform circles for the *Review* and its syndicate. They addressed the pressing social issues of the late nineteenth century such as women's suffrage, immigration, corporate monopoly, and racial discrimination. Frederick Douglass, Walt Whitman, Robert G. Ingersoll, John Boyle O'Reilly, Father Edward McGlynn, Henry George, David R. Locke, Thomas A. Edison, Benjamin F. Butler, George Washington Cable, and even Marion Harland, his infatuation from the early days of his first Southern travels, all wrote one or more articles for the *Review* during Redpath's tenure.[8] Redpath devoted long hours to recruiting authors for the *Review* and had to apologize to old friend John Devoy that he was "so frightfully overworked" by the *Review* that he had "neither time nor strength" to assist the Irish National League in early 1886.[9]

One interesting project that Redpath championed for *Review* readers was a series of articles on education for the southern freedpeople, a subject of much concern for him over the past two decades. Redpath encouraged James R. Gilmore to write an essay entitled "The Folly of Trying to Make Classical Scholars of the Negroes," saying in a private letter that he agreed with its premise, having "seen the bad results of it."[10] Finally, Redpath successfully recruited a article by Edward Kirke, entitled "How Shall the Negro Be Educated?" published in November 1886, that advocated industrial education as the best hope to make the freedman "a good citizen."[11]

Redpath also made the acquaintance of younger writers such as John Dimitry, who he managed to get published in the *Review* despite Rice's preference for established reputations. In September 1887, Dimitry sent Redpath a copy of his new book with thanks for literary advice. Redpath replied that it was a "pleasure & a privilege to aid men of genius in any way."[12]

Besides soliciting materials for the *Review* and its syndicate, Redpath worked with authors to edit those submissions into publishable condition. Redpath discovered that authors supplied articles of excessive length and that he had to endure some writers' wrath when attempting to pare them down. Redpath explained to an author that he had rejected a piece for "the reason of the apothecary—'my poverty' (of space) 'and not my willing consent.'"[13] In November 1886, Rice sold his syndicate to Whitelaw Reid of the *New York Tribune*, making Redpath's editorial job somewhat easier as he could focus exclusively on the *Review*.[14]

One of Rice's special publishing projects was an anthology of recollections of Abraham Lincoln by distinguished figures. Redpath collected sketches on Lincoln from a number of his old acquaintances from the abolitionist as well as lyceum days.[15] In 1885, Rice hoped to get permission to publish an excerpt from the deceased Ulysses S. Grant's diary, being edited by his son Frederick with Mark Twain's assistance. The younger Grant accepted a payment from Rice for the excerpt, but Twain tried to stop publication fearing it would harm the sales of the diary. Rice sent Redpath to Hartford to negotiate with Twain.

Redpath and Twain had remained friends since their association in the heyday of the lyceum in the early 1870s. In May 1885, Twain requested that Redpath come to Hartford to assist him in writing his autobiography. Twain had recently assisted Frederick Grant in arranging stenographic and editorial assistance in completing the memoirs of Ulysses S. Grant, his father. The general's painful experiences weighed heavily on Twain, and he wanted to complete his own work quickly. Twain realized the controversial nature of his role as publisher of Grant's highly profitable memoirs, and so went to great pains to keep records of that affair that he could use as self-vindication.[16]

Redpath wrote Twain back: "About the auto. When I do work by the week, I charge $100 a week for the best I can do."[17] Redpath's job was to serve as a stenographer but also to act as amanuensis by jogging Twain's memory with pertinent questions. Twain had planned to devote most of the summer to this project but managed to complete only a few chapters before he found the dictation procedure too foreign and abandoned the project.[18]

Twain later recalled that while he and Redpath were working: "Several 'toppy' telegrams arrived from Rice . . . one of them ordering Redpath 'not to concede too much.'"[19] Redpath, in fact, took his old friend's side and wired Rice back that publication of the Lincoln collection should be halted. Rice, however, pressured Fred Grant into asking Twain as "a personal favor" to drop his objections to publishing an excerpt of his father's diary. Finally Twain relented.

Redpath also gave longtime friend Walt Whitman unimpeded access to the *Review*'s columns to comment on social as well as literary trends. Redpath initially recruited Whitman to write for Rice's Lincoln series and a follow-up Civil War series. Redpath described Rice's Lincoln series to Whitman:

> He proposes to get every man of note now living who ever met Lincoln to write down in plain words and as accurately as human memory will record, just what Lincoln did; just how Lincoln looked; just what impression Lincoln made on him. However, he does not want the last clause (that is to say, the impression) recorded by anybody but only names that will go down in history. . . . Now, my dear Walt Whitman, won't you go to work at once because Rice is chained lightning in a dress suit and damned impatient.[20]

Whitman submitted a sketch for the Lincoln series and numerous articles for Rice's syndicate. Redpath informally acted as Whitman's agent with Rice syndicate and got him unusually high fees. Whitman wrote back thanking Redpath for his "services and affectionate good will."[21] Whitman similarly confided in his friend John Burroughs that "James Redpath, who manages things for A T R, has been very good to me—persistently so."[22]

Several years later in August 1888, when Horace Traubel was drawing out reminiscences from Whitman, the latter recalled: "Redpath was always partial to me—even went out of his way to curl my hair. He jumped in several times and saved me from bankruptcy—steered things my way that might have gone anywhere: interceded for me with Rice for instance, often, I suspect, at some cost to himself."[23]

Whitman also provided Traubel the following:

psychology of dear Jim Redpath, who was a friend among friends. Redpath said to me once when he was here: "Walt, if you have any money scrapes I want to help you out of 'em." This he did—did it again and again. Redpath was one of your radical crowd—he was way out and beyond in all his ideas—stalwart, searching—a sort of pioneer, going on and on, always in advance. Some men stay in the rear with the beef and beans but that was not Redpath's style.[24]

Redpath himself did relatively little writing for the *North American Review.* One important contribution was a brief essay advocating his employer's plan to introduce the secret, or "Australian," ballot to U.S. elections. Redpath noted that the current "system is nominally secret; but, practically, it is open." He then described ways that powerful interests could coerce voters. Endorsing the secret ballot, Redpath concluded that "we have no right to complain of the evils wrought by corrupt men and bad laws until we so perfect our political machinery that the will of the people shall be truthfully registered."[25] Redpath also penned a series of three "letters to the editor," signed with his former abolitionist pen name John Ball Jr., advocating protectionism over free trade.[26]

Another of Redpath's undertakings as managing editor of the *North American Review* was the recruitment of Jefferson Davis to write articles about the history of the Civil War. The unexpected friendship that developed between the former militant abolitionist and former Confederate president in the late 1880s and early 1890s is possibly the single most uncharacteristic act of Redpath's life. Explaining Redpath's action sheds light on broader intellectual trends at work in the nation at the end of the nineteenth century.

After a distinguished political career as a congressman, senator, governor, and secretary of war, Davis had been elected president of the seceding southern Confederacy in spring 1861. During the next four years, his leadership was the center of a storm of controversy, especially regarding his choice of generals to lead the main Confederate armies. After the fall of Richmond in

April 1865, Davis was captured by Union forces and spent the next two years in military prisons. Finally released on bond, ironically provided mainly by the John Brown backer Gerrit Smith, he was never brought to trial. During the next decade, Davis tried and failed at a number of business enterprises. In the late 1870s, he settled at Beauvoir, a Gulf Coast estate, given him by an admirer. There he prepared his massive two-volume, *The Rise and Fall of the Confederate Government,* which defended his presidential performance and mercilessly flayed his wartime opponents and postwar critics, especially former generals Joseph E. Johnston and P. G. T. Beauregard. Historian David Blight has described the 1,279 page tome as "what may be the longest and most self-righteous legal brief on behalf of a failed political movement ever done by an American."[27] Although Davis's book helped set the unapologetic tone for subsequent "Lost Cause" literature, it did not sell well. Davis remained financially strapped for his remaining years and looked to journalism as a way to remain solvent.

Redpath not only developed a close personal relationship with Jefferson Davis but also with Davis's wife and youngest daughter, both named Varina. Varina Anne Howell Davis was Davis's second wife, marrying him in 1845, ten years after the death of his first spouse. Varina was the mother of four children but still managed to reign as one of Washington's social leaders, especially during her husband's time heading the War Department under President Franklin Pierce. In Richmond, during the Civil War, Varina Davis was accused of championing the careers of her political and military favorites, particularly Judah P. Benjamin. Suffering from deep depression and hypochondria after the war, Varina lived apart from Jefferson for long periods, until the family reunited at Beauvoir in the late 1870s.[28]

The younger Varina Davis, generally known by her nickname "Winnie," had been born in Richmond in the waning months of the Confederacy. Educated mainly in Europe, she displayed a precocious love for literature and history. Frequently traveling across the South with her father in the 1880s, Winnie was introduced to a Georgia audience as the "Daughter of the Confederacy," a title that followed her for the remainder of her life. Forbidden by her mother from marrying a New York lawyer, she never married. Winnie instead channeled her energies into writing for magazines and later produced a biography of Irish nationalist Robert Emmet and two novels.[29]

Redpath had first met Jefferson Davis in September 1875 when he had unsuccessfully attempted to recruit the older man as a speaker for his lyceum bureau. The two men had talked amicably about Redpath's proposal while both were passengers on a train from Memphis to St. Louis.[30] Davis never became one of Redpath's lecturers and there is no surviving evidence of contact between the two men during the following decade.

Prior to Redpath's employment at the *North American Review,* Rice had encouraged Davis to prepare an article on Indian affairs during his antebellum term in the War Department. In September 1886, Redpath wrote

Jefferson Davis about the status of that article. In this initial correspondence, Redpath also noted that the *Review* was planning to publish an article by former Confederate general Joseph Johnston critical of Davis's management of the war in the western theater. Redpath inquired if Davis would be interested in preparing some form of rebuttal to Johnston's piece. Davis responded that he would quickly finish and submit the piece on the Indians, but ignored the suggestion that he enter into a public dispute with Johnston. In their exchanges of letters at this time, Redpath passed along copyediting suggestions to Davis's daughter, Winnie, who had submitted an unwieldy magazine piece on Irish history.[31]

This renewed contact between Redpath and Davis made a favorable impression on the old Confederate. In February 1888, Davis wrote Redpath to say that he had read press notices of the latter's recent ill-health, what was most likely a mild stroke. Davis reported that "my Daughter Miss Varina [that is Winnie] mindful of your courteous consideration feels sensibly your affliction and as my wife and myself is anxious to know how you are."[32]

In the summer of 1888, Redpath traveled to Davis's home in Beauvoir, Mississippi, to negotiate with Davis for a number of literary projects for the *Review*. Redpath first sought an article on the notorious Andersonville Prison. He also wanted a sketch of Robert E. Lee. At first hesitant to be drawn into the certain controversy such topics would provoke, Davis succumbed to a combination of Redpath's charm and persistence and the offer of a badly needed $250 for the Lee essay.[33] Redpath assured Davis that the $250 was much above the average paid for such articles and confided that "there are so many 'bigger men than Gen Grant' in the world who expect General's fees that it is sometimes embarrassing for an Editor to deal with them!"[34]

Redpath stayed at the Davis home for several weeks. The visit had not been without tension, as Varina Davis later recalled Redpath's "graceful silence . . . when we disagreed about your horrid 'puritan saint' [John Brown]."[35] During this visit, Davis confided in Redpath that he desired that some historian write a first-rate short history of the Confederacy, defending the cause of the South. Redpath persuaded Davis that only the former president could do justice to the task and recommended that he prepare an abridged version of his earlier mammoth work. Before returning northward in late August, Redpath had gotten Davis started on that short history as well as three articles for the *North American Review*.[36]

Another thing Redpath accomplished on this visit was to develop a friendship with Davis's wife Varina. After leaving Beauvoir, he had traveled on to New Orleans and then wrote back to the Davises before returning to New York City. Varina Davis wrote back, saying "your love was reverently delivered to [Mr. Davis], and warmly welcomed. Please accept our affectionate acknowledgments, and reciprocation to you." Varina also expressed the hope that Redpath's southern travels had aided his recovery of health and prepared him to return to "the eternal grind" at the *Review*. She wrote that the Davis family "missed you greatly after your departure. We left so much unsaid and unheard that some time we must finish our talk facing the Mississippi sound, with the sunshine filtering through the trees."[37]

In the same letter, Varina Davis wrote Redpath that the article on General Lee already was finished. She related that she had worked with Davis and "insisted upon popularizing the article as much as possible, for I thought it was not a military critique you wanted." The essay avoided controversial questions regarding the performance of Lee or his subordinates, especially the issue of James Longstreet's performance at Gettysburg. Instead, Davis's piece tried to show "the heart of the man through the eyes of one who knew and loved him."[38]

After returning to his editorial desk, Redpath published an article on his "interview" with Davis. He stated that Jefferson Davis was as deferential toward his wife "as if she were presiding at a tournament in the olden time." He judged her "quite as noteworthy a personage as her husband—a woman of large brain and great heart, highly educated, of marvellous insight into character, with the rarest conversational powers, bright, brilliant, witty and sympathetic."[39]

About this time, Redpath received the Lee article from Davis and wrote them of his satisfaction. In her reply, Varina reported "many thanks for the tender way in which your approval of Mr. Davis was spoken in your interview. He deserves all you said but 'apples of gold in pictures of sliver' are rare nowadays." Varina gave Redpath the welcome news that her husband was on the verge of agreeing to write the Andersonville piece. She also expressed "thanks for your kind opinion of me. I *do not* deserve it, but glory in your errors on this score." The letter was signed "Affectionately your friend."[40] About this time, Winnie Davis visited New York City, and Redpath introduced her among literary circles to assist her aspiring writing career.

Redpath took a brief leave from the *Review* from mid January to mid April 1889. He contracted with the Republican morning newspaper, the *New York Press* to arrange a tour of Ireland and send back reports on new developments there. The *Press* promised readers that from Redpath's dispatches they "will learn not only a good deal of the present condition of Ireland but of the hopes and aims of the Irish people for their future."[41] The British press began interviewing him as he disembarked his steamship. He met Michael Davitt and learned that the old quarrels between him and Charles Parnell had been healed.[42] Redpath also met Thomas Sherlock, the former Dublin correspondent of his old *Redpath's Weekly*. In an interview, Sherlock helped Redpath explain to readers the evolution in Irish-British political relations during the 1880s. While the land reform issue still remained important, Irish leaders had shifted the bulk of their efforts to demanding local Home Rule within the British Empire.[43]

Redpath reported that the biggest change in Irish politics was the support that Parnell and other nationalists felt that Home Rule was receiving from English liberals led by William Gladstone. In 1886, Gladstone had caused serious defections from his Liberal Party and lost the prime minister's post when he unsuccessfully introduced Home Rule legislation in Parliament. Nonetheless Gladstone believed his best hope to return the Liberals to power was a parliamentary alliance with Parnell's Irish nationalists followers on a platform pledged to make another attempt to enact Home Rule. Redpath opined that while "it is all right, of course, to give even the devil his due . . . Gladstone, therefore, in strict historical veracity instead of having 'conquered Ireland' by his political strategy, surrendered to the Irish political purpose."[44]

While in Dublin, Redpath interviewed younger Irish political leaders who had "come to the front" since his visits in the early 1880s. He reported on the arrest of one of them by English authorities and assured his readers: "The Irish will hold out—'the devil a fear of that,' as they say here."[45] Redpath predicted that the latest wave of repression would backfire politically and assist the Liberals to topple the Tory government at the next election.[46]

Redpath reported that English authorities sent plain clothes policemen to shadow his movement during a trip to western Ireland to report on the ongoing confrontation between tenants and landlords. He addressed several meetings in the western counties where sympathizers in the audiences often pointed out the police to him. Redpath joked, "It was very amusing this experience, but what a travesty on sane government this is! Imagine our government ordering a half-paralyzed foreigner to be followed by a policeman all across the country. This is an opera bouffe government—with Victoria as La Grande Duchesse."[47]

Redpath returned to New York City in mid April. He was interviewed by the American press and engaged in newspaper disputes with supporters of the English government. In one interview he left a clue that his mind was returning to his earlier literary project: "I fear that as an 'adopted Irishman' I am in the mental condition of some of the friends of my friend Jefferson Davis—I need a little reconstructing."[48]

During his absence, a quarrel had occurred between Davis and Rice about the Andersonville article that Redpath had commissioned. Davis had sent the piece to the *Review* in early 1889, and Rice had paid him the agreed $250 fee. After reading the piece carefully, Rice found that it dealt so harshly with Davis's former enemies that he postponed its publication indefinitely. When Redpath returned to the United States in April, Davis wrote him to discover why the piece had not appeared. He also thanked Redpath for sending materials regarding Ireland to his daughter, Winnie, and invited the journalist to visit his home in Beauvoir again.[49]

In the *Review*'s May issue, over Redpath's protests, Rice published an article by British general Viscount Woolsey, severely critical of Davis's handling of military affairs during the Civil War. Rice did allow Redpath to commission Davis to write a rebuttal and the heated exchange generated much popular comment. His resentment against the Woolsey article, nevertheless, soon drove Redpath to quit the *Review*.[50]

When first word of Redpath's actions reached the Davises, Varina wrote immediately to him:

> We have worried "out of our propriety" for fear you have given up your connexion [*sic*] with Mr. Rice because of the Andersonville prison article in some way. . . . Now do not suffer anything in our behalf. As our old nurse used to say "burnt brandy would not save us." We are in the trough of the sea and the waves will drown us, but we will die game. So there will be no moans made. Yet we both affectionately thank you for your efforts to save us.[51]

By then Redpath had found another employer in the Belford publishing firm.[52] The original Belford company had been founded in Toronto in 1872 by Charles, Robert, and Alexander Belford, three brothers who had immigrated to Canada from Ireland. This firm generated more than a million dollars of business a year by the later 1870s by selling cheap, pirated copies of books by American and British authors. In 1879, Robert Belford began managing a New York City branch of the business on Broadway. In 1888, Robert split from the parent firm and started his own publishing company. Robert soon launched the monthly *Belford's Magazine,* which featured a mix of political essays, literary reviews, and original fiction and poetry. *Belford's* was originally edited by Donn Piatt, long a leading Democratic Party journalist, but a quarrel with Belford over politics led to his firing in June 1889. In Piatt's place, Belford hired the twenty-eight-year-old journalist Alvah Milton Kerr. Kerr had just attracted notoriety for a novelistic exposé of Mormonism and in later years would write three more novels and eventually one of the first movie screenplays for a "western."[53] Belford had been an active supporter of Henry George in the 1886 mayoral campaign and that connection might have led the publisher to select Redpath as a veteran journalist to assist Kerr.[54]

Redpath wrote irregularly for the *Belford's Monthly*. His most substantial contribution was a November 1890 essay on "The Rights of Property," signed by John Ball Jr. The essay shows the influence of Henry George's anti–land monopoly ideology remained strong on Redpath. Redpath argued that a citizen has "right in his property; but the property itself neither has nor confers rights." He condemned the contrary notion because it was being used to support efforts to disenfranchise landless southern freedmen and to protect capitalists from governmental regulations. He compared the latter to the slaveholder's claimed right to own property in man. Redpath's essay concluded: "The slave-holder has gone; the capitalistic despot must go. Equal rights for all; special privileges for none!"[55]

Redpath explained to friends that his job for Belford's was not writing but "reading," that is, finding suitable manuscripts for the periodical.[56] Redpath persuaded his new employer to contract with Davis to prepare an abridged edition of his rambling *History of the Confederacy*. When Redpath wrote Davis about this plan and told him that Belford had volunteered the former abolitionist's editorial assistance, the old Confederate wrote back: "The sooner you come and the longer you stay the better it will please us."[57]

For nearly four months in 1889, Redpath lived in Davis's Mississippi household and assisted him with this editorial task. The *Short History of the Confederate States*, published by the Belford Company the following year, lacked the partisan venom of Davis's earlier work and presented a much more balanced account of the war. Critics generally acknowledged that it displayed genuine literary quality.[58] Redpath also helped Davis to start an autobiography.[59] In an article in *Belford's Monthly*, Redpath wrote a laudatory account of his intimate acquaintance with Davis:

> Before I had been with Mr. Davis three days every preconceived idea of him utterly and forever disappeared. Nobody doubted Mr. Davis's intellectual capacity, but it was not his mental power that most impressed me. It was his goodness, first of all, and then his intellectual integrity. I never saw an old man whose face bore more emphatic evidences of a gentle, refined, and benignant character. He seemed to me the ideal embodiment of "sweetness and light."[60]

The Davises, in turn, enjoyed the lengthy visits of the energetic journalist and appreciated his efforts to help them retain their financial independence through publication ventures. In November 1889, Varina Davis assured her concerned children that Redpath was an "agreeable" houseguest.[61]

Meanwhile Rice had died.[62] Probably at Davis's request, Redpath, who had returned to New York City in October 1889, approached the *Review* to discover its intentions regarding the Andersonville piece. The new editor of the *Review*, Lloyd Bryce, requested that Davis delete the personal attacks in his "Andersonville" essay on his former warden at Fortress Monroe General Nelson Miles.[63] Redpath dismissed Bryce as "a coward" and noted that the editor had "begged me to assure you that he entertained the most friendly sentiments toward you. For myself, I don't value such a kind of friend." Redpath promised Davis that *Belford's Monthly* "stands ready to accept pay for and publish the article without any mutilation."[64]

Redpath also reported that his own "health has been uninterruptedly good." Although he had been away from his wife Caroline for a third of a year, Redpath indicated his impatience to leave New York City and return to the Davis's home: "I was amazed to day to be told that I had been here two weeks already, I have had so many things to do that I have not noticed the rapid passing of the days. But I have done nothing that it was not needful to do in order that my mind might be at ease for the greater work before me at Beauvoir which I am eager to renew."[65]

Encouraged by Redpath's support, Davis refused to make any changes for Bryce and demanded his article back.[66] The old Confederate wrote to Redpath authorizing him to claim the manuscript, explaining that "I would rather not appear as a correspondent of the *North American Review,* as it puts me in company I do not care to keep."[67] Redpath then got the *Belford's Monthly* to reimburse the *Review* for the fee already paid to Davis and publish the essay.[68] Shortly after this incident, the eighty-one-year-old Davis's health deteriorated rapidly as a consequence of exhaustion and overexposure from a wintertime trip to inspect what remained of his plantation lands at Davis Bend.[69]

Unaware of the severity of Davis's condition, Redpath, now acting editor of *Belford's Monthly* due to a dispute over politics between Belford and Piatt in June, wrote him to request a new preface for the Andersonville piece, describing his treatment by the *North American Review.* On 28 November 1889, Varina wrote him back that "Mr. Davis can do absolutely nothing. We sit up with him every night and he is a very ill man. He could not write his name, still less read a proof." She also confided in Redpath that "I do not want the household told, but am miserably anxious."[70]

Davis never recovered and died on 6 December 1889. After his death, Davis's widow and children were burdened with considerable debts.[71] In her grief following her husband's funeral, Varina discovered the draft chapters of the autobiography that her husband had begun at Redpath's urging.[72] These inspired her to write her own memoirs as an extension of her husband's uncompleted one and as a means of defending Davis's historical reputation. For this task, she enlisted the assistance of her daughter Winnie and of New Orleans novelist John Dimitry, son of a longtime family friend.[73]

Varina also invited Redpath to Beauvoir only a few weeks after Davis's death to help her with the memoir. Before his arrival, she wrote him: "I am trying to get through my letters before you come, but am ready to try a beginning whenever you can come here. . . . I am worried *out of heart by many things* but everything is so small beside the great woe that I do not dwell on the small troubles."[74]

The Belford Company authorized Redpath to travel to Beauvoir to assist Varina, and he resided again at the Davis home for several months. He soon tired of the "lonely drudgery" of reading through old pamphlets and newspapers to locate useful materials for Varina and complained to Dimitry that "it is very evident to me that I was never intended to be an historian."[75] Exhausted, Redpath began to write friends for a recommendation of a "young gentleman who is a confident stenographer and typewriter," to come to Beauvoir to relieve him. If no such person could be located, he grieved that "I am in honor bound to stay here until the book is done & to have no personal business but only in the interest of the book."[76]

During this southern sojourn, Redpath befriended Leona Queyrouze (pseudonym Constant Beauvais), a Creole writer, poet, essayist, and musician. He first made her acquaintance when he traveled to New Orleans to try to recruit her brother as a typist for the notes of Varina Davis. The two exchanged notes that spring and summer. Redpath confided to Queyrouze his growing dismay at the commitment he had made to Varina's book: "Duty, for example, is a fetish that robs life of half its joys & yet we rank in our esteem in proportion as they do their duty and sacrifice their pleasure." Redpath mused that if he were younger: "I shd like to start a sect of Earth-lovers whose highest joys wd be to extol our own planet & see in it glories besides which the . . . glories of the New Jerusalem wd seem tame & tawdry."[77] As he did with many of his friends, Redpath solicited Queyrouze to write sketches for *Belford's,* assuring her that "you will one day make a name & gain fame in literature."[78] The possibility that this budding literary relationship might have developed more serious personal dimensions similar to Redpath's earlier one with Sherwood Bonner was cut short by strong disagreements about Davis's published attacks on Queyrouze's favorites, Joseph Johnston and Pierre Beauregard.[79]

Redpath finally returned to New York City and his work for the *Belford's Monthly* in late August 1890.[80] Varina Davis still relied on Redpath to shepherd the two-volume, 1,632-typed-page manuscript through the printing process. This proved no easy task, as other editors at the Belford Company complained that Varina's work was as "big as a dictionary" and "looked like the devil."[81] Concerned that no errors inadvertently enter the book, Varina and Winnie moved to New York City to correct the page proofs of the *Memoirs.* Ultimately this work proved a financial failure for both the author and publisher.[82] The Belford Company went bankrupt the following year and few copies of Varina's *Memoir* ever were distributed. Both women then turned to journalism and managed a respectable livelihood.[83]

Redpath left two lengthy published accounts of his relationship with the Davises. The first was an article in the *Commonwealth Magazine,* later republished as a small pamphlet. The other was his own posthumously published review of Jefferson Davis's book in *Belford's Monthly* (March 1891).

Redpath expressed a deep personal admiration for Jefferson Davis. Aware that his portrayal did not match the ex-Confederate's public image, Redpath declared, "Lest any foreigner should read this article let me say for his benefit that there are two Jefferson Davises in American History." Attempting to rebut the widely circulated characterization of Davis as quarrelsome and vindictive, Redpath described the man he had known as "in his old age at least . . . an incarnation of sweetness and light, to whom cruelty or even intolerance of opinion, was incompatible and indeed impossible."[84] Redpath also praised Davis's "intellectual integrity" and declared him "a man of whom all his countrymen . . . without distinction of creed political, are proud, and proud that he *was* their countrymen."[85]

Redpath even went as far as to declare that Davis had persuaded him that "whether the Southern people were justified in seceding has nothing to do with the fact or the right of secession. . . . I think that the South was justified in seceding, from the same point of view that the North held in suppressing its secession."[86] But instead of announcing his apparent conversion to the Confederate's "Lost Cause," which historian David Blight has documented was gaining hold among many other Northerners in the 1890s on account of sentimentalism toward defeated foes as well as its conservative ideology, the aging abolitionist made clear that he remained steadfast in his antislavery principles. About Jefferson Davis's *Short History*, Redpath declared,

> in reading this last history of the war, I feel inclined to add, thank God it was fought—slavery is abolished; thank God it was well fought—for both sides retired with honor; and thank God it was honorably fought—for its memories carry no hatred or regrets, only the memory of a misunderstanding which had no other solution than a fight to settle it.[87]

The Redpath-Davis friendship is cited by both Davis's and Redpath's biographers and by many other historians as evidence of the trend toward sectional reconciliation as Civil War memories faded.[88] A close reading of Redpath's statements, however, do not lead to the conclusion that the former biographer of John Brown had softened his abolitionist principles even following years of the most intimate contact and ultimately friendship with the family of Jefferson Davis. Although Redpath came to respect the old Confederate's uncompromising position on the doctrine of states' rights, he never made any concession to Davis's views on race. In private correspondence during this period, Redpath often complained about the stifling intellectual conservatism of the Davis household. Redpath began to regret the large amount of his waning energy he was devoting to helping the old Confederates defend their former cause and promised himself "to put the taste of this Conservatism out of my mouth forever. When I get through this work I shall popularize the most radical book on Socialism that I can find."[89] In this one case, at least, there were ideological obstacles to sectional reconciliation that no amount of "southern hospitality" could overcome.

In February 1891, Redpath was struck by a horse-drawn trolley car while hurrying across Park Avenue in New York City to reach the post office. The car ran over Redpath's left arm, the same one left partially paralyzed by his strokes and gave him a deep gash along his head. He did not lose consciousness but was taken to the Chambers Street Hospital by passersby for care. Doctors treated the lacerations and predicted a speedy recovery. The police arrested the trolley operator, William McGowan, for reckless driving but Carrie Redpath refused to make a complaint and so he was released.

When Redpath's condition began to worsen after two days, Carrie had Redpath transferred to the St. Luke's Hospital. Doctors there determined

that Redpath had endured serious internal injuries in the accident. According to press reports, an alarming accumulation of "pus and extravasated
blood" caused by crushed bones and blood vessels was discovered in his left
arm and "blood poisoning" (infection) had set in. Now realizing the gravity
of his injuries, Redpath instructed that if he died that funeral arrangements
be kept simple, and made a request that the song "America" be sung. He
died quietly and without sign of pain in St. Luke's at midmorning on
10 February 1891. At the hour of his passing, Redpath was attended by his
wife, one of her two adult daughters, Mrs. Estelle Sanner, and Dr. Robert
Abbe from the hospital staff.[90]

Funeral services were conducted for Redpath as his home at 242 West
14th Street. An American and an Irish flag were draped over the house's
front door. As Redpath had requested, no flowers were displayed. The
Reverend Robert Collyer, a Unitarian minister, presided and recalled how
Redpath had been instrumental in helping him raise funds for rebuilding
a former church of his in Chicago that had been destroyed by that city's
famous 1872 fire. Father McGlynn gave the principal eulogy and declared
that Redpath was "always a friend of the down-trodden" and always "the
first man to state the cause of the oppressed."[91]

Only a small number of mourners could enter the house for the services,
but delegations from the New York press corps, Irish American associations, the Knights of Labor, the Anti-Poverty Society, the Twilight Club, and
several black organizations all stood silent vigil outside. They stood at attention as pallbearers carried the casket from the house to a hearse waiting
to carry the body to Fresh Pond, Long Island, for cremation.

The attendance of representatives of such varied groups at Redpath's
funeral paid tribute to a forty-year career battling the injustices of his era.
He had enjoyed the celebrity, perversely even the notoriety, and had occasionally profited from his crusading; but Redpath's tireless exertion on
behalf of so many causes bore witness to the sincerity of the man's reform
principles. If he had pronounced a credo, it would have been the description he gave of his response to the Haitian government's demanding ex-
pectations on his labors: "Something like superhuman energy from me &
by Jove they'll have it too."[92] The characteristically frenzied approach that
the diminutive reformer brought to his professional, political, and personal
lives often blurred the boundaries between the three in the eyes of observ-
ers and in some instances even in Redpath's mind. Redpath repeatedly
overextended his resources and sometimes as a result failed badly, but
he nevertheless accomplished considerable good on behalf of many worthy causes. His critics were probably correct that he might have achieved
more, and thereby established a more conventional historical reputation,
if he had focused his energies on one or a few goals, but that prudent approach to life would have risked extinguishing the spark that was James
Redpath.

Notes

Preface and Acknowledgments

1 Helen Beal Woodward, *The Bold Women* (New York: Farrar, Straus, and Young, 1953), 218–19, 235–36; Robert E. Spiller et al., eds., *Literary History of the United States,* 4th ed. (New York: Macmillan, 1974), 800–801; Theodore Morrison, *Chautauqua: A Center for Education, Religion, and the Arts in America* (Chicago: University of Chicago Press, 1974), 176–78; John E. Tapia, *Circuit Chautauqua: From Rural Education to Popular Entertainment in Early Twentieth Century America* (Jefferson, N.C.: McFarland, 1997), 15; Carl Bode, *The American Lyceum: Town Meeting of the Mind* (New York: Oxford University Press, 1956), 200, 249.

2 James C. Malin, *John Brown and the Legend of Fifty-Six,* 2 vols. (Philadelphia: American Philosophical Society, 1942), 1:303–5;

3 Jane H. Pease and William H. Pease, *They Who Would Be Free: Blacks' Search for Freedom, 1830–1861* (New York: Athenaeum, 1974), 68–69, 82–92; James B. Stewart, *Holy Warriors: The Abolitionists and American Slavery* (New York: Hill and Wang, 1976), 125–30 Jeffrey Rossbach, *Ambivalent Conspirators: John Brown, the Secret Six, and a Theory of Slave Violence* (Philadelphia: University of Pennsylvania Press, 1982), 8–9; Jane H. Pease and William H. Pease, "Ends, Means, and Attitudes: Black-White Conflict in the Antislavery Movement," *Civil War History* 18 (June 1972): 117–28. Recent authors arguing for a reappraisal of this negative view include John Stauffer, *The Black Hearts of Men: Radical Abolitionists and the Transformation of Race* (Cambridge, Mass.: Harvard University Press, 2002), in passim; Stanley Harrold, *Subversives: Antislavery Community in Washington, D.C., 1828–1865* (Baton Rouge: Louisiana State University Press, 2003), 24–25, 253–57, and *American Abolitionists* (New York: Pearson Education, 2001), 51–60.

4 David W. Blight, *Race and Reunion: The Civil War in American Memory* (Cambridge, Mass., Cambridge University Press, 2001), 98–138; James M. McPherson, *The Abolitionist Legacy: From Reconstruction to the NAACP* (Princeton, N.J.: Princeton University Press, 1975), 100–102, 112–14.

5 Eric Foner, "Class, Ethnicity and Radicalism in the Gilded Age: The Land League and Irish-America," *Marxist Perspectives* 1 (summer 1978): 6, 45.

6 The best source on this topic remains John L. Thomas, *Alternative America: Henry George, Edward Bellamy, Henry Demarest Lloyd, and the Adversary Tradition* (Cambridge, Mass.: Belknap Press, 1983).

7 Richard J. Hinton, "Pens that Made Kansas Free," *Kansas State Historical Society Collections*, vol. 6 (1897–1900) (Topeka: Kansas State Historical Society, 1900), 379.

8 James B. Pond, *Eccentricities of Genius: Memories of Famous Men and Women of the Platform and Stage* (New York: G. W. Dillingham, ca. 1900), 538.

9 For example, two black abolitionists, Mary Ann Shadd and Martin Delany, made such charges against Redpath's Haitian activities, and these have been echoed by contemporary historian Chris Dixon. Redpath's motivation for supporting John Brown has been called self-serving by such historians as James G. Malin, Tilden Edelstein, and Edward Rehehan. Chris Dixon, *African America and Haiti: Emigration and Black Nationalism in the Nineteenth Century* (Westport, Conn.: Greenwood, 2000), 192, 201; Tilden Edelstein, *Strange Enthusiasm: A Life of Thomas Wentworth Higginson* (New Haven, Conn.: Yale University Press, 1968), 226–27; Edward J. Renehan Jr., *The Secret Six: The True Tale of the Men Who Conspired with John Brown* (New York: Crown, 1995), 221; Malin, *John Brown*, 1:230–31.

10 Charles F. Horner, *The Life of James Redpath and the Development of the Modern Lyceum* (New York: Barse and Hopkins, 1926).

11 John R. McKivigan, "James Redpath and Black Reaction to the Haitian Emigration Bureau," *Mid-America: An Historical Review* 69 (October 1987): 139–53, "John Ball, Jr., alias 'The Roving Editor,' alias James Redpath," *Manuscripts*, part I: 40 (fall 1988): 307–17; part II: 41 (winter 1989): 19–29, "James Redpath, John Brown, and Abolitionist Advocacy of Slave Insurrection," *Civil War History* 37(December 1991): 293–313, and "James Redpath in South Carolina: An Abolitionist Odyssey in the Reconstruction South," in *The Historical Moment: Essays on American Character and Regional Identity*, edited by Randall M. Miller and John R. McKivigan (Westport, Conn.: Greenwood Press, 1994), 188–210. Also James Redpath, *The Roving Editor; or, Talks with Slaves in the Southern States*, edited by John R. McKivigan (University Park: The Pennsylvania State University Press, 1996).

Chapter 1. The Roving Editor

1 F. M. Cowe, *Berwick upon Tweed: A Short Historical Guide* (Berwick upon Tweed, UK: J. D. Cowe, 1984), 1–4, 51–57; *Pigot's Directory for Northumberland . . . (1822)* (n.p., 1822), 573.

2 George F. Black, *The Surnames of Scotland: Their Origin, Meaning, and History* (New York: New York Public Library, 1946), 687; *Dictionary of National Biography*, 21 vols. (London: Cambridge University Press, 1921–22), 16:1178–81, hereinafter cited as *DNB*.

3 *Who Was Who in America with World Notables* (Chicago: A. N. Marquis, 1943–), 4:461.

4 *Pigot's Directory for Northumberland . . . (1822)*, 574; *Robson's Commercial Directory . . . (1841)*, 2 vols. (London, 1841), 2:36, 44; *Portrait and Biographical Record of Kalamazoo, Allegan, and Van Buren Counties, Michigan, etc.* (Chicago: Chapman Bros., 1892), 514–15; Janet D. Crowe, "The Development of Education in Berwick upon Tweed to 1902" (M.Ed. thesis, University of Durham, 1969), 545–46.

5 J. Wilson, *Land of Scott: Or the Tourist Guide to the Vale of the Tweed* (n.p., n.d.), 32; Frederick Sheldon, *History of Berwick upon Tweed* (n.p., 1849), 309–11; Crowe, "Development of Education in Berwick upon Tweed," 543–56.

6 "Burgess Roll of the Burgesses of the Municipal Borough of Berwick on Tweed," 1835, 1836, 1837, 1838, Berwick Public Records Office; *Pigot's Directory for Northumberland . . . (1834)* (n.p., 1834), 571.

7 Berwick upon Parish Marriage Register, EP 38/10.

8 *Pigot's Directory . . . (1834)*, 573.

9 "Register of Baptism Belonging to the Congregation of Protestant Dissenters that meets in Golden Square, Berwick-upon-Tweed., 1771–1837," Berwick Public Records Office, 353.

10 Charles F. Horner, *The Life of James Redpath and the Development of the Modern Lyceum* (New York: Barse and Hopkins, 1926), 7.

11 1841 British Census, Spittal, British Museum 25: 12, 13.

12 Only one mile from Berwick, the village of Spittal had a distinct character. Located at the mouth of the Tweed River on its south shore, Spittal fishermen had taken salmon and herring from local waters since the thirteenth century. By the 1840s, the village was attracting numerous visitors to its mineral spas and its wide sandy beach. A large iron foundry also began operation in Spittal in 1838. The combined population of Spittal and the adjacent village of Tweedmouth numbered a little over four thousand in 1841. *Robson's Commercial Directory . . . (1841)*, 32; Cowe, *Berwick upon Tweed*, 54–57; Crowe, "Development of Education in Berwick upon Tweed," 419, 426; *Robson's Commercial Directory . . . (1841)* (London, 1841), 2:44; Francis White and Co., *General Directory* (n.p., 1847), 722.

13 The British and Foreign Society schools were supported through a combination of the subscriptions of students' parents and grants from the society. Traveling agents ensured the quality of instruction met society standards. G. F. Bartle, "The Agents and Inspectors of the British and Foreign School Society, 1826–1884," *Bulletin of the History of Education Society* (1984): 19–30.

14 Crowe, "Development of Education in Berwick upon Tweed," 419–26; Wilson, *Land of Scott*, 47.

15 *New York Herald*, 11 February 1891; Helen Beal Woodward, *The Bold Women* (New York: Farrar, Straus and Young, 1953), 218–19; Horner, *James Redpath*, 10–12.

16 White, *General Directory . . . (1847)*, 727; Horner, *James Redpath*, 12; *DNB*, 16:1178.

17 George Ridpath, *The Border History of England and Scotland Deduced from the Earliest Times to the Union of the Two Crowns* (1776; Berwick, 1848).

18 Crowe, "Development of Education in Berwick upon Tweed," 422.

19 Bartle, "Agents and Inspectors of the British and Foreign School Society," 19–30.

20 Cowe, *Berwick upon Tweed*, 3.

21 Gordon Donaldson, *The Scots Overseas* (London: Robert Hale, 1966), 111–17; John Bodnar, *The Transplanted: A History of Immigrants to Urban America* (Bloomington: Indiana University Press, 1985), 4, 16.

22 *History of Allegan and Barry Counties, Michigan* (Philadelphia: D. W. Ensign, 1880), 272, 277, 344; *Portrait and Biographical Record of Kalamazoo, Allegan, and Van Buren Counties, Michigan, etc.*, 514–15.

23 For an indication of the younger James Redpath's gratitude to his uncle, see the dedication to James Redpath, *A Guide to Hayti* (Boston: Thayer and Eldridge, 1861), 3; Henry H. Thomas, *A Twentieth Century History of Allegan County, Michigan* (Chicago: Lewis, 1907), 589; *History of Allegan and Barry Counties, Michigan*, 272, 277.

24 George Torrey, "The Press of Kalamazoo," *Michigan Pioneer and Historical Society* 17 (1892): 369–91; David Fisher and Frank Little, eds., *Compendium of History and Biography of Kalamazoo County, Mich[igan]* (Chicago: A. W. Bowen, 1925), 79; Horner, *James Redpath*, 13–15.

25 Torrey, "Press of Kalamazoo," 388–90; Tom S. Applegate, "A History of the Press of Michigan," *Michigan Pioneer and Historical Collections* 6 (1883): 63–64.

26 Horner, *James Redpath*, 16–18.

27 *Savannah Daily Morning News*, 23 May 1854; *St. Louis Daily Missouri Democrat*, 27 March 1856; Robert W. Jones, *Journalism in the United States* (New York: E. P. Dutton, 1947), 266–70; Jeter Allen Iseley, *Horace Greeley and the Republican Party, 1853–1861: A Study of the New York Tribune* (Princeton, N.J.: Princeton University Press, 1947), 6–14; Horner, *James Redpath*, 19–22.

28 *Savannah Daily Morning News*, 12, 23 May 1854; *St. Louis Daily Missouri Democrat*, 15 June 1855, 27 March 1856; *Twentieth Century Biographical Dictionary of Notable Americans*, 10 vols. (Boston: The Biographical Society, 1904), n.p.

29 James Redpath to William H. Seward, 4 August 1852(?), Thomas A. Jenckes Papers, Manuscript Division, Library of Congress.

30 *Savannah Daily Morning News*, 23 May 1854.

31 *St. Louis Daily Missouri Democrat*, 27 March 1856; Redpath indirectly alluded to these editorials in an article in the *Savannah Daily Morning News* on 23 May 1854. He later reprinted these editorials as an appendix to his book-length collection of public tributes to John Brown. James Redpath, ed., *Echoes of Harper's Ferry* (Boston: Thayer and Eldridge, 1860), 457–513.

32 The group also held Fitz-James O'Brien, an Irish writer who had squandered his inheritance and come to New York, where he wrote poetry, plays, and literary essays. O'Brien occasionally wrote pieces for the recently founded *New York Times*. Two of O'Brien's colleagues at the *Times*, Charles C. B. Seymour, another English expatriate and drama editor for the paper, and Augustus Maverick, son of the famed engraver Peter Maverick and an assistant political editor, also joined this social circle. Albert Perry, *Garrets and Pretenders* (New York: Dover, 1933), 38–61.

33 *Liberator*, 8 September 1854; also see *Savannah Daily Morning News*, 12 May 1854.

34 *St. Louis Daily Missouri Democrat*, 27 March 1856; James Redpath to W. Whitelaw Reid, either 1879 or 1880.

35 Some examples of these articles can be found in the *New York Tribune*, 15, 16 February 1854.

36 Redpath is not reported in attendance at any abolitionist convention in New York City in the early 1850s. In his correspondence with leading abolitionists later in the decade he invariably had to introduce himself. James Redpath to William Lloyd Garrison, 26 July 1854, William Lloyd Garrison Papers, Boston Public Library (hereafter cited as Garrison Papers); James Redpath to Sydney Howard Gay, 6, 17 November 1854, Sydney Howard Gay Collection, Columbia University Library (hereafter cited as Gay Collection); James Redpath to Gerrit Smith, ca. March 1856, Gerrit Smith Papers, George Arents Research Library (hereafter cited as Smith Papers); *Liberator,* 8 December 1854.

37 Testimony of James Redpath, 24 December 1863, American Freedmen's Inquiry Commission Documents, Box 1054 A, O 328 (1863), Folder 7, National Archives.

38 James Redpath, *The Roving Editor; or, Talks with Slaves in the Southern States,* edited by John R. McKivigan (1859; University Park: Pennsylvania State University Press, 1996), 20; also see Testimony of James Redpath, 24 December 1863, American Freedmen's Inquiry Commission Documents, Box 1054 A, O 328 (1863), Folder 7, National Archives; Redpath to William Lloyd Garrison, 26 July 1854, Garrison Papers.

39 James L. Huston, "The Experiential Basis of the Northern Antislavery Impulse," *Journal of Southern History* 56 (November 1990): 609–40.

40 Frederick Law Olmsted, *The Cotton Kingdom: A Traveller's Observations on Cotton and Slavery in the American Slave States,* edited by Arthur M. Schlesinger (1860; New York: Alfred A. Knopf, 1954), ix–xxvii, 571–76; Broadus Mitchell, *Frederick Law Olmsted: A Critic of the Old South,* Johns Hopkins University Studies, ser 42, no. 2 (Baltimore: John Hopkins University, 1924), 71–72, 127–28. Modern critiques of Olmsted's evaluation of slavery can be found in Robert William Fogel, *Without Consent or Contract: The Rise and Fall of American Slavery* (New York: W. W. Norton, 1989), 73, 158, 194; Peter Kolchin, *American Slavery, 1619–1877* (New York: Hill and Wang, 1993), 74–75, 181.

41 The two free blacks specifically described discriminatory practices in Richmond's First African Baptist Church. *Liberator,* 11 August 1854; reprinted in Redpath, *Roving Editor,* 28–37; Marie Tyler-McGraw and Gregg D. Kimball, *In Bondage and Freedom: Antebellum Black Life in Richmond, Virginia* (Chapel Hill: University of North Carolina Press, 1988), 37–40.

42 [Mary Virginia Terhune], *Marion Harland's Autobiography: The Story of a Long Life* (New York: Harper and Brothers, 1910), 264–69; Edward T. James et al., *Notable American Women, 1607–1950: A Biographical Dictionary,* 3 vols. (Cambridge, Mass.: The Belknap Press of Harvard University Press, 1971), 3:439–41.

43 Redpath, *Roving Editor,* 77; Herbert Wender, *Southern Commercial Conventions, 1837–1859* (Baltimore: Johns Hopkins University Press, 1930), 119–46; John McCardell, *The Ideas of Southern Nationalism: Southern Nationalists and Southern Nationalism, 1830–1860* (New York: W. W. Norton, 1979), 91–132; Fogel, *Without Consent,* 105.

44 *New York Tribune,* 19 April 1854; Wender, *Southern Commercial Conventions,* 144–46.

45 *New York Tribune,* 15 April 1854; Wender, *Southern Commercial Conventions,* 119.

46 In his *Roving Editor,* Redpath claims to have persuaded this individual to introduce the resolution. Redpath, *Roving Editor,* 77–82.

47 *New York Herald,* 16 April 1854; *New York Tribune,* 17, 19 April 1854; Redpath, *Roving Editor,* 80–82.

48 Redpath, *Roving Editor,* 81.

49 Ibid., 58, also see 58–65; *Liberator,* 8 September 1854.

50 *Savannah Daily Morning News,* 17 April 1854; AFIC Report, p. 1.

51 Charles C. Jones, *History of Savannah, Ga.* (Syracuse, N.Y.: D. Mason, 1890), 519–20; F. D. Lee and J. L. Agnew, *Historical Record of the City of Savannah* (Savannah, Ga.: J. H. Estill, 1869), 194–96; *Dictionary of American Biography,* 20 vols. (New York, 1928–36), 9:479–80, hereinafter cited as *DAB.*

52 Tweed also prepared a series of sketches of Savannah's charitable institutions accompanied by the young reporter's own thoughts about the nature of poverty and philanthropy. Redpath complimented Savannah, declaring that "no city surpasses it in practical zeal for the cause of the poor and helpless." *Savannah Daily Morning News,* 29 April 1854; 4, 11, 12 May 1854.

53 *Savannah Daily Morning News,* 6 June 1854.

54 Ibid., 23 May 1854.

55 These letters were filled with news of sensational court trials, exhibits at Barnum's museum, accounts of the latest novels, and biting gossip about the inner workings of New York's newspapers. Berwick paid great attention to activities of the theater, including an expression of regret about the closing of a play by Redpath's friend, William North. *Savannah Daily Morning News,* 12, 13, 15, 16, 17, 22, 23, 24, 26, 27, 30 May 1854; 2, 5, 7 June 1854.

56 Ibid., 17 May 1854.

57 Ibid., 22 May 1854.

58 Ibid., 19 June 1854.

59 Ibid., 19 June 1854.

60 Redpath, *Roving Editor,* xv–xvi.

61 Redpath to William Lloyd Garrison, 26 July 1854, Garrison Papers, BPL.

62 *DNB,* 1:993–94, 19:1347–48; Redpath, *Roving Editor,* 248.

63 *Liberator,* 4 August 1854.

64 Redpath to Garrison, 26 July 1854, Garrison Papers.

65 *Liberator,* 4, 11 August 1854; 1, 8 September 1854.

66 Redpath to Sydney Howard Gay, 6, 17 November 1854, Gay Collection.

67 *National Anti-Slavery Standard,* 14, 21, 28 October 1854; 11, 25 November 1854; 2, 16, 23 December 1854; 27 January 1855; 17, 31 March 1855; 7, 14 April 1855.

68 Redpath to Sydney Howard Gay, 6 November 1854, Gay Collection.

69 *National Anti-Slavery Standard,* 20 January 1855; 3, 17 February 1855; 3, 17 March 1855.

70 Articles definitely written by Redpath while in the South can be found in the *New York Daily Tribune,* 13, 15, 16, 17, 18 April 1854; 16 February 1855; 24 March 1855.

71 Redpath to Gay, 17 November 1854, Gay Collection.

72 Ibid., 6, 17 November 1854; 23 January 1855, Gay Collection.

73 *National Anti-Slavery Standard,* 16 December 1854; 10 February 1855.

74 Redpath, *Roving Editor,* 87–137; *National Anti-Slavery Standard,* 21 October, 11 November, 2 December 1854.

75 Redpath, *Roving Editor,* 134, also 132–37; *Augusta Daily Constitutionalist and Republican,* 10 November 1854.

76 *Augusta Daily Constitutionalist and Republican,* 15 December 1854, also 17 November 1854; Redpath to Sydney Howard Gay, 6, 17 November 1854, Gay Papers; Redpath, *Roving Editor,* 137, 143, 149.

77 *National Anti-Slavery Standard,* 9 December 1854; Redpath to Sydney Howard Gay, 23 January 1855, Gay Papers; Isaac Wheeler Avery, *The History of the State of Georgia from 1850 to 1881* (New York: Brown and Derby, 1881), 30–31, 33–35, 610; Allen D. Candler and Clement Evans, eds. *Georgia,* 3 vols. (Atlanta: State Historical Association, 1906), 3:100–102.

78 Redpath, *Roving Editor,* 149; Redpath to Sydney Howard Gay, 6, 17 November 1854, Gay Papers.

79 Redpath to Sydney Howard Gay, 23 January 1855, Gay Papers; *National Anti-Slavery Standard,* 27 January 1855; Redpath, *Roving Editor,* 156–71.

80 *New Orleans Daily Picayune,* 30 January 1855; *New York Daily Tribune,* 16, 17, 18, 20 January 1855.

81 Redpath to Sydney Howard Gay, 23 January 1855, Gay Papers.

82 *St. Louis Daily Missouri Democrat,* 13, 15 June 1855; Redpath to Sydney Howard Gay, c. February, 1855.

83 [Terhune], *Marion Harland's Autobiography,* 264–65.

84 *New Orleans Bee,* 3 February 1855. Two other likely pieces by Redpath are notices of literary works by his friends William North and Marion Harland. *New Orleans Bee,* 25 March 1855; 10, 14 May 1855.

85 [James Redpath], *Shall We Suffocate Ed. Green?* (Boston: James Redpath, 1864), 34–39.

86 *St. Louis Daily Missouri Democrat,* 13 June 1855.

87 Ibid. Another friend, J. V. Thomas of the *Bee,* later became a mercenary in Central America. [Redpath], *Shall We Suffocate Ed. Green?* 34, 38–39.

88 Redpath to Editor of *Graham's Monthly,* 1 April [1855], Historical Society of Pennsylvania; *Augusta Daily Constitutionalist and Republican,* 17 November 1854; *Graham's Monthly* 46 (May 1855): 418–28, 462; 46 (June 1855): 561–62.

89 In *The Roving Editor,* Redpath corrects some of the false addresses and dates he had originally used in the John Ball Jr. letters to help to conceal his identity. *National Anti-Slavery Standard,* 16 December 1854; Redpath, *Roving Editor,* 128–30.

90 *National Anti-Slavery Standard,* 17 March 1855.

91 Redpath to Smith, November 1854, Smith Papers. The actual number of full-scale interviews recorded in Redpath's articles includes those with 29 slaves, 5 free blacks, and 7 slave owners.

92 *Liberator,* 11 August 1854.

93 *National Anti-Slavery Standard,* 9 December 1854; Redpath, *Roving Editor,* 141.

94 *National Anti-Slavery Standard,* 9 December 1854; Redpath, *Roving Editor,* 140–41.

95 To minimize the chances of detection, Redpath would approach the slave quarters late in the evening and depart before work began the following morning. *National Anti-Slavery Standard,* 2 December 1854; Redpath, *Roving Editor,* 126–27.

96 Redpath, *Roving Editor,* 20; also see *Liberator,* 1 September 1854.

97 *Liberator,* 11 August 1854.

98 Ibid., 1, 8 September 1854; *National Anti-Slavery Standard,* 2 December 1854.

99 *Liberator,* 1, 8 September 1854; *National Anti-Slavery Standard,* 14 October 1854; Redpath, *Roving Editor,* 39–40, 50–53, 55, 69–72, 93, 111.

100 *Liberator,* 11 August 1854; Redpath, *Roving Editor,* 32–33. Eugene Genovese attacks Redpath for his castigation of slave religion: "Some northern abolitionists and southern slaveholders alike doubted the depth of the slaves' Christian commitment. . . . for some northern critics, the slave system was so vicious that no one could possibly expect the slaves to be capable of understanding the Christian message. Thus [stated] James Redpath, whose youth may excuse his insufferable self-righteousness." Eugene D. Genovese, *Roll, Jordan, Roll: The World the Slaves Made* (1974; New York: Vintage Books, 1976), 214. Also see, Fogel, *Without Consent,* 171; Kolchin, *American Slavery,* 143–48.

101 *National Anti-Slavery Standard,* 28 October 1854; 10 February 1855; Redpath, *Roving Editor,* 111–12, 158–59.

102 Redpath, *Roving Editor,* 35, also 43–44, 63. *Liberator,* August 11 1854; September 8, 1854.

103 Redpath, *Roving Editor,* 42, 62–63, 92. A helpful summary of the historical debate regarding slave "contentment" can be found in Kolchin, *American Slavery,* 154–66.

104 Redpath, *Roving Editor,* 248.

105 *Liberator,* 8 September 1854; reprinted with minor revisions in Redpath, *Roving Editor,* 59.

106 *Liberator,* 8 September 1854; Redpath, *Roving Editor,* 62.

107 *Liberator,* 8 September 1854; reprinted with minor revisions in Redpath, *Roving Editor,* 59–60. Redpath noted that urban slaves often were hired out and could act with little supervision of whites. Richard C. Wade, *Slavery in the Cities: The South, 1820–1860* (New York: Oxford University Press, 1964), 48; Redpath, *Roving Editor,* 164–65. See also Douglas R. Egerton, *He Shall Go Free: The Lives of Denmark Vesey* (Madison, Wis.: Madison House, 1999), 126–53; Kolchin, *American Slavery,* 176.

108 *Liberator,* 11 August 1854; 8 September 1854; *National Anti-Slavery Standard,* 21 October 1854; 11 November 1854; Redpath, *Roving Editor,* 30–31, 120–21. See also Kolchin, *American Slavery,* 65–66.

109 *Liberator,* 1 September 1854; reprinted in Redpath, *Roving Editor,* 55. Herbert Aptheker cites Redpath as his principal authority for making a similar claim in his study of slave insurrections. Herbert Aptheker, *American Negro Slave Revolts* (New York: Columbia University Press, 1943), 115–16.

110 *National Anti-Slavery Standard,* 9 December 1854.

111 Ibid., 11 November 1854; reprinted in Redpath, *Roving Editor,* 120.

112 *Liberator,* 8 September 1854; reprinted with significant revisions in Redpath, *Roving Editor,* 73–74.

113 *National Anti-Slavery Standard,* 2 December 1854; also see *Liberator,* 1 September 1854.

114 *National Anti-Slavery Standard,* 11 November 1854; reprinted in Redpath, *Roving Editor,* 119, also see 109–10, 117.

115 *Liberator,* 1 September 1854; *National Anti-Slavery Standard,* 27 January 1855.

116 *National Anti-Slavery Standard,* 11 November 1854; reprinted with revisions in Redpath, *Roving Editor,* 121.

117 *National Anti-Slavery Standard,* 11 November 1854; reprinted in Redpath, *Roving Editor,* 119–20.

118 Stanley Harrold and I have examined the issue of the extent of pacifism in the early abolitionist movement in the introduction to our edited volume: John R. McKivigan and Stanley Harrold, *Antislavery Violence: Sectional, Racial, and Cultural Conflict in Antebellum America* (Knoxville: University of Tennessee Press, 1999), 1–22.

119 At sale at the Banks Arcade were 261 slaves who composed the estate of a deceased Louisiana planter. Redpath reported that the slaves were crying at the prospect of the imminent separation from their friends and families and noted "many a sympathetic tear in the audience." Moved by the sad spectacle, Redpath claimed that it was "impossible for me to give you a faithful description of the scene, as no pen can picture the horrors of it." Redpath's exposé of this slave auction was part of a recurring theme in abolitionist literature dating back at least to Benjamin Lundy. *New York Tribune,* 16 February 1855; 24 March 1855; *New Orleans Daily Picayune,* 19, 23 January 1855; Redpath, *Roving Editor,* 161; Huston, "Experiential Basis," 621.

120 *New Orleans Delta,* n.d., as quoted in *National Anti-Slavery Standard,* 31 March 1855.

121 Redpath, *Roving Editor,* 161. The yellow fever toll in the New Orleans vicinity in 1853 also had amounted to 7,790 fatalities. It usually ravaged the Mississippi Delta from July to October during the 1850s. Alcee Fortier, ed., *Louisiana,* 3 vols. (n.p.: Century Historical Association, 1914), 1:207–8; Sarah Searight, *New Orleans* (New York: Stein and Day, 1973), 240–41.

Chapter 2. The Crusader of Freedom

1 James Redpath, *The Roving Editor; or, Talks with Slaves in the Southern States* (New York: A. B. Burdick, 1859), 300.

2 Edwin C. McReynolds, *Missouri: A History of the Crossroads State* (Norman: University of Oklahoma Press, 1962), 156–62, 171; Jim Allee Hart, *A History of the St. Louis Globe-Dispatch* (Columbia: University of Missouri Press, 1961), 1.

3 Walter B. Stevens, *St. Louis: The Fourth City, 1764–1909* (St. Louis: S. J. Clarke, 1909), 210–12; William Ernest Smith, *The Francis Preston Blair Family in Politics,* 2 vols. (New York: Macmillan, 1933), 1:291–94, 301–3; Hart, *St. Louis Globe-Democrat,* 2–15.

4 Stevens, *St. Louis,* 221–22; Jim A. Hart, "James Redpath, Missouri Correspondent," *Missouri Historical Review* 57 (October 1962): 70–78; *National Cyclopaedia of American Biography* (New York: J. T. White, 1898–), 12:11, hereinafter cited as *NCAB.*

5 *St. Louis Daily Missouri Democrat,* 15 June 1855, also see 13 June 1855.

6 Ibid., 15 June 1855, also 25, 29 June 1855; 3 July 1855. Redpath mistakenly identifies Warner as "Miss A.B. Warren."

7 James A. Rawley, *Race and Politics: 'Bleeding Kansas' and the Coming of the Civil War* (Philadelphia: J. P. Lippincott, 1969), 32–33, 58–60, 79–85; William F. Zornow, *Kansas: A History of the Jayhawk State* (Norman: University of Oklahoma Press, 1957), 67–70; A. T. Andreas, *History of the State of Kansas*, 3 vols. (Chicago: A. T. Andreas, 1883), 1:85, 87–91, 93–99.

8 Richard J. Hinton, "Pens that Made Kansas Free," *Kansas State Historical Society Collections* 6 (1897–1900): 371–82; David W. Johnson, "Freesoilers for God: Kansas Newspaper Editors and the Antislavery Crusade," *Kansas History* 2 (summer 1979): 74–85; Lloyd Lewis, "Propaganda and the Kansas-Missouri War," *Missouri Historical Review* 34 (October 1939): 3–17; Bernard A. Weisberger, "The Newspaper Reporter and the Kansas Imbroglio," *Mississippi Valley Historical Review* 36 (March 1950): 633–56.

9 James Ford Rhodes, *History of the United States from the Compromise of 1850*, 9 vols. (New York: Macmillan, 1900–28), 2:218.

10 James C. Malin, *John Brown and the Legend of Fifty-Six*, 2 vols. (Philadelphia: American Philosophical Society, 1942), 1:221, also see 1:211, 213, 258–59.

11 Weisberger, "Kansas Imbroglio," 655–56.

12 Charles Robinson, *The Kansas Conflict* (Lawrence, Kan.: Journal, 1898), 182; Hart, "James Redpath," 77.

13 Hinton, "Pens That Made Kansas Free," 377–78.

14 Jay Monaghan, *Civil War on the Western Border, 1854–1865* (Boston: Little, Brown and Company, 1955), 25–27; Andreas, *Kansas,* 1:101–3; Zornow, *Kansas,* 70.

15 *St. Louis Daily Missouri Democrat,* 23 July 1855; 24 August 1855; Hart, "James Redpath," 71–72.

16 *St. Louis Daily Missouri Democrat,* 23 July 1855.

17 Ibid., 23, 30, 31 July 1855; 8, 9, 10, 13, 29, 31 August 1855; 3, 4 September 1855; Rawley, *Race and Politics,* 91–92; Andreas, *Kansas,* 1:101–6; Hart, "James Redpath," 72–74.

18 *St. Louis Daily Missouri Democrat,* 25 August 1855, also see 8, 22 August 1855.

19 Ibid., 28 July 1855; 14, 15 August 1855; Hart, "James Redpath," 74–75.

20 *St. Louis Daily Missouri Democrat,* 8 September 1855.

21 For example see *National Anti-Slavery Standard,* 1 September 1855; *New York Daily Tribune,* 5 September 1855; *St. Louis Daily Missouri Democrat,* 13 September 1855; Hart, "James Redpath," 77.

22 *St. Louis Daily Missouri Democrat,* 30 August 1855, also 13, 23 August 1855; Hinton, "Pens that Made Kansas Free," 378.

23 As quoted in *St. Louis Daily Missouri Democrat,* 13 September 1855. This Stringfellow was the brother of Benjamin F. Stringfellow, a Missouri politician and leading Border Ruffian. McReynolds, *Missouri,* 189–90.

24 The trails and much of the landscape, Redpath reported, could instantly change from dust to mud. Redpath praised the quality of the Kansas farmland and his accounts abounded with advice to would-be settlers. He also visited both pro- and antislavery towns and found none very impressive. The appearance of the year-old, free-state settlement of Lawrence, in fact, filled Redpath with "disappointment and doubt." The "resolute, earnest, and religious character of its inhabitants," however, reassured him and he prophetically declared that "it is a village with a

'backbone.'" *St. Louis Daily Missouri Democrat,* 23 October 1855, also see ibid., 10, 22, 24, 26, 27 October 1855; 9 November 1855.

25 Ibid., 23 July 1855.

26 Ibid., 30 July 1855.

27 Ibid.

28 Ibid., n.d., as reprinted in *National Anti-Slavery Standard,* 22 September 1855; also see Rawley, *Race and Politics,* 92–93, 96–97.

29 *St. Louis Daily Missouri Democrat,* 10 November 1855, also see 10, 22 October 1855.

30 Ibid., 13 September, 10 November 1855, 22 February 1856; also see G. Douglas Brewerton, *The War in Kansas: A Rough Trip to the Border* (1856; Freeport, N.Y.: Books for Libraries Press, 1971), 347.

31 Andreas, *Kansas,* 1:110–11; Zornow, *Kansas,* 70–71.

32 Redpath received $174 for his services as the convention's reporter. Daniel W. Wilder, *The Annals of Kansas* (Topeka: George W. Martin, 1875), 65; "The Topeka Movement," *Collections of the Kansas State Historical Society* 13 (1913–14): 148, 160; Andreas, *Kansas,* 1:111–12.

33 *St Louis Daily Missouri Democrat,* 14 November 1855, also see 9, 13, 14, 17, 20, 21, 23, November 1855; Zornow, *Kansas,* 71; Andreas, *Kansas,* 1:106–7, 111–12.

34 *St. Louis Daily Missouri Democrat,* 21 November 1855.

35 *New York Daily Tribune,* 8, 19 January 1856; Brewerton, *War in Kansas,* 345–49; Andreas, *Kansas,* 1:112.

36 *New York Daily Tribune,* 19 January 1856.

37 Ibid., 29 January 1856; Frank W. Blackmar, *The Life of Charles Robinson: The First State Governor of Kansas* (Topeka: Crane and Company, 1902), 190–93; Weisberger, "Kansas Imbroglio," 637.

38 Blackmar, *Charles Robinson,* 190–91.

39 *St. Louis Daily Missouri Democrat,* 8, 10 December 1855.

40 Ibid., 12 December 1855.

41 Ibid., 27 December 1855; *Chicago Tribune,* 4 June 1856; Zornow, *Kansas,* 71–72; Andreas, *Kansas,* 1:115–20.

42 Brewerton, *War in Kansas,* 392; Weisberger, "Kansas Imbroglio," 642–43; Andreas, *Kansas,* 1:121.

43 *New York Daily Tribune,* 19 January 1856, also see 4 February 1856; *St. Louis Daily Missouri Democrat,* 5 December 1855; 29 January 1856; 6 February 1856.

44 *New York Daily Tribune,* 19 January 1856; quoted in Oswald Garrison Villard, *John Brown, 1800–1859: A Biography Fifty Years After* (Boston: Houghton Mifflin Co., 1910), 139.

45 *St. Louis Daily Missouri Democrat,* 5, 7, 8 February 1856. At Redpath's suggestion, the *Missouri Democrat* replaced him in Kansas with Albert Deane Richardson, later famous as a Civil War correspondent for the *New York Tribune.* See Stevens, *St. Louis,* 222; *DAB,* 15:562–63.

46 Some of Redpath's observations were purely humorous. Terre Haute, he observed, was "not a fast, unsubstantial, gaudily-decorated, gilt-gingerbread concern, such as Young America delights in building up, by way of recreation, between dinner and dusk—but a broad-breasted, strong, healthy, richly-plain dressed individual

of middle age." *St. Louis Daily Missouri Democrat,* 21 February 1856; also 15, 18, 21, 23, 25, 29 February 1856; 1, 3, 7, 21, 29 March 1856; 1 April 1856.

47 Ibid., 3 March 1856.

48 *National Anti-Slavery Standard,* 22 March 1856; *Liberator,* 28 March 1856.

49 *St Louis Daily Missouri Democrat,* 29 February 1856.

50 Gordon S. Kleeberg, *The Formation of the Republican Party as a National Political Organization* (1911; New York: Burt Franklin, 1970), 28–38; William E. Gienapp, *The Origins of the Republican Party, 1852–1856* (New York: Oxford University Press, 1987), 254–59; Rawley, *Race and Politics,* 145–46.

51 Vaughan had edited the *Louisville Examiner* in the 1840s and promoted the general idea of emancipation. Either while at the convention in Pittsburgh or shortly thereafter, Vaughan hired Redpath to cover Kansas events for the *Chicago Tribune.* Richard S. Sewell, *Ballots for Freedom: Antislavery Politics in the United States, 1837–1860* (New York: W. W. Norton, 1976), 314; Lloyd Wendt; *Chicago Tribune: The Rise of a Great American Newspaper* (Chicago: Rand McNally, 1979), 63, 65, 72–73, 78–79.

52 *New York Daily Tribune,* 25 February 1856.

53 *Chicago Tribune,* 14 April 1856; Francis Curtis, *The Republican Party: A History of Its Fifty Years' Existence and A Record of Its Measures and Leaders, 1854–1904,* 2 vols. (New York: G. P. Putnam's Sons, 1904), 1:250–55; Gienapp, *Origins of the Republican Party,* 265–71; Rawley, *Race and Politics,* 144–46.

54 Redpath to Gerrit Smith, ca. March 1856, Gerrit Smith Papers, George Arents Library, Syracuse University (hereafter cited as Smith Papers).

55 *St. Louis Daily Missouri Democrat,* 20, 27, 28 March 1855; 1, 8 April 1855.

56 Ralph Volney Harlow, *Gerrit Smith: Philanthropist and Reformer* (New York: Holt, 1939), 234–35, 242–49; John R. McKivigan and Madeleine L. McKivigan, "'He Stands Like Jupiter': The Autobiography of Gerrit Smith," *New York History* 65 (April 1984): 193–94.

57 James Redpath to Gerrit Smith, ca. March 1856; 23 April 1856, Smith Papers; also see *St. Louis Daily Missouri Democrat,* 8 April 1856.

58 James Redpath to William H. Seward, 10 April 1856, William H. Seward Papers, University of Rochester Library.

59 Redpath to William Penn Clarke, 27 October 1856, Chicago Historical Society; *Chicago Tribune,* 15 May 1856; Wendt, *Chicago Tribune,* 65–67.

60 *Chicago Tribune,* 16 May 1856; Bernard A. Weisberger, *Reporters for the Union* (Boston: Little, Brown, 1953), 38–39.

61 *Chicago Tribune,* 17 May 1856; also see 15, 22 May 1856.

62 Ibid., 22 May 1856; Monaghan, *Civil War on the Western Border,* 53; McReynolds, *Missouri,* 192–93; Weisberger, "Kansas Imbroglio," 643–44.

63 *New York Tribune,* 9, 12 June 1856; Zornow, *Kansas,* 72–73; McReynolds, *Missouri,* 193; Weisberger, *Reporters for the Union,* 34–35, and "Kansas Imbroglio," 645–46; Andreas, *Kansas,* 1:129–31.

64 Malin, *John Brown,* 1:52–62; Stephen B. Oates, *To Purge This Land with Blood: A Biography of John Brown* (New York: Harper and Row, 1970), 126–37; Zornow, *Kansas,* 73–74.

65 Hill Peebles Wilson, *John Brown, Soldier of Fortune: A Critique* (Lawrence, Kan.: H. P. Wilson, 1913), 138–39.

66 Otto J. Scott, *The Secret Six: John Brown and The Abolitionist Movement* (New York: Times Books, 1979), 196.

67 An even younger reporter, James B. Pond, who after the Civil War became Redpath's partner in the lyceum business, claimed to have accompanied him on this trip. Redpath never acknowledged Pond's presence at the interview with Brown. James B. Pond, *Eccentricities of Genius* (London: Chatto and Windus, 1901), 534.

68 *Boston Atlas and Bee*, 22 October 1859; James Redpath, *The Public Life of Captain John Brown* (Boston: Thayer and Eldridge, 1860), 109–11.

69 Redpath, *Captain John Brown*, 112–14; *Boston Atlas and Bee*, 22 October 1859; Robert Penn Warren, *John Brown: The Making of a Martyr* (New York: Payson and Clarke, 1929), 180–83; Oates, *To Purge This Land*, 159–61.

70 One member of Brown's band recalled that Redpath was "very cheerful" and "declared that it showed well for the settlers that, in spite of the great rewards offered, nobody had, as yet, been found to pilot the enemy to our camp. He asked us to remain in good spirits; that while we alone represented the aggressive anti-slavery agitation of the United States, also on our perseverance alone depended the ultimate victory of the good cause." August Bondi, "With John Brown in Kansas," *Transactions of the Kansas State Historical Society* 8 (1903–4): 285.

71 Franklin Benjamin Sanborn, *The Life and Letters of John Brown: Liberator of Kansas, and Martyr of Virginia* (Boston: Roberts Brothers, 1891), 294–97; Redpath, *Captain John Brown*, 112–14; Villard, *John Brown*, 199–200.

72 Salomon Brown, "John Brown and His Sons in Kansas Territory," *Indiana Magazine of History* 31 (June 1935): 142–50.

73 Jeffrey Rossbach, *Ambivalent Conspirators: John Brown, the Secret Six, and a Theory of Slave Violence* (Philadelphia: University of Pennsylvania Press, 1982), 175–78; Warren, *John Brown*, 182–83.

74 *Chicago Tribune*, n.d., reprinted in *New York Tribune*, 12 June 1856.

75 James Townsley, "The Pottawatomie Tragedy: John Brown's Connection with It," in *John Brown: The Making of a Revolutionary*, edited by Louis Ruchames (New York: Grosset and Dunlap, 1969), 205–11; George W. Brown, *False Claims of Kansas Historians Truthfully Corrected* (Rockford, Ill.: George W. Brown, 1902), 125–27; Robinson, *Kansas Conflict*, 324.

76 August Bondi, one of Brown's followers, contends that Redpath had assured Brown that armed rifle companies would soon ride to his aid. Bondi, "With John Brown in Kansas," 285; Wilson, *John Brown*, 140–41.

77 Oates, *To Purge This Land*, 151–54; Wilson, *John Brown*, 140–41.

78 Andreas, *Kansas*, 1:132–33; Oates, *To Purge This Land with Blood*, 152–54; Wilson, *John Brown*, 139–41.

79 As quoted in *Chicago Tribune*, 15 July 1856; also see *Boston Atlas and Bee*, 24 October 1859; Malin, *John Brown*, 1:100–101.

80 Redpath had not entirely abandoned journalism. He was present in Topeka to report that federal cavalry under orders from Governor Shannon had forced the free-state legislature to disperse in the tradition of "Cromwell and Napoleon." He also reported many incidents of violence against northern settlers that summer, such as the tarring and feathering of the Reverend Pardee Butler and two alleged rapes of free-state women. *New York Tribune*, 19 June 1856; *Chicago Tribune*,

15 May 1856; 15 July 1856; Hinton, "Pens that Made Kansas Free," 377; Andreas, *Kansas*, 1:140; Villard, *John Brown*, 174; Wendt, *Chicago Tribune*, 73; Weisberger, "Kansas Imbroglio," 637, 643–45, 648. This photograph is in possession of the Kansas State Historical Society.

81 *Chicago Tribune*, 15 July 1856; William Elsey Connelley, "The Lane Trail," *Collections of the Kansas State Historical Society* 13 (1913–14): 268; Rawley, *Race and Politics*, 158–59; Andreas, *Kansas*, 1:135–38; Monaghan, *Civil War on the Western Border*, 90–91; Weisberger, *Reporters for the Union*, 36.

82 *Chicago Tribune*, 22 August 1856, also 18, 20 August 1856.

83 Glenn Noble, *John Brown and the Jim Lane Trail* (Broken Bow, Neb.: Purcells, 1977), 54; Hinton, *John Brown*, 116–17.

84 A second party led by Preston B. Plumb always traveled within sight of Redpath's vanguard. Leverett Wilson Spring, *Kansas: The Prelude to the War for the Union* (Boston: Houghton, Mifflin and Company, 1885), 170; Wendell Holmes Stephenson, "The Political Career of General James H. Lane," *Publications of the Kansas State Historical Society* 3 (1930): 82; Connelley, "Lane Trail," 275; Hinton, *John Brown*, 116–18; Andreas, *Kansas*, 1:141; Noble, *John Brown and the Jim Lane Trail*, 56; Alice Nichols, *Bleeding Kansas* (New York: Oxford University Press, 1954), 163.

85 Redpath, *Captain John Brown*, 145; Rawley, *Race and Politics*, 158–60; Zornow, *Kansas*, 74–75; Andreas, *Kansas*, 1:141, 147.

86 S. H. Fairfield," Getting Married and the Ague," *Collections of the Kansas State Historical Society* 11 (1909–1910): 609–13.

87 Higginson incorrectly identifies the place of their arrest as Lawrence. Thomas Wentworth Higginson, *A Ride through Kansas* (New York: American Anti-Slavery Society, 1856), 7–8, and *Cheerful Yesterdays* (Boston: Houghton and Mifflin Company, 1898), 204–7; *Lawrence Herald of Freedom*, 1 November 1856; Andreas, *Kansas*, 1:153; R. G. Elliott, "The Twenty-First of May," *Transactions of the Kansas State Historical Society* 7 (1902): 527.

88 James Redpath to Preston B. Plumb, 27 September 1856, Redpath Papers, Kansas State Historical Society; Noble, *John Brown and the Jim Lane Trail*, 56; Andreas, *Kansas*, 1:153.

89 Higginson, *Ride Through Kansas*, 9.

90 In his biography of Brown, Redpath wrote a greatly exaggerated account of Brown's activities at Lawrence, which contemporary critics and later historians have seized on as evidence of his irresponsible journalism. Brown, *False Claims*, 30–31; Andreas, *Kansas*, 1:150–51; Malin, *John Brown*, 1:302; Weisberger, *Reporters for the Union*, 645–46.

91 Sanborn, *John Brown*, 340–41; Noble, *John Brown and the Jim Lane Trail*, 340–41; McReynolds, *Missouri*, 194.

92 Rawley, *Race and Politics*, 159–60.

93 James Redpath to W. Penn Clarke, 27 October 1856, Gunther Collection, Chicago Historical Society; James Redpath to William Hutchinson, 28 October 1856, Redpath Papers, Kansas State Historical Society.

94 Redpath to Gerrit Smith, 26 October 1856, Smith Papers.

95 *New York Daily Tribune*, 14 November 1856; Gienapp, *Origins of the Republican Party*, 413–48.

96 *New York Daily Tribune*, 14 November 1856.

97 *New York Daily Tribune,* 14 November 1856; also see Malin, *John Brown,* 1:240.

98 Redpath to William H. Seward, 17 December 1856, Seward Papers, University of Rochester Library; Sanborn, *John Brown,* 353–54. Redpath's friend Richard Hinton has written that Redpath found work as a reporter for the *Boston Daily Advertiser* during his stay in Boston but no confirmation of this has been located. Hinton, "Pens that Made Kansas Free," 378.

99 *New York Daily Tribune,* 12 January 1857; Printed Circular, February 1857, James Redpath Papers, Kansas State Historical Society.

100 Redpath to Thomas Wentworth Higginson, 5 February 1860, James Redpath Papers or Higginson Papers, Kansas State Historical Society; also Redpath to William H. Seward, 11 February 1857, Seward Papers; Charles Sumner to Redpath, 10 January 1857, in *The Works of Charles Sumner,* 15 vols. (Boston: Lee and Shepard, 1874–83), 4:390–91; Charles Sumner to Redpath, 7 March 1857, in Boston *Liberator,* 20 March 1857.

101 Redpath to Thomas W. Higginson, November 1856, Redpath Papers, Kansas State Historical Society.

102 Redpath reported Brown's address to the Massachusetts legislature on the outrages against free-state settlers in the territory, including his own family. *New York Daily Tribune,* 12 January 1857; also quoted in Scott, *Secret Six,* 230. Also see Wilder, *Annals of Kansas,* 115–16; Wilson, *John Brown,* 191–96.

103 As quoted in Scott, *Secret Six,* 230; Arthur J. Bolster Jr. *James Freeman Clarke: Disciple to Advancing Truth* (Boston: Beacon Press, 1954), 248.

104 *New York Daily Tribune,* 17, 19, 21, 28 January 1857; *Liberator,* 23 January 1857; *National Anti-Slavery Standard,* 24 January 1857; Jane H. Pease and William H. Pease, "Confrontation and Abolition in the 1850s," *Journal of American History* 58 (March 1972): 932–34; John Demos, "The Antislavery Movement and the Problem of Violent 'Means,'" *New England Quarterly* 37 (December 1964): 522–23.

105 Sanborn, *John Brown,* 351–54.

106 Redpath also allowed John Ball Jr. a final appearance in the abolitionist press in two letters that attacked politicians with ambivalent stands on slavery. He complained that his former employer on the *Missouri Democrat,* Frank Blair Jr., opposed the spread of slavery to Kansas but nonetheless favored the deportation of free blacks to Liberia. When Kansas governor Geary finally had broken with the proslavery minority and tried to reorganize the territorial government to represent popular will, "John Ball Jr." declared him trying to play a desperate "double game" because he had not yet learned he could not "serve God and Mammon, nor Liberty and Slavery." *National Anti-Slavery Standard,* 7 March 1857; also *Liberator,* 20 February 1857.

107 *Boston Daily Advertiser,* 16 April 1857.

108 Horner makes an oblique reference at one point to Redpath's stepdaughter, Caroline Mae Kidder Morse, but never directly to her mother. Charles F. Horner, *The Life of James Redpath and the Development of the Modern Lyceum* (New York: Barse and Hopkins, 1926), 127–29.

109 *Doniphan Crusader of Freedom,* 19 December 1857.

110 *Boston Evening Transcript,* 14, 21 August 1914; *New York Times,* 22 August 1914; *Boston Directory for 1851/53* (Boston, 1852), 157; U.S. Bureau of

the Census, 1850 Census Tract; U.S. Bureau of the Census, *Eighth Federal Census (1860)* Record Group 29, M 653, Reel 506, 117.

111 Redpath to Wendell Phillips, 29 April 1857, Wendell Phillips Papers, Houghton Library, Harvard University. Redpath, his wife, and her children probably settled temporarily in New Hampton, New Hampshire, from which Caroline later wrote to Redpath in January 1858. *Doniphan Crusader of Freedom*, 20 January 1858.

112 *Boston Daily Evening Traveller*, 23 May 1857; 6, 13 June 1857.

113 *St. Louis Daily Morning Democrat*, 27 July 1857.

114 Ibid., 1 August 1857.

115 Ibid., 11 September 1857, also see 18, 24 August 1857.

116 Ibid., 24 August 1857, also see 27, 31 August 1857.

117 Ibid., 31 August 1857, also see 27 August 1857.

118 Ibid., 30 July 1857; 1, 10, 14, 27, 31 August 1857; also see William A. Phillips to James Redpath, 4 April 1857; Redpath Papers, Kansas State Historical Society; Don W. Wilson, *Governor Charles Robinson of Kansas* (Lawrence: University Press of Kansas, 1975), 67.

119 Horner, *James Redpath*, 95–96.

120 Rawley, *Race and Politics*, 208–10, 213–14; Zornow, *Kansas*, 76–77.

121 *St. Louis Daily Missouri Democrat*, 1 September 1857.

122 Ibid., 5 September 1857, also see 2, 10, 11 September 1857; *Boston Daily Advertiser*, 15 September 1857; Brown, *False Claims*, 29–31; Andreas, *Kansas*, 1:162; Villard, *John Brown*, 296; Nichols, *Bleeding Kansas*, 197; Robert Gaston Elliott, "The Grasshopper Falls Convention and the Legislature of 1857," *Collections of the Kansas State Historical Society* 10 (1907–1908): 177.

123 Redpath to John Brown, 20 September 1857, as quoted in Villard, *John Brown*, 301. Brown at this time was based in Tabor, Iowa, where he was training a small fighting band. He did not enter Kansas to meet Lane until November. Oates, *To Purge This Land*, 215, 219.

124 *St. Louis Daily Missouri Democrat*, 5 October 1857.

125 Redpath to Gerrit Smith, 24 October 1857, Smith Papers; "The Kansas Territorial Election of October 1857," *Collections of the Kansas State Historical Society* 13 (1913–1914): 257.

126 *St. Louis Daily Missouri Democrat*, 11 November 1857.

127 *Doniphan Crusader of Freedom*, 19 December 1857.

128 *Lawrence Herald of Freedom*, 10, 24 April 1858.

129 *New York Daily Tribune*, 14 December 1857, also 11 December 1857; *Lawrence Herald of Freedom*, 5 December 1857.

130 *Doniphan Crusader of Freedom*, 16 December 1857; 30 January, 6 March 1858; P. L. Gray, *Gray's Doniphan County History* (Bendena, Kan.: Roycroft Press, 1905), 15–16, 68.

131 Noble L. Prentiss, *Kansas Miscellanies* (Topeka: Kansas Publishing House, 1889), 103–5; *DAB*, 12:341–42.

132 *Lawrence Herald of Freedom*, 2 January 1858; *Doniphan Crusader of Freedom*, 19 December 1857, 20 January 1858; James Redpath and Richard J. Hinton, *Handbook to Kansas Territory* (New York: J. H. Colton, 1859), n.p.; Gray, *Doniphan County History*, 15–16, 43–44.

133 *Doniphan Crusader of Freedom,* 19 December 1857; 20 January, 6 March 1858.

134 *Boston Atlas and Bee,* 25 October 1859.

135 Redpath to Orville C. Brown, 21 May 1858, Redpath Papers, Kansas State Historical Society.

136 *Doniphan Crusader of Freedom,* 19 December 1857.

137 G. Raymond Gaeddert, *The Birth of Kansas* (Lawrence: University of Kansas Press, 1940), 7–16; Zornow, *Kansas,* 71, 73n, 81.

138 *Doniphan Crusader of Freedom,* 30 January 1858, also see 6 March 1858; Zornow, *Kansas,* 77; Malin, *John Brown,* 2:708–90; McReynolds, *Missouri,* 195.

139 *Lawrence Herald of Freedom,* 13, 27 February 1858.

140 *Doniphan Crusader of Freedom,* 30 January 1858; also see *Lawrence Herald of Freedom,* 3 April 1858.

141 *Doniphan Crusader of Freedom,* 30 January 1858; also see 19 December 1857.

142 *Lawrence Herald of Freedom,* 3 April 1858, also see 10 April 1858. Brown repeated these charges forty-five years later. Brown, *False Claims,* 28–29.

143 *Doniphan Crusader of Freedom,* 19 December 1857.

144 Ibid., 19 December 1857; Rawley, *Race and Politics,* 223–31.

145 *Lawrence Herald of Freedom,* 26 December 1857; *Geary City* (Kan.) *Era,* 2 January 1858; Horner, *James Redpath,* 87–88; G. Merlin Welch, *Border Warfare in Southeastern Kansas, 1856–1859* (Pleasanton, Kan.: Linn County Publishers, 1977), 169.

146 Quoted in *Lawrence Herald of Freedom,* 30 January 1858.

147 Ibid., 16 January 1858, also 23, 30 January 1858.

148 *Doniphan Crusader of Freedom,* 6 March 1858, as quoted in Malin, *John Brown,* 1:708–10.

149 *Lawrence Herald of Freedom,* 16 January 1858.

150 *Doniphan Crusader of Freedom,* 3 February 1858, also see *New York Times,* 19 February 1858; *Lawrence Herald of Freedom,* 20 February 1858; Wendell Holmes Stephenson, "The Political Career of General James H. Lane," *Publications of the Kansas State Historical Society* 3 (1930): 15.

151 *Lawrence Herald of Freedom,* 29 May 1858; 5 June 1858; Gray, *Doniphan County History,* 38.

152 *Doniphan Crusader of Freedom,* 17 May 1858, as quoted in Gray, *Doniphan County History,* 37, 68; Weekly Kansas Chief, *Illustrated Doniphan County* (Troy, Kan.: Weekly Kansas Chief, 1916), 216.

153 Monaghan, *Civil War on the Western Border,* 126; Gray, *Doniphan County History,* 37.

154 *Doniphan Crusader of Freedom,* 17 May 1858, as quoted in Gray, *Doniphan County History,* 38; also see *Lawrence Herald of Freedom,* 5 June 1858.

155 *Doniphan Crusader of Freedom,* n.d., as quoted in *Lawrence Herald of Freedom,* 3 April 1858, also see 24 April 1858.

156 *Lawrence Herald of Freedom,* 10 April 1858.

157 Joseph G. Waters, "Fifty Years of the Wyandotte Constitution," *Collections of the Kansas State Historical Society* 11 (1909–1910): 48.

158 *Doniphan Crusader of Freedom,* n.d., as quoted in *Lawrence Herald of Freedom,* 24 April 1858.

159 Gray, *Doniphan County History,* 37–38; Nichols, *Bleeding Kansas,* 213–14.

160 *Doniphan Crusader of Freedom,* 17 May 1858, as quoted in *Lawrence Herald of Freedom,* 5 June 1858.

161 *Lawrence Herald of Freedom,* 3, 24 April 1858. Brown added further salt to the wounds by giving a mock endorsement to Lane's presidential aspiration. Ibid., 29 May, 5 June 1858.

162 Gray, *Doniphan County History,* 37–38, 68.

163 Redpath, *Captain John Brown,* 199–200; Oates, *To Purge This Land,* 253; Richard J. Hinton, *John Brown and His Men* (1894; Funk and Wagnalls, 1965), 205–6; Franklin B. Sanborn, *Life and Letters of John Brown* (Boston: Roberts Brothers, 1885), 471–72; Villard, *John Brown,* 345.

164 Redpath, *Captain John Brown,* 200–202; Sanborn, *John Brown,* 352.

165 *Boston Atlas and Bee,* 30 October 1859; Redpath, *Captain John Brown,* 205; Sanborn, *John Brown,* 472–73.

166 Hinton, *John Brown,* 252–53.

167 Rossbach, *Ambivalent Conspirators,* 175–78; Oates, *To Purge This Land,* 238.

168 Redpath, *The Roving Editor,* iv.

169 This is also the conclusion of Redpath's close friend and fellow Kansas reporter, Richard J. Hinton. Hinton, *John Brown,* 41.

170 *Boston Atlas and Bee,* 21 October 1859.

Chapter 3. Echoes of Harpers Ferry

1 Henry C. Binford, *The First Suburbs: Residential Communities on the Boston Periphery, 1815–1860* (Chicago: University of Chicago Press, 1985), 21, 35, 39, 96, 141–42, 149, 220.

2 Manuscript of the Eighth Federal Census (1960), Record Group 29, M653, Reel 506, 117; Redpath to John Brown Jr., 28 March, 5 April 1860, John Brown Jr. Papers, Rutherford B. Hayes Historical Center.

3 Justin Kaplan, *Walt Whitman: A Life* (New York: Simon and Schuster, 1980), 247, 255; Albert Perry, *Garrets and Pretenders* (New York, 1933), 38–61; *Boston Evening Transcript,* 21 August 1914; *Malden Evening News,* 21 August 1914, 12 August 1976.

4 Stephen B. Oates, *To Purge This Land with Blood: A Biography of John Brown* (New York: Harper and Row, 1970), 238; Richard J. Hinton, *John Brown and His Men* (New York: Funk and Wagnalls Company, 1894), 130–31; Jeffery Rossbach, *Ambivalent Conspirators: John Brown, The Secret Six, and a Theory of Slave Violence* (Philadelphia: University of Pennsylvania Press, 1982), 146, 205–6, 210, 214; Edward J. Renehan Jr., *The Secret Six: The True Tale of the Men Who Conspired with John Brown* (New York: Crown, 1995), especially 145–46.

5 Thomas Wentworth Higginson, *Cheerful Yesterdays* (Boston: Houghton Mifflin, 1896), 206; Rossbach, *Ambivalent Conspirators,* 71.

6 Redpath to Gerrit Smith, November 1858, Smith Papers.

7 Rossbach, *Ambivalent Conspirators,* 175–78, 188, 199–202.

8 James Redpath, *The Public Life of Captain John Brown* (Boston: Thayer and Eldridge, 1860), 28, 190; Hinton, *John Brown,* 464–65; Charles F. Horner, *The Life of James Redpath and the Development of the Modern Lyceum* (New York: Barse and Hopkins, 1926), 80–81, 129.

9 Hugh T. Lefler, *Hinton Rowan Helper: Advocate of a "White America"* (Charlottesville, Va.: Historical Publishing, 1934), 19–20; John R. McKivigan, "John Ball Jr., Alias the Roving Editor Alias James Redpath," *Manuscripts* 40 (fall 1988): 307–17; 41 (winter 1989): 19–29.

10 Ralph V. Harlow, *Gerrit Smith: Philanthropist and Reformer* (New York: Henry Holt, 1939), 67–69, 234–35, 242–49; John R. McKivigan and Madeleine L. McKivigan, "'He Stands Like Jupiter': The Autobiography of Gerrit Smith," *New York History* 65 (April 1984): 193–94, 196.

11 Redpath to Gerrit Smith, November 1858, Smith Papers.

12 *Boston Atlas and Bee,* 22 October 1859.

13 James Redpath, *The Roving Editor; or, Talks with Slaves in the Southern States* (University Park: Pennsylvania State University Press, 1996), 119.

14 Redpath, *Roving Editor,* 239–46, 248–54; Rossbach, *Ambivalent Conspirators,* 177; Merton L. Dillon, *Slavery Attacked: Southern Slaves and Their Allies, 1619–1865* (Baton Rouge: Louisiana State University Press, 1990), 236–37.

15 Redpath, *Roving Editor,* 86. Redpath defended the propriety and morality of encouraging slave rebellion: "I do not hesitate to urge the friends of the slave to incite insurrections, and encourage, in the North, a spirit which shall ultimate in civil and servile wars. I think it unfair that the American bondsman should have no generous Lafayette. What France was to us in our hour of trial, let the North be to the slave to-day. If the fathers were justified in *their* rebellion, how much more will the slaves be justifiable in *their* insurrection? Ibid., 3–4.

16 Ibid., 87.

17 Ibid., 249, 252, 258; James C. Malin, *John Brown and the Legend of Fifty-Six,* 2 vols. (Philadelphia: American Philosophical Society, 1942), 1:239–41.

18 Redpath, *Roving Editor,* 4.

19 *New York Daily Tribune,* 5 March 1859.

20 *Frederick Douglass' Paper,* 8 April 1859.

21 *The Journals of Bronson Alcott,* edited by Odell Shepard (Boston: Little, Brown, 1938), 323.

22 *New York Daily Tribune,* 12 April 1859; *Frederick Douglass' Paper,* 22 April 1859.

23 *Boston Atlas and Bee,* 30 October 1859; James Redpath, *A Guide to Hayti* (Boston: Thayer and Eldridge, 1860), 10; U.S. Senate, 30th Congress, *Report,* 135–36.

24 James Redpath and Richard J. Hinton, *Hand-Book to Kansas Territory and the Rocky Mountains' Gold Regions* (New York: J. H. Colton, 1859), iii–iv; William E. Connelly, "Col. Richard J. Hinton," *Transactions of the Kansas State Historical Society* 7 (1901–1902): 486–93; Weisberger, "Newspaper Reporter," 639.

25 Redpath and Hinton, *Hand-Book to Kansas Territory,* 3, 20.

26 Ibid., 107.

27 Redpath to Preston J. Plumb, 7 April 1859, James Redpath Papers, Kansas State Historical Society.

28 *Boston Atlas and Bee,* 30 October 1859; Redpath, *Guide to Hayti,* 10.

29 *Boston Atlas and Bee,* 30 October 1859; Francis J. Merriam to John Brown, 23 December 1858, in U.S. Senate, 30th Congress, *Report,* 66–67; Hinton, *John Brown,* 464–65; Oswald Garrison Villard, *John Brown, 1800–1859: A Biography Fifty Years After* (Boston: Houghton Mifflin, 1910), 421; Rossbach, *Ambivalent Conspirators,* 71; Hill Peebles Wilson, *John Brown, Soldier of Fortune: A Critique* (Lawrence, Kan.: Hill P. Wilson, 1913), 342.

30 Brown's party included three of his sons and five black men. Richard O. Boyer, *John Brown: A Biography and a History* (New York: Knopf, 1973), 8–9, 16–18; Oates, *To Purge This Land,* 274–80, 287–302.

31 Redpath, *Captain John Brown,* 7; also see *New York Herald,* 29 October 1859; 10 November 1859; Oates, *To Purge This Land,* 312–15; Tilden C. Edelstein, *Strange Enthusiasm: A Life of Thomas Wentworth Higginson* (New Haven, Conn.: Yale University Press, 1968), 222–27; John R. McKivigan and Madeleine Leveille, "The 'Black Dream' of Gerrit Smith, New York Abolitionist," *Syracuse University Library Associates Courier* 20 (fall 1985): 51–76.

32 *Boston Atlas and Bee,* 21, 24, 28, 29, 30 October 1859; *Lawrence* (Kan.) *Republican,* 10 November 1859; Redpath, *Captain John Brown,* 7; Edelstein, *Strange Enthusiasm,* 226–27; Malin, *John Brown,* 1:284.

33 *Boston Atlas and Bee,* 21 October 1859.

34 Ibid., 24 October 1860.

35 Redpath to William Lloyd Garrison, 13 January 1860, in Boston *Liberator,* 20 January 1860.

36 *Boston Atlas and Bee,* 30 October 1859; also 21, 22, 24, 25, 26 October 1859.

37 Ibid., 28 October 1859; Edelstein, *Strange Enthusiasm,* 226–27.

38 John R. McKivigan, "His Soul Goes Marching On: The Story of John Brown's Followers after the Harpers Ferry Raid," in *Antislavery Violence: Sectional, Racial, and Cultural Conflict in Antebellum America,* edited by John R. McKivigan and Stanley Harrold (Knoxville: University of Tennessee, 1999), 278.

39 Redpath to Thomas Wentworth Higginson, 8, 13 November 1859, Higginson-Brown Collection, Boston Public Library; Hinton, *John Brown,* 374; Rossbach, *Ambivalent Conspirators,* 226.

40 Edelstein, *Strange Enthusiasm,* 227–30; Villard, *John Brown,* 517; Rossbach, *Ambivalent Conspirators,* 226; Oates, *To Purge This Land,* 314–16, 335; O. E. Morse, "An Attempted Rescue of John Brown from the Charleston [*sic*], Va. Jail," *Transactions of the Kansas State Historical Society* 8 (1903–4): 213–26; Wilson, *John Brown,* 384–85; Hinton leaves a very different account. See his *John Brown,* esp. 380–86.

41 W. W. Thayer Autobiography, Laurel C. Thayer Papers, Manuscripts Department, Indiana State Library; also Redpath, *Captain John Brown,* 8. Also see, John R. McKivigan, ed., "The Reminiscences of William Wild Thayer, Boston Publisher and Abolitionist," *Proceedings of the Massachusetts Historical Society* 103 (1991): 138–56.

42 He had entered into the arrangement no later than 8 November 1860. Redpath to Thomas Wentworth Higginson, 8 November 1860, Higginson Papers, Boston Public Library; Redpath, *Captain John Brown,* 9.

43 Redpath, *Captain John Brown,* 8.

44 *New York Daily Tribune,* n.d., as quoted in Malin, *John Brown,* 1:296.

45 Malin, *John Brown,* 1:294; Paul Finkelman, "Manufacturing Martyrdom: The Antislavery Response to John Brown's Raid," in *His Soul Goes Marching On: Responses to John Brown's Raid,* edited by Paul Finkelman (Charlottesville: University of Virginia Press, 1995), 54–58.

46 *Lawrence Herald of Freedom,* 19 November 1859; also see *New York Herald,* 5 November 1859; Malin, *John Brown,* 1:295.

47 *New York Daily Tribune,* 7 November 1859, also see 11, 30 November 1859.

48 Redpath to Thomas Wentworth Higginson, 13 November 1859, Higginson Papers, Boston Public Library; James Foreman to Redpath, 28 September 1859, in Louis Ruchames, ed., *John Brown: The Making of a Revolutionary* (New York: Grosset and Dunlap, 1969), 171–76; Redpath, *Captain John Brown,* 9–10; Malin, *John Brown,* 1:297–98.

49 *Journals of Bronson Alcott,* 323; Sanborn, *John Brown,* 18; Edelstein, *Strange Enthusiasms,* 231; Redpath, *Captain John Brown,* 27–35, 60–72.

50 Redpath, *Captain John Brown,* 9–10; Paul Finkelman, "Manufacturing Martyrdom," 65, n72. Redpath originally had requested Higginson to obtain these for his research. Redpath to Thomas Wentworth Higginson, 8, 13 November 1860, Higginson Papers, Boston Public Library.

51 Redpath to Thomas Wentworth Higginson, 13 November 1859, Higginson-Brown Papers, Boston Public Library, as quoted in Edelstein, *Strange Enthusiasms,* 230.

52 Redpath to Thomas Wentworth Higginson, 15 December 1859, Higginson Papers, Boston Public Library.

53 Malin, *John Brown,* 1:296; McKivigan, "William Wild Thayer," 142.

54 Redpath, *Captain John Brown,* 5–6.

55 Ibid., 8. In his biography of Thomas W. Higginson, Tilden Edelstein contends that Redpath intentionally omitted an advocacy of massive slave insurrection in *Public Life of Captain John Brown,* a contention I believe the above quoted passage refutes. Edelstein, *Strange Enthusiasm,* 226–27; Malin, *John Brown,* 1:230–31: Renehan, *Secret Six,* 221.

56 Redpath, *Captain John Brown,* 82.

57 Redpath to Thomas Wentworth Higginson, 13 November 1859, Higginson-Brown Papers, Boston Public Library. Renehan, *Secret Six,* 218.

58 Francis B. Sanborn related that Redpath stubbornly clung to this incorrect view until his death. Redpath, *Captain John Brown,* 115–20, 126–35, 143–68; Sanborn, *John Brown,* 261.

59 This comment might be overly rhetorical since Brown and Smith had a close relationship. Redpath, *Captain John Brown,* 104–5.

60 Ibid., 238.

61 Ibid., 243–44; American Anti-Slavery Society, *Annual Report . . . for 1860* (1860; New York: Negro Universities Press, 1969), 78; Horace Greeley, *The American Conflict: A History of the Great Rebellion in the United States of America, 1860–1865,* 2 vols. (Hartford, Conn.: O. D. Case, 1864–66), 1:289.

62 Redpath, *Captain John Brown,* 246.

63 Ibid., 253–54.

64 Ibid., 254–55.

65 Ibid., 334; also 275, 292, 296, 309.

66 Ibid., 404; also see 344–407. James C. Malin correctly faults Redpath for helping to perpetuate the legend of John Brown kissing a baby while on his way

to the gallows. See Redpath to C. H. Brainard, 1 June 1860, in *Liberator,* 15 June 1860; James C. Malin, "The John Brown Legend in Pictures," *Kansas Historical Quarterly* 8 (November 1959): 339–45.

67 Redpath, *Captain John Brown,* 3–4.

68 McKivigan, 'William Wild Thayer," 143; Thayer, "Autobiography," 12; *New York Tribune,* 28 January 1860; *British and Foreign Anti-Slavery Reporter,* ser. 3, 8 (June 1860): 143; Allan Nevins, *The Emergence of Lincoln,* 2 vols. (New York: Charles Scribner's Son, 1950), 2:100; Agnes Rush Burr, *Russell H. Conwell and His Work: One Man's Interpretation of Life* (Philadelphia: John C. Winston, 1926), 321; Renehan, *Secret Six,* 221.

69 *Frank Leslie's Illustrated Newspaper,* 25 February 1860. The *New York Daily Tribune* published a lengthy summary of the book rather than a critical review. *New York Tribune,* 21 January 1860.

70 Advertising supplement bound with Redpath, *Guide to Hayti,* 2–3.

71 *Atlantic Monthly* 5 (March 1860): 378–81.

72 *Liberator,* n.d., reprinted in advertising supplement bound with Redpath, *Guide to Hayti,* 9–10.

73 This undated letter to the editor of *Atlantic Monthly* was never published and eventually came into the possession of Thomas Wentworth Higginson. Thomas Wentworth Higginson Papers, Kansas State Historical Society. Also see, Malin, *John Brown,* 1:303.

74 Franklin B. Sanborn to Henry D. Thoreau, 16 January 1860, in *Companion to Thoreau's Correspondence,* edited by Keith Walter Cameron (Hartford, Conn.: Transcendental Books, [1964?]), 179–80.

75 *British and Foreign Anti-Slavery Reporter,* ser. 3, 8 (June 1860): 143.

76 *The Dial* (Cincinnati), 1 (March 1869): 200; Moncure Daniel Conway, *Autobiography, Memories and Experiences,* 2 vols. (Boston: Houghton, Mifflin, 1904), 1:302–3.

77 Greeley, *American Conflict,* 1:282; *Lewisburg* (Pa.) *Star and Chronicle,* n.d., reprinted in advertising supplement bound with Redpath, *Guide to Hayti,* 6.

78 Malin, *John Brown,* 1:303–5; also see, W. E. Burghardt DuBois, *John Brown* (Philadelphia: George W. Jacobs, 1909), 72–73, 147–48, 181; Oates, *To Purge This Land,* 317; Paul Finkelman, "John Brown and His Raid," in *His Soul Goes Marching On: Responses to John Brown's Raid,* edited by Paul Finkelman (Charlottesville: University of Virginia Press, 1995), 4.

79 Redpath to Henry David Thoreau, 6 February 1860, in *The Correspondence of Henry David Thoreau,* edited by Walter Harding and Carl Bode (New York: New York University Press, 1958), 574–75.

80 I have described this plot in my essay, "His Soul Goes Marching On," 274–97. Also see Redpath to Thomas Wentworth Higginson, 19 January 1860, Higginson Papers, Boston Public Library; Hinton, *John Brown,* 520–22; Villard, *John Brown,* 574; Edelstein, *Strange Enthusiasms,* 234–36; Renehan, *Secret Six,* 214–20, 247, 252–62; Morse, "Attempted Rescue of John Brown," 219–20; McKivigan, "William Wild Thayer," 147–50.

81 U.S. Senate, 30th Congress, *Report of the Select Committee of the Senate Appointed to Inquire into the Late Invasion and Seizure of the Public Property at Harper's Ferry,* 198, also 19, 30, 31, 33–34, 66–67, 135–37, 200–201, 250; Renehan, *Secret Six,* 236–51.

82 Redpath to James Murray Mason, 1 February 1860, in *New York Herald,* 6 February 1860; Renehan, *Secret Six,* 257.

83 U.S. Senate, 30th Congress, *Report of the Select Committee of the Senate Appointed to Inquire into the Late Invasion and Seizure of the Public Property at Harper's Ferry,* 33–34; *New York Daily Tribune,* 16 February 1860; Villard, *John Brown,* 582.

84 Redpath to John Brown Jr., 5 February 1860; 28 March 1860, John Brown Jr. Papers, Rutherford B. Hayes Historical Center; Redpath to Henry David Thoreau, 6 February 1860, in *Correspondence of Henry David Thoreau,* 574–75; Redpath to Wendell Phillips, 13 February 1860, Crawford Blagden Collection, Houghton Library, Harvard University; *Life in Letters of William Dean Howells,* edited by Mildred Howells, 2 vols. (Garden City, N.Y.: Doubleday, Doran, 1928), 1:26–27; Renehan, *Secret Six,* 212–13; McKivigan, "His Soul," 278–80.

85 Redpath to James H. Lane, 8 March 1860, in *Lawrence* (Kan.) *Republican,* 22 March 1860.

86 Ibid., also 29 March 1860; G. Raymond Gaeddert, *The Birth of Kansas* (Lawrence: University of Kansas, 1940), 9–13, 80–84. William Phillips also made public statements upholding Redpath's side in the controversy and attacking Robinson's general credibility. William A. Phillips to Redpath, 24 February 1869, in Hinton, *John Brown,* 44–45.

87 Redpath to John Brown Jr., 5 April 1860, John Brown Jr. Papers, Rutherford B. Hayes Historical Center; also see Redpath to H. N. Rust, 15 April 1860, Manuscripts Department, The Huntington; Rossbach, *Ambivalent Conspirators,* 261–64; McKivigan, "William Wild Thayer," 151–53.

88 Redpath to Thomas Wentworth Higginson, 20 April 1860, Redpath Papers, Kansas State Historical Society.

89 "William Handy" [William W. Thayer] to Thomas Wentworth Higginson, 3, 6, 16 April 1860, Higginson Papers, Kansas State Historical Society; McKivigan, "William Wild Thayer," 151–53.

90 Redpath to John Brown Jr., 26 April 1860; 10 May 1860, John Brown Jr. Papers, Rutherford B. Hayes Library; *Douglass' Monthly* 3 (June 1860), 288.

91 Mason Committee Report, 19.

92 From Thoreau, Redpath received not only permission to reprint his lecture on John Brown but an invitation for the abolitionist and his wife to dine with him in Concord. Redpath to Henry David Thoreau, 6 February 1860, in *Correspondence of Henry David Thoreau,* 574–75; Redpath to Maria Weston Chapman, 12, 17 January 1860, Maria Weston Chapman Papers, Boston Public Library; Redpath to Thomas Wentworth Higginson, 20 April 1860, Redpath Papers, Kansas State Historical Society.

93 James Redpath, *Echoes of Harper's Ferry* (Boston, 1860); John Tebbell, *A History of Book Publishing in the United States,* 4 vols. (New York: R. R. Bowker, 1972), 1:444–45; Redpath to John Brown Jr., 5 February 1860; 28 March 1860, John Brown Jr. Papers; William W. Thayer to Thomas Wentworth Higginson, 6 April 1860, Higginson Papers, Kansas State Historical Society; Redpath to Thomas Wentworth Higginson, 20 April 1860, Redpath Papers, Kansas State Historical State; Wendy Hamand Venet, " 'Cry Aloud and Spare Not': Northern Antislavery Women and John Brown's Raid," in *His Soul Goes Marching On: Responses*

to *John Brown's Raid*, edited by Paul Finkelman (Charlottesville: University of Virginia Press, 1995), 105, 110.

94 Redpath, *Echoes*, 9.

95 Redpath dedicated the book to Fabre Geffrard, the president of Haiti, the only black nation to have won its independence from European domination through rebellion. Ibid., x.

96 Ibid., 7.

97 Redpath to William Lloyd Garrison, 13 January 1860, in Redpath, ibid., 310–11; also see *Liberator,* 20 January 1860.

98 Redpath, *Echoes*, 385–34. The book contains an odd appendix of *New York Tribune* editorials on slavery and the union from 1854, which Redpath hints that he helped prepare. Ibid., 457–513.

99 *New York Times,* 19 May 1860 (Supplement).

100 Redpath to Walt Whitman, 25 June 1860, in Horace Traubel, *With Walt Whitman,* 5 vols. (Boston: Small, Maynard, 1906–64), 3:460–61; Kaplan, *Walt Whitman,* 247–56; McKivigan, "William Wild Thayer," 143.

101 James Redpath, *Southern Notes for National Circulation* (Boston: Thayer and Eldrige, 1860), 3.

102 Ibid., 80.

103 Ibid., 94.

104 The dedication was dated 4 July 1860. Ibid., 3, 132.

105 Redpath to John Brown Jr., 2 July 1860, in *Liberator,* 27 July 1860.

106 Redpath publicized notices asking for information on these men but never wrote the book. *Liberator,* 29 June 1860; also see Redpath to Horatio Nelson Rust, 23 January 1860, Horatio Nelson Rust Papers, Huntington Library; Redpath to Henry David Thoreau, 6 February 1860, in *Correspondence of Henry David Thoreau,* 574–75.

107 Redpath to John Brown Jr., 5 February 1860; 5 April 1860, John Brown Jr. Papers, Rutherford B. Hayes Historical Center; Thaddeus Hyatt to Friends, 16 July 1860, in *New York Weekly Tribune,* 28 July 1860; advertising supplement bound with Redpath, *Guide to Hayti,* 1; Nevins, *Emergence of Lincoln,* 2:100.

108 C. H. Brainard to Redpath, 1 July 1860, in *Liberator,* 27 July 1860; also Redpath to William Lloyd Garrison, 28 June 1860, Garrison Papers, Boston Public Library.

109 *Liberator,* 27 July 1860. Henry David Thoreau and Frederick Douglass also sent noteworthy letters to be read. Hinton, *John Brown,* 506.

110 Redpath to John Brown Jr., 2 July 1860, in *Liberator,* 27 July 1860; Redpath to H. N. Rust, 11 July 1860, Rust Papers, Huntington Library; *Douglass' Monthly* 3 (September 1860), 331–33; Hinton, *John Brown,* 506.

111 *Liberator,* 30 November 1860; *National Anti-Slavery Standard,* 1 December 1860; *New York Weekly Tribune,* 8 December 1860. Ralph Waldo Emerson had been invited but instead spoke at a similar service in Concord on the same day. Garrison declined for medical reasons. James Miller McKim and Gerrit Smith also declined Redpath's invitation. James McKim to James Redpath, 23 November 1860, Department of Rare Books, Cornell University Library; Redpath to Gerrit Smith, 28 November 1860, Smith Papers; Garrison to Redpath, 1 December 1860, Garrison Papers, Boston Public Library; *Liberator,* 7 December 1860; Ralph L. Rusk, *Letters of Ralph Waldo Emerson,* 6 vols. (New

York: Columbia University Press, 1939), 5:182; Thomas H. O'Connor, *Civil War Boston: Home Front and Battlefield* (Boston: Northeastern University Press, 1997), 42–44.

112 Henry Wilson to James Redpath, 27 November 1860, in *Liberator,* 14 December 1860.

113 *New York Daily Tribune,* 3 December 1860, also see 7 December 1860; *Liberator,* 7 December 1860; Wendell Phillips, *Speeches, Lectures, and Letters* (Boston: James Redpath, 1863), 319–42; O'Connor, *Civil War Boston,* 42–43.

114 *Boston Post,* 4 December 1860.

115 Phillips, *Speeches, Lectures, and Letters,* 339; O'Connor, *Civil War Boston,* 43–44; McKivigan, "William Wild Thayer," 153–56.

116 Villard, *John Brown,* 583.

117 In addition, Redpath wrote *Guide to Hayti.*

Chapter 4. Commissioner Plenipotentiary for Haiti

1 Chris Dixon, *African America and Haiti: Emigration and Black Nationalism in the Nineteenth Century* (Westport, Conn.: Greenwood, 2000), 2–3, 31–32; Robert S. Levine, *Martin Delany, Frederick Douglass, and the Politics of Representative Identity* (Chapel Hill: University of North Carolina Press, 1997), 50.

2 Redpath to Wendell Phillips, 13 February [1860], Crawford Blagden Collection, Houghton Library, Harvard University; James Redpath, *A Guide to Hayti* (Boston: Haytian Bureau of Emigration, 1861), 9; James Brewer Stewart, *Wendell Phillips: Liberty's Hero* (Baton Rouge: Louisiana State University Press, 1986), 104, 184, 199; Dixon, *African America and Haiti,* 102–3. Phillips's lecture powerfully argued for the ability of black slaves to rise up against their masters and prove their right to be free: "Some doubt the courage of the negro. Go to Hayti, and stand on [the] fifty thousand graves of the best soldiers France ever had, and ask them what they think of the negro's sword. . . . There never was a race that weakened and degraded by such chattel slavery, unaided, tore off its fetters, forged them into swords, and won its liberty on the battlefield, but one, and that was the black race of St. Domingo." Wendell Phillips, *Speeches, Lectures, and Letters* (Boston: James Redpath, 1863), 491–92.

3 *Boston Atlas and Bee,* 30 October 1859.

4 The first article in the *New York Tribune* was written on 23 January 1859 and appeared in the issue of 12 April 1859. The first *National Anti-Slavery Standard* article was written a day later but appeared on 26 March 1859.

5 *New York Daily Tribune,* 12 April 1859; also *National Anti-Slavery Standard,* 26 March 1859; *Frederick Douglass' Paper,* 22, 29 April 1859; *New York Weekly Tribune,* 7 May 1859.

6 *New York Daily Tribune,* 12 April 1859, *Frederick Douglass' Paper,* 22 April 1859; *New York Weekly Tribune,* 7 May 1859; *National Anti-Slavery Standard,* 26 March 1859.

7 *New York Weekly Tribune,* 7 May 1859. Also see David Nicholls, *From Dessalines to Duvalier: Race, Colour, and National Independence in Haiti* (New Brunswick, N.J.: Rutgers University Press, 1979), 12, 69–71, 82–85, 107; Dixon, *African America and Haiti,* 134.

8 *New York Daily Tribune,* 12, 30 April 1859; 14 May 1859; 25 June 1859; *New York Weekly Tribune,* 7, 14, 28 May 1859; 2, 9 July 1859; *National Anti-Slavery Standard,* 14 May 1859.

9 *New York Daily Tribune,* 25 June 1859.

10 Ibid., 14 May 1859; 22 October 1859; *Frederick Douglass' Paper,* 27 May 1859; *New York Weekly Tribune,* 9 July 1859.

11 *New York Daily Tribune,* 25 June 1859; also 30 April 1859; *Frederick Douglass' Paper,* 20 May 1859; *New York Weekly Tribune,* 28 May 1859.

12 *New York Daily Tribune,* 12 April 1859; also 30 April 1859; *Frederick Douglass' Paper,* 22, 29 April 1859; 20 May 1859; *New York Weekly Tribune,* 7 May 1859. See also Nicholls, *From Dessalines to Duvalier,* 68–69.

13 *New York Daily Tribune,* 30 April 1859; 25 June 1859; *Frederick Douglass' Paper,* 20 May 1859. On abolitionist environmentalism, see Paul Goodman, *Of One Blood: Abolitionism and the Origins of Racial Equality* (Berkeley: University of California Press, 1998), 9, 20, 57–61.

14 Redpath, *Guide to Hayti,* 164.

15 *New York Daily Tribune,* 22 October 1859; also 12 April 1859; *Frederick Douglass' Paper,* 29 April 1859; *New York Weekly Tribune,* 14 May 1859; Redpath, *Guide to Hayti,* 164–67.

16 *New York Daily Tribune,* 12 April 1859; 25 May 1859; Rochester *Frederick Douglass' Paper,* 22 April 1859; 17 June 1859; *New York Weekly Tribune,* 7 May 1859. When the two white men stayed at the cabin of a West-Indian-born black who spoke good English, Redpath recounted their conversations in detail. More often, he had to rely on Merriam or other Americans and Europeans he encountered in Haiti to communicate with the black natives. *New York Daily Tribune,* 14 May 1859; 22 October 1859; 1 November 1859; *Frederick Douglass' Paper,* 27 May 1859; *New York Weekly Tribune,* 9 July 1859.

17 *New York Daily Tribune,* 12 April 1859; *Frederick Douglass' Paper,* 29 April 1859; *New York Weekly Tribune,* 14 May 1859.

18 *New York Daily Tribune,* 30 April 1859; *Frederick Douglass' Paper,* 20 May 1859; *New York Weekly Tribune,* 2 July 1859. There were several exceptions that Redpath made to his otherwise high appraisal of the Haitian character. He criticized the loose sexual practices of Haitians of all classes. Describing the frequency of concubinage and "free love" practices, he argued that such practices exploited women: "Unfitted by her sensitive and delicate nature to cope with man—in the various modes of obtaining a subsistence, women require all the protection which the most stringent legal and religious forms and obligations can give to the sacred institution of marriage. Let reformers who doubt this truth, come here and see the results of their system. It corrupts man and degrades women." *New York Daily Tribune,* 18 April 1859; *Frederick Douglass' Paper,* 13 May 1859; *New York Weekly Tribune,* 28 May 1859.

19 *New York Daily Tribune,* 30 April 1859; 25 June 1859; *Frederick Douglass' Paper,* 20 May 1859; *New York Weekly Tribune,* 2 July 1859; *National Anti-Slavery Standard,* 14 May 1859.

20 *New York Daily Tribune,* 25 May 1859; *Frederick Douglass' Paper,* 17 June 1859; *National Anti-Slavery Standard,* 14 May 1859.

21 *National Anti-Slavery Standard,* 14 May 1859.

22 *National Anti-Slavery Standard,* 14 May 1859. A slave who rose to be a general in the Haitian revolution for independence, Jean Jacques Dessalines (1758–1806)

proclaimed himself emperor in 1804 and ruled until being assassinated two years later. Nicholls, *From Dessalines to Duvalier,* 33–40.

23 *New York Daily Tribune,* 13 July 1859; also 25 June 1859.

24 Ibid., 25 June 1859; also *National Anti-Slavery Standard,* 14 May 1859.

25 *New York Daily Tribune,* 25 June 1859.

26 Geffrard did exercise his constitutional power to dissolve the legislature in June 1863. H. P. Davis, *Black Democracy: The Story of Haiti* (New York: Dial Press, 1929), 119–25; Robert Debs Heinl Jr. and Nancy Gordon Heinl, *Written in Blood: The Story of the Haitian People, 1492–1971* (Boston: Houghton Mifflin, 1978), 209–26; Nicholls, *From Dessalines to Duvalier,* 83–85; Dixon, *African America and Haiti,* 193.

27 Floyd J. Miller, *The Search for a Black Nationality: Black Emigration and Colonization, 1787–1863* (Urbana, Ill.: University of Illinois Press, 1975), 236, 238; Heinl and Heinl, *Written in Blood,* 223; Willis D. Boyd, "James Redpath and American Negro Colonization in Haiti, 1860–1862," *The Americas* 12 (October 1955): 170, 172.

28 Miller, *Search for a Black Nationality,* 236.

29 Redpath to "The Free Persons of Color in Missouri and the North," 23 April 1859, in *New York Daily Tribune,* 30 April 1859; *Frederick Douglass' Paper,* 6 May 1859; *National Anti-Slavery Standard,* 7 May 1859.

30 Jane H. Pease and William H. Pease, *They Who Would Be Free: Blacks' Search for Freedom, 1830–1861* (New York: Antheneum, 1974), 21–22, 255; Goodman, *Of One Blood,* 11–28; Levine, *Martin Delany, Frederick Douglass,* 80, 91; Dixon, *African America and Haiti,* 20–24.

31 Robert A. Warner, *New Haven Negroes, A Social History* (New Haven: Yale University Press, 1940), 108; Dixon, *African America and Haiti,* 66–67; Howard H. Bell, "The Negro Emigration Movement, 1849–1854: A Phase of Negro Nationalism," *Phylon* 20 (summer 1959): 134, 141–42, and "Negro Nationalism: A Factor in Emigration Projects, 1858–1861," *Journal of Negro History* 47(January 1962): 42.

32 David W. Blight, *Frederick Douglass' Civil War: Keeping Faith in Jubilee* (Baton Rouge: Louisiana State University Press, 1989), 128–31; Miller, *Search for a Black Nationality,* 115–33, 192–93, 228–31; Pease and Pease, *They Who Would Be Free,* 267–72.

33 Vincent Harding, *There Is a River: The Black Struggle for Freedom in America* (New York: Harcourt, Brace, Jovanich, 1981), 184–92; Pease and Pease, *They Who Would Be Free,* 262–66, 272–75; Miller, *Search for a Black Nationality,* 93–94, 124–29, 160, 171–83, 201–15; Levine, *Martin Delany, Frederick Douglass,* 24–26; Blight, *Frederick Douglass's Civil War,* 128; Dixon, *African America and Haiti,* 75–77, 116–17.

34 The society hoped to aid Africa by sending it talented black farmers, artisans, and preachers to elevate their civilization. Garnet also claimed that such an emigration could assist in the production of free-labor cotton in Africa thereby undercutting the economic props of slavery in the United States. Pease and Pease, *They Who Would Be Free,* 267–70; Benjamin Quarles, *Black Abolitionists* (New York: Oxford University Press, 1969), 217–21. Miller, *Search for a Black Nationality,* 191–93; Blight, *Frederick Douglass's Civil War,* 128; Dixon, *African America and Haiti,* 117–18.

35 Pease and Pease, *They Who Would Be Free,* 270, 271–72; Miller, *Search for a Black Nationality,* 153–66; Dixon, *African America and Haiti,* 77–82, 119–20.

36 Waldo E. Martin, Jr., *The Mind of Frederick Douglass* (Chapel Hill: University of North Carolina Press, 1984), 89; Earl Ofari, *"Let Your Motto Be Resistance": The Life and Thought of Henry Highland Garnet* (Beacon: Beacon Press, 1972), 100–101; Boyd, "James Redpath," 169.

37 The Haitian government, in return, made official pronouncements praising the courage shown by John Brown and his followers at Harpers Ferry. Dixon, *African America and Haiti*, 133, 154–55.

38 The self-proclaimed Haitian emperor Faustin I had even encouraged southern slaveholders to consider sending manumitted slaves to Haiti. *National Anti-Slavery Standard*, 4 May 1859; Dixon, *African America and Haiti*, 34–35, 47; Heinl and Heinl, *Written in Blood*, 215.

39 Theodore P. Holly, "Thoughts on Hayti," *The Afro-American Magazine* 1 (1859–60), 185; James O. Horton and Lois E. Horton, *Black Bostonians: Family Life and Community Struggle in the Antebellum North* (New York: Holmes and Meier, 1977), 122; Benjamin Quarles, *Lincoln and the Negro* (New York: Oxford University Press, 1962), 119; Dixon, *African America and Haiti*, 74, 106, 141–45, 156–57, Miller, *Search for a Black Nationality*, 237–38; Pease and Pease, *They Who Would Be Free*, 274–75; Bell, "Negro Nationalism," 44–46; Dixon, *African America and Haiti*, 8–9, 67–68, 95–97, 103–13, 141–45; David M. Dean, *Defender of the Race: James Theodore Holly, Black Nationalist Bishop* (Boston: Lambeth Press, 1979), 20–30, 34.

40 *New York Daily Tribune*, 2 May 1859; Redpath, *Guide to Hayti*, 10.

41 *New York Daily Tribune*, 16, 18, 23 April 1859; 4 May 1859.

42 *Boston Atlas and Bee*, 30 October 1859.

43 Redpath, *Guide to Hayti*, 10.

44 Ibid., 10; *Boston Atlas and Bee* 31 October 1859; Redpath *Guide to Hayti*, 10, 166.

45 *Douglass' Monthly* 3(September 1860); *Liberator*, 5 October 1860; also *New York Daily Tribune*, 22 October 1859.

46 *Liberator*, 5 October 1860; *Douglass' Monthly* 3 (November 1860), 358–60; Redpath to Geffrard, 4 August 1860, Redpath, *Guide to Hayti*, 9, 120–26.

47 *New York Daily Tribune*, 9 November 1860; *Douglass' Monthly* 3 (January 1861), 399; Redpath, *Guide to Hayti*, 63–64. Most secondary accounts note the initial Haitian plan to settle emigrants as sharecroppers but not the later homestead legislation. For example, see Ofari, *Henry Highland Garnet*, 99; Miller, *Search for a Black Nationality*, 236–37; Boyd, "James Redpath," 171.

48 Redpath to Victorien Pleasance, 7 April, 11 August, 14 September 1861, in "James Redpath, Letters and Reports as General Agent of Emigration to Haiti, March 31 to December 27, 1861" (Manuscripts Division, Library of Congress); Redpath to William Lloyd Garrison, 2 July 1861, in *Liberator*, 12 July 1861.

49 Redpath to Victorien Pleasance, 24 June 1864, HEB Letterbook, Library of Congress; Redpath, *Guide to Hayti*, 110–11, 120–24; Dixon, *African America and Haiti*, 146; Dean, *Defender of the Race*, 34.

50 Boyd, "James Redpath," 172; Dixon, *African America and Haiti*, 146. Redpath's correspondence with these two Haitian officials as well as that with his agents in the United States can be found in four separate letterbooks in the following libraries: the Library of Congress (Manuscripts Division), the Boston Public Library, the New York Public Library (Schomburg Branch), and the William R. Perkins Library, Duke University.

51 *Liberator,* 2 November 1860; also "Weekly Report of James Redpath, General Agent of Emigration to Hayti," No. 1, 3 November 1860, Haitian Emigration Letterbook, Boston Public Library.

52 Redpath to John Brown Jr., 17 October 1860, John Brown Jr. Papers, Rutherford B. Hayes Research Center; *Liberator,* 5 October 1860.

53 *New York Daily Tribune,* 9 November 1860; *Weekly Anglo-African,* 27 April 1861; *Douglass' Monthly* 3 (October 1860), 341; 3 (November 1860), 358–60; 3 (May 1861), 463–64; 4 (September 1861), 720; "Weekly Report of James Redpath, General Agent of Emigration to Hayti," No. 29, HEB Letterbook, Library of Congress.

54 Weekly Report of James Redpath, General Agent of Emigration to Hayti," no. 1, 3 November 1860, HEB Letterbook, Boston Public Library; "Weekly Report of James Redpath, General Agent of Emigration to Hayti," no. 29, HEB Letterbook, Library of Congress; Redpath to John Brown Jr., 10 February 1861, John Brown Jr. Papers, Rutherford B. Hayes Research Center; Redpath to Frederick Douglass, 30 March 1861, HEB Letterbook, Duke University.

55 Redpath to August Elie, 23 February 1861, HEB Letterbook, Duke University.

56 For examples, see Redpath to James H. Hall, 25 February 1861, Redpath to H. Griffin, 2 March 1861, Duke Letterbook; "Weekly Report of James Redpath, General Agent of Emigration to Hayti," no. 7, 1 December 1860; no. 11, 18 December 1860, HEB Letterbook, Boston Public Library; "Weekly Report of James Redpath, General Agent of Emigration to Hayti," no. 28, 31 March 1861, Library of Congress.

57 "Weekly Report of James Redpath, General Agent of Emigration to Hayti," no. 2, 12 November 1861; no. 9, 9 December 1860; no. 11, 18 December 1860, HEB Letterbook, Boston Public Library; Redpath to Victorien Pleaseance, 24 June 1861. See also John Tebbel, *A History of Book Publishing in the United States,* 4 vols. (New York: R. R. Bowker, 1972), 1:444.

58 Redpath, *Guide to Hayti,* 3, also 10.

59 Ibid., 11.

60 The *Pine and Palm* also was published in an awkward manner. Lawrence and Hinton in New York composed the editorial materials but then shipped them to Boston where Redpath's corresponding secretary, A. E. Newton, oversaw the newspaper's printing and distribution. Redpath to John Brown Jr., 16 March 1861, John Brown Jr. Papers, Rutherford B. Hayes Research Center; Redpath to Richard J. Hinton, 18 March 1861; 1, 3 April 1861, Redpath to James N. Holmes, 3 April 1861, Redpath to George L. Lawrence, 8 April 1861; 15 May 1861, HEB Letterbook, Duke University; "Weekly Report of James Redpath, General Agent of Emigration to Hayti," no. 7, 1 December 1860; no. 19, 2 February 1861; no. 24, 7 March 1861; no. 26, 16 March 1861; no. 27, 23 March 1861, HEB Letterbook, Boston Public Library; "Weekly Report of James Redpath, General Agent of Emigration to Hayti," no. 28, 31 March 1861, 27 May 1861, 24 June 1861, HEB Letterbook, Library of Congress; *Douglass' Monthly* 3 (January 1861), 389, 399 (April 1861), 438; *Weekly Anglo-African,* March 16, 1861; Ludwell Lee Montague, *Haiti and the United States, 1714–1938* (Durham, N.C.: Duke University Press, 1940), 74; Penelope L. Bullock, *The Afro-American Press, 1838–1909* (Baton Rouge: Louisiana State University Press, 1981), 57–63, 72; Horton and Horton, *Black Bostonians,* 122; Dean, *Defender of the Race,* 35–36.

61 *Weekly Anglo-African,* 27 April 1861; Redpath to H. Highland Garnet, 24 February 1861, HEB Letterbook, Duke University.

62 Redpath, *Guide to Hayti,* 172. Also see, *Pine and Palm,* 12 June 1862; Sharon Ann Carroll, "Elitism and Reform: Some Antislavery Opinion Makers in the Era of Civil War and Reconstruction" (Ph.D. Diss., Cornell University, 1970), 95–97, 99.

63 Redpath, *Guide to Hayti,* 175; also Redpath to C. W. Jacobs, 25 March 1861, HEB Letterbook, Duke University; Dixon, *African America and Haiti,* 158.

64 Redpath, *Guide to Haiti,* 9, also see 174; Dixon, *African America and Haiti,* 160–61.

65 Redpath, *Guide to Hayti,* 9.

66 Ibid., 10; also see "Weekly Report of James Redpath, General Agent of Emigration to Hayti," no. 18, 3 February 1861, HEB Letterbook, Boston Public Library; Dixon, *African America and Haiti,* 161; Boyd, "James Redpath," 173.

67 I have been influenced in drawing this conclusion by Dixon, *African America and Haiti,* 161–65.

68 "Weekly Report of James Redpath, General Agent of Emigration to Hayti," no. 8, 7 December 1860; no. 11, 18 December 1860, HEB Letterbook, Boston Public Library.

69 Redpath to Charles Sumner, 17 March 1861, Letters of Application and Recommendation during the Administrations of Abraham Lincoln and Andrew Johnson, M 650, Reel 41; "Weekly Report of James Redpath, General Agent of Emigration to Hayti," no. 26, 16 March 1861, HEB Letterbook, Boston Public Library; Redpath to John Greenleaf Whittier, 1 June 1861, G. W. Pickard Collection, Houghton Library, Harvard University.

70 *Pine and Palm,* 6 July 1861, also 31 August 1861; 9 November 1861. Two months later, Redpath anticipated other antislavery radicals by editorially endorsing John C. Frémont as a replacement for Lincoln on the next Republican ticket. *Pine and Palm,* 21 September 1861; also see 19 October, 3 November 1861.

71 Redpath to Auguste Elie, 6 May 1861, as quoted in Boyd, "James Redpath," 173; also see *Pine and Palm,* 2, 22 June 1861; 3 November 1861.

72 Other agents included J. Dennis Harris, the Reverend Samuel V. Berry, and the Reverend John B. Smith. James Redpath and Richard J. Hinton, *Hand-book to Kansas Territory and the Rocky Mountains' Gold Region* (New York: J.H. Colton, 1859); Redpath to Richard J. Hinton, 18 March 1861; 17, 23, 30 May 1861, Redpath to George Lawrence, June 5, 1861, HEB Letterbook, Duke University; Robin W. Winks, *The Blacks in Canada: A History* (Montreal: McGill-Queen's University Press, 1971), 164–65; Boyd, "James Redpath," 175; Miller, *Search for a Black Nationality,* 238; Dixon, *African America and Haiti,* 147–48 150, 153–54, 157, 169, 183.

73 Redpath to H. Ford Douglas, 12 May 1861, HEB Letterbook, Duke University; also "Weekly Report of James Redpath, General Agent of Emigration to Hayti," 24 June 1861, HEB Letterbook, Library of Congress.

74 Redpath to John Brown Jr., 10 February 1861, John Brown Jr. Papers, Rutherford B. Hayes Research Center; R. L. Harris, "H. Ford Douglas: Afro-American Antislavery Emigrationist," *Journal of Negro History* 62 (July 1977): 228.

75 Redpath to Richard J. Hinton, 10 November 1860; "Weekly Report of James Redpath, General Agent of Emigration to Hayti," no. 4, 17 November 1860; no. 8, 7 December 1860; no. 10, 12 December 1860; no. 24, 7 March 1861,

HEB Letterbook, Boston Public Library; "Weekly Report of James Redpath, General Agent of Emigration to Hayti," 24 June 1861, HEB Letterbook, Library of Congress.

76 *Douglass' Monthly* 3 (December 1860), 373; Redpath to Ad. Ackermann, 20 November 1860, "Weekly Report of James Redpath, General Agent of Emigration to Hayti," no. 9, 9 December 1860; no. 11, 18 December 1860; no. 15, 12 January 1861, HEB Letterbook, Boston Public Library; Redpath to Ad. Ackermann, 2, 6 March 1861, HEB Letterbook, Duke University; Dixon, *African America and Haiti*, 136–39, 196.

77 *Pine and Palm*, 25 May 1861; "Weekly Report of James Redpath, General Agent of Emigration to Hayti," no. 27, 23 March 1861, HEB Letterbook, Boston Public Library.

78 Redpath to John Brown Jr., 17 October, 12 December 1860, John Brown Jr. Collection, Rutherford B. Hayes Presidential Center; "Weekly Report of James Redpath, General Agent of Emigration to Hayti," no. 16, 21 January 1861; no. 19, 2 February 1861, HEB Letterbook, Boston Public Library.

79 Redpath to C. B. Cellew [?], 21 May 1861, HEB Letterbook, Duke University.

80 The *Weekly Anglo-African* also reprinted Holly's "Thoughts on Hayti." *Weekly Anglo-African*, 6, 20, 27 April 1861; Redpath to James Theodore Holly, 9 November 1860, "Weekly Report of James Redpath, General Agent of Emigration to Hayti," no. 15, 12 January 1861; no. 26, 16 March 1861, HEB Letterbook, Boston Public Library; Miller, *Search for a Black Nationality*, 240–41; Dean, *Defender of the Race*, 34; Dixon, *African America and Haiti*, 148; Stefan Cohen, "Holly for Haiti: James Theodore Holly and the Haitian Emigration Bureau" (Unpublished senior's honor thesis, Yale University, 1986), 2, 6, 11–14.

81 As quoted in Dixon, *African America and Haiti*, 154. See also "Weekly Report of James Redpath, General Agent of Emigration to Hayti," no. 12, 23 February 1861, HEB Letterbook, Boston Public Library; Redpath to H. Ford Douglas, 12 May 1861, HEB Letterbook, Duke University; Harris, "H. Ford Douglas," 228.

82 Quoted in Martin B. Pasternak, "Rise Now and Fly to Arms: The Life of Henry Highland Garnet" (Ph.D. diss., University of Massachusetts, 1981), 167–68. Pasternak, "Henry Highland Garnet," 168. See also *Weekly Anglo-African*, 27 April 1861; Blight, *Frederick Douglass' Civil War*, 128–31; Dixon, *African America and Haiti*, 148–49, 158–59.

83 Brown had visited Haiti in the early 1840s but had never previously favored schemes of mass emigration for blacks. Besides lecturing, Brown also wrote reports on the conditions of blacks in the communities where he visited and historical articles on the exploits of two slave rebels, Nat Turner and Madison Washington, for the *Pine and Palm*. *Pine and Palm*, 3, 17 August 1861; Edward Farrison, *William Wells Brown: Author and Reformer* (Chicago: University of Chicago Press, 1969), 336.

84 *Pine and Palm*, 1 June 1861. See also Dixon, *African America and Haiti*, 149, 152–53, 154–55.

85 *Pine and Palm*, 3 August 1861, also 21, 28 September 1861. See also Dixon, *African America and Haiti*, 149, 150–52, 157–58; Levine, *Martin Delany, Frederick Douglass*, 216–17.

86 Douglass had editorialized against Haitian emigration as late as May 1859. *Douglass' Monthly* 1 (May 1859), 70. Also see, Levine, *Martin Delany, Frederick*

Douglass, 216–17; Martin, *Mind of Frederick Douglass,* 74; Dixon, *African America and Haiti,* 167; Bell, "Negro Emigration Movement," 135, 138.

87 *Douglass' Monthly* 3 (January 1861), 386–87; "Weekly Report of James Redpath, General Agent of Emigration to Hayti," no. 20, 9 February 1861, HEB Letterbook, Boston Public Library. See also, Blight, *Frederick Douglass' Civil War,* 131.

88 *Douglass' Monthly* 3 (March 1861), 420; Redpath to Frederick Douglass, 30 March 1861, HEB Letterbook, Duke University. See also, Blight, *Frederick Douglass' Civil War,* 110

89 As quoted in Dixon, *African America and Haiti,* 167.

90 *Douglass' Monthly* 3 (May 1861), 449–50; Redpath to Frederick Douglass, 20 March, 5 April 1861, HEB Letterbook, Duke University; Joel Schor, *Henry Highland Garnet: A Voice of Black Radicalism in the Nineteenth Century* (Westport, Conn.: Greenwood Press, 1977), 176–77; Blight, *Frederick Douglass' Civil War,* 132–33; Dixon, *African America and Haiti,* 167–68. The other leading black editor, Robert Hamilton of the *Weekly Anglo-African,* before its purchase by Redpath, took no "official position" on Haitian emigration but published letters from Garnet and others advocating it. *Weekly Anglo-African,* 29 December 1860. It is noteworthy that Redpath rejected a similar request by white abolitionist Daniel Monecure Conway for free passage to Haiti to inspect the achievements of American emigrants to there, claiming financial reasons. Redpath to Daniel Monecure Conway, 20 May 1861, HEB Letterbook, Duke University.

91 Blight, *Frederick Douglass' Civil War,* 133–34. Schor, *Henry Highland Garnet,* 175–77; Miller, *Search for a Black Nationality,* 239; Harding, *There is a River,* 214; Harris, "H. Ford Douglas," 228; Bell, "Negro Nationalism," 43, 47–50.

92 Redpath to H. H. Garnet, 22 February, 2 March 1861, HEB Letterbook, Duke University; "Weekly Report of James Redpath, General Agent of Emigration to Hayti," no. 16, 21 January 1861; No. 24, 7 March 1861, HEB Letterbook, Boston Public Library; Miller, *Search for a Black Nationality,* 243; Dixon, *African America and Haiti,* 200–201.

93 *Weekly Anglo-African,* 28 September; 19, 26 October; 9 November; 14, 28 December 1861; 15 February, 5 April 1862; Jason H. Silverman, *"Unwelcome Guests": Canada West's Response to American Fugitive Slaves, 1800–1865* (Millwood, N.Y.: Associated Faculties Press, 1985), 59–60, 113–19; Dixon, *African America and Haiti,* 201.

94 *National Anti-Slavery Standard,* 15 December 1860, 5 January 1861.

95 *Pine and Palm,* 26 July 1861; *Liberator,* 9 August 1861. Garrison had earlier criticized the Haitian movement in response to a letter from Boston blacks. See *Liberator,* 17 May 1861; A. E. Newton to George L. Lawrence, 23 May 1861, HEB Letterbook, Duke University.

96 *Pine and Palm,* 26 July 1861; *Weekly Anglo-African,* 17 August 1861. Also see *Liberator,* 12 July 1861; *The Letters of William Lloyd Garrison,* edited by Walter M. Merrill and Louis Ruchames (Cambridge, Mass.: Harvard University Press, 1971–81), 5:24–26.

97 *Liberator,* 25 October 1861; also *Weekly Anglo-African,* 19 October 1861; 21 December 1861. The group was the American Baptist Missionary Convention. John R. McKivigan, *The War against Proslavery Religion: Abolitionism and the Northern Churches, 1830–1865* (Ithaca, N.Y.: Cornell University Press, 1984), 107–9.

98 *New York Times,* 28 February 1861; also see Philadelphia *Public Ledger,* 18 October 1861.

99 *Liberator,* 17 May 1861, also 19 July 1861. See also Merrill and Ruchames, *Letters of Garrison,* 5:25. Thomas Wentworth Higginson, one of the Secret Six who had aided Brown, wrote a letter that Garrison published in the *Liberator* likewise warning blacks of the "mischief" caused by even selective emigration: "Let one family go, and it seems to infect all the rest with the desire to go,—while whites immediately begin to fancy that it would be very convenient to have them go." *Liberator,* 19 July 1861.

100 *Liberator,* 19 July 1861. Francis B. Sanborn also offered what Redpath labeled "kindly criticism . . . against the Haytian scheme" but remained encouraging. Redpath to Francis B. Sanborn, 18 May 1861, HEB Letterbook, Duke University.

101 *Weekly Anglo-African,* 16 November 1861.

102 Ibid., 24 August 1861. Garrison expressed a similar opinion in a lecture to a black group. See *Liberator,* 9 August 1861. Also see *Liberator,* 2 May 1862; Horton and Horton, *Black Bostonians,* 123.

103 *Weekly Anglo-African,* 16 November 1861. See also, Blight, *Frederick Douglass' Civil War,* 133–34.

104 *Douglass' Monthly* 4 (July 1861), 484. See also, Levine, *Martin Delany, Frederick Douglass,* 189; Dixon, *African America and Haiti,* 197; Blight, *Frederick Douglass' Civil War,* 133–34.

105 "Weekly Report of James Redpath, General Agent of Emigration to Hayti," 20 July 1861, HEB Letterbook, Library of Congress.

106 *Chatham Planet,* 15 February 1861, quoted in Miller, *Search for a Black Nationality,* 241; "Weekly Report of James Redpath, General Agent of Emigration to Hayti," no. 16, 21 January 1861, HEB Letterbook, Boston Public Library; Redpath to the Editor of the *Chatham Planet,* 13 March 1861, HEB Letterbook, Duke University; William P. Newman to Editor of the Anglo-African, 21 August 1861, in *Weekly Anglo-African,* 31 August 1861; Redpath to the Editor of the *Chatham Planet,* 27 August 1861, in *Pine and Palm,* 7 September 1861.

107 *Weekly Anglo-African,* 2 November 1861, also 17 August 1861; "Weekly Report of James Redpath, General Agent of Emigration to Hayti," no. 19, 2 February 1861, HEB Letterbook, Boston Public Library; Dixon, *African America and Haiti,* 192; Dean, *Defender of the Race,* 34–35.

108 *Chatham Planet,* 15 February 1861, as quoted in Miller, *Search for a Black Nationality,* 241. See also Dean, *Defender of the Race,* 34–35.

109 Ofari, *Henry Highland Garnet,* 100; Victor Ullman, *Martin R. Delany: The Beginnings of Black Nationalism* (Boston: Beacon, 1971), 254.

110 The newspaper declared the action signified that "the *controlling* religious *influence must be white,* which requires nothing but *time,* to make the entire *political* influence also *white,* when the liberty of the black race must be at an end." *Weekly Anglo-African,* 2 November 1861.

111 *Weekly Anglo-African,* 1 February 1862.

112 Ibid., 16 November 1861.

113 Ibid., 5, 12, 19 January 1861, quoted in Pasternak, "Henry Highland Garnet," 167–68: James M. McPherson, The *Negro's Civil War: How American Negroes Felt and Acted During the War for the Union* (Princeton, N.J.: Princeton University Press, 1965), 83–84.

114 *Weekly Anglo-African,* 12 April 1862, also 21 December 1861. Frederick Douglass described Garnet's Haitian agency as still another "adventuristic scheme" designed to make money for Garnet. Quoted in Pasternak, "Henry Highland Garnet," 167.

115 Redpath to Henry Highland Garnet, 29 March 1861, HEB Letterbook, Duke University; *Weekly Anglo-African,* 9, 16 February; 6 April 1861; Pasternak, "Henry Highland Garnet," 168–69.

116 *Weekly Anglo-African,* 12 April 1862.

117 Ibid., 21 December 1861.

118 Ibid., 29 March 1862. See also Dixon, *African America and Haiti,* 191–92.

119 Redpath to William Lloyd Garrison, 2 July 1861, in *Liberator,* 12 July 1861.

120 Redpath to John Jones, 15 March 1861, HEB Letterbook, Duke University.

121 "Weekly Report of James Redpath, General Agent of Emigration to Hayti," no. 19, 2 February 1861, HEB Letterbook, Boston Public Library.

122 As quoted in Dixon, *African America and Haiti,* 199.

123 "Weekly Report of James Redpath, General Agent of Emigration to Hayti," no. 12, 23 December 1860; no. 13, 6 January 1861, HEB Letterbook, Boston Public Library; Redpath to Auguste Elie, 15 July 1861, HEB Letterbook, DLC.

124 "Weekly Report of James Redpath, General Agent of Emigration to Hayti," no. 9, 9 December 1860; no. 11, 18 December 1860; no. 16, 21 January 1861; no. 19, 2 February 1861; no. 23, 23 February 1861, HEB Letterbook, Boston Public Library; *Liberator,* 15 March 1861.

125 *New York Times,* 28 February 1858; "Weekly Report of James Redpath, General Agent of Emigration to Hayti," no. 4, 17 November 1860; no. 9, 9 December 1860; no. 16, 21 January 1861; no. 17, 27 January 1861; no. 21, 16 February 1861, HEB Letterbook, Boston Public Library; Redpath to H. Ford Douglas, 23 February 1861, Redpath to Louis Pouille, 15 March 1861, HEB Letterbook, Duke University; Michael P. Johnson and James L. Roark, *Black Masters: A Free Family of Color in the Old South* (New York: Norton, 1984), 284–86, 294–95; Quarles, *Lincoln and the Negro,* 119–20; Montague, *Haiti and the United States,* 75; Dixon, *African America and Haiti,* 135–39, 196.

126 Redpath to Theodore Holly, 27 February 1861; 14 March 1861, HEB Letterbook, Duke University; "Weekly Report of James Redpath, General Agent of Emigration to Hayti," no. 26, 16 March 1861, HEB Letterbook, Boston Public Library; "Weekly Report of James Redpath, General Agent of Emigration to Hayti," 27 May 1861, HEB Letterbook, Library of Congress; *Weekly Anglo-African,* 23 March 1861; 27 April 1861; Warner, *New Haven Negroes,* 108; Dean, *Defender of the Race,* 37–38, 40–41; Dixon, *African America and Haiti,* 189–91, Cohen, "Holly for Haiti," 24–28.

127 Redpath to Simon Cameron, 1 June 1861; 13 August 1861, Letters Received by the Secretary of War, Irregular Series, 1861–66, DNA, M 492, Reel 12, frames 775–78, M 221, Roll 194, frames 248–50; also *Weekly Anglo-African,* 15 February 1862.

128 "Weekly Report of James Redpath, General Agent of Emigration to Hayti," no. 28, 31 March 1861, Library of Congress; R. L. Harris, "H. Ford Douglas: Afro-American Antislavery Emigrationist," *Journal of Negro History* 62 (July 1977): 228.

129 Redpath to John Jay, Jr., 9 September 1861, Jay Family Papers, Columbia University Libraries.

130 "Weekly Report of James Redpath, General Agent of Emigration to Hayti," no. 28, 31 March 1861, Library of Congress; Redpath to John V. Thomas, 26 March, 27 May 1861, HEB Letterbook, Duke University.

131 "Weekly Report of James Redpath, General Agent of Emigration to Hayti," no. 13, 6 January 1861; no. 20, 9 February 1861; no. 25, 8 March 1861, HEB Letterbook, Boston Public Library; "Weekly Report of James Redpath, General Agent of Emigration to Hayti," no. 28, 31 March 1861, 1 July 1861, Redpath to Auguste Elie, 8, 16 May 1861, HEB Letterbook, Library of Congress; Redpath to Messers. Walden and Booth, 23 May, 7 June 1861, Redpath to Auguste Elie, 30 May 1861, A.E. Newton to George Lawrence, 3 June 1861, HEB Letterbook, Duke University.

132 Redpath to Theodore Holly, 27 February 1861, HEB Letterbook, Duke University.

133 "Weekly Report of James Redpath, General Agent of Emigration to Hayti," no. 13, 6 January 1861; no. 20, HEB Letterbook, Boston Public Library; *Pine and Palm,* 22 June 1861; 26 October 1861; *Weekly Anglo-African,* 23 March 1861; 27 April 1861; Quarles, *Lincoln and the Negro,* 120; Warner, *New Haven Negroes,* 108.

134 Redpath to [William C.] Howells, 18 February 1861, William Dean Howells Collection, Hayes Presidential Center, Frémont, Ohio.

135 "Weekly Report of James Redpath, General Agent of Emigration to Hayti," no. 3, 15 November 1860; no. 10, 12 December 1860; no. 11, 18 December 1860; no. 26, 16 March 1861; no. 27, 23 March 1861, Redpath to Montgomery Blair, 16 November 1860, Redpath to Charles Sumner, 17 March 1861, HEB Letterbook, Boston Public Library; Redpath to John A. Andrew, [March 1861], John A. Andrew Papers, Massachusetts Historical Society; "Weekly Report of James Redpath, General Agent of Emigration to Hayti," no. 29, 6 April 1861, HEB Letterbook, Library of Congress.

136 *Congressional Globe,* 37th Congress, Second Session, 23 April 1862, vol. 42: 1773–75; Redpath to Montgomery Blair, 16 November 1860, Redpath to Victorien Pleasance, 12 December 1860, Redpath to Charles Sumner, 17 March 1861, HEB Letterbook, Boston Public Library; Redpath to Charles Sumner, 17 March 1861, Letters of Application and Recommendation during the Administrations of Abraham Lincoln and Andrew Johnson, M 650, Reel 41; "Weekly Report of James Redpath, General Agent of Emigration to Hayti," no. 30, 16 April 1861, Redpath to William H. Seward, 25 May 1861, Redpath to Victorien Pleasance, 15 June, 24 August 1861, HEB Letterbook, DLC: Frederic W. Seward to Redpath, 17 August 1861, Domestic Letters of the Department of State, DNA, M 40, Reel 52, 548; *Weekly Anglo-African,* 27 August 1861; Dixon, *African America and Haiti,* 146–47; Charles H. Wesley, "The Struggle for the Recognition of Haiti and Liberia as Independent Republics," *Journal of Negro History* 4 (October 1917): 380–82; Quarles, *Lincoln and the Negro,* 99–100.

137 *Douglass' Monthly* 4 (November 1862), 744; Redpath to Victorien Pleasance, 29 April 1862, "Correspondence of James Redpath, Commercial agent of Hayti for Philadelphia, Joint commissioner plenipotentiary of Hayti to the government of the U.S. & General agent of emigration to Hayti for the U.S. and Canada," New York Public Library, Schomburg Branch, hereafter cited as HEB Letterbook, Schomburg; *Weekly Anglo-African,* 27 April 1861.

138 *Douglass' Monthly* 4 (November 1862), 744; Quarles, *Lincoln and the Negro,* 100. Haiti ultimately selected Ernest Roumain, a twenty-seven-year-old black army colonel, as its first official diplomatic representative to the United States. Thanks to the improved relations between the two nations, the U.S. Navy was able to utilize Haiti as a refueling station for its efforts to suppress blockade running from ports in British and French ports in the Caribbean. Heinl and Heinl, *Written in Blood,* 222, 224–25; Dixon, *African America and Haiti,* 146.

139 Redpath to G. R. Heywood, 10 April 1861, HEB Letterbook, Library of Congress.

140 *Liberator,* 12 July 1861; "Weekly Report of James Redpath, General Agent of Emigration to Hayti," No. 29, 6 April 1861, HEB Letterbook, Library of Congress; Rayford W. Logan, *The Diplomatic Relations of the United States with Haiti, 1776–1891* (Chapel Hill: University of North Carolina Press, 1941), 296; Dixon, *African America and Haiti,* 192–93; Heinl and Heinl, *Written in Blood,* 220–21.

141 *Liberator,* 12 April 1861; *Douglass' Monthly* 3 (May 1861), 460–61. *Pine and Palm,* 26 June 1861; Redpath to Auguste Elie, 30 May 1861, Redpath to Victorien Pleasance, 27 May, 20 July, 1 October 1861, HEB Letterbook, DLC.

142 Redpath to Editor of the *New York Tribune,* n.d., in *New York Tribune,* 20 May 1861; *Pine and Palm,* 1 June 1861; Redpath to William F. Seward, 27 May 1861, HEB Letterbook, Duke University.

143 "Weekly Report of James Redpath, General Agent of Emigration to Hayti," 27 May 1861; 20 July 1861, HEB Letterbook, Library of Congress; *Pine and Palm,* 1 June 1861. See also Dixon, *African America and Haiti,* 192.

144 Redpath to John Brown Jr., 9 August 1861, John Brown Jr. Papers, Rutherford B. Hayes Research Center.

145 Redpath to John Brown Jr., 10 February 1861; 16, 25 March 1861; 12 July 1861; 9 August 1861, John Brown Jr. Papers, Rutherford B. Hayes Research Center; *Pine and Palm,* 22 June 1861; Winks, *Blacks in Canada,* 164–65; Boyd, "James Redpath," 175.

146 Dixon, *African America and Haiti,* 194–95. See also Dean, *Defender of the Race,* 37.

147 "Weekly Report of James Redpath, General Agent of Emigration to Hayti," no. 20, 9 February 1861, HEB Letterbook, Boston Public Library; "Weekly Report of James Redpath, General Agent of Emigration to Hayti," no. 30, 16 April 1861, HEB Letterbook, Library of Congress.

148 "Weekly Report of James Redpath, General Agent of Emigration to Hayti," no. 19, 2 February 1861, HEB Letterbook, Boston Public Library.

149 Redpath to H. Ford Douglas, 30 May 1861, HEB Letterbook, Duke University; Redpath to John Brown Jr., 12 July 1861, John Brown Jr. Papers, Rutherford B. Hayes Research Center.

150 Redpath to George L. Lawrence, 5 June 1861, HEB Letterbook, Duke University.

151 Redpath to Richard J. Hinton, 17 May 1861, HEB Letterbook, Duke University.

152 Ibid., 23 May 1861, HEB Letterbook, Duke University.

153 Ibid., 30 May 1861, Redpath to George Lawrence, 4, 5 June 1861, HEB Letterbook, Duke University. Redpath's alienation of long-time collaborator

Hinton tends to confirm Dixon's assessments of the young abolitionist's
psychological shortcomings in managing a large reform enterprise. Having
succeeded to that point in time largely on his personal powers of persuasion,
Redpath could not tolerate criticism of his vision for the emigration movement
from within his inner circle of advisors when the bureau began to falter. Whether
this should be interpreted as evidence of a deeper psychological imbalance in
Redpath or just the failings of an unseasoned young leader depends on
examining the longer trajectory of Redpath's career. For an assessment of
this incident very critical of Redpath, see Dixon, *African America and Haiti,*
194–95.

154 Redpath to George L. Lawrence, 17 May 1861, HEB Letterbook, Duke
University.

155 Ibid., 5 June 1861, HEB Letterbook, Duke University.

156 *Pine and Palm,* 1 June 1861.

157 Ibid., 22, 29 June 1861; 6, 13 July 1861; 3, 10 August 1861.

158 Ibid., 14 December 1861; also see *Weekly Anglo-African,* 11 January 1862;
8 February 1862; 29 March 1862.

159 *Weekly Anglo-African,* 11 January 1862; 8 February 1862; 29 March
1862; 12 April 1862.

160 Redpath to John Brown Jr., 12 July 1861, John Brown Jr. Papers,
Rutherford B. Hayes Research Center; also Redpath to James T. Rapier, 14 May
1861, Redpath to Alexander Tate and John Brown Jr., 18 May 1861, HEB Letterbook, Duke University; "Weekly Report of James Redpath, General Agent of Emigration to Hayti," no. 21, 16 February 1861; no. 22, 23 February 1861, HEB Letterbook, Boston Public Library; "Weekly Report of James Redpath, General Agent
of Emigration to Hayti," 27 May, 8 June, 20 July 1861, HEB Letterbook, Library
of Congress. See also Dixon, *African America and Haiti,* 195.

161 *Weekly Anglo-African,* 31 August 1861; 5 October 1861; 14 December
1861.

162 Ibid., 5 April 1862; Redpath to Auguste Elie, 22 August 1861, Redpath
to Victorien Pleasance, 20 August 1861, 7 September 1861, 26 April 1861, HEB
Letterbook, DLC; Quarles, *Lincoln and the Negro,* 120; Boyd, "James Redpath,"
178; Miller, *Search for a Black Nationality,* 246; Dixon, *African America and
Haiti,* 178–82.

163 Dean, *Defender of the Race,* 41–44; Dixon, *African America and Haiti,*
182; Miller, *Search for a Black Nationality,* 246–47.

164 Redpath to Victorien Pleasance, 13 October 1861, HEB Letterbook, DLC;
Redpath to George Lawrence, 29 February 1862, HEB Letterbook, Schomburg;
Miller, *Search for a Black Nationality,* 246–47.

165 Redpath to Victorien Pleasance, 29 April 1861; 10 October 1861; 11,
22 November 1861, Redpath to Auguste Elie, 20 October 1861, HEB Letterbook,
DLC; Redpath to Auguste Elie, 2 February 1862, Redpath to Victorien Pleasance,
10 March 1862, HEB Letterbook, Schomburg.

166 Redpath to Auguste Elie, 15 June 1861, HEB Letterbook, Library of
Congress.

167 Montague, *Haiti and the United States,* 76; Dixon, *African America and
Haiti,* 183–84.

168 *Pine and Palm,* 28 December 1861.

169 "Weekly Report of James Redpath, General Agent of Emigration to Hayti," 27 May 1861; 8 June 1861; 20 July 1861, HEB Letterbook, Library of Congress.

170 Redpath to Auguste Elie, 21 May 1862, HEB Letterbook, Schomburg. See also Dixon, *African America and Haiti*, 205.

171 *Liberator*, 3 October 1862; 7 November 1862; Miller, *Search for a Black Nationality*, 247; Boyd, "James Redpath," 181.

172 *Pine and Palm*, n.d., as quoted in Dixon, *African America and Haiti*, 207.

173 Miller, *Search for a Black Nationality*, 248; Pease and Pease, *They Who Would Be Free*, 276.

174 Miller, *Search for a Black Nationality*, 247; Montague, *Haiti and the United States*, 76; James M. McPherson, "Abolitionist and Negro Opposition to Colonization during the Civil War, *Phylon* 26 (winter 1965): 88.

175 Bell, "Negro Nationalism," 53.

176 Montague, *Haiti and the United States*, 76; Dixon, *African America and Haiti*, 206–7; Jason H. Silverman, " 'In Isles Beyond the Main': Abraham Lincoln's Philosophy on Black Colonization," *Lincoln Herald* 80 (fall 1978): 115–21; McPherson, "Opposition to Colonization," 391–92.

177 This is also the conclusion of other scholars. See Miller, *Search for a Black Nationality*, 249; Davis, *Black Democracy*, 125; McPherson, "Opposition to Colonization," 88.

178 McPherson, *Negro's Civil War*, 88; Miller, *Search for a Black Nationality*, 249; Davis, *Black Democracy*, 125; Bell, "Negro Nationalism," 53.

179 For a more negative assessment of Redpath, see Dixon, *African America and Haiti*, 185, 195.

180 *Liberator*, 3 October 1862; *Douglass' Monthly* 4 (July 1861), 484.

Chapter 5. The Radical Publisher

1 Thayer and Eldridge Insolvency #704, Suffolk County Probate Court and Court of Insolvency, Boston, December 1860; John R. McKivigan, ed., "The Reminiscences of William Wild Thayer, Boston Publisher and Abolitionist," *Proceedings of the Massachusetts Historical Society* 103 (1991): 139, 142–44, 150–51; Justin Kaplan, *Walt Whitman: A Life* (Toronto: Bantam Books, 1980), 246–47.

2 Madeleine B. Stern, "James Redpath and His 'Books for the Times,' " *Publisher's Weekly* 148 (December 1945): 2649. This essay was reprinted in Madeleine B. Stern, *Imprints on History: Book Publishers and American Frontiers* (Bloomington: Indiana University Press, 1956), 76–83.

3 John Tebbel, *A History of Book Publishing in the United States*, 4 vols. (New York: R. R. Bowker, 1972), 1:444.

4 Cathy N. Davidson, *Revolution and the Word: The Rise of the Novel in America* (New York: Oxford University Press, 1986), 13–25, 52–54, 70–79; Hellmut Lehmann-Haupt, *The Book in America: A History of the Making and Selling of Books in the United States*, 2d ed. (New York: R. R. Bowker, 1952), 80–88, 117–19; Carl Bode, *The Anatomy of American Popular Culture, 1840–1861* (Berkley: University of California Press, 1960), 110.

5 Lehmann-Haupt, *Book in America*, 121–22; E. Douglass Branch, *The Sentimental Years, 1836–1860: A Social History* (New York: Hill and Wang, 1934), 110–11.

6 Michael Winship, *American Literary Publishing in the Mid-Nineteenth Century: The Business of Ticknor and Fields* (Cambridge, Mass.: Cambridge University Press, 1995), 19–21, 52–53; Lehmann-Haupt, *Book in America*, 126–29, 215, 229; Tebbel, *Book Publishing*, 1:242–45; Bode, *American Popular Culture*, 111.

7 Bode, *American Popular Culture*, 110–19; Lehmann-Haupt, *Book in America*, 131–36, 241–59; Tebbel, *Book Publishing*, 1:158–60.

8 Albert Johannsen, *The House of Beadle and Adams and Its Dime and Nickel Novels: The Story of a Vanished Literature* (Norman: University of Oklahoma Press, 1950), 1–4. Ralph Adamari, "The House that Beadle Built, 1859–1869," *American Book Collector* 4 (December 1933): 228–91.

9 Madeleine Stern, *Publishers for Mass Entertainment in Nineteenth-Century America* (Boston: G. K. Hall, 1980), 261–63; Tebbel, *Book Publishing*, 444.

10 As quoted in *American Publishers' Circular* 1 (1 September 1863), 348; (15 September 1863), 378.

11 Stern, *Publishers for Mass Entertainment*, 263, and "James Redpath," 2651; Tebbel, *Book Publishing*, 444.

12 *American Publishers' Circular* 1 (1 September 1863), 346, 348; 1 (15 September 1863), 378; 1 (15 October 1863), 439; Stern, "James Redpath," 2651.

13 Adamari, "House that Beadle Built," 288–90; Johannsen, *House of Beadle*, 48.

14 "Beadle's Dime-Books," *North American Review* 99 (July 1864): 309.

15 *American Literary Gazette*, 15 April 1864; *Legends of the Infancy and Boyhood of Jesus Christ* (Boston: James Redpath, 1864), rear cover; Tebbel, *Book Publishing*, 445.

16 *National Anti-Slavery Standard*, 20 February 1864; Stern, "James Redpath," 2652.

17 *American Literary Gazette*, 1 March 1864; also quoted in Stern, *Publishers for Mass Entertainment*, 264.

18 *Liberator*, 18, 25 March 1864; 8, 22 April 1864; J. Noel Heermance, *William Wells Brown and Clotelle: A Portrait of the Artist in the First Negro Novel* (n.p.: Archon Books, 1969), 192–93.

19 Advertisements as quoted in Stern, *Publishers for Mass Entertainment*, 265.

20 *American Publishers' Circular* 1 (15 October 1863), 439; 1 (15 December 1863), 153; *American Literary Gazette*, 15 April 1864; Stern, *Publishers for Mass Entertainment*, 265.

21 Tebbel, *Book Publishing*, 444–45.

22 *National Anti-Slavery Standard*, 20 February 1864; David Kaser, *Books and Libraries in Camp and Battle: The Civil War Experience* (Westport, Conn.: Greenwood Press, 1984), 94–95; Tebbel, *Book Publishing*, 445.

23 Louis Ruchames, "Wendell Phillips' Lovejoy Address," *New England Quarterly* 41 (March 1974): 108–17. For a differing conclusion, see James Brewer Stewart, *Wendell Phillips: Liberty's Hero* (Baton Rouge: Louisiana State University Press, 1986), 58–63.

24 Wendell Phillips, *Speeches, Lectures, and Letters* (Boston: James Redpath, 1863), iii–iv; Thomas Wentworth Higginson, *Contemporaries* (Boston: Houghton and Mifflin, 1900), 265; Stewart, *Wendell Phillips*, 184, 199, 222, and *William Lloyd Garrison and the Challenge of Emancipation* (Arlington Heights, Ill.: Harlan Davidson, 1992), 161.

25 Curtis W. Ellison and E. W. Metcalf Jr., *William Wells Brown and Martin R. Delany: A Reference Guide* (Boston: G. K. Hall, 1978), 4–5; Heermance, *William Wells Brown and Clotelle*, 191.

26 *Pine and Palm,* 1 June 1861; 3, 17 August 1861; John R. McKivigan, "James Redpath and Black Reaction to the Haitian Emigration Bureau," *Mid-America: An Historical Review* 69 (October 1987): 145–46; Edward Farrison, *William Wells Brown: Author and Reformer* (Chicago: University of Chicago Press, 1969), 336.

27 Brown, *Clotelle,* 104; *Liberator,* 12 February 1864; Curtis and Metcalf, *William Wells Brown,* 5, 93; M. Guilia Fabi, "The 'Unguarded Expressions of the Feelings of the Negroes': Gender, Slave Resistance, and William Wells Brown's Revisions of Clotel," *African American Review* 27 (winter 1993): 647–49.

28 Redpath to Louisa May Alcott, 23 January 1864, Louisa May Alcott Papers, University of Virginia Library, hereinafter cited as Alcott Papers.

29 *American Publishers' Circular* (1 September 1863), 346; Tebbel, *Book Publishing,* 444; Stern, *Publishers for Mass Entertainment,* 261.

30 *American Publishers' Circular* 1 (15 September 1863), 378.

31 *Liberator,* 27 November 1863; Farrison, *William Wells Brown,* 369–71.

32 *Douglass' Monthly,* n.d., quoted in Curtis and Metcalf, *William Wells Brown,* 92.

33 *Liberator,* 18 March 1864; also *American Publishers' Circular* 1 (15 September 1863), 378; 1 (15 October 1863), 439.

34 John R. Beard, *Toussaint L'Ouverture: Biography and Autobiography* (Boston: James Redpath, 1863), iii–vi.

35 Ibid., iv–v.

36 [Henry Ward Beecher], *England and America: Speech of Henry Ward Beecher at the Free-trade Hall, Manchester, October 9, 1863* (Boston: J. Redpath, 1863).

37 *The Journals of Bronson Alcott,* edited by Odell Shepard (Boston: Little, Brown, 1938), 323; Louisa May Alcott to Alfred Whitman, 5 April 1860, in *The Selected Letters of Louisa May Alcott,* edited by Joel Myerson, Daniel Shealy, and Madeleine B. Stern (Boston: Little Brown, 1987), 52–54; Madeleine B. Stern, *Louisa May Alcott* (Norman: University of Oklahoma Press, 1950), 95, 98; Martha Saxton, *Louisa May: A Modern Biography of Louisa May Alcott* (Boston: Houghton, Mifflin, 1977), 232.

38 Madeleine L. Stern, *Critical Essays on Louisa May Alcott* (Boston: G. K. Hall, 1984), 27–28, and *Louisa May Alcott,* 134–35; *Selected Letters of Louisa May Alcott,* xxiv–xxv.

39 Louisa May Alcott to Redpath, [July 1863], in *Selected Letters of Louisa May Alcott,* 86. Also see Redpath to Louisa May Alcott, 26 June, 8 August 1863, Alcott Papers; Saxton, *Louisa May,* 263; Stern, *Alcott,* 134, and *Publishers for Mass Entertainment,* 263–64.

40 *Louisa May Alcott: Her Life, Letters, and Journals,* edited by Ednah D. Cheney (Boston: Roberts Brothers, 1890), 151–52; Stern, *Critical Essays,* 27–28, and *Louisa May Alcott,* 134–35; Saxton, *Louisa May,* 263.

41 As quoted in Cheney, *Louisa May Alcott,* 152–53; also see Redpath to Louisa May Alcott, 26 June 1863; 8 August 1863, Alcott Papers; *American Publishers' Circular* 1 (1 September 1863), 346; Stern, *Publishers for Mass Entertainment,* 263–64.

42 Louisa May Alcott to Redpath, 28 August 1863, in *Selected Letters of Louisa May Alcott,* 88–89; also quoted in Saxton, *Louisa May,* 264.

43 Louisa May Alcott to Samuel Joseph May, 10 September 1863, in *Selected Letters of Louisa May Alcott,* 93–94.

44 Redpath to Louisa May Alcott, 1 December 1863, Alcott Papers; Stern, *Alcott,* 135.

45 Redpath to Louisa May Alcott, 23 January 1864, in Alcott Papers.

46 As quoted in Saxton, *Louisa May,* 264.

47 Louisa May Alcott to Redpath, [early September 1863], in *Selected Letters of Louisa May Alcott,* 90–91.

48 Ibid., 24 January 1864, in *Selected Letters of Louisa May Alcott,* 100–101, also see 88–93.

49 Redpath to Louisa May Alcott, December 1863, Alcott Papers.

50 Louisa May Alcott to Redpath, 28 August 1863, in *Selected Letters of Louisa May Alcott,* 88–89.

51 Cheney, *Louisa May Alcott,* 153–55; Stern, *Publishers for Mass Entertainment,* 264, and "James Redpath," 2652.

52 Louisa May Alcott to Redpath, 24 January 1864, in *Selected Letters of Louisa May Alcott,* 100–101.

53 Cheney, *Louisa May Alcott,* 155; Stern, *Alcott,* 136, 139.

54 Louisa May Alcott to Redpath, [early September 1863], in *Selected Letters of Louisa May Alcott,* 90–91.

55 Redpath to "Messrs. Roberts Bros.," 27 April 1864, Alcott Papers; also see Louisa May Alcott to Redpath, [spring? 1864], in *Selected Letters of Louisa May Alcott,* 104–5.

56 Louisa May Alcott to Alfred Whitman, 2 January 1864, in *Selected Letters of Louisa May Alcott,* 99–100.

57 Ibid., [February 1864], in *Selected Letters of Louisa May Alcott,* 102–3.

58 Ibid.

59 As quoted in Saxton, *Louisa May,* 269.

60 Redpath to Louisa May Alcott, 1 December 1863, 19 August 1864, Alcott Papers; Cheney, *Louisa May Alcott,* 156; Saxton, *Louisa May,* 269–70, 274–82; Stern, *Alcott,* 140–41, 143; *Selected Letters of Louisa May Alcott,* 100–101, 104–5.

61 Redpath to Louisa May Alcott, 19 August 1864, Alcott Papers.

62 *Louisa's Wonder Book—An Unknown Alcott Juvenile,* edited by Madeleine L. Stern (Mount Pleasant: Central Michigan University, 1975); Saxton, *Louisa May,* 269–70, 274–82; Stern, *Alcott,* 140–41, 143; *Selected Letters of Louisa May Alcott,* 101.

63 Redpath to Louisa May Alcott, 1 December 1863, 23 January 1864, Alcott Papers; Stern, *Publishers for Mass Entertainment,* 264; Saxton, *Louisa May,* 265–66.

64 Ralph Waldo Emerson to Redpath, 23 February 1863, as quoted in Francis B. Dedmond, " 'Here among the Soldiers in Hospital': An Unpublished letter from Walt Whitman to Lucia Jane Russell Briggs," *New England Quarterly* 59 (December 1986): 544–45.

65 Redpath to Walt Whitman, 10 March. 1860;, 5 May 1860; 25 June 1860, in Horace Traubel, *With Walt Whitman in Camden,* 5 vols. (Boston: Small, Maynard, 1906–64), 3:143, 145, 460–61; *The Letters of Ralph Waldo Emerson,* 6 vols. (New York: Columbia University Press, 1939), 5:314, 316; Thomas Donaldson,

Walt Whitman: The Man (New York: Francis P. Harper, 1896), 143–53; Kaplan, *Walt Whitman*, 255, 276.

66 Emerson to Redpath, 9 August 1863, as quoted in Dedmond, "Here among Soldiers," 545.

67 Redpath to Walt Whitman, 8 October 1863, in *Walt Whitman: The Correspondence*, edited by E. H. Miller, 8 vols. (Boston: Houghton, Mifflin, 1959–70), 1:164.

68 Ibid.

69 Miller, *Correspondence of Walt Whitman*, 1:171–72; George Fredrickson, *The Inner Civil War: Northern Intellectuals and the Crisis of the Union* (New York: Harper Torchbooks, 1965), 93; Roy Morris Jr., *The Better Angel: Walt Whitman in the Civil War* (New York: Oxford University Press, 2000), 146–47; Kaplan, *Walt Whitman*, 277–78.

70 Redpath to Walt Whitman, 28 October 1863, in Traubel, *With Walt Whitman*, 418.

71 Walt Whitman, *Memoranda during the War* (Camden, N.J.: Author, 1875); Kaplan, *Walt Whitman*, 277–78; Morris, *Better Angel*, 147–48.

72 As quoted in Traubel, *With Walt Whitman*, 4:418; also see 2:73–77. Thanks to Redpath's championing of Alcott and Whitman, when William Henry Channing began work on a biography of Henry David Thoreau, who died in December 1862, he considered Redpath's firm as the most suitable press to publish it. Channing began publishing preliminary portions of this work in the *Boston Commonwealth* the following December but never completed a book manuscript for Redpath.

73 *New York Times*, 9 February 1864; 26 April 1864; 12 June 1864; [James Redpath], *Shall We Suffocate Ed. Green? By a Citizen of Malden* (Boston: James Redpath, 1864), 19, 22–23, 55; Henry Greenleaf Pearson, *The Life of John A. Andrew: Governor of Massachusetts, 1861–1865*, 2 vols. (Boston: Houghton, Mifflin, 1904), 2:219.

74 Steven Mintz, *Moralists and Modernizers: America's Pre–Civil War Reformers* (Baltimore: The Johns Hopkins University Press, 1995), 93–94; David Brion Davis, "The Movement to Abolish Capital Punishment in America, 1787–1861," *American Historical Review* 63 (October 1957): 28–34.

75 Louis P. Masur, *Rites of Execution: Capital Punishment and the Transformation of American Culture, 1776–1865* (New York: Oxford University Press, 1989), 118–22, 128–29, 157–58; Davis, "Abolish Capital Punishment," 42, 44–45.

76 Masur, *Rites of Execution*, 120–21, 128–29; Alan Rogers, "'Under Sentence of Death': The Movement to Abolish Capital Punishment in Massachusetts, 1835–1849," *New England Quarterly* 66 (March 1993), 27–46; Davis, "Abolish Capital Punishment," 34, 42, 44–45.

77 As quoted in Pearson, *John A. Andrew*, 2:219–21; Louis Filler, "Movements to Abolish the Death Penalty in the United States," in *Capital Punishment*, edited by Thorsten Sellin (New York: Harper and Row, 1967), 111, 114.

78 [Redpath], *Shall We Suffocate Ed. Green?*, 30–31, 58–59.

79 Ibid., 48, also 46–47, 49–51.

80 Redpath also guided his readers to books by John L. O'Sullivan and Robert Rantoul, although confessing that he himself had not read them. [Redpath], *Shall We Suffocate Ed. Green?*, 24, 32–34.

81 Ibid., 38; also see 34–39, 47.

82 Ibid., 8, 56–57; also see 7–15, 50.

83 Ibid., 57–58.

84 Ibid., 9–10, 47. Also see Emanuel Swedenborg, *Arcana Coelestia,* Passages 1009–12.

85 Ibid., 26, also 24, 28, 29, 59.

86 Pearson, *John A. Andrew,* 2:225–26; Davis, "Abolish Capital Punishment," 46.

87 Redpath to Louisa May Alcott, 1 December 1863, Alcott Papers.

88 Ibid., 23 January 1864, Alcott Papers.

89 Stern, *Publishers for Mass Entertainment,* 265.

90 Redpath to Louisa May Alcott, 13 August 1864, Alcott Papers.

91 Cheney, *Louisa May Alcott,* 151–52.

Chapter 6. Abolitionizing the South

1 Redpath to Louisa May Alcott, 13 August 1864, Alcott Papers; Redpath to Sydney Howard Gay, 6 March 1865, Sydney Howard Gay Papers, Manuscripts Collection, Columbia University Libraries; *Liberator,* 6 January 1865; *National Anti-Slavery Standard,* 11, 18 March 1865.

2 J. Cutler Andrews, *The North Reports the Civil War* (Pittsburgh: University of Pittsburgh Press, 1955), 60–63; Louis M. Starr, *Bohemian Brigade: Civil War Newsmen in Action* (Madison: University of Wisconsin Press, 1987), 61; Brayton Harris, *Blue and Gray in Black and White: Newspapers in the Civil War* (Washington, D.C.: Brassey's, 1999), 119–27.

3 As quoted in John F. Marszalek, *Sherman's Other War: The General and the Civil War Press* (Memphis: Memphis State University Press, 1981), 163; see also Harris, *Blue and Gray,* 242.

4 *Boston Daily Journal,* 26 December 1864.

5 Ironically, Redpath's identity was verified by none other than General John W. Geary, the same man who once had arrested him in Kansas as a free-state agitator. *Boston Daily Journal,* 2 September 1864, also see 31 October 1864.

6 *New York Tribune,* 22 February 1865; Charles Carleton Coffin, *The Boys of 1861; or, Four Years of Fighting* (Boston: Dana Estes, 1901), 482–507; James M. Perry, *A Bohemian Brigade: The Civil War Correspondents* (New York: John Wiley, 2000), 261–62; Andrews, *North Reports the Civil War,* 621–24.

7 Redpath to Sydney Howard Gay, 6 March 1865, Gay Papers.

8 For examples, see *Boston Daily Journal,* 28, 31 October 1864; 3, 10, 11, 12, 14, 30 November 1864; 1 December 1864.

9 Marszalek, *Sherman's Other War,* 164–65; also see David P. Conyngham, *Sherman's March through the South* (New York: Sheldon, 1865), 74–77; Bernard A. Weisberger, *Reporters for the Union* (Boston: Little, Brown, 1953), 120–24; Harris, *Blue and Gray,* 242, 321.

10 *Boston Daily Journal,* 10 November 1864, also see 17 November 1864; Starr, *Bohemian Brigade,* 350–51; Harris, *Blue and Gray,* 141–45.

11 *New York Times,* 6 May 1864; John C. Waugh, *Reelecting Lincoln: The Battle for the 1864 Presidency* (New York: Crown, 1997), 172–81; Allan Nevins, *Frémont: Pathmarker of the West* (New York: D. Appleton-Century, 1939), 573; James Brewer Stewart, *Wendell Phillips: Liberty's Hero* (Baton Rouge: Louisiana State University Press, 1998), 250–53.

12 *Boston Daily Journal,* 28 October 1864. Thoughtful analyses of the political significance of the capture of Atlanta in the 1864 presidential election is found in James M. McPherson, "American Victory, American Defeat," and Archer Jones, "Military Means, Political Ends: Strategy," both in *Why the Confederacy Lost,* edited by Gabor S. Boritt (New York: Oxford University Press, 1992), 39–41, 71–73.

13 *Boston Daily Journal,* 17 November 1864.

14 Starr, *Bohemian Brigade,* 250–51.

15 Redpath to Sydney Howard Gay, 6 March 1865, Gay Papers; Starr, *Bohemian Brigade,* 251.

16 Redpath to Sydney Howard Gay, 6 March 1865, Gay Papers.

17 This title appeared on five dispatches. See *Boston Daily Journal,* 26, 27 August 1864; 1, 2, 6 September 1864.

18 *Boston Daily Journal,* 1 September 1864.

19 Ibid., 1 September 1864; *New York Tribune,* 2 March 1865.

20 *Boston Daily Journal,* 27 August 1864; 30 November 1864; 24 December 1864.

21 Ibid., 1 September 1864.

22 Ibid., 26 December 1864.

23 Ibid., also see 14, 21 October 1864; 8 February 1865.

24 Ibid., 1 September 1864; 31 October 1864.

25 Ibid., 22 December 1864; Peter Maslowski, *Treason Must Be Made Odious: Military Occupation and Wartime Reconstruction in Nashville, Tennessee, 1862–65* (Millwood, N.Y.: KTO Press, 1975), 109–10.

26 *New York Tribune,* 2, 11 March 1865; see also Donald Yacovone, *A Voice of Thunder: A Black Soldier's Civil War* (Urbana: University of Illinois Press, 1997), 81.

27 *Boston Daily Journal,* 9 December 1864, reprinted in *New York Tribune,* 12 December 1864; also see *Liberator,* 7 October 1864; *Boston Daily Journal,* 26 October 1864; John V. Cimprich and Robert Mainfort, "The Fort Pillow Massacre: A Statistical Note," *Journal of American History* 75 (December 1989): 830–37.

28 *Boston Daily Journal,* 31 October 1864.

29 Ibid., 21 October 1864.

30 Ibid., 6 September 1864; Joseph T. Glatthaar, *Forged in Battle: The Civil War Alliance of Black Soldiers and White Officers* (New York: Macmillan, 1990), 6–7, 10, 12–18.

31 *Boston Daily Journal,* 14 October 1864.

32 Ibid., 6 September 1864, also see 12 November 1864; *National Anti-Slavery Standard,* 10 December 1864.

33 *Boston Daily Journal,* 11 November 1864. Redpath also blamed the civilian casualties in Atlanta on Confederate general John Bell Hood's failure to order noncombatants to evacuate the city. *Boston Daily Journal,* 3 November 1864.

34 Ibid., 11 November 1864.

35 *New York Tribune,* 2 March 1864; also reprinted in *National Anti-Slavery Standard,* 11 March 1864.

36 *Boston Daily Journal,* 14 November 1861, also see 3 November 1864.

37 Ibid., 26 October 1864, also see 26 November 1864.

38 Ibid., 8 February 1865, also see *National Anti-Slavery Standard,* 10 December 1864.

39 *Boston Liberator,* 6 January 1865, also 7 October 1864.

40 *Richmond Enquirer*, n.d., as quoted in *New York Tribune*, 16 March 1865.

41 *Boston Daily Journal*, 20 August 1864.

42 Ibid., 14 November 1864.

43 Ibid., 30 November 1864.

44 *New York Tribune*, 28 March 1864, also reprinted in *National Anti-Slavery Standard*, 1 April 1865, also see 10 December 1864.

45 Eric Foner, *Reconstruction: America's Unfinished Revolution, 1863–1877* (New York: Harper and Row, 1988), 67–70, 96–100, 233–37.

46 *New York Tribune*, 11, 28 March 1865; LaWanda Cox, *Lincoln and Black Freedom: A Study in Presidential Leadership* (Columbia: University of South Carolina Press, 1981), 15–19, 40–41.

47 *New York Tribune*, 11 March 1865.

48 *Boston Daily Journal*, 10 November 1864, also see 26 November 1864; 23, 26 January 1865; also reprinted in *Liberator*, 27 January 1865; *National Anti-Slavery Standard*, 27 January, 8 February 1865; John Cimprich, *Slavery's End in Tennessee, 1861–1865* (University: University of Alabama Press, 1985), 105–7, 115–17.

49 Cimprich, *Slavery's End in Tennessee*, 114–17.

50 *Boston Daily Journal*, 14 November 1864.

51 *Boston Daily Journal*, 17 November 1864. Redpath offered the same assessment in South Carolina. See *New York Tribune*, 2, 11, 28 March 1865; *National Anti-Slavery Standard*, 18 March 1865.

52 *New York Tribune*, 2 March 1865; reprinted in *National Anti-Slavery Standard*, 11 March 1865.

53 Redpath to Mrs. Pillsbury, 9 March 1865, in *Freedmen's Record* 1 (April 1865): 61; Bernard E. Powers Jr., *Black Charlestonians: A Social History, 1822–1885* (Fayetteville: University of Arkansas Press, 1994), 137.

54 Redpath to the Editor of the Standard, 12 July 1865, in *National Anti-Slavery Standard*, 22 July 1865.

55 *Charleston Daily Courier*, 2 March 1865.

56 Redpath to Mrs. Pillsbury, 9 March 1865, in *Freedmen's Record* 1 (April 1865): 61.

57 *New York Tribune*, 18 March 1865; Powers, *Black Charlestonians*, 137.

58 Ibid.

59 Ibid.

60 *Freedmen's Record* 1 (May 1865): 73.

61 *Charleston Daily Courier*, 17 May 1865.

62 *Charleston Daily Courier*, 6 April 1865; Robert C. Morris, *Reading, 'Riting, and Reconstruction: The Education of Freedmen in the South, 1861–1870* (Chicago: University of Chicago Press, 1976), 131; Powers, *Black Charlestonians*, 138.

63 *Charleston Daily Courier*, 6 April 1865; 17 May 1865; *New York Times*, 16 April 1865; *New York Tribune*, 10, 18 March 1865; 16 April 1865; Wilbert L. Jenkins, *Seizing the New Day: African Americans in Post-Civil War Charleston* (Bloomington: Indiana University Press, 1998), 72–73; Martin Abbott, "The Freedmen's Bureau and Negro Schooling in South Carolina," *South Carolina Historical Magazine* 57 (April 1956): 68.

64 *Charleston Daily Courier*, 6 April 1865; W. F. Allen to unknown correspondent, 23 May 1865, as reprinted in *Freedmen's Record* 1 (July 1865): 112–13; *Charleston Daily Courier*, 17 May 1865.

65 Thomas W. Cardozo to Michael E. Strieby, 29 April 1865, as quoted in Edmund L. Drago, *Initiative, Paternalism, and Race Relations: Charleston's Avery Normal Institute* (Athens: University of Georgia Press, 1990), 45–47.

66 Willie Lee Rose, *Rehearsal for Reconstruction: The Port Royal Experiment* (New York: Vintage, 1964), 333–37.

67 Redpath to William Gurney 30 April 1865, in *Charleston Daily Courier,* 17 May 1865; *Freedmen's Record* 1 (June 1865), 97; *National Anti-Slavery Standard,* 29 July 1865.

68 W. F. Allen to unknown correspondent, 23 May 1865, in *Freedmen's Record* 1 (July 1865): 112–13.

69 "M.C." to unknown correspondent, 25 April 1865, reprinted in *Freedmen's Record* 1 (June 1865): 99–100.

70 *Freedmen's Record* 1 (May 1865): 70–71.

71 "Mazeel" to the Editors of the Boston Daily Advertiser, 30 June 1865, in *Boston Daily Advertiser,* 7 July 1865.

72 Joel Williamson, *After Slavery: The Negro in South Carolina during Reconstruction, 1861–1877* (Chapel Hill: University of North Carolina Press, 1965), 216.

73 William F. Allen quoted in Morris, *Reading, 'Riting, and Reconstruction,* 131.

74 T. P. O'Neale to R. H. Gourdin, 3 June 1865, R. H. Gourdin Papers, as quoted in Williamson, *After Slavery,* 216.

75 Redpath to the Editor of the Standard, 12 July 1865, in *National Anti-Slavery Standard,* 22 July 1865.

76 Redpath to William Gurney, 30 April 1865, in *Charleston Daily Courier,* 17 May 1865; Jenkins, *Seizing the Day,* 37.

77 *New York Tribune,* 8 April 1865; *Freedmen's Record* 1 (May 1865): 97; Redpath to the Editor of the Standard, in *National Anti-Slavery Standard,* 22 July 1865; personal correspondence between author and Dr. Marvin M. Dulaney, 15 March 2004, in author's possession; Jenkins, *Seizing the New Day,* 103; Powers, *Black Charlestonians,* 241.

78 Redpath to the Editor of the Standard, 12, 20 July 1865, in *National Anti-Slavery Standard,* 22, 29 July 1865.

79 *New York Tribune,* 20 April 1865, also see 17, 18, 22 April 1865; 22 May 1865; *The Letters of William Lloyd Garrison,* edited by Walter M. Merrill, and Louis Ruchames, 6 vols. (Cambridge, Mass.: Harvard University Press, 1971–81), 5:265–70; James Brewer Stewart, *William Lloyd Garrison and the Challenge of Emancipation* (Arlington Heights, Ill.: Harlan Davidson, 1992), 191–92; Powers, *Black Charlestonians,* 70–71.

80 Mary R. Dearing, *Veterans in Politics: The Story of the G.A.R.* (Baton Rouge: Louisiana State University Press, 1952), 177; Paul H. Buck, *The Road to Reunion, 1865–1900* (Boston: Little, Brown, 1937), 116; Lloyd Lewis, *Myths after Lincoln* (New York, Readers Club, 1941), 304–7; Elizabeth G. Rice, "A Yankee Teacher in the South: An Experience in the Early Days of Reconstruction," *Century Magazine* 62 (May 1901): 154.

81 Buck, *Road to Reunion,* 116.

82 *New York Tribune,* 8 April 1865.

83 *Charleston Daily Courier,* 2 May 1865; Redpath to the Editor of the Standard, in *National Anti-Slavery Standard,* 22 July 1865, and *Malden Mirror,* 28 August 1914; Jenkins, *Seizing the New Day,* 37.

84 Quoted in *Malden Evening News,* 12 August 1976; see also *Malden Mirror,* 28 August 1914.

85 Rice, "Yankees Teacher in the South," 154; also see *Charleston Daily Courier,* 2 May 1865; *New York Tribune,* 13 May 1865; *Malden Evening Mirror,* 24 August 1914; *Malden Mirror,* 28 August 1914; Jenkins, *Seizing the New Day,* 37.

86 *Charleston Daily Courier,* 2 May 1865; *New York Tribune,* 13 May 1865.

87 *New York Times,* 22 May 1865; *Charleston Daily Courier,* 8 July 1865.

88 *Charleston Daily Courier,* 8 July 1865.

89 Redpath to Editor of the Standard, 20 July 1865, in *National Anti-Slavery Standard,* 29 July 1865.

90 John C. Chavis to James Redpath, 20 June 1865, John C. Chavis Papers, South Caroliniana Library.

91 *Charleston Daily Courier,* 17 June 1865.

92 Ibid., 1 July 1865.

93 O. O. Howard to James Redpath, 15 July 1865, O. O. Howard Papers, Bowdoin College Library; Martin Abbott, *The Freedmen's Bureau in South Carolina, 1865–1872* (Chapel Hill: University of North Carolina Press, 1967), 4–5, 9, 12–13.

94 James Redpath to O. O. Howard, 21 July 1865, RBRFAL.

95 Powers, *Black Charlesonians,* 78; Jenkins, *Seizing the New Day,* 140.

96 Redpath to William Lloyd Garrison, n.d., published in *Liberator,* 21 July 1865.

97 Redpath to the Editor of the Standard, 12 July 1865, in *National Anti-Slavery Standard,* 22 July 1865; Redpath to the Editor of the Standard, 20 July 1865, in *National Anti-Slavery Standard,* 29 July 1865.

98 Redpath to Andrew Johnson, 3 August 1864, in *The Papers of Andrew Johnson,* edited by Leroy P. Graf et al. (Knoxville: University of Tennessee Press, 1967–), 7:71–72; (New York) *Nation,* 17 August 1865.

99 LaWanda Cox and John Cox, *Politics, Principle, and Prejudice, 1865–1866: Dilemma of Reconstruction America* (1963; New York, Free Press, 1969), 151–71; Hans L. Trefousse, *Andrew Johnson: A Biography* (New York: W. W. Norton, 1989), 214–33; Foner, *Reconstruction,* 180–202.

100 Redpath to Howard, 5 September 1865, Howard Papers; also see Redpath to Howard, 15 September 1865, BRFAL.

101 Howard to Redpath, 13 September 1865, Howard Papers.

102 Howard to Rufus Saxton, 15 September 1865, Howard Papers; also see Redpath to Howard, 15, 18 September 1865, BRFAL; Joseph A. Selden to Redpath, 15 September 1865, Howard Papers.

103 Morris, *Reading, 'Riting, and Reconstruction,* 39; William S. McFeely, *Yankee Stepfather: General O. O. Howard and the Freedmen* (New York: W. W. Norton, 1968), 39; Powers, *Black Charlestonians,* 138, 141, 147; Drago, *Avery Normal Institute,* 76–77; Williamson, *After Slavery,* 211; Martin, *Freedmen's Bureau,* 85–87.

104 McFeely, *Howard,* 65, 132; also see Morris, *Reading, 'Riting, and Reconstruction,* 39.

105 *Nation,* 21 December 1865, as noted in Williamson, *After Slavery,* 217. Abbott, *Freedmen's Bureau,* 93–97; Jenkins, *Seizing the New Day,* 70–91, has the

most complete assessment of the education of Charleston's black population during Reconstruction.

106 Thomas Holt, *Black over White: Negro Political Leadership in South Carolina during Reconstruction* (Urbana: University of Illinois Press, 1977), 10–14.

Chapter 7. The Redpath Lyceum Bureau

1 James Redpath to Sydney Howard Gay, [undated] 1865, Gay Papers.

2 Gay to Redpath, 25 February 1866; Richard Kluger, *The Paper: The Life and Death of the New York Herald Tribune* (New York: Knopf, 1986), 121, 124.

3 For examples, see *New York Tribune*, 25 November 1865; 2, 16 December 1865; 20 January 1866; *National Anti-Slavery Standard*, 23 December 1865.

4 Paul H. Buck, *The Road to Reunion, 1865–1900* (Boston: Little, Brown, 1937), 15–21; A. A. Taylor, "The Confusion of the Transition," *Journal of Negro History* 9 (July 1924): 259–79.

5 *New York Tribune*, 2 December 1865; also see 28 October 1865; 25 November 1865. In these articles, Redpath repeated his earlier calls for confiscation of the lands of ex-Confederates and its distribution to the blacks.

6 *New York Tribune*, 28 October 1865; also see 2 December 1865.

7 Redpath to Editor of the Standard, 18 June 1866, in *National Anti-Slavery Standard*, 7 July 1866; also see Redpath to unknown recipient, 22 March 1866, William R. Perkins Library, Duke University; Redpath to Editor of the *Nation*, 30 March 1867, in *Nation*, 4 April 1867; *National Anti-Slavery Standard*, 14 September 1867; *New York Tribune*, 20 January 1866; *Nation*, 28 March 1867. For an interesting account of abolitionist reaction to the unexpected conservatism of the *Nation* on matters of Reconstruction, see James M. McPherson, *Abolitionist Legacy: From Reconstruction to the NAACP* (Princeton, N.J.: Princeton University Press, 1975), 38–40.

8 *New York Tribune*, 31 March 1866; 21 June 1866; *National Anti-Slavery Standard*, 23, 30 March 1867; 13, 20 April 1867; 11 May 1867; 29 June 1867; 6, 13 July 1867.

9 *Youth's Companion*, 16, 23 February 1865; 1, 8 June 1865; 8, 17, 31 August 1865; 21 September 1865; 5, 26 October 1865; 14, 21, 28 December 1865.

10 David Donald, *Charles Sumner and the Rights of Man* (New York: Alfred A. Knopf, 1970), 301–2; *Boston Daily Advertiser*, 2 April 1868; *National Anti-Slavery Standard*, 18 April 1868.

11 Charles Lowe to Benjamin F. Butler, 7 June 1865, in *Private and Official Correspondence of Gen. Benjamin F. Butler during the Period of the Civil War*, 5 vols. (n.p. 1917), 5:629; Hans L. Trefousse, *Ben Butler: The South Called Him BEAST!* (New York: Octagon Books, 1974), 186–88; Robert S. Holzman, *Stormy Ben Butler* (New York: Macmillan, 1965), 161–63; Howard P. Nash Jr., *Stormy Petrel: The Life and Times of General Benjamin F. Butler, 1818–1893* (Rutherford, N.J.: Fairleigh Dickinson University Press, 1969), 224–29.

12 *New York Tribune*, 29 September 1866; see also *Boston Evening Traveller*, 25, 27, 28, 29 September 1866; Murray M. Horowitz, "Ben Butler: The Making of a Radical" (Ph.D. diss., Columbia University, 1955), 306–8.

13 *National Anti-Slavery Standard*, 26 January 1867, also see 10 November 1866; 2 March, 14 September 1867; *Boston Daily Advertiser*, 7 December 1866; *New York Times*, 25 January 1867; *Nation*, 28 March 1867; 4 April 1867; L. T. Merrill, "General Benjamin F. Butler in Washington," *Records of the Columbia Historical Society* 39 (1938): 84–88; Horowitz, "Ben Butler," 308–11.

14 *National Anti-Slavery Standard*, 28 March 1868; also see *Boston Daily Advertiser*, 2 April 1868. Ben Butler also hoped to defeat Grant and win the Republican presidential nomination. Samuel Shapiro, " 'Aristocracy, Mud, and Vituperation': The Butler-Dana Campaign in Essex County in 1868," *New England Quarterly* 31 (September 1958): 341; Merrill, "Benjamin F. Butler," 89–91.

15 *National Anti-Slavery Standard*, 28 March 1868; 4, 11 April 1868.

16 Redpath to Gay, June 1866, Gay Papers, Columbia University Library.

17 *Boston Daily Advertiser*, 3, 6, 26 November 1866; 4, 7 December 1866; 9 July 1867; *National Anti-Slavery Standard*, 10 November 1866, 20 July 1867; *Congressional Globe*, 1st Sess., 40th Cong., 515–17, 522; Roy Z. Chamlee Jr., *Lincoln's Assassins: A Complete Account of their Capture, Trial, and Punishment* (Jefferson, N.C.: McFarland, 1990), 511–30; Robert Werlich, *"Beast" Butler: The Incredible Career of Major General Benjamin Franklin Butler* (Washington, D.C.: Quaker Press, 1962), 127–28; George Fort Milton, *The Age of Hate: Andrew Johnson and the Radicals* (1930; Hamden, Conn.: Archon Books, 1965), 412–16; Nash, *Stormy Petrel*, 231–32; Holzman, *Stormy Ben Butler*, 163–64; Shapiro, "Butler-Dana Campaign," 340–41.

18 David Miller DeWitt, *The Impeachment and Trial of Andrew Johnson* (1903; Madison: State Historical Society of Wisconsin, 1967), 237–39, 280–81; Lately Thomas, *The First President Johnson: The Three Lives of the Seventeenth President of the United States of America* (New York: William Morrow, 1968), 530–31, 550–51; Trefousse, *Ben Butler*, 191–92.

19 *New York Times*, 19 April 1868; Mark E. Neely Jr., *The Abraham Lincoln Encyclopedia* (New York: McGraw Hill, 1982), 171–73; Ruth Painter Randall, *Mary Lincoln: Biography of a Marriage* (Boston: Little, Brown, 1953), 414–15, 509; John E. Washington, *They Knew Lincoln* (New York: E. P. Dutton, 1942), 234–36, 239; Carolyn Sorisio, "Unmasking the Genteel Performer: Elizabeth Keckley's *Behind the Scenes* and the Politics of Public Wrath," *African American Review* 34 (spring 2000): 19–38.

20 One exception was recruiting aid for Southern freedmen. See Redpath to John A. Andrew, c. January 1867, John A. Andrew Papers, Massachusetts Historical Society; *National Anti-Slavery Standard*, 11 July 1868.

21 *Boston Daily Advertiser*, 21, 22, 24 August 1867.

22 Ibid., 6 August 1868; also see 5, 7, 8 August 1868. The junket took a total of sixteen days to travel to Utah and back. Redpath recounted that the bored travelers discharged pistols at any sign of game on the prairie and visited "dancing halls" and "keg houses" at various stops. He lectured his Boston readers: "Whatever discomfort and expenses may attend a trip across the continent are more than paid back by the knowledge you have gained of the vastness of area, or resources, and of capacities, that our country contains. It greatly erases your local prejudices, it teaches you that, after all, Massachusetts and New England are only a small fragment of our nation domain; that whether we dread it or regret it, the sceptre of political power is surely and rapidly passing from us into the hands of the bold and daring pioneers and capitalists of the great West." In the early fall of 1868,

Redpath described a steamship excursion to Nova Scotia and Prince Edward's Island accompanying a U.S. congressional delegation, including Ben Butler. Redpath advised Congress to adopt a trade policy to tie that region economically to the United States and insure its eventual annexation. He noted deep division in the Atlantic provinces over the proposed Dominion of Canada and jingoistically predicted that most "Canadians, as well as Nova Scotians, are convinced that their true interest lies, not in establishing a new nationality, but in blending their political fortunes with ours." *Boston Daily Advertiser,* 6 August 1868; 7 November 1868; also see 3, 6, 10, 14, 17 October 1868.

23 *Boston Daily Advertiser,* 20 June 1868, also see 6, 17 June 1868; 11 July 1868, 2 October 1868; 12, 22 December 1868.

24 Ibid., 12 October 1867; also see 13, 14 February 1868; Redpath to Anna Dickinson, 19 February 1868, Anna Dickinson Papers, Manuscripts Division, Library of Congress; Redpath to Caroline H. Dall, 29 February 1868, Caroline H. Dall Papers, Massachusetts Historical Society.

25 *Boston Daily Advertiser,* 13 February 1868.

26 *National Anti-Slavery Standard,* 2 October 1868; *Boston Daily Advertiser,* 12 December 1868.

27 *Boston Daily Advertiser,* 21 April 1868; also see 1 April 1868.

28 Ibid., 20 November, 3 December 1867; Charles F. Horner, *The Life of James Redpath* (New York: Barse and Hopkins, 1926), 127–28.

29 Irving Wallace, *The Twenty-seventh Wife* (New York: Simon and Schuster, 1961), 349.

30 Horner, *James Redpath,* 129, 136–39.

31 Carl Bode, *The American Lyceum: Town Meeting of the Mind* (New York: Oxford University Press, 1956), 249.

32 Horner, *James Redpath,* 127.

33 Marjorie Harrell Eubank, "The Redpath Lyceum Bureau from 1868 to 1901" (Ph.D. diss., University of Michigan, 1968), 97–98.

34 The Reverend Josiah Holcomb as quoted in Vern Wagner, "The Lecture Lyceum and the Problem of Controversy," *Journal of the History of Ideas* 15 (January 1954): 123; see also Donald M. Scott, "The Popular Lecture and the Creation of a Public in Mid-Nineteenth-Century America," *Journal of American History* 66 (March 1980): 791–809.

35 Scott, "Popular Lecture," 800–805; Mary Kupiec Cayton, "The Making of an American Prophet: Emerson, His Audiences, and the Rise of the Culture Industry in Nineteenth-Century America," *American Historical Review* 92 (June 1987): 597–620; R. Laurence Moore, "Religion, Secularization, and the Shaping of the Culture Industry in Antebellum America," *American Quarterly* 41 (June 1989): 216–42.

36 Charles Dickens Jr., "Lyceums and Lecturing in America," *All the Year Round* (4 March 1871): 317–18; *Scribner's Monthly,* 1 (March 1871): 560; Justin Kaplan, *Mr. Clemens and Mark Twain* (New York: Simon and Schuster, 1966), 84–85; Irving H. Bartlett, "Wendell Phillips and the Eloquence of Abuse," *American Quarterly* 4 (winter 1959): 509–20; Eubank, "Redpath Lyceum Bureau," 53–61.

37 For example, see Will Carleton to Redpath, 9 February 1874, Historical Society of Pennsylvania; James C. Austin, *Petroleum V. Nasby (David Ross Locke)* (New York: Twayne, 1965), 37; see also *St. Louis Democrat,* 20 February 1875;

San Francisco Chronicle, 30 November 1879; Cyril Clemens, *Josh Billings, Yankee Humorist* (Webster Grove, Mo.: International Mark Twain Society, 1933), 68–72; Harrison, *Locke,* 186–87; Eubank, "Redpath Lyceum Bureau," 65–70.

38 Thomas Wentworth Higginson, "The American Lecture-System," *Every Saturday* 5 (18 April 1868): 492; Eubank, "Redpath Lyceum Bureau," 76–81.

39 For example, the humorous travel lecturer Ralph Keeler requested that Redpath act as his agent in February 1869. Others who came forward that first year included George P. Deming, Mr. Moore of Lawrence, and the Reverend W. F. Mallaiieu. Ralph Keeler to Redpath, 22 February 1869, Ralph Keeler Papers, Manuscripts Department, William R. Perkins Library, Duke University; William Ralph Emerson to Redpath, 16 April 1869, New York Historical Society; Charles C. Deming to Redpath, 19 April 1869, Manuscript Department, William R. Perkins Library, Duke University; George P. Deming to Redpath, 14 December 1869, New York Historical Society; George Hepworth to Redpath, 9, 25 May 1869, Manuscript Department, William R. Perkins Library, Duke University; W. F. Mallalieu to Redpath, 24 May 1869, Manuscripts Department, William R. Perkins Library, Duke University; Redpath to "Lyceums in New England," printed circular, May 1869, Massachusetts Historical Society; *San Francisco Chronicle,* 11 January 1880.

40 For example, Mr. Parson encouraged Professor S. W. Draper to offer popular lectures on chemistry. Wendell Phillips recruited General Samuel Armstrong. S. W. Draper to Redpath, 25 November 1869, New York Historical Society; Wendell Phillips to Redpath, 31 January 1871, Henry E. Huntington Library.

41 Eubank, "Redpath Lyceum Bureau," 114.

42 Ibid., 117, also see 118–21, 133–37, 142–47.

43 Bode, *American Lyceum,* 249; John E. Tapia, *Circuit Chautauqua: From Rural Education to Popular Entertainment in Early Twentieth Century America* (Jefferson, N.C.: McFarland, 1997), 15; Horner, *James Redpath,* 226; Kaplan, *Mr. Clemens and Mark Twain,* 85; Eubank, "Redpath Lyceum Bureau," 104. Some lecturers desired to retain a measure of independence (e.g., not pay an agent's fee when they arranged a lecture on their own). See Edward Eggleston to Redpath, 7 March 1874, University of Virginia Library.

44 Redpath to O. O. Howard, 3 April 1869, O. O. Howard Collection, Bowdoin College Library.

45 *Redpath Lyceum* (1875): 6; Boston Lyceum Bureau printed circular, 20 August 1870, Samuel Paley Library, Temple University.

46 Redpath to Henry Ward Beecher, 24 May 1874; 12 June 1874, Manuscripts and Archives, Yale University Library; A. Augustus Wright, *Who's in the Lyceum* (Philadelphia: Pearson Brothers, 1906), 29.

47 Giraud Chester, *Embattled Maiden: The Life of Anna Dickinson* (New York: G. P. Putnam and Sons, 1951), 85.

48 *San Francisco Chronicle,* 28 December 1879; J. Matthew Gallman, *America's Joan of Arc: The Life of Anna Elizabeth Dickinson* (New York: Oxford University Press, 2006), 66–68; Austin, *Petroleum V. Nasby,* 37; Chester, *Embattled Maiden,* 86; Wallace, *Twenty-seventh Wife,* 350.

49 Wendell Phillips to Redpath, 21 December 1870, also see Redpath to Wendell Phillips, 25 November 1869, Memorandum, 21 September 1870, Wendell Phillips to Redpath, 25 October 1870, undated c.1870, December 1871, 3 July 1873,

Miscellaneous Manuscripts Collection, Manuscript Division, Library of Congress; *San Francisco Chronicle,* 11 January 1880; Wallace, *Twenty-seventh Wife,* 350.

50 *St. Louis Democrat,* 20 February 1875.

51 Fred Harvey Harrington, *Fighting Politician: Major General N. P. Banks* (Philadelphia: University of Pennsylvania Press, 1948), 203.

52 Mark Twain to Redpath, 14 December 1871, as quoted in Eubank, "Redpath Lyceum Bureau," 107.

53 As quoted in Eubank, "Redpath Lyceum Bureau," 113; *Who Was Who in America, 1897–1942,* 2 vols. (Chicago: A. N. Marquis Company, 1943), 1:534; Horner, *James Redpath,* 137–38, 156–57, 226.

54 *San Francisco Chronicle,* 30 November 1879. The New York City–based American Literary Bureau absorbed the Associated Western Literary Societies in the early 1870s to become Redpath's chief competitor. Eubank, "Redpath Lyceum Bureau," 128–29.

55 Horner, *James Redpath,* 147–48.

56 Redpath to Elias Nason, 10 April 1874, as quoted in Donald, *Charles Sumner,* 575; also see 461; see also Eubank, "Redpath Lyceum Bureau," 137.

57 *San Francisco Chronicle,* 4 December 1879.

58 John B. Gough to Redpath, 6 August 1873, John B. Gough Papers, Amherst College Library; *St. Louis Democrat,* 20 February 1875; *San Francisco Chronicle,* 4 December 1879; Nevins, *American Culture,* 238; Wallace, *Twenty-seventh Wife,* 349; Austin, *Petroleum V. Nasby,* 37; Kaplan, *Mr. Clemens and Mark Twain,* 85.

59 Frederick Douglass to Redpath, 9 November 1869, Anti-Slavery Collection, Boston Public Library; also see Frederick Douglass to Redpath, 10 April 1869, University of Illinois at Chicago Library; Redpath to Frederick Douglass, 17 April 1869, Reel 2, frame 461, Frederick Douglass Papers, Library of Congress.

60 Frederick Douglass to Redpath, 29 July 1871, Alfred W. Anthony Papers, New York Public Library.

61 *St. Louis Democrat,* 20 February 1875.

62 Redpath to Henry Ward Beecher, 24 May 1874; 12 June 1874, Manuscripts and Archives Department, Yale University Library; Wright, *Who's in the Lyceum,* 29.

63 *San Francisco Chronicle,* 15 February 1880. Redpath directly managed the lecturing of a few key clients such as Henry Ward Beecher and ran his own "star course" in Boston each season. Eubank, "Redpath Lyceum Bureau," 172.

64 Mary A. Livermore, *The Story of My Life; or, The Sunshine and Shadow of Seventy Years* (Hartford, Conn.: A. D. Worthington, 1899), 485; Horner, *James Redpath,* 143–46.

65 Eubank, "Redpath Lyceum Bureau," 221–22.

66 Stanton lectured for the bureau in 1869; Anthony in 1870 and 1874; Howe in 1869, 1872, 1874, and 1875. Deborah Pickman Clifford, *Mine Eyes Have Seen the Glory: A Biography of Julia Ward Howe* (Boston: Little, Brown, 1978), 208–9; James B. Pond, *Eccentricities of Genius: Memories of Famous Men and Women of the Platform and Stage* (New York: G. W. Dillingham, ca. 1900), 232; Wallace, *Twenty-seventh Wife,* 350. Eubanks, "Redpath Lyceum Bureau," 295–303.

67 Susan B. Anthony to Redpath, 1 January 1870; 23 December 1870, Elizabeth Cady Stanton to James Redpath, 28 February 1870, Susan B. Anthony Collection, Vassar College Library.

68 *National Anti-Slavery Standard,* 2 October 1869.

69 Livermore, *Story of My Life,* 485–86, 494–95; Eubank, "Redpath Lyceum Bureau," 299. Redpath also performed a similar mentoring service for novice lecturer Emma Carter. John M. Carter to Redpath, 16 April 1869, New York Historical Society.

70 Even Ralph Waldo Emerson, at the close of his long career on the lyceum circuit, lectured under the Redpath Bureau's management. Horner, *James Redpath,* 130–43.

71 John Hay to Redpath, 27 June 1871, Beinecke Rare Book and Manuscript Library, Yale University; John Hay to Redpath, 20 October 1871, John Hay Papers, Manuscripts Division, Library of Congress; *St. Louis Democrat,* 20 February 1875.

72 Circular of the Redpath Lyceum Bureau, 20 August 1870, Samuel Paley Library, Temple University; Merle Curti, *The Growth of American Thought* (New York: Harper, 1943), 581. In a brief autobiographical note at the end of his book, *Acres of Diamonds,* Conwell related that his first contact with Redpath had been in the 1860s when he had been a sales agent for Redpath's biography of John Brown. Russell H. Conwell, *Acres of Diamonds* (New York: Harper and Brothers, 1915), n.p.; Eubank, "Redpath Lyceum Bureau," 225.

73 Redpath to Moses Coit Tyler, 29 December 1874, Department of Rare Books, Cornell University Library.

74 *The Lyceum* (1870): 5; Edward E. Hale read his lecture entitled "He Did His Level Best." Redpath to Edward E. Hale, 24 October 1871; Redpath to Edward E. Hale, 1, 9 November, 10 December 1872, Edward E. Hale Papers, New York State Library; Eubank, "Redpath Lyceum Bureau," 160–61.

75 Kaplan, *Mr. Clemens and Mark Twain,* 86.

76 James Parton to Redpath, 10 October 1870, Beinecke Rare Book and Manuscript Library, Yale University.

77 *Malden Mirror and Messenger,* 17 May 1873; Horner, *James Redpath,* 159.

78 Edward Jenkins to Redpath, 2 April 1872, 22 April, 5 July, 8 August 1873, Manuscript Autobiography of Edward Jenkins, c. 1872, University of Iowa Library.

79 *St. Louis Democrat,* 20 February 1875; Horner, *James Redpath,* 159–60.

80 *Charles Kingsley's American Notes: Letters from a Lecturer Tour, 1874,* edited by Robert Bernard Martin (Princeton, N.J.: Princeton University Press, 1958), 7–8, 20–21, 25; Robert Bernard Martin, *The Dust of Combat: A Life of Charles Kingsley* (London: Faber and Faber, 1959), 281–83.

81 *Charles Kingsley's American Notes,* 23.

82 Horner, *James Redpath,* 152.

83 John Stoddard was another popular travel lecturer. Redpath to "Lyceums in New England," printed circular, May 1869, Massachusetts Historical Society; Curti, *American Thought,* 581.

84 *National Anti-Slavery Standard,* 2 October 1869.

85 Ibid.; Horner, *James Redpath,* 176; Walter Blair, "The Popularity of Nineteenth-Century American Humorists," *American Literature* 3 (May 1931): 175–94.

86 John Billings to Redpath, 25 April 1869, Manuscripts Department, University of Virginia; *San Francisco Chronicle,* 18 January 1880.

87 *San Francisco Chronicle,* 18 January 1880; Albert Bigelow Paine, *Mark Twain: A Biography,* 3 vols. (New York: Harper, 1912), 1:445–46.

88 David R. Locke to Redpath, 9 September 1871, 2 August 1872, 13 February 1873, James Redpath Papers, New York Historical Society; *San Francisco*

Chronicle, 21 December 1879; Austin, *Petroleum V. Nasby,* 37–38: Blair, "American Humorists," 189

89 Cyril Clemens, *Petroleum Vesuvius Nasby* (Webster Groves, Mo.: International Mark Twain Society, 1936), 111.

90 [Samuel Langhorne Clemens], *The Autobiography of Mark Twain* (1912; New York: Harper Perennial, 1980), 173; Paine, *Mark Twain,* 1:373; Paul Fatout, *Mark Twain on the Lecture Circuit* (Bloomington: University of Indiana Press, 1960), 103–4; Edgar M. Branch, " 'The Babes in the Wood': Artemus Ward's 'Double Health' to Mark Twain," *Proceedings of the Modern Language Association* 93 (October 1978): 955–92; Fred W. Lorch, "Mark Twain's Lecture Tour of 1868–1869: 'The American Vandal Abroad,' " *American Literature* 26 (January 1955): 515–27.

91 Redpath continued to act as an informal literary promoter for Twain for several more years. Redpath to Samuel L. Clemens, 24 April 1869, University of Iowa Library; Samuel L. Clemens to Redpath, ca. 1870, Beinecke Rare Book and Manuscript Library, Yale University; Fred W. Lorch, *The Trouble Begins at Eight: Mark Twain's Lecture Tours* (Ames: University of Iowa Press, 1966), 98–99.

92 Samuel L. Clemens to Redpath, 10 June 1871, New York Historical Society; Delancey Ferguson, *Mark Twain: Man and Legend* (Indianapolis: Bobbs-Merrill, 1943), 141; Lorch, *Trouble Begins at Eight,* 103–4; Fatout, *Mark Twain,* 103–4, 121–29; Kaplan, *Mr. Clemens and Mark Twain,* 98.

93 Kaplan, *Mr. Clemens and Mark Twain,* 98; Fatout, *Mark Twain,* 121.

94 Fatout, *Mark Twain,* 140–41.

95 *Mark Twain's Letters,* edited by Albert B. Paine, 2 vols. (New York: Harper and Brothers, 1929), 1:172; see also Paine, *Mark Twain,* 1:409–10; Ferguson, *Mark Twain,* 154–55; Lorch, *Trouble Begins at Eight,* 113.

96 As quoted in Lorch, *Trouble Begins at Eight,* 113.

97 Samuel Clemens to Redpath, 27 June 1871; 10, 20 July 1871; 15, 26 September 1871 in *Mark Twain's Letters,* 189–90; see also Lorch, *Trouble Begins at Eight,* 114–15, 118; Ferguson, *Mark Twain,* 153–55; Fred W. Lorch, "Mark Twain's 'Artemus Ward' Lecture on the Tour of 1871–1872," *New England Quarterly* 25 (September 1952): 327–43.

98 Samuel Clemens to Redpath, 8 August 1871, in *Mark Twain's Letters,* 190; also see Samuel Clemens to William D. Howells, 27 February 1874, in *Mark Twain-Howells Letters: The Correspondence of Samuel L. Clemens and William D. Howells, 1872–1910,* 2 vols., edited by Henry Nash Smith and William M. Gibson (Cambridge, Mass.: Belknap Press of Harvard University Press, 1960), 1:14–15; Paine, *Mark Twain,* 1:441; Fatout, *Mark Twain,* 150; Ferguson, *Mark Twain,* 158.

99 As quoted in Ferguson, *Mark Twain,* 159.

100 Samuel Clemens to Redpath, 2 January 1872, in *Mark Twain's Letters,* 193–94.

101 As quoted in Paine, *Mark Twain,* 1:473; see also Fatout, *Mark Twain,* 173; Lorch, *Trouble Begins at Eight,* 136.

102 Dennis Welland, *Mark Twain in England* (London: Chatto and Windus, 1978), 53; Fatout, *Mark Twain,* 173–75, 188.

103 As quoted in Paine, *Mark Twain,* 1:502; Ferguson, *Mark Twain,* 173. See also *Mark Twain-Howells Letters,* 1:14, 15.

104 Kaplan, *Mr. Clemens and Mark Twain*, 185; Ferguson, *Mark Twain*, 140–41; Paine, *Mark Twain*, 2:527–29; *Mark Twain-Howells Letters*, 1:14, 36.

105 [Clemens], *Autobiography of Mark Twain*, 162.

106 Quoted in Eubank, "Redpath Lyceum Bureau," 147.

107 Samuel Clemens to Redpath, 12 January 1872, University of Iowa Libraries; Samuel Clemens to Redpath, 13 February 1874, Beinecke Rare Book and Manuscript Library, Yale University; Horner, *James Redpath*, 168, 172–74; Dixon Wecter, *Mark Twain to Mrs. Fairbanks* (San Marino, Calif.: Huntington Library, 1948), 183.

108 Lorch, *Trouble Begins at Eight*, 116–17.

109 *Boston Evening Journal*, 29 January 1921; Pond, *Eccentricities of Genius*, 232; Horner, *James Redpath*, 129.

110 Clemens, *Josh Billings*, 85; Pond, *Eccentricities of Genius*, 232–33; Paine, *Mark Twain*, 1:444–45, and *Mark Twain's Letters*, 1:166.

111 [Clemens], *Autobiography of Mark Twain*, 166; Paine, *Mark Twain*, 1:444–45.

112 [Clemens], *Autobiography of Mark Twain*, 166.

113 Ibid.; also see Paine, *Mark Twain*, 1:444–45.

114 *Malden Evening Transcript*, 21 August 1914; *Malden Mirror*, 28 August 1914.

115 *Boston City Directories: 1867*, 422; *1868*, 491; *1869*, 511; *1871–72*, 581; *1875–76*, 745; *1877–78*, 745; *1878–79*, 740; *1879–80*, 765; *1882–83*, 868; *1883–84*, 896; *Boston Evening Transcript*, 21 August 1914.

116 *Malden Evening News*, 21 August 1914.

117 *Malden Free Press*, 28 August 1914.

118 Ibid., 28 August 1914.

119 *Malden Tribune*, 21 September 1872.

120 Harriet Hanson Robinson Diary, 26 January 1868, 9 April 1869, Robinson-Shattuck Papers, Schlesinger Library, Radcliff College; *DAB*, 16:58–59; *ANB*, 18:655–56.

121 Butler also had the strong support of another prominent Massachusetts abolitionist, Wendell Phillips. Holzman, *Stormy Ben Butler*, 186–88, 191, 198–99; Nash, *Stormy Petrel*, 264–66; Trefousse, *Ben Butler*, 224–25; Donald, *Sumner*, 2:522–23; William D. Mallam, "Butlerism in Massachusetts," *New England Quarterly* 33 (June 1960): 186–206; Shapiro, "Butler-Dana Campaign," 357–60; Merrill, "Benjamin F. Butler," 89–91.

122 *Malden Tribune*, 7 September 1862.

123 Ibid., 14, 28 September 1872; 10, 12 October 1872; *Malden Evening News*, 12 August 1976.

124 *Malden Tribune*, 28 September 1872; 19, 26 October 1872; 2, 9, 16 November 1872.

125 Ibid., 16 November 1872.

126 Ibid., 23, 30 November 1872; 7 December 1872.

127 Ibid., 16, 30 November 1872.

128 *Malden Evening News*, 12 August 1976. In 1873, Butler was able to exact some revenge against his intraparty enemies when he successfully plotted to have Redpath's Malden friend, William Robinson, removed from his patronage post as clerk of the Massachusetts house of representatives. For more detail on

Massachusetts politics in this era, see Margaret S. Thompson, "Ben Butler versus the Brahmins: Patronage and Politics in Early Gilded Age Massachusetts," *New England Quarterly* 55 (June 1982): 163–86; Merrill, "Benjamin F. Butler," 91; *ANB*, 18:655–56; *DAB*, 16:58–59.

Chapter 8. Entertainment Innovator

1 Allan Nevins, *The Emergence of Modern America* (New York: Macmillan, 1927), 239; Irving Wallace, *The Twenty-seventh Wife* (New York: Simon and Schuster, 1961), 350–51.

2 George C. D. Odell, *Annals of the New York Stage*, 15 vols. (New York: Columbia University Press, 1927–49), 9:476; Nevins, *Modern America*, 239.

3 *San Francisco Chronicle*, 30 November 1879.

4 *St. Louis Democrat*, 20 February 1875.

5 Ibid.

6 Ibid.; *San Francisco Chronicle*, 30 November 1879.

7 Robert Bernard Martin, *The Dust of Combat: A Life of Charles Kingsley* (London: Faber and Faber, 1959), 283.

8 *Charles Kingsley's American Notes: Letters from a Lecture Tour, 1874*, edited by Robert Bernard Martin (Princeton, N.J.: Princeton University Press, 1958), 25.

9 Ibid., 7–8, 20–25, 27, 30.

10 *The Lyceum*, n.d., as quoted in Eubank, "Redpath Lyceum Bureau," 292.

11 A. Augustus Wright, *Who's in the Lyceum* (Philadelphia: Pearson Brothers, 1906), 30; Charles F. Horner, *The Life of James Redpath and the Development of the Modern Lyceum* (New York: Barse and Hopkins, 1926), 214; Paul Fatout, *Mark Twain on the Lecture Circuit* (Bloomington: University of Indiana Press, 1960), 190; Marjorie Harrell Eubank, "The Redpath Lyceum Bureau from 1868 to 1901" (Ph.D. diss., University of Michigan, 1968), 190–91, 195–96, 209.

12 Nevins, *Modern America*, 239.

13 Ibid.; Wallace, *Twenty-seventh Wife*, 352; Horner, *James Redpath*, 213–14; Eubank, "Redpath Lyceum Bureau, 209–12.

14 John E. Tapia, *Circuit Chautauqua: From Rural Education to Popular Education in Early Twentieth Century America* (Jefferson, N.C.: McFarland, 1997), 16.

15 *St. Louis Democrat*, 20 February 1875.

16 Justin Kaplan, *Mr. Clemens and Mark Twain* (New York: Simon and Schuster, 1966), 86; Horner, *James Redpath*, 198; *NCAB*, 14:221–22.

17 Kaplan, *Mr. Clemens and Mark Twain*, 86; Arthur Quinn, *Hell with the Fire Out: A History of the Modoc War* (Boston: Faber and Faber, 1997), 195. Also in the summer of 1875, Redpath attempted unsuccessfully to persuade the former military and governmental leaders of the Union and Confederate sides in the Civil War to participate in a series of joint lectures in cities across the country. Nathaniel P. Banks to Jefferson Davis, 30 August 1875, Jefferson Davis to Redpath, 6 September 1875, in *Jefferson Davis, Constitutionalist: His Letters, Papers, and Speeches*, edited by Dunbar Rowland, 10 vols. (Jackson, Miss.: Mississippi Department of Archives and History, 1923), 7:452–56.

18 Redpath to Edna D. Cheney, 1 May 1875, Sophia Smith Collection; Robert E. Spiller et al., *Literary History of the United States,* 4th ed. (New York: Macmillan, 1974), 800; Horner, *James Redpath,* 198.

19 Redpath to Theodore Tilton, ca. 10 April 1873, University of California at Los Angeles.

20 J. B. Pond, *Eccentricities of Genius: Memories of Famous Men and Women of the Platform and Stage* (London: Catto and Windus, 1901), 188–89. See also *San Francisco Chronicle,* 4 January 1880.

21 Pond, *Eccentricities of Genius,* 189. Also see Thomas Nast to Redpath, 30 June 1873, Thomas Nast Papers, Rutherford B. Hayes Presidential Center, Fremont, Ohio; *San Francisco Chronicle,* 4 January 1860.

22 Redpath to Thomas Nast, 3 October 1874, Otis Norcross Papers, Massachusetts Historical Society; *St. Louis Democrat,* 20 February 1875; San Francisco Chronicle, 4 January 1860; Albert Bigelow Paine, *Th. Nast: His Period and His Pictures* (New York: Macmillan, 1904), 275–85; Pond, *Eccentricities of Genius,* 188–89.

23 Redpath to Vinnie Ream, 19 May 1871, Library of Congress.

24 Mark Twain and Charles Dudley Warner, *The Gilded Age: A Tale of Today* (1873; New York: Penguin Books, 2001), 413.

25 Pond had accompanied Redpath at the time of the latter's first newspaper interview of Kansas free-state guerrilla leader John Brown in 1855. After service in the Union Army, Pond had migrated to Utah and engaged in the mercantile business. *DAB,* 15:60–61; *NCAB,* 1:240–41; *Who Was Who in America, 1897–1942,* 2:981.

26 Ann Eliza Young, *Wife No. 19; or the Story of a Life in Bondage* (Chicago: Dustin, Gilman, 1875), chap. 28; also see *St. Louis Democrat,* 20 February 1875; Joan Smyth Iversen, *The Antipolygamy Controversy in U.S. Women's Movements, 1880–1925* (New York: Garland, 1997), 102–3.

27 Wallace, *Twenty-seventh Wife,* 269–71, 304–50; Edward T. James et al., *Notable American Women, 1607–1950: A Biographical Dictionary,* 3 vols. (Cambridge, Mass.: Harvard University Press, 1971), 3:696–97 (hereinafter cited as *NAW.*).

28 As quoted in Fatout, *Mark Twain,* 103.

29 *Scribner's Monthly* 1 (March 1871): 560; see also Fatout, *Mark Twain,* 142–43; Eubank, "Redpath Lyceum Bureau," 127–28, 263–68.

30 Horner, *James Redpath,* 192, 196.

31 As quoted in Dixon Wecter, *Mark Twain to Mrs. Fairbanks* (San Marino: Huntington Library, 1949), 146–47; see also Fatout, *Mark Twain,* 143.

32 Allan Nevins, as quoted in Eubank, "Redpath Lyceum Bureau," 131.

33 *Autobiography of Mark Twain,* 161–62.

34 *St. Louis Democrat,* 20 February 1875; Pond, *Eccentricities of Genius,* 351.

35 Neil Harris, *Humbug: The Art of P. T. Barnum* (Chicago: The University of Chicago Press, 1973), 194–95; Tapia, *Circuit Chautauqua,* 15.

36 *San Francisco Chronicle,* 28 December 1879.

37 Redpath to Anna Dickinson, 16 December 1869; 30 May 1870; 8, 19, 24 August 1870; 11 February 1872.

38 Giraud Chester, *Embattled Maiden: The Life of Anna Dickinson* (New York: G. P. Putnam and Sons, 1951), 145–46; J. Matthew Gallman, *America's Joan of*

Arc: The Life of Anna Elizabeth Dickinson (New York: Oxford University Press, 2006), 66–68, 131; Odell, *Annals,* 10:261–62; *Mark Twain–Howells Letters: The Correspondence of Samuel L. Clemens and William D. Howells, 1872–1910,* edited by Henry Nash Smith and William M. Gibson, 2 vols. (Cambridge, Mass.: Harvard University Press, 1960), 1:7.

39 *St. Louis Democrat,* 20 February 1875; *San Francisco Chronicle,* 21 December 1879.

40 Quoted in Horner, *James Redpath,* 183.

41 Redpath to William C. Howells, 6 November 1874, James Redpath Collection, Huntington Library. See also *St. Louis Democrat,* 20 February 1875. In the summer of 1873, Redpath attempted to diversify his investments by purchasing a newspaper, the *Chronicle,* in nearby Charlestown, Massachusetts. *Malden Mirror and Messenger,* 26 July 1873.

42 Richard Wrightman Fox, *Trials of Intimacy: Love and Loss in the Beecher-Tilton Scandal* (Chicago: University of Chicago Press, 1999), 386–87; Barbara Goldsmith, *Other Powers: The Age of Suffrage, Spiritualism, and the Scandalous Victoria Woodhull* (New York: Alfred A. Knopf, 1998), 410–21.

43 Two years later, when called as a witness in the civil case, however, there were unsubstantiated imputations that Redpath had at first joined Tilton and Moulton in attempting to blackmail Beecher. *New York Tribune,* 1 April 1875; [*New York Times*], *The Beecher Trial: A Review of the Evidence* (New York: New York Times, 1875); J. E. P. Doyle, *Plymouth Church and Its Pastor; or, Henry Ward Beecher and His Accusers* (Hartford, Conn.: Park, 1874).

44 *New York Tribune,* 2 April 1875. Also see *New York Times,* 1 April 1875.

45 *New York Tribune,* 2 April 1875. Also see *Boston Daily Advertiser,* 1, 2 April 1875; *New York Times,* 2, 23 April 1875; 23 June 1875.

46 *New York Tribune,* 2 April 1875. Also see *New York Times,* 25 April 1875; 23 June 1875.

47 Robert Shaplen, *Free Love and Heavenly Sinners* (New York: Knopf, 1954), 185–260; Fatout, *Mark Twain,* 194–95.

48 *Mark Twain–Howells Letters,* 1:100–102.

49 Earl Marble, "James Redpath," *Cottage Hearth* 4 (February 1877): 29.

50 As quoted in Daniel E. Sutherland, "Some Thoughts Concerning the Love Life of Sherwood Bonner," *Southern Studies* 26 (1987): 116; Hubert Horton McAlexander, *The Prodigal Daughter: A Biography of Sherwood Bonner* (Baton Rouge: Louisiana State University Press, 1981), 131.

51 Sutherland, "Sherwood Bonner," 119, 126; McAlexander, *Sherwood Bonner,* 80.

52 The entire text is reproduced and analyzed in Anne Razey Gowdy, ed., *A Sherwood Bonner Sampler, 1869–1884: What a Bright, Educated, Witty, Lively, Snappy Young Woman Can Say on a Variety of Topics* (Knoxville: University of Tennessee Press, 2000), 409–14. Also see McAlexander, *Sherwood Bonner,* 68–71; Sutherland, "Sherwood Bonner," 121–22.

53 Quoted in Gowdy, *Sherwood Bonner Sampler,* xlvi.

54 Redpath carried a letter of introduction to Davis from Nathaniel P. Banks. In early September, Redpath traveled to Memphis but narrowly missed seeing the ex-Confederate president. N. P. Banks to Jefferson Davis, 30 August 1875, Jefferson Davis to James Redpath, 6 September 1875, in *Jefferson Davis, Constitutionalist:*

His Letters, Papers and Speeches, edited by Dunbar Rowland, 10 vols. (Jackson, Miss.: Torgerson Press, 1923), 7:452–53, 455–56.

55 As quoted in McAlexander, *Sherwood Bonner,* 80, also see 79.

56 Ibid., 80.

57 As quoted in Sutherland, "Sherwood Bonner," 123, see also 119–20; McAlexander, *Sherwood Bonner,* 120.

58 Gowdy, *Sherwood Bonner Sampler,* xlix; *DAB,* 33–34; McAlexander, *Sherwood Bonner,* 95–96.

59 *Boston Daily Advertiser,* 6 October 1875. Also see Wallace, *Twenty-seventh Wife,* 352; *DAB,* 15:60–61; *Who's Who in American History, 1897–1942,* 534.

60 *San Francisco Chronicle,* 29 October 1879.

61 McAlexander, *Prodigal Daughter,* 97.

62 Hugh A. Orchard, *Fifty Years of Chautauqua: Its Beginnings, Its Development, Its Message, and Its Life* (Cedar Rapids, Iowa: Torch Press, 1923), 113, 152–55; Spiller et al., eds., *Literary History of the United States,* 800–801; Theodore Morrison, *Chautauqua: A Center for Education, Religion, and the Arts in America* (Chicago: University of Chicago Press, 1974), 176–78; Tapia, *Circuit Chautauqua,* 15; Carl Bode, *The American Lyceum: Town Meeting of the Mind* (New York: Oxford University Press, 1956), 200; Horner, *James Redpath,* 180, 226; Fatout, *Mark Twain,* 193.

63 Merle Curti, *The Growth of American Thought* (New York: Harpers, 1943), 581. See also, Jack Poggi, *Theater in America: The Impact of Economic Forces* (Ithaca, N.Y.: Cornell University Press, 1966), 3–11.

64 Robert C. Allen, *Horrible Prettiness: Burlesque and American Culture* (Chapel Hill: University of North Carolina Press, 1991), 178–85.

65 See Harris, *Humbug,* 280–81.

66 Eric Foner, *Reconstruction: America's Unfinished Revolution, 1863–1877* (New York: Harper and Row, 1988), 558–63.

67 Robert F. Durden, *James Shepherd Pike: Republicanism and the American Negro, 1850–1882* (Durham, N.C.: Duke University Press, 1957), 183–219; Foner, *Reconstruction,* 524–28; James M. McPherson, *The Abolitionist Legacy: From Reconstruction to the NAACP* (Princeton, N.J. Princeton University Press, 1975), 24–34, 41–42.

68 *New York Independent,* 2, 23 March 1876; McPherson, *Abolitionist Legacy,* 24–34, 41–42.

69 *New York Times,* 3, 8, 27, 31 July 1876; 5, 8, 14, 21, 28 August 1876; 1, 2, 11 September 1876; *Mississippi in 1875, Report of the Select Committee to Inquire into the Mississippi Election of 1875, Senate Reports,* #527, 44th Cong., 1st Sess., 2 vols., Washington, D.C., 1876; James Wilford Garner, *Reconstruction in Mississippi* (1901; Baton Rouge: Louisiana State University Press, 1968), 408–10; McPherson, *Abolitionist Legacy,* 51.

70 Sherwood Bonner to Ruth Bonner, 4 February 1876, as quoted in McAlexander, *Prodigal Daughter,* 97.

71 *New York Independent,* 3 August 1876; *American Missionary* 20 (September 1876): 205–6.

72 *New York Independent,* 3 August 1876; also see *American Missionary* 20 (September 1876): 204–5.

73 *New York Independent,* 31 August 1876.

74 Ibid., 28 September 1876; McPherson, *Abolitionist Legacy,* 52.

75 Hugh Talmage Lefler and Albert Ray Newsome, *North Carolina: The History of a Southern State,* 3d ed. (Chapel Hill: University of North Carolina Press, 1973), 497–501.

76 *New York Tribune,* 6 November 1876. Also see Redpath to W. Whitelaw Reid, 9 November 1876, W. Whitelaw Reid Papers, DLC; Richard H. Abbott, *For Free Press and Equal Rights: Republican Newspapers in the Reconstruction South* (Athens: University of Georgia Press, 2004), 87–90, 129–30.

77 *New York Tribune,* 6 November 1876.

78 Lefler and Newsome, *North Carolina,* 500–501.

79 *New York Times,* 17, 20, 22, 25 November 1876; 1, 4, 11, 26 December 1876.

80 Ibid., 20 November 1876.

81 Ibid., 1 December 1876.

82 McPherson, *Abolitionist Legacy,* 84–86.

83 *New York Times,* 15, 16 January 1877; Alfred B. Williams, *Hampton and His Red Shirts: South Carolina's Deliverance in 1876* (Charleston, S.C.: Walker, Evans, and Cogsewell, 1935), 435.

84 Redpath to W. Whitelaw Reid, 24 March 1877, W. W. Reid Collection, Manuscripts Division, Library of Congress. Also see Bingham Duncan, *Whitelaw Reid: Journalist, Politician, Diplomat* (Athens: University of Georgia Press, 1975), 66–69.

85 Roy Morris, Jr., *Fraud of the Century: Rutherford B. Hayes, Samuel Tilden, and the Stolen Election of 1876* (New York: Simon and Schuster, 2003), 286–93; Foner, *Reconstruction,* 575–82.

86 Redpath blamed the final collapse of southern Reconstruction on the new president's capitulation to the Democrats: "One word, constantly in Hayes' mouth, reveals his character. That word is—*Policy.* That word is the shibboleth of his motley horde of scamp-followers. Once, the inspiration of the Republicans was—Principle. The party was a warrior of the Lord then with a light from God's Throne on its forehead. As far as Hayes represents it, the party, now, is a leprous lazarus, whining for the votes that fall from the Southern Democratic table." Redpath to M[errimon] Howard, 14 April 1877, Hayes Papers; Vernon Lane Wharton, *The Negro in Mississippi, 1865–1900* (1947; New York: Harper and Row, 1965), 169.

87 Redpath acknowledged the need for a degree of compromise with responsible Democrats. He approved of Hayes's appointment of southern Democrat David M. Keyes to his cabinet but asked why neither native southern white Republicans nor a black Republican, such as Frederick Douglass, were included as well. Redpath argued: "No man opposes conciliation. Every decent man desires it. That is Part the First of Hayes' Policy. But Part the Second is Surrender. It means the acquiescence of the National Government in the rule of the majority by the minority; because that minority of citizens has a majority of property, intelligence and military power. . . . Republicanism means not the rule of respectability but the rule of the majority; and Hayes' Gulf State policy is the suicide of republicanism. . . . Hayes says, or is reported to have said, that 'if the rebels do not act in good faith he will soon change his policy.' This is boy's talk, or worse. How *can* he change his policy after he yields his power?" Redpath to M[errimon] Howard, 14 April 1877, Hayes Papers; Wharton, *Negro in Mississippi,* 169.

88 James Redpath to M. Howard, 14 April 1877, Published Circular Letter, Rutherford B. Hayes Papers, Rutherford B. Hayes Presidential Center.

89 Ibid.

90 Ibid.

91 Ibid. See also *Martinsburg Statesman* (WV), 8 May 1877.

92 One southerner wrote the new president that Redpath was "one of the original Exeter Hall agents of Abolitionism sent to this country in the British East-India interests, to foment fratricidal strife, and to destroy the organized system of labour in the Southern states then successfully applied to the production of rivalling staples to those of the East Indies." Donald C. Henderson to Rutherford B. Hayes, 30 April 1877, John Tyler, Jr. to Rutherford B. Hayes, 19 April 1877, Hayes Papers; *Chicago Inter-Ocean,* 18 April 1877.

93 McPherson, *Abolitionist Legacy,* 84–139, 113.

94 Robert W. Jones, *Journalism in the United States* (New York: E. P. Dutton, 1947), 352–61; James Melvin Lee, *History of American Journalism* (Boston: Houghton Mifflin, 1917), 275–76; James G. Smart, "Information Control, Thought Control: Whitelaw Reid and the Nation's News Services," *Public Historian* 3 (spring 1981): 23–42.

95 *San Francisco Chronicle,* 30 November 1879; C. H. Cramer, *Royal Bob: The Life of Robert G. Ingersoll* (Indianapolis: Bobbs-Merrill, 1952), 116, see also 104–8, 114; Herman E. Kittredge, *Ingersoll: A Biographical Appreciation* (New York: Dresden, 1911), 91–109; David D. Anderson, *Robert Ingersoll* (New York: Twayne, 1972), 61–70, 116–18; Robert Waters, *Intellectual Pursuits or Culture by Self-Help* (New York: Worthington, 1892), 350–51; *The Works of Robert Ingersoll,* Dresden edition, 12 vols. (New York: C. P. Farrell, 1900), 8:128; McAlexander, *Prodigal Daughter,* 115; Wallace, *Twenty-seventh Wife,* 352.

96 Walter L. Welch and Leah Brodbeck Stenzel Burt, *From Tinfoil to Stereo: The Acoustic Years of the Recording Industry, 1877–1929* (Gainesville: University Press of Florida, 1994), 5–21; Neil Baldwin, *Edison: Inventing the Century* (New York: Hyperion, 1995), 76–68; Andre Millard, *Edison and the Business of Innovation* (Baltimore: Johns Hopkins University Press, 1990), 63–64.

97 Redpath to Thomas A. Edison, 22 June 1878, Edison National Historic Site, West Orange, New Jersey; Frank Lewis Dyer, *Edison: His Life and Inventions* (New York: Harper Brothers, 1929), 103; Matthew Josephson, *Edison* (New York: McGraw-Hill, 1959), 172–73; Baldwin, *Edison,* 90–92; Millard, *Edison,* 64: Lisa Gitelman, "The First Phonographs: Reading and Writing with Sound," *Biblion: The Bulletin of the New York Public Library* 8 (fall 1999): 3–16.

98 Francis Jehl, *Menlo Park Reminiscences,* 2 vols. (1937; New York: Dover, 1990), 1:176–79; Dyer, *Edison,* 107.

99 *New York Tribune,* 18 September 1879; *San Francisco Chronicle,* 29 October 1879; *New York Times,* 30 October 1879; Odell, *Annals of the New York Stage,* 11:180.

100 Sutherland, "Sherwood Bonner," 121–23; McAlexander, *Sherwood Bonner,* 130–32.

101 McAlexander, *Sherwood Bonner,* 115; Sutherland, "Sherwood Bonner," 122.

102 McAlexander, *Sherwood Bonner,* 117–19; Sutherland, "Sherwood Bonner," 123–24.

103 *New York Tribune,* 18 September 1879; *New York Times,* 19 September 1879; *New York Herald,* 19 September 1879.

104 Sutherland, "Sherwood Bonner," 124; McAlexander, *Sherwood Bonner,* 150–51.

105 *New York Tribune,* 18, 20 September 1879.

106 Sutherland, "Sherwood Bonner," 124; McAlexander, *Sherwood Bonner,* 150–51.

107 *New York Times,* 19 September. Also see *New York Tribune,* 18, 19, 20 September 1879; 18 October 1879; *New York Herald,* 19 September 1879.

108 Thomas Nast spoke for many close acquaintances when he declared: "Had it been any other man than James Redpath, I could at least form some conjecture as to where he would be most likely to go and where he is now; but Redpath is so peculiar in his mind and methods, so different from others, that I have no idea about it." As quoted in the *New York Tribune,* 20 September 1879. Also see *New York Times,* 19 September 1879; *New York Herald,* 19 September 1879.

109 *San Francisco Chronicle,* 29 October 1879. See also *New York Tribune,* 18 October 1879.

110 Horner, *James Redpath,* 254–55.

111 McAlexander, *Sherwood Bonner,* 223; *NAW,* 461–62.

112 *San Francisco Chronicle,* 29 October 1879.

113 More than any other documents, the *Chronicle* articles disclose Redpath's philosophy of public entertainment and provide a means of assessing his contribution to the development of the entertainment industry. Presented as "interviews," the whole articles appear to be the product of Redpath's hand. See *San Francisco Chronicle,* 30 November 1879; 7, 14, 21, 28 December 1879; 4, 11, 18, 25 January 1880; 1, 8, 15, 22, 29 February 1880; 7 March 1880.

Chapter 9. The Adopted Irishman

1 John R. McKivigan and Thomas J. Robertson, "The Irish American Worker in Transition, 1877–1914: New York City as a Test Case," in *The New York Irish,* edited by Ronald H. Bayor and Timothy J. Meagher (New York: Johns Hopkins University Press, 1996), 301–3; William Leonard Joyce, "Editors and Ethnicity: A History of the Irish-American Press, 1848–1883" (Ph.D. diss., University of Michigan, 1974), 151.

2 Richard Kluger, *The Paper: The Life and Death of the New York Herald Tribune* (New York: Alfred A. Knopf, 1986), 122, 140–45.

3 Bingham Duncan, *Whitelaw Reid: Journalist, Politician, Diplomat* (Athens: The University of Georgia Press, 1975), 37–39, 46–49. Kluger, *The Paper,* 122–24, 132–39.

4 Redpath to W. Whitelaw Reid, 29 January 1880, W. Whitelaw Reid Papers, Manuscripts Division, Library of Congress.

5 Redpath to Reid, 4 April 1879, also see 29 June 1880, Reid Papers.

6 Redpath to Reid, 29 January 1880, Reid Papers.

7 Kerby A. Miller, *Emigrants and Exiles: Ireland and the Irish Exodus to North America* (New York: Oxford University Press, 1985), 347–52, 380–81, 385–89, 398–400; T. W. Moody, "Fenianism, Home Rule, and the Land War (1850–1921)," in *The Course of Irish History,* edited by T. W. Moody and

F. X. Martin, 2d ed. (Cork, Ire.: The Mercer Press, 1984), 275, 280–81; T. H. Corfe, "The Troubles of Captain Boycott," *History Today* 14 (November 1964): 760–61.

8 For background on the Irish Land League see Moody, "Fenianism, Home Rule, and the Land War," 285–88; Norman D. Palmer, *The Irish Land League Crisis* (New Haven: Yale University Press, 1940), 72; Miller, *Emigrants and Exiles,* 443–44.

9 Moody, "Fenianism, Home Rule, and the Land War," 253–54.

10 *New York Tribune,* 23 March 1880; also see 5, 8, 12, 17, 19, 26 March 1880; 3, 9, 11, 12, 17, 19, 21, 27 April 1880; 1, 3, 15, 23 May 1880. These reports were reprinted in *Boston Pilot,* 3, 17, 24 April 1880; 1 May 1880; *New York Irish World and Industrial Liberator,* 17 April, 8 May 1880, hereinafter cited as *Irish World.*

11 Redpath to Reid, 24 February 1880, Reid Papers.

12 Churchill was a junior minister in Benjamin Disraeli's Conservative Party government. Redpath to W. W. Reid, 27 February 1880, Reid Papers.

13 Michael Davitt, *The Fall of Feudalism in Ireland* (New York: Harper Brothers, 1904), 224; T. W. Moody, *Davitt and Irish Revolution, 1846–82* (Oxford, Eng.: Clarendon Press, 1981), 367.

14 Davitt, *Fall of Feudalism,* 224.

15 *New York Irish World,* 19 June 1880. Also see, Redpath to Reid, 24, 27 February 1880, Reid Papers.

16 *Boston Pilot,* 24 April 1880, also see 17 April 1880; 8 May 1880; 24 July 1880; *New York Tribune,* 3, 11 April 1880; 3 October 1880. In another article Redpath charged that the Irish peasants were "more miserable than ever were our Southern slaves as far as their physical comforts are. If the Southern slaveholder had not had the right of sale—if he could not have robbed the laborer's cradle and sent the young girl or wife to the auction block—the negroes of our South would not have exchanged places with Lord Sligo's tenants." *New York Tribune,* 3 April 1880.

17 *New York Tribune,* 11 April 1880.

18 *New York Irish World,* 12 June 1880; clipping hand dated as *Cork Constitution* (Ire.), 22 March 1880.

19 Redpath to Reid, n.d. [c. April 1880], Reid Papers. This is the only expression of anti-Semitism in Redpath's published writings or surviving correspondence.

20 Redpath to Reid, 1 June 1880, Reid Papers.

21 *Boston Pilot,* 24 April 1880.

22 Redpath to Reid, 9, 19 April 1880, Reid Papers; *Boston Pilot,* 24 April 1880.

23 *Boston Pilot,* 8 May 1880, also see 15, 22 May 1880; *New York Tribune,* 7 May 1880; *New York Times,* 7 May 1880; *New York Irish World,* 22 May 1880; 19 June 1880; 10, 24 July 1880; Redpath to Reid, 1 June 1880, Reid Papers.

24 *New York Times,* 7 May 1880; *Boston Pilot,* 15, 22 May 1880; *New York Irish World,* 22 May 1880. In June 1880, Redpath wrote a widely circulated public letter, advising Americans not to contribute to the famine relief committees sponsored by British officials. He declared that "the Queen, the Duchess of Marlborough, and the Lord Mayor of Dublin deserve no thanks from America. They deserve reproaches for their miserly contributions for the relief of Irish distress." Quoted in Palmer, *Irish Land League Crisis,* 99.

25 Redpath to Reid, 1 June 1880, see also Redpath to Reid, 5 May 1880, Reid Papers.

26 *New York Irish World,* 5 June 1880. At one occasion, Redpath called Davitt the William Lloyd Garrison of the Irish people. Thomas N. Brown, *Irish-American Nationalism, 1870–1890* (Philadelphia: Lippincott, 1966), 109; Michael Allen Gordon, "Studies in Irish and Irish-American Thought and Behavior in Gilded Age New York City" (Ph.D. diss., University of Rochester, 1977), 453.

27 Davitt names the secretary as "Mr. Bacon, of Boston." Davitt, *Fall of Feudalism,* 251; Moody, *Davitt,* 386.

28 Diary, 12 June 1880, Michael Davitt Papers, Trinity College, Dublin; John Boyle O'Reilly to John Devoy, 13 April 1880, *Devoy's Post Bag,* 2 vols. (Dublin: Fallon, 1948): 1:513; *New York Irish World,* 26 June 1880; Davitt, *Fall of Feudalism,* 267; Moody, *Davitt,* 396.

29 *New York Irish World,* 3, 17 July 1880; 14 August 1880; 11 September 1880; *Chicago Inter-Ocean,* 12, 22 July 1880; *Boston Pilot,* 24 July 1880; 7, 21 August 1880; 2 October 1880; *New York Tribune,* 15, 22, 29 August 1880; 3, 10 September 1880; 2, 8, 14 October 1880; 16 November 1880; Redpath to Reid, 19 April, 1 June, 23 August 1880, Reid Papers.

30 Redpath to Reid, 23 August 1880, Reid Papers.

31 Moody, *Davitt,* 396.

32 *New York Tribune,* 15 August 1880; see also 22 August 1880. The prolandlord *Dublin Mail* denounced Redpath's reporting as a poorly veiled effort to incite Irish Americans to arm the Irish peasantry for an uprising. *Dublin Mail,* n.d., as quoted in *New York Irish World,* 7, 14, 21 August 1880.

33 R. Barry O'Brien, *The Life of Charles Stewart Parnell, 1846–1891* (1898; New York: Greenwood Press, 1969), 1:237–39; Moody, *Davitt,* 419.

34 T. H. Corfe, "The Troubles of Captain Boycott," *History Today* 14 (November 1964): 762–63; Robert Kee, *The Laurel and the Ivy: The Story of Charles Stewart Parnell and Irish Nationalism* (London: Hamish, Hamilton, 1993), 211, 254, 276. 280.

35 *New York Irish World,* 25 September 1880, also quoted in Corfe, "Captain Boycott," 763 and Davitt, *Fall of Feudalism,* 267–68. Also see James Redpath, *Talks about Ireland* (New York: P. J. Kennedy, 1881), 90–93; *New York Irish World,* 28 August 1880; 11 September 1880; 9 October 1880; 6, 17 November 1880; *Boston Pilot,* 23 October 1880; Brown, *Irish-American Nationalism,* 107–9; Moody, *Davitt and Irish Revolution,* 41, 367, 381; Palmer, *Irish Land League Crisis,* 200; A. D. Vinton, "The History of Boycotting," *Magazine of Western History* 5 (December 1886): 212.

36 *Boston Pilot,* 9 October 1880.

37 Redpath, *Talks about Ireland,* 81–82; Davitt, *Fall of Feudalism,* 276; Palmer, *Irish Land League Crisis,* 200; Corfe, "Captain Boycott," 858.

38 William O'Brien, *Recollections* (New York: Macmillan, 1905), 333; David R. Locke, *Nasby in Exile: or, Six Months of Travel in England, Ireland, Scotland, France, Germany, Switzerland and Belgium* (Toledo, Ohio: Locke, 1882), 411–12; Norman Dunbar Palmer, *The Irish Land League Crisis* (New Haven, Conn.: H. Milford, 1940), 102; Gordon, "Irish and Irish-American Thought and Behavior," 365–66. Redpath's activities won him praise from Irish and Irish Americans. The *Kerry Sentinel* declared that Redpath's "most generous sympathies were enlisted on behalf of the people of Erin, and we say—truly say—of him that he is now *ipsis Hibernis, hibernior,* more Irish than the Irish themselves." The New York

City–based *Irish World* praised the speeches Redpath made in Ireland: "Mr. Redpath is really a God-send to the Irish people. . . . [H]e minces no words, nor restrains the passion of his heart in speaking of the heartless land-robbers." *New York Irish World*, 4, 18 December 1880; Conor Cruise O'Brien, *Parnell and His Party, 1880–90* (Oxford, Eng.: Clarendon Press, 1957), 53–55.

39 *New York Irish World*, 4 December 1880; Davitt, *Fall of Feudalism*, 272; Kee, *Parnell*, 280; O'Brien, *Parnell*, 55–56.

40 *New York Irish World*, 6, 27 November 1880; *New York Tribune*, 9 November, 4 December 1880; O'Brien, *Parnell*, 254–55; Palmer, *Irish Land League Crisis*, 280–81; Miller, *Emigrants and Exiles*, 444; T. W. Moody, "Anna Parnell and the Land League," *Hermathena* 117 (summer 1974): 5–17; Moody, "Fenianism, Home Rule, and the Land War," 288–89.

41 *New York Tribune*, 30 November 1880; 13 December 1880; 11 January, 5 May 1881; *New York Irish World*, 4, 11, 25 December 1880; 1, 8, 15, 22 January 1881; 26 February 1881; 5, 19 March 1881; *Boston Pilot*, 8 January 1881; *Chicago Tribune*, 18 February 1881; Roland A. Alpiser and Clarence Miller, *Forty Years of Long Ago: Early Annals of the Mercantile Library Association and Its Public Hall, 1846–1886* (St. Louis: St. Louis Mercantile Library, 1900), 123; O'Brien, *Parnell*, 55–59. Two days after his return to the United States, Redpath appeared with the mother of Charles Parnell at a rally to organize the Newark, New Jersey, branch of the Land League. He praised Parnell and Davitt as "'leaders of the modern type'—as executor's of the people's will" and claimed that the land movement could not be defeated by their arrest because it was "not a leader's agitation but the uprising of the Irish Democracy." *New York Irish World*, 11, 25 December 1880; also see *New York Tribune*, 30 November 1880.

42 *New York Irish World*, 22 January 1881; also see ibid., 1, 15 January 1881; 12, 26 February 1881; 5, 12, 19, 26 March 1881; *Boston Pilot*, 8 January 1881; *New York Tribune*, 11 January 1881; 4, 5 May 1881; *Chicago Tribune*, 17, 18 February 1881.

43 *New York Times*, 2 June, 27 July 1881; *New York Tribune*, 2 June 1881; 17 July 1881; *London Times*, 21, 29 June 1881; *Boston Pilot*, 23, 30 July 1881; 5 November 1881; 3, 24 December 1881.

44 *Proceedings at a Farewell Dinner Given by the Land League of New York to James Redpath Prior to His Departure for Ireland, at Delmonico's, June 1, 1881* (New York: Bradstreet Press, 1881), 7–10, 10–19; also see *New York Times*, 2 June 1881; *New York Tribune*, 2 June 1881; Joyce, "Editors and Ethnicity," 157–61.

45 *Proceedings of a Farewell Dinner*, 10–19.

46 *London Times*, 21, 29 June 1881; *New York Tribune*, 17 July 1881; *Boston Pilot*, 23 July 1881; *New York Times*, 27 July 1881.

47 Additional details of Redpath's activities during this tour can be gleaned from the following: *London Times*, 21, 29 June 1881; *New York Tribune*, 17 July 1881; *New York Times*, 27 July 1881; *Boston Pilot*, 30 July 1881; *Chattanooga Daily Times* (Tenn.), 4 October 1881.

48 *Connaught Telegraph*, 30 July 1881; as cited in Palmer, *Irish Land League Crisis*, 280–301.

49 *Boston Pilot*, 14 January, 4 March 1882.

50 Quoted in Palmer, *Irish Land League Crisis*, 303; see also *Boston Pilot*, 25 February 1882; 4, 18, 25 March 1882.

51 *Boston Pilot*, 24 December 1881; see also ibid., 30 July 1881; 5 November 1881; 3, 31 December 1881; 25 February, 25 March 1882. *London Times*, 21 June 1881.

52 *Boston Pilot*, 25 February 1882.

53 *New York Irish World*, 18 December 1880; Palmer, *Irish Land League Crisis*, 112; Charles Callan Tansill, *America and the Fight for Irish Freedom, 1866–1912* (New York: Devin-Adair, 1957), 54.

54 *Boston Pilot*, 5 November 1881.

55 Ibid., 31 December 1881. Locke later wrote a book about this trip and credited Redpath with opening his eyes to Ireland's ills. Locke, *Nasby in Exile*, 374–77.

56 *Boston Pilot*, 14 January 1882; 25 February 1882; *New York Times*, 27 February 1882; Published circular of the Redpath Lyceum Bureau, reprinted in Redpath, *Talks about Ireland*, 99–100.

57 *Boston Pilot*, 3 December 1881.

58 Redpath to John Devoy, n.d. [late 1881], *Devoy's Post Bag*, 2:102–3.

59 *New York Herald*, 13 May 1882; also see *New York Tribune*, 11 May 1882; *New York Times*, 13 May 1882; *Boston Pilot*, 20 May 1882.

60 *Boston Pilot*, 27 May 1882.

61 Smalley actually was married to Phillips's ward, not his natural daughter. Smalley remained one of the *Tribune*'s star reporters until the century's end. Redpath denounced another prolandlord American reporter in Ireland as "a religious Ku-klux, and his statements about Irish outrages are about as reliable as those of a Cyclops of the Ku-klux Klan would be in relation to outrages by negroes in our own South." *New York Tribune*, 16 July 1882, see also 4, 9 July 1882; Redpath, *Talks about Ireland*, 70, 73; Duncan, *Whitelaw Reid*, 112–13.

62 *McGee's Illustrated Weekly*, 8, 15 July 1882.

63 *Redpath's Illustrated Weekly*, 12 January 1883; N. W. Ayer and Son's American Newspaper Annual (Philadelphia: N. W. Ayer and Son, 1883), 66; *Hubbard's Newspapers and Bank Directory of the World*, 3 vols. (New Haven, Conn.: H. P. Hubbard, 1883–84), 3:552.

64 *Redpath's Illustrated Weekly*, 30 September 1882.

65 *Boston Pilot*, 10 March 1883; 5 May 1883; 15 September 1883; 3 November 1883; *New York Tribune*, 26, 28 April 1883; *New York Times*, 28 April 1883; *John Swinton's Paper* (New York), 13 April 1884; N. W. Ayer and Son's American Newspaper Annual, 66; Hubbard's Newspaper and Bank Directory, 2:552; Moody, "Anna Parnell," 5–17; Moody, "Fenianism, Home Rule, and the Land War," 288–89.

66 *Proceedings of a Farewell Dinner*, 10–19; *Boston Pilot*, 27 May 1882; 15 March 1884; *New York Tribune*, 11 May 1882, 2 March 1883; *New York Herald*, 13 May 1882; *New York Times*, 13 May 1882; 3, 4 August 1882; *Redpath's Weekly*, 7 April 1883; William D'Arcy, "The Fenian Movement in the United States: 1858–1886" (Ph.D. diss., Catholic University, 1947), 398–407; Joyce, "Editors and Ethnicity," 179.

67 *Redpath's Weekly*, 3 March 1883.

68 Ibid., 12 July 1883; also see 3 March 1883. British authorities accused Redpath of condoning the murder of landlords and arrested at least one Irish newspaper editor, Richard Kelly of the *Tuam Herald*, for republishing his writing. *Redpath's Weekly*, 26 August 1882; *Proceedings of a Farewell Dinner*, 10–19;

Boston Pilot, 27 May 1882; 15 March 1884; *New York Tribune,* 11 May 1882; 2 March 1883; *New York Herald,* 13 May 1882; *New York Times,* 13 May 1882; 3, 4 August 1882; D'Arcy, "Fenian Movement," 398–407; Joyce, "Editors and Ethnicity," 179.

69 *Redpath's Weekly,* 3 March 1883; also see ibid., 12 July 1883. Perhaps not entirely coincidentally, Redpath's friend Mark Twain also had a heated dispute with Reid in 1882. The preceding fall, while Reid had been honeymooning in Europe, Twain had persuaded the paper's acting editor, John Hay, to publish a favorable, unsigned review of *The Prince and the Pauper,* by Twain's close friend William Dean Howells. Although Twain had published some of his early newspaper dispatches in the *Tribune,* later republished as *Innocents Abroad,* that newspaper had panned two other of his earlier books, *Roughing It* and *The Gilded Age.* Reid came to regard Twain as crude and greedy. When Reid learned of the Howell's review, he wired Hay that employing a "warm personal friend" to review an author "isn't good journalism." Twain devoted three weeks to starting a "dynamatic" biography of "Outlaw Reid," before finally calming down. Reid remained in control of the *Tribune* until 1905, restoring much of its antebellum luster and influence, and saw to it that neither Redpath nor Twain wrote for his paper again. Justin Kaplan, *Mr. Clemens and Mark Twain: A Biography* (1966; New York: Simon and Schuster, 1983), 167, 240–42; Kluger, *The Paper,* 120, 125; Duncan, *Whitelaw Reid,* 54.

70 *Redpath's Illustrated Weekly,* 7 December 1882. Redpath also used his *Weekly* to attack the efforts of northern Irish Protestants to dissociate themselves from the nationalist forces unleashed by Parnell's land agitation. He denied that Irish Catholics had demonstrated religious intolerance against Protestants and compared the latter with the urban slaves of antebellum America who vainly tried to ingratiate themselves with the whites by ridiculing the manners of rural slaves. Redpath lectured the Protestant Irish that "no man who is ashamed of his own race is respected by any race! The Orangemen want to separate themselves from their race, and therefore they earn the hearty contempt of all free peoples. *They* are the "town niggers of Ireland!' " He cited the examples of Parnell and earlier of Daniel O'Connell as Irish Protestants who found common cause with the Catholic majority in resisting British oppression. Ibid.; *Boston Pilot,* 16 February 1884.

71 The newspaper continued: "It is not pertinent at all to the case to allege that Davitt has made mistakes, as the best meaning men that ever lived have done; the accusation is none the less cowardly and indefensible and the man who uttered it should be made feel that the Irish people cannot be turned against an old friend, even at the dictation of a bureau lecturer who has traded upon Irish patriotism, at the rate of a hundred dollars a night." *Catholic Telegraph,* 22 December 1882.

72 Redpath to John Devoy, 7 May 1883, *Devoy's Post Bag,* 2:196. One exception was John Boyle O'Reilly of the *Boston Pilot,* who endorsed Redpath's as the best Irish American newspaper in New York City. *Boston Pilot,* 3 November 1883.

73 *New York Tribune,* 2 March 1883.

74 *New York Herald,* 28 April 1883. See also *New York Tribune,* 28 April 1883; *New York Times,* 28 April 1883; *Redpath's Illustrated Weekly,* 4 May 1883; *Boston Pilot,* 5 May 1883; Joyce, "Editors and Ethnicity," 170.

75 Ibid; *New York Times,* 28 April 1883; *Boston Pilot,* 5 May 1883; Miller, *Emigrants and Exiles,* 444–45, 544–48; Gordon, "Irish and Irish-American

Thought and Behavior," 485–86, Joyce, "Editors and Ethnicity," 170. In the *Weekly*, he editorialized: "No one had reason to be dissatisfied with the result of the compromise effected both as to the platform and the officers. *The majority ruled.* The hour for discussion has passed. Our army is formed and officered, and our plan of battle is adopted, and every man who now revolts against the decisions of the Irish Convention should be regarded as a rebel against the organized majesty of the Irish race. Toleration of differences ceases when the battle begins." *Redpath's Weekly*, 18 May 1883.

76 *Redpath's Illustrated Weekly*, 22 July 1882.

77 Ibid., 2 September 1882.

78 Ibid., 5 August 1882. This editorial is an early clue of the influence of Henry George's ideas on political economy on Redpath.

79 *Redpath's Weekly*, 18 October 1882; 9, 16 November 1882.

80 Ibid., 23 January 1883.

81 Ibid., 3 March 1883.

82 Despite the quarrels among Irish and Irish American factions, Redpath still editorially assisted nearly every fund-raising campaign to relieve economic distress in Ireland. *Redpath's Illustrated Weekly*, n.d., as quoted in *Boston Pilot*, 20 January 1883. See also *New York Herald*, 27 February 1883; *Boston Pilot*, 10 March 1883; Redpath to John Devoy, 7 May 1883, *Devoy's Post Bag*, 2:196.

83 *Redpath's Illustrated Weekly*, 12 January 1883; also see ibid., 23 November 1882; *Redpath's Weekly*, 26 January 1883.

84 To compensate Irish American readers who missed the *Weekly*'s original supply of Irish news, Redpath arranged for them to receive discounted subscriptions to the pro-Parnell publication, *United Ireland. Redpath's Weekly*, 22 March 1884.

85 *Redpath's Weekly*, 22 March 1884.

86 *Boston Pilot*, 18 March 1882, 27 September 1884; *New York Tribune*, 18 August 1884.

87 *Boston Pilot*, 27 September 1884.

88 *Devoy's Post Bag*, 2:252.

89 *New York Sun*, n.d., as quoted in *Boston Pilot*, 3 January 1885; see also *Catholic Herald*, n.d., as quoted in *Boston Pilot*, 7 March 1885; *Catholic World*, n.d., as quoted in *Boston Pilot*, 18 April 1885.

90 For example, see his letter of 18 December 1884 to *John Swinton's Paper*, published on 21 December 1884.

91 *Boston Pilot*, 3 January 1885; 7 March 1885; 18 April 1885; *New York Press*, 24 February 1889; 3, 10, 17, 24, 31 March 1889; 7, 14 April 1889.

92 Redpath also drew interesting parallels between Britain's oppressive rule over Ireland and the North's treatment of the South following the Civil War: "Our North overthrew our South; yet to-day the South is loyal. If there had been no other problem to settle there than the political problem, the moral effects of the civil war would have been effaced within a decade of Appomattox. It is because so many of the Southern people believed—unjustly but honestly believed—that our policy of reconstruction was a *nagging* policy, that we liberated and enfranchised the blacks in order to humiliate the whites, that it needed decades to fully restore unity of national sentiment as well as unity of national power. If our North had adopted the English policy in Ireland our South to-day would have been more disloyal than when her boys in gray rallied under the banners of Jackson and Lee.

'Your magnanimity,' said fiery Roger Pryor, 'disarmed us!' " [James Redpath], "Ireland's Moderation," *Catholic World* (April 1885), 101; see also the positive response to these articles in *Boston Pilot,* 7 March 1885; 18 April 1885.

93 Historian Eric Foner contends that Redpath and Wendell Phillips of Boston were the only two prominent abolitionists to play a significant role in postbellum movements dealing with the problems of immigrants and laborers. Eric Foner, "Class, Ethnicity and Radicalism in the Gilded Age: The Land League and Irish-America," *Marxist Perspectives* 1 (summer 1978): 6, 45; and "Class, Ethnicity, and Radicalism in the Gilded Age: The Land League and Irish America," in *Politics and Ideology in the Age of the Civil War,* edited by Eric Foner (New York: Oxford University Press, 1980), 157, 164–66, 177

94 *New York Herald,* 11 February 1891; *New York Times,* 11 February 1891.

95 Foner, *Politics and Ideology,* 157, 164–66, 177; Michael Gordon, "The Labor Boycott in New York City, 1800–1886," *Labor History* 16 (spring 1975): 185–86.

96 Edwin G. Burrows and Mike Wallace, *Gotham: A History of New York City to 1898* (New York: Oxford University Press, 1999), 986–87, 1012–13; McKivigan and Robertson, "Irish American Worker in Transition," 303–4.

97 Terrence V. Powderly, *The Path I Trod* (New York: Columbia University Press, 1940), 181; Leon Fink, *Workingmen's Democracy: The Knights of Labor and American Politics* (Urbana, Ill.: University of Illinois Press, 1983), xii, 4; David Montgomery, "The Irish and the American Labor Movement," in *America and Ireland, 1776–1976: The American Identity and the Irish Connection,* edited by David Noel Doyle and Owen Dudley Edwards (Westport, Conn.: Greenwood Press, 1976), 216.

98 *John Swinton's Paper,* 28 February 1886; Gordon, "Irish and Irish-American Thought and Behavior," 451, Montgomery, "Irish and the Labor Movement," 214–15; McKivigan and Robertson, "Irish American Worker in Transition," 304–5.

99 *Frank Leslie's Illustrated Newspaper,* 62:1464 (13 October 1883); *John Swinton's Paper,* 23, 30 December 1882; Kluger, *The Paper,* 147–48.

100 In fall 1883, Redpath printed a list of the city's newsdealers carrying his paper, which included a full sampler of Celtic last names such as Ryan, Connelly, Kiernan, Boylan, Flynn, Regan, Doolan, Clancy, Finnegan, Tobin, Donovan, Rooney, Costello, and Brennan, in addition to an even larger number of surnames with "O" and "Mc" antecedents. Several of these individuals became leaders of local newsdealers associations formed during the strike. *Redpath's Weekly,* 10 November 1883.

101 *New York Tribune,* 3 October 1883.

102 *New York Herald,* 3 October 1883; see also *New York Times,* 3 October 1883.

103 The New York City newsdealers' position remained precarious and similar boycotts and strikes continued well into the next century. *Frank Leslie's Illustrated Newspaper,* 62:1464 (13 October 1883); *John Swinton's Paper,* 30 March 1884; Steven D. Lyons, "James Gordon Bennett, Jr.," in *American Newspaper Journalists, 1873–1900: Dictionary of Literary Biography,* vol. 23, edited by Perry J. Ashley (Detroit: Gale Research Group, 1983), 13.

104 As quoted by Gordon, "Labor Boycott," 184; also see *John Swinton's Paper,* 11 May 1884.

105 *New York Times,* 7 April 1889; see also Gordon, "Labor Boycott," 188–93, 206–7.

106 In particular, a strike in March 1886 by horse-car workers to decrease their sixteen-hour workday produced a pitched street battle between the police and supporters of the strikers. The city leaders also were concerned about the popularity in some German American neighborhoods of small socialist political groups and an even tinier circle of anarchists advocating a violent confrontation with capitalism. The nationally publicized accounts of the explosion of a bomb in the ranks of Chicago policemen attempting to disperse a labor rally at Haymarket Square on 4 May 1886 raised suspicions about all signs of worker assertiveness. Bruce C. Nelson, *Beyond the Martyrs: A Social History of Chicago's Anarchists, 1870–1900* (New Brunswick, N.J.: Rutgers University Press, 1988), 156–65, 170–73, 177–200; Bruce Laurie, *Artisans into Workers: Labor in Nineteenth-Century America* (Urbana: University of Illinois Press, 1989), 168–73; Burrows and Wallace, *Gotham,* 1095–98.

107 *The Boycotter,* 31 January 1885; 31 October 1885; *John Swinton's Paper,* 11 May 1884, 9 May 1886; 11 July 1886; Bureau of Labor Statistics, *Fourth Annual Report,* 744–82; Gordon, "Studies in Irish and Irish American Thought and Behavior," 551–59, 571–77; David Ray Papke, *The Pullman Case: The Clash of Labor and Capital in Industrial America* (Lawrence: University of Kansas Press, 1999), 51, 96–98.

108 *Fourth Annual Report,* 745–48, 752–56; John R. Commons et al., *History of Labour in the United States* (New York: Macmillan, 1918), 444–45; Burrows and Wallace, *Gotham,* 1098; Gordon, "Labor Boycott," 221–23, and "Irish and Irish-American Thought and Behavior," 571–73: Ronald Mendel, "Workers in Gilded Age New York and Brooklyn, 1886–1898" (Ph.D. diss., City University of New York, 1989), 95–96.

109 *New York Times,* 20 July 1886; Bureau of Labor Statistics, *Fourth Annual Report,* 761–82; Gordon, "Labor Boycott," 228–29, and "Irish and Irish-American Thought and Behavior," 577.

110 Bureau of Labor Statistics, *Fourth Annual Report,* 771–74.

111 Ibid., 774–80. After Hill's action, Redpath's committee called on the Central Labor Union to end the boycott of Theiss's establishment, which it did. Ibid., 781–82.

112 While Irish American votes bolstered Tammany's strength, that organization still needed the financial support of wealthy Protestant businessmen and professionals, often tied to the Democrats on account of national issues like low tariffs and hard money, rather than local concerns. Prominent among these "Swallowtail" Democrats were banker August Belmont, corporate lawyer and past party presidential candidate Samuel Tilden, and iron and steel manufacturer Abram Hewitt. The Tammany-Swallowtail alliance was a fragile one, however, making the Democratic hold over the city government potentially vulnerable. Stephen P. Erie, *Rainbow's End: Irish-Americans and the Dilemmas of Urban Machine Politics, 1840–1985* (Berkeley: University of California Press), 55–51; Thomas M. Henderson, *Tammany Hall and the New Immigrant* (New York: Arno Press, 1976), 87; Miller, *Emigrant and Exile,* 496; Commons, *History of Labour,* 443–44; Gordon, "Labor Boycott," 200–201, and "Studies in Irish and Irish American Thought and Behavior," 491–92, 556–60. Burrows and Wallace, *Gotham,* 1103–4.

113 Erie, *Rainbow's End,* 56–57, 60–63; Robert Emmett Curran, "The McGlynn Affair and the Shaping of the New Conservatism in American Catholicism, 1886–1894," *Catholic Historical Review* 66 (April 1980): 187; Gordon, "Irish and Irish-American Thought and Behavior," 405–30.

114 Commons, *History of Labour,* 446–50; Burrows and Wallace, *Gotham,* 1098–99; John L. Thomas, *Alternative America: Henry George, Edward Bellamy, Henry Demarest Lloyd, and the Adversary Tradition* (Cambridge, Mass.: Belknap Press, 1983), 231–32, 320.

115 Patrick Ford of the *New York Irish World* had been impressed by the book and hired George as a special correspondent to tour Ireland and report on its economic distress. Briefly arrested by British authorities, George's land reform ideas became intensely popular among such influential Irishmen on both sides of the Atlantic as Michael Davitt and Father McGlynn in the early 1880s. Howard H. Quint, *The Forging of American Socialism: Origins of the Modern Movement* (Indianapolis, Ind.: Bobbs-Merrill, 1953), 38–40; Thomas, *Alternative America,* 231–32, 320; Burrows and Wallace, *Gotham,* 1092–95; McKivigan and Robertson, "Irish American Worker in Transition," 307–8; Gordon, "Labor Boycott," 201–2.

116 *John Swinton's Paper,* 14 December 1886. An intriguing letter from Elizabeth Cady Stanton hints that Redpath had visited Tenafly, New Jersey, in the company of George and Irish nationalist Michael Davitt in mid August 1886. Elizabeth Cady Stanton to Redpath, 10 August [1886], Alfred W. Anthony Collection, New York Public Library.

117 The national Knights of Labor leader Powderly was of Irish descent and already had sponsored George's lectures in New York and nationwide. George's faith in the fundamental harmony of labor and capital blended easily with the Knights' doctrine of producing class unity. The economist accepted Powderly's personal invitation to join the Knights in 1883. The most active element backing George in the city was the heavily middle class District Assembly #49, especially its informal leadership clique, the "Home Club." District Assembly #91, representing mainly Irish American shoemakers, sponsored a rally for George at Irving Hall on 27 October. Redpath spoke and vouched that George was a "good friend of Ireland." *New York Tribune,* 28 October 1886; Samuel L. Gompers, *Seventy Years of Life and Labor* (New York: E. P. Dutton, 1925), 186; Louis F. Post, *The Prophet of San Francisco: Personal Memories and Interpretations of Henry George* (New York: Vanguard Press, 1930), 170; Gordon, "Labor Boycott," 201–2; Thomas, *Alternative America,* 183–84.

118 Gompers of the Cigar Makers union privately voiced his misgivings about the headlong rush into political action, but observed the enthusiasm among workers for George enlisted in the campaign. As Gompers told the Central Labor Union: "I have been working for organized labor for twenty-five years and have never declared myself a politician. Now I come out for George as a trade unionist and intend to support him with all my might." Gompers, *Seventy Years,* 185.

119 Mary Jo Buhle, Paul Buhle, and Dan Georgakas, eds., *Encyclopedia of the American Left* (Urbana: University of Illinois Press, 1990), 528, 711–14. Thomas, *Alternative America,* 181.

120 James P. Rodechko, "An Irish-American Journalist and Catholicism: Patrick Ford of the *Irish World,*" *Church History* 39 (December 1970): 533.

121 Commons, *History of Labour,* 450; Gompers, *Seventy Years,* 185; Mendel, "Workers in Gilded Age New York and Brooklyn," 35.

122 *New York Sun,* 31 October 1886; Commons, *History of Labour,* 451–52.

123 *New York Tribune,* 25 September 1886; *New York Sun,* 25 September 1886.

124 *New York Tribune,* 6 October 1886.

125 *New York Sun,* 14, 21 October 1886.

126 Louis F. Post and Fred C. Leubuscher, *An Account of the George-Hewitt Campaign in the New York Municipal Election of 1886,* rev. ed. (New York: Henry George School, 1961), 115–18.

127 *New York Sun,* 19 October 1886. See also ibid., 14 October 1886.

128 Ibid.

129 *John Swinton's Paper,* 19 December 1886; see also 2 March 1884, 7 February 1885, 14 September 1886.

130 Post and Leubuscher, *Henry George's 1886 Campaign,* 133.

131 *New York Tribune,* 28 October 1886.

132 George had drawn well among second- and third-generation Irish American voters as well as other longer established immigrant groups, such as German Americans. Despite the opposition of the hierarchy, he had done best in heavily Catholic wards on the city's Lower East Side and Hell's Kitchen. Only among the poorest slum districts, filled with the most recent and desperate immigrant arrivals, had a combination of church warnings and Tammany Hall patronage put Hewitt ahead of George. Roosevelt's vote was about 20,000 below usual Republican totals in the city's silk-stocking and middle-class wards. Apparently the fear of the victory of a labor candidate had persuaded many Republicans to vote for the economically safe Hewitt. Commons, *History of Labour,* 453; Burrows and Wallace, *Gotham,* 1106; McKivigan and Robertson, "Irish American Worker in Transition," 309.

133 Originally Professor David R. Scott was the third man chosen for the executive committee along with McMackin and McGlynn. When Scott declined the appointment due to ill-health, Redpath was given the seat. *New York Standard,* 8 January 1887.

134 Ibid.; *New York Sun,* 7 November 1886; Commons, *History of Labour,* 454–55.

135 *New York Tribune,* 7 January 1887; Quint, *American Socialism,* 43–49; Thomas, *Alternate America,* 228–31.

136 Gompers, *Seventy Years,* 187–88; Charles Albro Barker, *Henry George* (New York: Oxford University Press, 1955), 484; Mendel, "Workers in Gilded Age New York and Brooklyn," 40.

137 *John Swinton's Paper,* 8 May, 26 June 1887; Thomas, *Alternative America,* 231–32, 320.

138 Quoted in Barker, *Henry George,* 492.

139 Pentecost later became a good friend of anarchist Emma Goldman. Barker, *Henry George,* 492–93; Post, *Prophet of San Francisco,* 90–92.

140 As quoted in Post, *Prophet of San Francisco,* 94–95.

141 In that *Standard* article, Redpath ironically reminisced about his old lyceum star, Henry Ward Beecher, who had died just weeks before of a stroke not dissimilar to Redpath's. *New York Standard,* 12 March 1887; *New York Times,* 7 September 1888.

142 Commons, *History of Labour,* 456–57.

143 *New York Times,* 11 July 1887; *New York Tribune,* 11 July 1887.

144 Curran, "McGlynn Affair," 188, 193–94.

145 In 1888, McGlynn publicly denounced Powderly's active courting of Catholic prelates, such as James Cardinal Gibbons of Baltimore, as well as the Grand Master Workman's opposition to clemency for the Haymarket bombers. McGlynn actively courted support among New York City Knights, especially in District Assembly #49. McGlynn's attacks on Powderly weakened him just as he was attempting to stem a wave of defections from the Knights to trade unions belonging to the newly founded American Federation of labor headed by Gompers. The damage produced by the McGlynn-Powderly feud led pro-Powderly editor John Swinton to declare that McGlynn "has done more mischief to the cause of labor by hurling the religious firebrand into Labor's camp than has been done by all the attacks of its capitalist enemies." *John Swinton's Paper,* 29 May 1887, see also 3 July 1887. Also see Robert E. Weir, "A Fragile Alliance: Henry George and the Knights of Labor," *American Journal of Economics and Sociology* 56 (October 1997): 47–51; Laurie, *Artisans into Workers,* 174–75.

146 In 1887, the society sponsored a multiday "Labor Fair" at Madison Square Garden that raised more than $20,000 for George's campaign. Despite their political falling out, privately McGlynn and George remained friends. Thomas, *Alternative America,* 320–22, 334; Post, *Prophet of San Francisco,* 86–92.

147 *New York Tribune,* 7 September 1888; Jefferson Davis to Redpath, 3 February, 24 April 1888, Jefferson Davis Papers, New York Historical Society.

148 Laurie, *Artisans into Workers,* 164; Weir, "Fragile Alliance," 54; Foner, "Land League and Irish America,"198–200.

149 *New York Tribune,* 7 September 1888.

150 The account continued: "She is well known in the society of Washington, where she lived for many years and is the widow of Major Chorpenning, who figured rather conspicuously in official circles at Washington during the Grant administration." *New York Herald,* 7 September 1888.

Chapter 10. Jefferson Davis's Ghostwriter

1 Redpath to George W. Cable, 19, 20 March 1885; 3 April 1885, George W. Cable Collection, Howard-Tilton Memorial Library, Tulane University.

2 Henry Adams and Henry Cabot Lodge, "The 'Independents' in the Canvass," *North American Review* 123 (October 1876): 426–67; Frank Luther Mott, A *History of American Magazines,* 5 vols. (Cambridge, Mass.: Harvard University Press, 1938–68), 2:247–49.

3 Lloyd Bryce, "Tributes to Allen Thorndike Rice," *North American Review* 149 (July 1889): 114–18.

4 Redpath to James R. Gilmore, 2 April, 16 June, 24 July, 20 September 1886, Gilmore Collection, Johns Hopkins University; Bryce, "Tributes to Allen Thorndike Rice," 115.

5 Mott, *American Magazines,* 2: 249–54.

6 Rice financed archeological expeditions to Central America and bought a newspaper in Paris. In 1886, the same year as the Henry George mayoral

campaign, Rice had been an unsuccessful Republican candidate for Congress from Manhattan. He felt cheated out of victory by election fraud and had worked with the United Labor Party leaders in demanding institution of the secret ballot in the state. Rice's death at thirty-six in May 1889, just as he was about to leave for the post of U.S. ambassador to Russia, shocked the journalistic and political worlds. By then, Rice and Redpath had quarreled over editorial issues, and the latter had found new employment at the rival *Belford's Monthly* magazine. Redpath to R. H. Thurston, 24 August 1887, Cornell University Libraries; *ACAB*, 5:233.

7 Redpath to Walt Whitman, 5 October 1886, in Horace L. Traubel, *With Walt Whitman in Camden*, 5 vols. (Boston: Small, Maynard, 1906–64), 2:226.

8 Benjamin F. Butler, "Vice-Presidential Politics in '64," *North American Review* 141 (October 1885): 331–35, and "Defenseless Canada," *North American Review* 147 (October 1888): 441–53; Walt Whitman, "Slang in America," *North American Review* 141 (November 1885): 430–36, "Robert Burns as Poet and Person," *North American Review* 143 (November 1886): 427–36, and "Some War Memoranda—Jotted Down at the Time," *North American Review* 142 (January 1887): 55–61; Robert G. Ingersoll, "Motley and Monarch," *North American Review* 141 (December 1885): 528–33, "Art and Morality," *North American Review* 146 (March 1888): 318–27, and "Professor Huxley and Agnosticism," *North American Review* 148 (April 1889): 403–17; John Boyle O'Reilly, "At Last!" *North American Review* 142 (January 1886): 104–11, and "The Coercion Bill," *North American Review* 144 (May 1887): 528–40; Thomas A. Edison, "The Air-Telegraph: System of Telegraphing to Trains and Ships," *North American Review* 146 (June 1888): 641–51, and "The Perfected Phonograph," *North American Review* 142 (January 1886): 104–11; Henry George, "More about American Landlordism," *North American Review* 142 (April 1886): 387–402, and "Labor in Pennsylvania," *North American Review* 143 (September 1886): 268–78; Frederick Douglass, "The Future of the Colored Race," *North American Review* 142 (May 1886): 437–41; Terrence V. Powderly, "Strikes and Arbitration," *North American Review* 142 (May 1886): 502–7, and "A Menacing Irruption," *North American Review* 147 (August 1888): 165–75; Mary A. Livermore, "Woman Suffrage," *North American Review* 143 (October 1886): 371–82; David R. Locke, "Prohibition," *North American Review* 143 (October 1886): 382–98, and "High License No Remedy," *North American Review* 145 (September 1887): 291–306; Edward McGlynn, "Lessons of the New York City Election," *North American Review* 143 (December 1886): 571–76, and "The New Know-Nothingness and the Old," *North American Review* 145 (August 1887): 192–206; Marion Harland, "Are Women to Blame?" *North American Review* 1482 (May 1889): 630–33, and "Minister's Wives," *North American Review* 149 (September 1889): 371–77; Redpath to Mary Abigail Dodge, 11, 17 May 1886; 13 October 1886, University of Virginia Library; Redpath to George W. Cable, 9 November 1885, Drew University Manuscripts. Old abolitionist friend Thomas W. Higginson sent Redpath a manuscript from black writer Charlotte Forten for consideration. Thomas W. Higginson to Redpath, 31 December 1885, Thomas W. Higginson Papers, Boston Public Library.

9 Redpath to John Devoy, 31 January 1886, in *John Devoy's Post Bag*, 2 vols. (Dublin: C. J. Fallon, 1948–53), 2:271–72.

10 Redpath to James R. Gilmore, 2 April, 16 June, 24 July, 20 September 1886, Gilmore Collection, Johns Hopkins University. The article was published in the

North American Review in November 1886; Redpath to Rev. Dr. Gilbert, 13 January 1886, Bowdoin College Library.

11 Edward Kirke, "How Shall the Negro Be Educated?" *North American Review* 143 (November 1886): 421–26.

12 Redpath to John Dimitry, 22 September 1887, also see 29 March 1886, Mayes-Dimitry-Stuart Papers, Mississippi Department of Archives and History. In another letter from the period, Redpath complained to Dimitry that an alderman wants to create "a low groggery right opposite my house." Redpath to John Dimitry, 28 July 1886, Mayes-Dimitry-Stuart Papers.

13 Redpath to Edward Atkinson, 13, 15, 30 September 1886, Edward Atkinson Papers, Massachusetts Historical Society.

14 Redpath to W. Whitelaw Reid, 22 November 1886, Manuscripts Division, Library of Congress. See also P. G. T. Beauregard to Redpath, 8, 11 October 1886, Dartmouth College Library.

15 Redpath to Sallie Jay White, 20 August 1885, Schlesinger Library, Radcliffe College; Redpath to Ward H. Lamon, 17 October 1885, Henry E. Huntington Library and Art Gallery.

16 Justin Kaplan, *Mr. Clemens and Mark Twain: A Biography* (New York: Simon and Schuster, 1966), 271–74.

17 As quoted in *Mark Twain's Notebooks and Journals*, edited by Frederick Anderson, 3 vols. (Berkeley: University of California Press, 1975–79), 3:112, see also 3:130.

18 Albert Bigelow Paine, *Mark Twain: A Biography*, 2 vols. (New York: Harper and Brothers, 1913), 2:818; *Mark Twain's Notebooks and Journals*, 3:118.

19 *Mark Twain, Business Man*, edited by Samuel Charles Webster (Boston: Little, Brown, 1946), 340–44.

20 Redpath to Walt Whitman, 16 July 1885, in Traubel, *With Walt Whitman*, 2:74–75. Also see Redpath to Walt Whitman, 30 June 1885, in Traubel, *With Walt Whitman*, 2:73–74.

21 Whitman to Redpath, 12 August 1885, in *Walt Whitman: The Correspondence*, edited by E. H. Miller, 5 vols. (New York: New York University Press, 1961–69), 3:403, and Traubel, *With Walt Whitman*, 2:76. See also Redpath to Whitman, 11 August 1885, in Traubel, *With Walt Whitman*, 2:75–76; Miller, *Whitman*, 3:412 Whitman to Redpath, 29 June 1886, Miller, *Whitman*, 4:36; and 10 July 1886, Miller, *Whitman*, 4:37; Whitman to Redpath, 28 July 1886, Miller, *Whitman*, 4:39.

22 Walt Whitman to John Burroughs, 18 March 1886, in Miller, *Whitman*, 4:21. He said the same to William D. O'Connor; Whitman to William D. O'Connor, 19 November 1886, Miller, *Whitman*, 4:54–55.

23 Traubel, *With Walt Whitman*, 2:226–27.

24 Ibid., 2:77–78.

25 *North American Review* 145 (October 1887): 451–53, 570.

26 Each letter warned of the potential harm to the American worker of adhering to "the brutal creed of free trade—that we ought to 'buy in the cheapest market and sell in the dearest.'" Instead Redpath argued: "American protectionists recognize the fact their first, chief and supreme duty is to take care of their own countrymen against all rivals; that cheap goods do not represent the best results of statesmanship; that it would be buying the whistle too dear to

purchase cheap foreign fabrics at the expense of transforming an intelligent and important class of citizens into ragged and dependent 'hands' or 'hinds,' or wandering and discontented tramps." *North American Review* 147 (January 1888): 106–8; also see Redpath, 146 (December 1887): 709–10; 147 (February 1888): 231–32.

27 David W. Blight, *Race and Reunion: The Civil War in American Memory* (Cambridge, Mass.: Harvard University Press, 2001), 259; Hudson Strode, *Jefferson Davis, Tragic Hero: The Last Twenty-Five Years, 1864–1889* (New York: Harcourt, Brace, and World, 1964); William C. Davis, *Jefferson Davis: The Man and His Hour, A Biography* (New York: Harper Collins, 1991); Robert McElroy, *Jefferson Davis: The Unreal and the Real*, 2 vols. (New York: Harper and Brothers, 1937); *DAB*, 5:123–31.

28 Gerry Van der Heuvel, *Crowns of Thorns and Glory: Mary Todd Lincoln and Varina Howell Davis* (New York: E. P. Dutton, 1988); Ishbel Ross, *First Lady of the South: The Life of Mrs. Jefferson Davis* (New York: Harper and Brothers, 1958); Eron Rowland, *Varina Howell: Wife of Jefferson Davis*, 2 vols. (New York: Macmillan, 1931); *NAW*, 1:447–48; *DAB*, 5:146.

29 Blight, *Race and Reunion*, 266; *DAB*, 5:145–46; *NAW*, 1:448.

30 Redpath had also used the same trip to unsuccessfully court Sherwood Bonner while the latter was at her parents' home in Holly Springs, Mississippi. Strode, *Jefferson Davis*, 407, 497; Hubert Horton McAlexander, *The Prodigal Daughter: A Biography of Sherwood Bonner* (Baton Rouge: Louisiana State University Press, 1981), 79–80.

31 Redpath to Jefferson Davis, 4 September 1886, Jefferson Davis Papers, Alabama Department of Archives and History (hereafter cited as Davis Papers, ADAH); Davis to Redpath, 16 September 1886, Jefferson Davis Papers, New York Historical Society (hereafter cited as Davis Papers, NYHS), and reprinted in Dunbar Rowland, *Jefferson Davis, Constitutionalist: His Letters, Papers and Speeches*, 10 vols. (Jackson: Mississippi Department of Archives and History, 1923), 9:470; Redpath to Davis, 24 September 1886, Davis Papers, ADAH; Davis to Redpath, 30 September 1886, Davis Papers, NYHS, and reprinted in Rowland, *Jefferson Davis*, 9:491–92.

32 Davis to Redpath, 3 February 1888, Davis Papers, NYHS, reprinted in Rowland, *Jefferson Davis*, 36.

33 Strode, *Jefferson Davis*, 497; McElroy, *Jefferson Davis*, 2:687. McElroy says Redpath dropped the Andersonville idea temporarily and instead got Davis started on the Lee essay.

34 Redpath to Jefferson Davis, 29 August 1888, Davis Papers, ADAH.

35 As quoted in McElroy, *Jefferson Davis*, 689. See also, Van der Heuvel, *Crowns of Thorns and Glory*, 250–51.

36 Strode, *Jefferson Davis*, 497.

37 McElroy, *Jefferson Davis*, 688–89.

38 Varina Davis to Redpath, 5 September 1888, Howard Tilton Library, Tulane University, as quoted in Strode, *Jefferson Davis*, 497; Ross, *First Lady*, 342.

39 As quoted in Ross, *First Lady*, 2:345.

40 As quoted in McElroy, *Jefferson Davis*, 690–91.

41 *New York Press*, 10 February 1889. Also see *London Times*, 16, 21 January 1889. There is a contradictory account of Redpath's departure from the *Review* in

Redpath to James R. Gilmore, ca. May 1889, Gilmore Collection, Johns Hopkins University Library.

42 *New York Press,* 24 February 1889.

43 Sherlock explained to Redpath the minimum that the Irish agitation sought was "complete and unfettered control of all purely Irish concerns by a native government responsible solely to a native legislature elected on a broad suffrage—manhood suffrage—for choice." Redpath told his readers "I cordially concur in all Mr. Sherlock said." *New York Press,* 31 March 1889.

44 Ibid., 7 April 1889. After returning to the United States, Redpath commented further on Gladstone, "While I am willing to praise his skill, I see no need of allotting high moral motives to an old political gambler. It is an insult to the Irish patriots, dead and living, to rank an expert old gambler with them." *New York Press,* 5 May 1889. Also see ibid., 3, 10 March 1889; Kerby A. Miller, *Emigrants and Exiles: Ireland and the Irish Exodus to North America* (New York: Oxford University Press, 1985), 445–47.

45 *New York Press,* 17, 24 March 1889; 21 April 1889.

46 Ibid., 24 March 1889.

47 Ibid., 14 April 1889.

48 Ibid., 28 April 1889.

49 Davis to Redpath, 24 April 1889, Davis Papers, NYHS; also in Rowland, *Jefferson Davis,* 108.

50 Jefferson Davis, "Lord Woolsey's Mistakes," *North American Review* 149 (October 1889): 472–83; Strode, *Jefferson Davis,* 500; McElroy, *Jefferson Davis,* 691–92.

51 Varina Davis to Redpath, 23 February 1889, as quoted in McElroy, *Jefferson Davis,* 692.

52 Redpath had first sought new employment with the *Cosmopolitan.* That magazine had been founded in 1886 as a "first-class family magazine" and had built its circulation up quickly. The parent publishing company that owned the magazine, however, had gone bankrupt in 1888 and the magazine foundered. Redpath met its acting editor, E. D. Walker, and concluded that "a radical change of editorial management was needed . . . before any one cd make that periodical a success." The following year, the magazine foundered until it was purchased by John Brisben Walker and quickly rebuilt its strength by introducing serialized fiction, book reviews, and color illustrations. Redpath to John Dimitry, [c. May 1889], Mayes-Dimitry-Stuart Papers, Mississippi Department of Archives and History.

53 Frank Luther Mott, *A History of American Magazines, 1885–1905* (Cambridge, Mass.: Harvard University Press, 1957), 45; Alvah Milton Kerr, *Trean, or the Mormon's Daughter* (Chicago: Belford, 1889); Peter Dzwonkosi, ed., *American Literary Publishing Houses,* 2 vols. (Detroit: Garland, 1986), 1:47; Marc La Terreur, ed., *Dictionary of Canadian Biography,* 12 vols. (Toronto, University of Toronto Press, 1966—), 10:43–44, 12:923.

54 *New York Tribune,* 25 September 1886.

55 *Belford's Monthly* 5 (November 1890): 899–901. Another short piece extolled the superior suitability of New York City as the choice for the proposed 400th Columbian anniversary celebration that ultimately was sited in Chicago. Ibid., 4 (December 1889): 21–23.

56 Redpath to James R. Gilmore, 5 June 1889, James Robert Gilmore Papers, Johns Hopkins University Library.

57 As quoted in McElroy, *Jefferson Davis,* 693. See also Redpath to John Dimitry, 21 June 1889, Mayes-Dimitry-Stuart Papers.

58 Davis, *Jefferson Davis,* 683; Strode, *Jefferson Davis,* 501.

59 Strode, *Jefferson Davis,* 501.

60 As quoted in Ibid., 501.

61 *Jefferson Davis, Private Letters, 1823–1889,* edited by Hudson Strode (New York: Harcourt, Brace, 1966), 560.

62 Redpath confided in a friend about the real tragedy of Rice's early passing: "Sadder still is the fact that he lived unloved and died absolutely unmourned. No tear as far as I know was shed for him. He led a purely selfish life; and his career was a personal failure. . . . Only tributes that can be bought—no others—were laid in his grave. God save us from such a fate." Redpath to John Dimitry, [c. May 1889], Mayes-Dimitry-Stuart Papers, Mississippi Department of Archives and History.

63 Lloyd Bryce to Jefferson Davis, 30 October 1889, in Rowland, *Jefferson Davis,* 10:158.

64 In the same letter, Redpath reported that he was eager to get back to Beauvoir and complete the final revisions on the *Short History.* Redpath to Jefferson Davis, 31 October 1889, in Rowland, *Jefferson Davis,* 10:158–59.

65 Redpath to Jefferson Davis, 31 October 1889, in Rowland, *Jefferson Davis,* 158–60.

66 Jefferson Davis to Lloyd Bryce, 3 November 1889, in Rowland, *Jefferson Davis,* 160–61.

67 As quoted in McElroy, *Jefferson Davis,* 694.

68 Jefferson Davis, "Andersonville and Other War Prisons," *Belford's Monthly* 4 (January 1890): 161–78: 4(February 1890): 337–53; Varina H. Davis, *Jefferson Davis, Ex-President of the Confederate States of America: A Memoir by His Wife,* 2 vols. (New York: Belford, 1890), 682–83; Strode, *Jefferson Davis,* 501; McElroy, *Jefferson Davis,* 694–95.

69 Strode, *Jefferson Davis,* 508; McElroy, *Jefferson Davis,* 695–96; Van der Heuvel, *Crowns of Thorns and Glory,* 251.

70 As quoted in Strode, *Jefferson Davis,* 509; McElroy, *Jefferson Davis,* 697.

71 Rowland, *Varina Howell,* 2:254–56.

72 Strode, *Jefferson Davis,* 527.

73 Redpath had been a longtime acquaintance of Dimitry, through his editorial work at the *Review.* The Belford Company apparently reimbursed Dimitry for his editorial labors. See Redpath to John Dimitry, 29 March 29 1886, 22 September 1887, Mayes-Dimitry-Stuart Papers, Mississippi Department of Archives and History; Ross, *First Lady,* 364–65; Van der Heuvel, *Crowns of Thorns and Glory,* 252.

74 Varina Davis to Redpath, 28 December 1889, as quoted in Ross, *First Lady,* 365.

75 Redpath to John Dimitry, ca. August 1890 and ca. June 1890, Mayes-Dimitry-Stuart Papers. By August 1890, Redpath reported that Varina was driving both of them with little rest: "Mrs. Davis has been at work herself and kept me at work, from morning to night. She is taking a very much more active part in the work than I expected. In fact, she works longer than, I fear, is good for her and

certainly longer than I like. But she is so nervous and anxious about the book that of the two evils she has probably chosen the least." Redpath to John Dimitry, August 1890, Mayes-Dimitry-Stuart Papers, also quoted in Ross, *First Lady*, 2:372; see also Redpath to Leona Queyrouze, 5 May 1890, Rosemonde E. and Emile Kuntz Collection, Manuscripts Section, Howard-Tilton Memorial Library, Tulane University.

76 Redpath to Leona Queyrouze, 2 May 1890, Kuntz Collection.

77 Redpath to Leona Queyrouze, 5, 21 May 1890, see also 13 March 1890; 23 April 1890, Rosemonde E. and Emile Kuntz Collection, Howard-Tilton Memorial Library, Tulane University.

78 Redpath to Leona Queyrouze, 25 June 1890.

79 Leona Queyrouze to Redpath, 2, 28 July 1890, Kuntz Collection.

80 Redpath to Dimitry, 23 August 1890, Mayes-Dimitry-Stuart Papers; Redpath to Queyrouze, 26 August 1890, Kuntz Collection.

81 Redpath to John Dimitry, 13 March 1890, Mayes-Dimitry-Stuart Papers; Rowland, *Varina Howell*, 2:526–28; Strode, *Jefferson Davis*, 527. Varina did not acknowledge Redpath's assistance anywhere in her book but only quoted his positive comments on her husband. Davis, *Jefferson Davis*, 2:935–39.

82 *NAW*, 1:448.

83 Van der Heuvel, *Crowns of Thorns and Glory*, 252–53; Ross, *First Lady*, 373–74; *NAW*, 1:448; *DAB*, 5: 146.

84 *Belford's Monthly* (March 1891): 556. In *Neither Traitor nor Rebel*, Redpath made a nearly identical statement: "I never saw an old man whose face bore more, or more emphatic, evidences of a gentle, refined and benignant character. He seemed to me the ideal embodiment of 'sweetness and light.'" Also see McElroy, *Jefferson Davis*, 693–94; Charles F. Horner, *The Life of James Redpath and the Development of the Modern Lyceum* (New York: Barse and Hopkins, 1926), 298–99.

85 *Neither Traitor nor Rebel*, as quoted in McElroy, *Jefferson Davis*, 693.

86 *Belford's Monthly* (March 1891): 558. Returning to his old Garrisonian beliefs, Redpath also observed that "I think that [the South] undoubtedly [had] a constitutional right to seek to extend slavery into the Territories." Ibid, 558–59.

87 *Belford's Monthly* (March 1891): 562. See Blight, *Race and Reunion*, 266–67.

88 For example, see Horner, *James Redpath*, 228–29; Strode, *Jefferson Davis*, 501; Edward J. Renehan, Jr., *The Secret Six: The True Tale of the Men Who Conspired with John Brown* (New York: Crown Publishers, 1995), 221.

89 Redpath to Leona Queyrouze, June 1890, see also 25 June 1890, Kuntz Collection.

90 *New York Herald*, 11 February 1891; *New York Tribune*, 11 February 1891; *New York Times*, 11 February 1891; Horner, *James Redpath*, 297.

91 As quoted in Horner, *James Redpath*, 299–300; also see *New York Tribune*, 11 February 1891.

92 Redpath to John Brown, Jr., 17 October 1860, John Brown Jr. Papers, Rutherford B. Hayes Research Center.

Index

Abbe, Robert, 191
abolition: in Brazil, 114; immediate goal
 of, 6, 19, 37, 70–71, 190; Redpath and,
 ix, 6, 19; violence and, 17–19
abolitionists: assist fugitive slaves, 17,
 45; John Brown supporters among, 21,
 44, 48, 51–53, 59–60, 213n; capital
 punishment and, 94–95; Civil War and,
 80, 87–89, 97, 100–101; colonization
 opposed by, 65; emigration opposed by,
 65–66, 71, 73–74, 80, 224–25nn; free
 blacks and, 15, 65, 71–72, 194n; from
 Great Britain, 89, 253n; Haiti and, 61,
 63, 66, 70, 78–79; ideology of, 63; Irish
 Land Leaguers compared to, 163, 165,
 167, 176; in Kansas, 19, 20–21, 23, 25,
 30–33, 44, 47, 56–57, 206n; Lincoln
 and, 180–81; as lyceum lecturers, xi, 61,
 87–88, 119–23, 127; in Massachusetts,
 30, 59–60, 93–95; meetings of, 9,
 59–60, 197n; mobbing of, 60; in New
 York, 9, 197n; pacifism and, 17–18,
 45, 48, 51, 53–54, 57, 80–81, 201n;
 postbellum attitudes of, xii–xiii, 261n;
 press of, x, 10, 20, 53; racial attitudes
 of, xii, 26; reconstruction and, xi–xii,
 106, 108, 111–12, 121, 143, 146, 148,
 176, 190, 240n; Republican Party and,
 26, 33–34, 59, 222n; slave insurrections
 and, xii, 16–17, 19, 34, 45–46, 48,
 56–57, 61, 211n; U.S. Constitution
 and, 271n; in Virginia, 17, 58; younger
 generation of, xii, 17–18. See also
 National Anti-Slavery Standard, Radical
 Abolition Party
Academy of Music (New York City), 174
Ackermann, Adolphus, 67, 71, 76, 79

Adams, Henry, 178
Adams, Robert, 85
Africa, 65, 74–75
African Civilization Society, 65, 74, 219n
Alabama: Civil War in, 101–2; Redpath
 travels in, 12, 14, 101–2; slaveholders
 in, 27; slaves in, 102, 104
Alabama River, 12
Alcott, Bronson, 46, 140
Alcott, Louisa May: Redpath befriends, x,
 87–92, 234n; writes Echoes of Harpers
 Ferry and, 57, 89–90; writes Hospital
 Sketches of, 86, 90–92; writes Little
 Women, 96; writes Moods, 92; writes
 On Picket Duty, 86, 91–92; writes Rose
 Family, The, 87, 91–92; writes Success,
 90–91
Aldridge, Ira, 89
Allegan County, Mich., 4
Alone (Harland), 7, 10, 11
Alton, Ill., 30
American Baptist Missionary Convention,
 224n
American Colonization Society, 65, 69–70,
 73–74, 207n
American Federation of Labor, 168, 265n
American Freedmen Inquiry Commission, 6
American Literary Bureau, 244n
American Missionary Association, 106
American Publishers Circular, 86
American Revolution, 94; battles of, 46,
 51, 103, 211n; principles of, 45–46, 51
American Slavery as It Is (Weld), 58
American Woman Suffrage Association,
 123
anarchists, 262n
Andersonville Prison, 183–88